P9-CLS-438

Frommer's™

Best Hiking Trips in Hawaii

My Hawaii
by Pam Wright & Diane Bair

NO MATTER HOW MANY TIMES WE VISIT THE ISLANDS, THEY ALWAYS CATCH

us by surprise. We know what to expect: waterfalls, rainforests, sea cliffs, ancient temples, swaths of white and black beaches, barren craters, and steaming volcanoes. Still. The sheer natural beauty and wild diversity of this island chain continues to stun us, and every time we trade our flip flops for hiking boots, we're rewarded with a new view. Getting off the beaten tourist path helps; no doubt, hikers see the best that these islands have to offer.

There are some absolutely must-do trails: the legendary Kalalau along the spectacular Na Pali Coast; the eerie Alaka'i Swamp through the world's highest rainforest; the Sliding Sands to the bottom of Haleakala crater; the Mauna Kea to the highest peak in the Pacific. And then there's the hike into the sacred Halawa Valley, site of 12 of Molokai's ancient temples; or the hike to Kalaupapa, home to Molokai's infamous leper colony. Of course, hike Diamond Head. Hit the Mahaulepu Heritage trail on Kauai early in the morning and you may spot endangered monk seals; in winter throughout the islands, watch for migrating whales. There are so many at times that the locals call it "whale soup." There are many more, from easy coastal walks and waterfall and rainforest hikes to rugged mountain and sea cliff treks. And still, you won't do it all. Come back, and be surprised and stunned—again.

First page: top, ©Mark Segal / Getty Images; bottom, ©iStockphoto.com

©Tor Johnson / Photo Resource Hawaii

DIAMOND HEAD (opposite page) is Oahu's most prominent and famous landmark. The two-hour hike outside of Waikiki takes you to the summit of the 750-foot volcano cone, where you'll find spectacular views of the island in every direction.

You don't have to travel far outside of Honolulu to find ridge hikes you'll have almost entirely to yourself. Climbing the **WILIWILINUI TRAIL (right)** gives you outstanding views of Honolulu and the Koko Crater on one side, and the white sand beaches of Waimanolo Bay on the other.

The massive peak of Big Island's **MAUNA KEA (below)** gives you outstanding views of Honolulu and the Koko Crater on one side, and the white sand beaches of Waimanolo Bay on the other.

©Kari Romaniuk

©David Thompson

One of the iconic hiking settings you'll find throughout Hawaii is the amazing **WATERFALLS (above)**. Big Island's Hamakua Coast is chock-full of them, including many that are hundreds of feet high.

Hawaii Volcanoes National Park is the state's only recognized World Heritage Site, and eruptions are still commonplace here. The **KILAUEA IKI TRAIL (right)** takes you through lush rainforest to the edge of a crater that was blasting lava nearly a mile into the sky only 50 years ago.

Haleakala National Park—one of the two national parks in the state—and its other-worldly landscapes are Maui's most popular tourist site, but still boasts some stunningly barren vistas. The **SLIDING SANDS TRAIL (below)** descends through cinder cones and lava flows to the massive floor of the Haleakala crater.

©Kari Romaniuk

KILAUEA IKI TRAI
Kilauea Iki   0
Thurston Lava Tube   2

©Pam Wright

No trip to Maui would be complete without some time spent strolling along its gorgeous **BEACHES (below).** A hike along the east side of the island will give you a chance to explore steep sea cliffs, blowholes, and sacred religious sites as you follow the footpaths of ancient Hawaiians.

There are few areas in the world that possess the natural grandeur of Kauai's stunning **NA PALI COAST** (right). For hikers, the famed Kalalua Trail is considered one of the best short hiking routes in the world, where challenging climbs are rewarded with sweeping ocean vistas, sea caves, tropical forests, and abundant waterfalls, culminating at a remote beach.

On the west side of Kauai, you can take a stroll along the 17-mile remote, windswept **POLIHALE BEACH** (below). The sweeping dunes and wild surf are a favorite of locals.

©iStockphoto.com

©Diane Bair

The remote island of Molokai doesn't boast much in the way of development, but it's home to more native Hawaiians than any other island and the scenery is second to none. Its few hiking trails are gems, including the dramatic **KALAUPAPA TRAIL (above)**, which drops nearly 2,000 feet over soaring sea cliffs before reaching the site of the former infamous Molokai leper colony.

©Jack Jeffrey

APAPANE

Size: Length 4–5 inches. Weight ½ ounce

Identifying features: A maroon bird with white feathers under the tail. Call and songs is a high pitched "deee-dit-dit-dit" call, as well as whistles, trills, squeaks, and buzzes

Best sighting times: Morning is best, but Apapane sing and are visible throughout the year and during the daylight hours

Where to see it: Apapane are found mostly in the Ohi'a tree canopy on any native forest trail above 3,000-ft. elevation on all islands

The 'Apapane (*ah-pa-pa-neh*) is one of the most common Hawaiian honeycreepers. Found on each of the main Islands, 'Apapane differ little on each island and are considered the same species throughout Hawaii. Adult 'Apapane, males and females, are scarlet red and look exactly alike, but juveniles are a brownish gray, sometimes with red blotches as they mature. All possess white undertail feathers and a black, slightly downward curving bill. 'Apapane can be found wherever there is Ohi'a bloom in the native forest. They feed on nectar, insects, and fruit. Quite the songsters, 'Apapane have over 60 songs and calls in their repertoire. Their red coloration helps them blend into the tops of the trees, looking like red Ohi'a blossoms to hawks and owls that may prey on them.

©Jack Jeffrey

I'IWI

Size: Length 5–6 inches. Weight ¾ ounce

Identifying features: A vermillion red bird with a distinctive long downcurved orange bill. Calls are a distinctive squeaky "toot-tweet" also rusty hinge–like squeaks and whistles.

Best sighting times: The I'iwi call and sing more in the morning hours but can be seen any time of day

Where to see it: Found in native forests over 4,500-ft. elevation on all islands except Lanai and Molokai

The spectacular scarlet-feathered I'iwi (*ee-ee-vee*) are the last of the Hawaiian sickle-billed honeycreepers. Before humans arrived in the islands, more than fifty different honeycreepers were known to have existed. Today, fewer than half remain, and most of these are endangered or threatened. I'iwi are still fairly abundant in the remaining high elevation native Koa-O'hia forests. The orange, long down-curved bill is a perfect match for the shape of the tubular flowers of many native plants, making I'iwi important pollinators of native plants. To see an I'iwi or to hear its loud distinctive call is an extraordinary experience and one that can only be had in a Hawaiian rainforest.

'AMAKIHI

Size: Length 4–5 inches. Weight
½ ounce

Identifying features: Yellow or gray-green bird with black down-curved bill The song is a rapid trill ("wichi-wichi-wichi-wichi-wichi-), while the call sound is a kitten-like "tzeeee"

Best sighting times: Can be seen any time of day but are more active in the early mornings and late afternoon

Where to see it: Any native forest trail above 2,000 feet on all islands except Lanai.

©Jack Jeffrey

The 'Amakihi (*ah-ma-kee-hee*) is one of the more common Hawaiian honeycreepers. The male 'Amakihi are yellow, while females and juveniles are dull grey green. All have a dark slightly downward curving bill, and dark lines through the eyes. Their song is a steady trill, and the call note is a high pitched "tzeeee." They breed almost year-round in stick nests high in the outer branches of Ohi'a trees. The 'Amakihi feed in the leafy branches of native forest trees and other native plants, feeding on insects, nectar, and fruit. 'Amakihi on each island are different enough to be recognized as either a distinct species or subspecies.

'ELEPAIO

Size: Length 5–6 inches. Weight
²/₃ ounce

Identifying features: Chestnut-brown bird with white barring on the wings, upright tail with white underneath

Best sighting times: Can be seen any time of day

Where to see it: Any native forest trail on Hawaii, Kauai, and Oahu, generally above 1,000-ft. elevation

©Jack Jeffrey

The 'Elepaio is endemic to the Hawaiian islands. This small chestnut-colored flycatcher is the only native bird with white bars on the wings, and it holds its tail upright. The males have black on the throat, while on the female, the throat is white. 'Elepaio are found on only three islands Hawaii, Oahu, and on Kauai. The Oahu subspecies is endangered. The Elepaio call is distinctive and sounds like its name, *E-lee-PAI-o*. The 'Elepaio feeds on flying insects, such as moths and beetles which it catches while in flight, but it also gleans insects and spiders from tree bark. 'Elepaio are very curious birds and will follow people hiking through the forest. Often they follow very closely, calling while catching insects stirred up by hikers.

©Jack Jeffrey

NENE

Size: Length 22–26 inches. Weight 4.5–5 lbs.

Identifying features: A medium-sized goose with buffy gray neck with darker furrows

Best sighting times: Any time of day

Where to see it: On all islands except Lanai, in open grassy areas, parks, and trail heads

The endangered Hawaiian Goose, or Nene (*ney-ney*), is Hawaii's state bird. In the 1950s, the nene population was reduced to only 25 individuals because of predation, habitat loss, and disease. Since that time, captive propagation and removal of non-native predators from nesting areas has increased the population to about 2,000 birds. Because of the absence of mongoose on Kauai, the Nene population on this island has increased dramatically. They can be seen from sea level near the airport, to the highest reaches of the Kokee in the mountains. The breeding season is from October to April for this ground nesting species, and the pairs nest for life. At the end of the breeding season the adults molt their flight feathers and become flightless, making them vulnerable to predation by introduced mammals such as mongoose, cats, and dogs. Please do not feed the nene, as feeding them makes them vulnerable to diseases and attracts them to roadsides and parking lots where they may be hit by cars.

©Jack Jeffrey

SMALL INDIAN MONGOOSE

Size: Length 20–25 inches. Weight 2–3 lbs.

Identifying features: A long, brown, pointy faced, short-legged mammal with a long furry tail

Best sighting times: Any time during the day

Where to see it: Often seen running across roads and trails on all islands except Kauai and Lanai

The Small Indian Mongoose was introduced to Hawaii in 1883 from India to control rats eating the sugar cane crop. However, they turned out to not be a good control method for rats, as mongooses feed during the day and rats feed at night. In the past, Hawaii had numerous bird species that nested on the ground, such as sea birds, rails, and the Hawaiian goose. Once the mongoose was introduced to Hawaii, it was not long before they decimated these ground nesting bird species, by eating eggs, nestlings, and adults, even causing the extinction of some species. Luckily the mongoose was not introduced to Kauai or Lanai. On Kauai, ground nesting sea birds flourish, as can be seen at Kilauea Point National Wildlife Refuge.

FERAL PIG

Size: Height 24–30 inches. Weight 50–200 lbs.

Identifying features: Large pigs generally black, with tusks 2–6 inches long

Best sighting times: Early mornings and twilight any time of year

Where to see it: Found on all islands and often seen on trails near any thickly forested areas

©Jack Jeffrey

The first pigs were brought to Hawaii by the Polynesians over a thousand years ago. These small pigs were raised and fed by the Hawaiians and stayed close to human habitation. In the late 1700s, the larger European pigs were introduced to Hawaii by explorers and whalers. These large pigs interbred with the smaller local pigs and over time their progeny moved into the forest areas. Today hundreds of thousands of feral pigs roam the forests on all of the islands, causing destruction, reduction in native forest habitat, and even the extinction of some native flora and fauna. Feral pigs are often seen along forest trails, but because they are hunted, the pigs are afraid of people and usually run away from hikers.

JAPANESE WHITE EYE

Size: Length 4 inches. Weight 1/3 ounce

Identifying features: Upper body is olive green, with lighter coloring below and with white ring around the eye. Call is a high pitched "zeeee" and the song a high pitched twitter

Best sightings time: The birds are more active in the early mornings and late afternoons

Where to see it: Just about any trail with vegetation from low to high elevations

©Jack Jeffrey

Native to Japan, the Japanese white-eye was originally brought to Hawaii as a caged bird, and was released on Oahu about 1929. Escaped birds quickly became established on other islands and are currently the most common bird on all the Hawaiian Islands. They range from sea level to forests high in the mountains. The white eye ring is a clear identifying mark on this tiny green bird. Sometimes traveling in small flocks, white-eyes feed on small insects, nectar, and fruit. They build small hanging nests made of spider webs and plant fibers in which they lay 2 to 4 small white eggs. The young birds are similar in color to the adults but lack the white eye ring.

©Jack Jeffrey

OHI'A TREE

Size: Medium to large trees up to 100 feet tall, with small round leaves and red pompom-like flowers

Identifying features: Trees with ¾- to 1-inch round leaves and 2- to 3- inch red pompom flowers

Best sighting times: In bloom year-round, but peaking in the spring

Where to see them: All native forests

The Ohi'a tree forest dominates the native forest landscapes of all of the main Hawaiian Islands, and makes up the oldest broadleaf forest in the Northern Hemisphere. Its blossoms, commonly various shades of red but also bright yellow to orange, provide nectar for many of Hawaii's forest birds. The scientific name of Ohi'a means "many forms" as can be seen in the varied shaped leaves as well as different colored flowers. The red flower or "Lehua" is considered sacred to the volcano goddess Pele'. Ohia grows very slowly, with a three-foot diameter tree being about 300 to 500 years old. The reddish-colored wood is very hard and was used by the ancient Hawaiians for statues, building construction, kapa cloth pounding mallets, and spears.

©Jack Jeffrey

KOA TREE

Size: Up to 4 feet in diameter and 90 feet tall

Identifying characteristics: 6-inch long sickle-shaped leaves

Best sighting times: In spring, half-inch yellow pompom blossoms form clusters at the branch ends

Where to see them: Native forests at elevations above 3,000 feet

Much revered by the ancient Hawaiians for canoes, bowls, and tools, the endemic Koa tree is found on all the main Hawaiian Islands. In ancient times giant Koa trees were a common sight, but today, cattle grazing, logging, and fires have reduced the once extensive Koa forests to only a few remnants. Koa takes nitrogen from the air and makes it available for use by other forest plants. The 6-inch long sickle-shaped leaves are expanded petioles called phyllodes that perform the same functions as leaves but protect the tree against drought. Tiny hairs on the leaves catch the rainforest mist and direct it down to the ground. The chestnut brown koa wood is now used for high end furniture, cabinetry and bowls.

HAPU'U, HAWAIIAN TREE FERN

Size: Up to 1 foot in diameter and 10 feet tall, with fronds extending out 10 or more feet

Identifying characteristics: Giant standing ferns

Best sighting times: The hapu'u have fronds all year round

Where to see them: Native rain forest

©Jack Jeffrey

The giant Hawaiian tree ferns are found in moist forests throughout the state. At Hawaii Volcanoes National Park, they provide a 20-foot canopy under the trees in the forest, with fronds extending 8–10 feet out from the main trunk. The young emerging fronds (or fiddle heads) are as large as an outstretched hand and are covered with a blond hair called *pulu*. In ancient times, the Hawaiians used the pulu as bandages, or for embalming the dead. The fiddle heads can be cooked and eaten and the starchy core also eaten after cooking and being leached of toxins. Today the trunks of hapu'u are shredded and used by horticulturists as a growing medium for orchids and anthuriums.

MAILE VINE

Size: ¼ inch in diameter stem and up to 10 feet tall; leaves 2–4 inches long

Identifying characteristics: Thin woody vine with elongated sweet fragrant dark green leaves

Best sighting times: Maile grows all year long

Where to see them: Native rain forest throughout the state

©Jack Jeffrey

Maile is a vine with shiny, fragrant leaves that grow in the remote forests of all of the main Hawaiian Islands. From ancient times until today, the placing of a *maile lei* on a person's shoulders shows respect and honor to the person receiving the long green leafy lei. Maile is associated with the goddess Laka, the goddess of hula. It is picked by pinching off the stem and striping off the leaves still attached to the thin flexible bark. Several vines are intertwined to make a maile lei. Maile lei are use for important occasions such as weddings, graduations, and, in olden times, a peace offering in battles.

©Jack Jeffrey

OHELO BERRY

Size: Small bushes up to 2 feet tall

Identifying characteristics: Similar to blueberries, but with red and yellow berries

Best sighting times: Ripe berries can be found in late spring and summer

Where to see them: Native forest and upland open areas

Related to blueberry and cranberry, the ohelo is bush that produces large amounts of tangy, edible red berries. The berries are regarded as the goddess Pele's fruit and legend says that fruit should be offered to Pele before picking it for yourself. The berries can be used in pies, jams, and jellies and the leaves steeped as a tea and drunk for chest colds. At Hawaii Volcanoes National Park, the berries should not be picked, as they are food for the endangered Nene or Hawaiian goose. The red berries of the poisonous Akia (one large seed) should not be confused with Ohelo berries (many tiny seeds).

©Jack Jeffrey

GUAVA

Size: Small trees can grow up to 20 feet tall

Identifying characteristics: Oval leaves with yellow, medium-sized fruit. Flesh pink with many seeds

Best sighting times: Fruits are seen all year long, but mostly in spring and summer

Where to see them: Lowland areas to 3,000-ft. elevation

Several species of guava have been introduced to Hawaii over the past 150 years. Originally brought to Hawaii from South America for it delicious fruit, they produce delicious apple-sized round or egg-shaped yellow fruit, with a sweet and tangy pink flesh that can be made into juice, jam, and jellies. Strawberry guava has become an invasive plant pest, producing prodigious amounts of small edible, golf-ball-size red or yellow fruits with hundreds of seeds that are spread by birds and pigs. The plant produces toxic chemicals in its leaves, prevents the growth and establishment of native plants, and destroys native forest habitat in Hawaii.

AFRICAN TULIP TREE

Size: Tall trees up to 75 feet tall; seed capsules 10 inches long

Identifying characteristics: Large tree with clumps of crimson-orange tulip-like flowers

Best sighting times: Flowers all year long, but more so in spring

Where to see them: Lowland areas, sea level to 3,000-ft. elevation

©Jack Jeffrey

Introduced from equatorial Africa, the African tulip tree (also known as the "flame of the forest") is an ornamental plant. These beautiful orange-flowered trees have escaped cultivation and become a pest weed tree in Hawaii. They grow below 3,000 feet in the wetter areas of all the main Islands, and can be seen in many valley settings dotting the forest with their crimson orange flowers. The long, bean-like, upright seed capsules contain hundreds of winged seeds, which are blown by the wind, spreading this plant into native forests, pastures, farmlands, and other areas where it is unwanted.

PANDANUS OR HALA (SCREWPINE)

Size: Small trees can be up to 25 feet tall

Identifying characteristics: Long, thin leaves up to 4 feet by 2 inches wide, with prop-roots from the trunk

Best sighting times: All year

Where to see them: Lowland areas, sea level to 3,000-ft. elevation

©Jack Jeffrey

Pandanus trees, or Screwpine, can be found at lower elevations and along many of the shoreline trails of all the main Hawaiian Islands. Known in Hawaii as "hala", the long, thin, saw-tooth edge leaves (4 feet long by 2 inches wide) and long "prop-roots" are distinctive. The 10-inch diameter fruit reminds many people of pineapples when ripe, but are not very tasty. The fruit are very fibrous, and separate into inedible sections with paintbrush like tips. The nuts in each of the sections are edible but difficult to get to. The leaves, after removing the tooth edge and dried, are used for weaving "lauhala" mats, hats, handbags, and baskets.

Frommer's™

Best Hiking
Trips in Hawaii

1st Edition

by Pamela Wright, Diane Bair,
David Thompson & Michael Tsai

Wildlife Guide by Jack Jeffrey

Here's what the critics say about Frommer's:

"Amazingly easy to use. Very portable, very complete."
—**BOOKLIST**

"Detailed, accurate, and easy-to-read information
for all price ranges."
—**GLAMOUR MAGAZINE**

"Hotel information is close to encyclopedic."
—**DES MOINES SUNDAY REGISTER**

"Frommer's Guides have a way of giving you
a real feel for a place."
—**KNIGHT RIDDER NEWSPAPERS**

John Wiley & Sons Canada, Ltd.

Published by:

JOHN WILEY & SONS CANADA, LTD.

6045 Freemont Blvd.
Mississauga, ON   L5R 4J3

ISBN: 978-0-470-16057-2

Editor: Gene Shannon
Project Manager: Elizabeth McCurdy
Project Editor: Lindsay Humphreys
Editorial Assistant: Katie Wolsley
Project Coordinator: Lynsey Stanford
Cartographer: Lohnes & Wright
Production by Wiley Indianapolis Composition Services

Front cover photo: Hiker on the Na Pali Coast trail on Kauai

For reseller information, including discounts and premium sales, please call our sales
department: Tel. 416-646-7992. For press review copies, author interviews, or other
publicity information, please contact our publicity department: Tel. 416-646-4582;
Fax: 416-236-4448.

Wiley also publishes its books in a variety of electronic formats. Some content that
appears in print may not be available in electronic formats.

Manufactured in the United States

1   2   3   4   5   RRD   13   12   11   10   09

CONTENTS

4 OAHU HIKES 39

by Michael Tsai

5 THE BIG ISLAND HIKES 91

by David Thompson

6 MAUI HIKES 142

by Diane Bair & Pamela Wright

7 KAUAI HIKES   182

by Diane Bair & Pamela Wright

8 MOLOKAI HIKES   222

by Diane Bair & Pamela Wright

APPENDIX A: FAST FACTS, TOLL-FREE NUMBERS & WEBSITES   238

APPENDIX B: THE HAWAIIAN LANGUAGE   249

APPENDIX C: OUTDOOR ACTIVITIES A TO Z   253

INDEX   258

Table of Hikes

Hike	Distance
Oahu	
Makapuu Tide Pools	2.5 miles round-trip
Koko Crater Stairs	1.25 miles
Kuliouou Ridge Trail	5 miles round-trip
Hawaiiloa Ridge	5 miles loop
Honolulu Mauka Trail System	9 miles loop
Manoa Falls	1.6 miles round-trip
Lanipo	7 miles round-trip
Diamond Head (Leahi)	1.7 miles round-trip
Aiea Loop Trail	4.5 miles loop
Moanalua Valley Trail	3.6 miles round-trip
Wiliwilinui Trail	5 miles round-trip
Kaiwa Ridge Hike	2 miles round-trip
MT. Olomana	5 miles round-trip
Maunawili Falls	3.5 miles round-trip
Puu Manamana	4.5 miles (horseshoe)
Kealia Trail and Access Road	6 miles round-trip
The Big Island	
Pololu Valley Trail	1 mile round-trip
Puukohola Trail at Puukohola Heiau National Historic Site	1.5 mile loop
Puako Petroglyph Trail (aka Malama Trail)	1.4 miles round-trip
Ala Kahakai Trail	15.4 miles one-way
Kiholo Bay	5.5 miles round-trip
Kaloko-Honokohau National Historical Park Loop	3.3 mile loop
Captain Cook Monument Trail	3.6 miles round-trip
Punaluu Coastal Trail	2 miles, round-trip
Kilauea Iki Trail in Hawaii Volcanoes National Park	4 mile loop trail
Napau Crater Trail in Hawaii Volcanoes National Park	14 miles round-trip
Akaka Falls Trail	0.4 mile loop trail
Puu Oo Trail	About 7.4 miles round-trip
Puu Laau Road	8.4 miles round-trip
Mauna Kea-Humuula Trail, AKA Mauna Kea Summit Trail	6 miles, one way
Maui	
Haleakala National Park Hikes:	
Sliding Sands Trail	18.6 miles round-trip to Paliku Cabin
Halemau'u Trail	20.6 miles round-trip to Paliku Cabin; there's a variety of shorter options, too

Difficulty	Best Time to Go	Star rating	Page number
Moderate/ Strenuous	8 to 10 a.m.	★★	41
Moderate	Before 9 a.m. or after 3 p.m.	★	44
Moderate	After 3 p.m.		47
Moderate/ Strenuous	8 to 10 a.m.	★★	50
Moderate	7 to 10 a.m.	★★★	52
Easy	June to September	★	55
Strenuous	August to October	★★	58
Easy	Before 9 a.m. or after 4 p.m.	★	61
Moderate	May to August	★★	64
Moderate	Noon to 3 p.m.	★★	66
Moderate	Avoid if rainy, but two days after rainfall the trail should be in good shape	★	69
Easy/Moderate	6 a.m. to 10 p.m.	★	72
Strenuous	May to September	★★★	75
Easy/Moderate	2 to 4 p.m.		78
Strenuous	March to September	★★	81
Moderate	8 to 11 p.m. April, May, and August	★	84
Moderate	Mornings offer the best chances of sunny, clear weather	★★	93
Easy	February at the height of whale-watching season	★	96
Easy	Late afternoon or early morning		99
Strenuous	February, when whale-watching season peaks		102
Moderate	Before 10 a.m. to beat the heat and hit the beach in its morning prime		106
Moderate	To avoid roasting in the lava desert section of this hike, go before 10 a.m. or after 4 p.m.	★★★	109
Strenuous	Before 10am, to beat the heat and catch the best snorkeling conditions		113
Moderate	Whale watching season, mid-December to mid-March		116
Moderate	On one of the two or three Tuesdays each month when After Dark in the Park is held	★★★	119
Strenuous	On one of the two or three Tuesdays each month when After Dark in the Park is held		123
Easy	October through April	★	127
Moderate	Early in the day to avoid rain and fog		130
Moderate	Weekdays to avoid the weekend hunters and ATV riders. For birders, go near dawn or sunset, when birds are most active		133
Strenuous	April through October. Start no later than 8am to get up and back before dark		136
Difficult	Midweek when it's less crowded	★★★	144
Strenuous	June–July, which is the best time to see silversword in bloom	★★★	148

Table of Hikes

Hike	Distance
Maui *(continued)*	
Hosmer Grove Trail	0.6 miles round-trip
Pa'kaoao Trail	0.5 mile round-trip
Pipiwai Trail	4 miles round-trip
Hana Area	
Hana-Waianapanapa Coastal Trail	6 miles round-trip
Waikamoi Forest Ridge Trail	0.8 miles round-trip, 1.5 miles round-trip with the extension
Iao Valley State Park	0.6 miles round-trip
Waihee Valley Swinging Bridge Trail	5 miles round-trip
Nakalele Blowhole	1.2 miles round-trip
Honolua Ridge and Maunalei Arboretum Trails	6 miles round-trip
Lahaina Pali Trail	5 miles round-trip to the summit peak; 5.5 miles one-way to hike the full length of the trail with shuttle pick-up on one end; 11 miles round-trip without pick-up
Hoapili Trail & La Perouse Bay	5.5 miles round-trip
Kauai	
North Shore	
Kalalau Trail	22 miles round-trip; 4 miles round-trip to Hanakapiai Beach
Hanakapi'ai Falls Trail	8 miles round-trip
Hanalei 'Okolehao Trail	2.5 miles round-trip
Hanalei River Trail	2 miles round-trip
East/Kapaa/Wailua Area	
Sleeping Giant (Nounou Mountain East)	3.5 miles round-trip
Kuilau Ridge Trail	4 miles round-trip to the Moalepe Trail junction
The Nature Trail (at Koke'e State Park)	880 feet round-trip
Pihea & Alaka'i Swamp Trails	7.4 miles round-trip
Awa'awapahi Trail	6.2 miles round-trip
Nu'alolo Trail & Nu'alolo Cliff Trail	7.6 miles round-trip to the Nu'alolo Cliff Trail junction; 10 miles round-trip combining Nu'Alolo and Nu'alolo Cliff trails; 10.5 miles round-trip looping to Awa'awapuhi Trail
Iliau Nature Loop	0.3 miles round-trip
Polihale Beach Trail	Up to 17 miles one way
Mahaulepu Heritage Trail	4 miles round-trip

Difficulty	Best Time to Go	Star rating	Page number
Easy	Early morning when the birds are most active		151
Easy	Sunrise or sunset		153
Moderate	Winter, when the waterfalls are most dramatic	★	155
Moderate	Midweek; avoid weekends when large local crowds congregate at the park		158
Easy	September to early December		160
Easy	Clear mornings, before the afternoon clouds roll in		163
Easy	The falls are best after a rain		165
Easy	When the tides are high and the winds are blowing		168
Moderate	During the annual Kapalua Community Whale-Watching Festival, held each February		170
Strenuous	Winter, from December to March, is great for whale watching		173
Easy to moderate	Early in the day before the tradewinds move in and churn up the water	★	176
Strenuous	May–October, when the weather tends to be drier	★★★	185
Strenuous	Dry, summer months, June–September, are best	★★	188
Moderate	Best in early morning, before the mercury climbs		191
Easy	Best just after a light rain, when it's ultra misty and the cascades and streams are flowing		193
Moderate	Early mornings when skies tend to be clearer	★	195
Moderate	All year, but the trail can get muddy January–March		197
Easy	Early morning hours when the flowers are fresh and the crowds are thin		200
Strenuous	March–October, during dry season	★★	203
Strenuous	March–October	★	205
Strenuous	March–October	★	208
Easy	Best in late afternoon when the setting sun lights up the canyon walls		210
Easy to Moderate	November–March is best because the beach can be extremely hot		213
Easy	November–March when humpback whales are migrating offshore	★	216

Table of Hikes

Hike	Distance
Molokai	
Pepeopae Trail	3 miles round-trip, loop
Kalaupapa Trail	4 miles round-trip
Mo'omomi Preserve Trail	2 miles, loop, or 8 miles, if you need to walk the road to access the trail head
Halawa Valley Trail	4 miles round-trip

Difficulty	Best Time to Go	Star rating	Page number
Moderate	April–October, when the access road is passable (with a four-wheel-drive vehicle)	★★★	224
Difficult	You'll need to be on the trail by at least 8 a.m. to catch the required tour		227
Easy	May–September		230
Moderate	To swim in the pools under the falls, April–October. To see the falls at their fullest, November–March	★	233

LIST OF REGIONAL MAPS

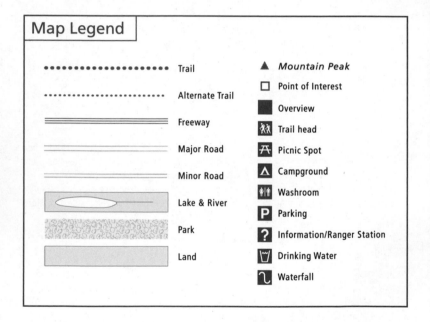

Map Legend

••••••••••••••••••••	Trail
•••••••••••••••••••	Alternate Trail
════════════	Freeway
────────────	Major Road
·············	Minor Road
	Lake & River
	Park
	Land

▲ Mountain Peak
□ Point of Interest
■ Overview
Trail head
Picnic Spot
△ Campground
Washroom
P Parking
? Information/Ranger Station
Drinking Water
Waterfall

AN INVITATION TO THE READER

In researching this book, we discovered many wonderful places—hotels, restaurants, shops, and more. We're sure you'll find others. Please tell us about them, so we can share the information with your fellow travelers in upcoming editions. If you were disappointed with a recommendation, we'd love to know that, too. Please write to:

Frommer's Best Hiking Trips in Hawaii, 1st Edition
John Wiley & Sons Canada, Ltd. • 6045 Freemont Blvd. • Mississauga, ON   L5R 4J3

AN ADDITIONAL NOTE

Please be advised that travel information is subject to change at any time—and this is especially true of prices. We therefore suggest that you write or call ahead for confirmation when making your travel plans. The authors, editors, and publisher cannot be held responsible for the experiences of readers while traveling. Your safety is important to us, however, so we encourage you to stay alert and be aware of your surroundings. Keep a close eye on cameras, purses, and wallets, all favorite targets of thieves and pickpockets.

ABOUT THE AUTHORS

New England–based writers **Diane Bair** and **Pam Wright** don't sit still for long. Whether they're researching a story or traveling for fun, the duo is usually found outdoors, scrambling a mountain summit, snowshoeing to a frozen waterfall or checking out antiquities from the back of a camel. Co-authors of more than two dozen travel books and hundreds of magazine stories, Diane and Pam have very well-traveled laptops! They also burn through several pairs of hiking boots each year. They're currently planning their next adventure, and their next trip to Hawaii.

David Thompson is the author of *Pauline Frommer's Alaska* and a co-author of *Pauline Frommer's Hawaii.* He lives, surfs and hikes in Hawaii.

Michael Tsai is an award-winning reporter and columnist for *The Honolulu Advertiser* and an instructor of English at the University of Hawaii at Manoa and Kapiolani Community College. In addition to climbing the highest mountains in Europe, Africa, and South America, he has explored nearly every public trail on Oahu.

Other Great Guides for Your Trip:

Frommer's Hawaii
Frommer's Honolulu & Oahu Day by Day
Frommer's Maui Day by Day

FROMMER'S STAR RATINGS, ICONS & ABBREVIATIONS

Every hotel, restaurant, and attraction listing in this guide has been ranked for quality, value, service, amenities, and special features using a **star-rating system.** In country, state, and regional guides, we also rate towns and regions to help you narrow down your choices and budget your time accordingly. Hotels and restaurants are rated on a scale of zero (recommended) to three stars (exceptional). Attractions, shopping, nightlife, towns, and regions are rated according to the following scale: zero stars (recommended), one star (highly recommended), two stars (very highly recommended), and three stars (must-see).

In addition to the star-rating system, we also use **six feature icons** that point you to the great deals, in-the-know advice, and unique experiences that separate travelers from tourists. Throughout the book, look for:

(Finds)	Special finds—those places only insiders know about
(Fun Facts)	Fun facts—details that make travelers more informed and their trips more fun
(Kids)	Best bets for kids, and advice for the whole family
(Moments)	Special moments—those experiences that memories are made of
(Tips)	Insider tips—great ways to save time and money
(Value)	Great values—where to get the best deals

The following **abbreviations** are used for credit cards:

AE	American Express	DISC	Discover	V	Visa
DC	Diners Club	MC	MasterCard		

FROMMERS.COM

Now that you have this guidebook to help you plan a great trip, visit our website at **www.frommers.com** for additional travel information on more than 4,000 destinations. We update features regularly to give you instant access to the most current trip-planning information available. At Frommers.com, you'll find scoops on the best airfares, lodging rates, and car rental bargains. You can even book your travel online through our reliable travel booking partners. Other popular features include:

- Online updates of our most popular guidebooks
- Vacation sweepstakes and contest giveaways
- Newsletters highlighting the hottest travel trends
- Podcasts, interactive maps, and up-to-the-minute events listings
- Opinionated blog entries by Arthur Frommer himself
- Online travel message boards with featured travel discussions

The Best of Hiking in Hawaii

The Hawaiian Islands . . . the mere mention of these sun-drenched, palm-fringed, lush islands can get you dreaming. They are the stuff of fantasies and fodder for Hollywood movies, a favorite destination for vacationers from around the world seeking fun and relaxation in the sun. They are stunning in their natural beauty: miles of beaches and secluded swaths of red, black, yellow, gold, and sugar-white sand, a paradise of tropical rainforests, hanging gardens, tumbling waterfalls, rugged canyons, deep valleys, and towering volcanoes. Beyond its beauty, Hawaii has a rich history, with deep ties to ancient cultures.

Alas, not all is perfect in paradise. We'll admit it: The islands also have their fair share of stifling crowds, traffic jams, overpriced tourist traps, and general schlock. But for those who are willing to leave the well-traveled road for a trail, there are few destinations that have as much to offer as Hawaii. Hikers—whether they're climbing jagged peaks or descending to a giant crater floor, bare-footing across a black sand beach or cooling their feet in a waterfall pool, crisscrossing a misty rainforest or rock-hopping soaring sea cliffs—see the best of Hawaii. Put on your hiking boots and you'll discover a new view of paradise.

The islands, each unique and geographically diverse, boast a variety of hikes and terrain to rival anywhere in the world. The most difficult part about hiking in Hawaii is deciding which trail to take. Do you head for the summit of a 13,000-foot volcano, where you may encounter snow and blooming silversword? Do you opt to walk deep into a wet, tropical forest to discover plants and birds found nowhere else in the world? Or, do you cross a hot, lava rock–strewn beach, passing ancient temples and, perhaps, a sleeping monk seal? No problem; not only can you do it all, you may be able to do it all in 1 day!

We've included more than 55 hikes on five islands, showcasing Hawaii's astounding diversity and neck-snapping beauty. Here we highlight some of the best.

1 THE BEST FAMILY HIKES

- **Manoa Falls Trail** (Oahu): Marrying easy access with a host of natural attractions, Manoa Falls is the island's most popular public trail. The trail is relatively short and aggressively managed to appeal to hikers of all ages and skill levels. See p. 55.
- **Kiholo Bay** (Big Island): A dusty hike through arid South Kohala kiawe brush to the coast and a beautiful, turtle-rich, blue lagoon. Take a swim, and then continue hiking along the beach, to a lava tube and a spring-fed lava-rock pond known as Queen's Bath, where yes, queens really did bathe. See p. 106.
- **Pa Kaoao Trail** (Maui): It's not much of a hike—you can do it up and back in less than a half-hour—but it's a great

way to take in some wonderful views of Maui's volcanic basin. The short trail goes to the summit of Pa Kaoao, one of the highest viewpoints in Haleakala National Park. You'll have great views of the stark Haleakala volcanic wilderness and, on clear days, neighboring Big Island's tallest peaks. See p. 153.

- **Waihee Valley Swinging Bridge Trail** (Maui): What could be more fun on a hot Hawaiian day than hiking an impossibly lush rainforest, crossing two swinging bridges, and ending at a perfect swimming hole? Walk through misty and verdant Waihee Valley, with rippling streams, cascades, and waterfalls. See p. 165.
- **Nakalele Blowhole Trail** (Maui): Set on Maui's northern coast, Nakalele

Point is an otherworldly scene of twisted lava and hissing ocean. Water surges through a hole in the lava shelf, erupting like a geyser and sending seawater some 100 feet or more into the air. Rocky coastline and ocean views abound, and easy walking makes it a good family stop. See p. 168.

- **Mahaulepu Heritage Trail** (Kauai): Rugged sea cliffs, secluded coves, dunes, tide pools, sculpted lava formations, native plants, and petroglyphs are found along this ancient coastal route. The beach was also site of a legendary battle during the 1300s, has prime whale watching in the winter, and is a favorite hangout for endangered monk seals. See p. 216.

2 THE BEST EASY HIKES

- **Diamond Head** (Oahu): When locals give directions, they use Diamond Head as a direction; such is the significance of Oahu's most recognizable geographic landmark to the Hawaiian sense of place. It's hard to resist this hike to the top of this well-known volcanic crater, and with railings and handholds on steeper sections, it's easier than you might think to reach the top. See p. 61.
- **Puako Petroglyph Trail** (Big Island): A short, hot trek through dry kiawe woods takes you to the Puako petroglyph field, one of the most extensive assemblies of ancient rock carvings in the Pacific. While the trail itself can be a scorcher, the trail head is at a little oasis of a beach park, a lovely spot for picnicking, tide pooling, and sitting in the shade. See p. 99.
- **Waikamoi Forest Ridge Trail** (Maui): Want to get into the rainforest, without having to do much work? This

short nature walk, off of scenic Hana Highway, travels through a thick bamboo and fern forest, with valley-to-ocean views of the Keanae Peninsula. See p. 160.

- **Iliau Nature Loop** (Kauai): This easy-to-do, roadside stroll offers a nice sampling of Hawaii's indigenous and endemic plants, along with awesome Waimea Canyon views. Interpretive signs identify the plants and explain their medicinal and ancient cultural uses. It's a great introduction to some of the plants that you'll spot on other trails. See p. 210
- **Mo'omomi Preserve Trail** (Molokai): Walk along the most intact beach and sand dune area in the main Hawaiian Islands. Wild, remote, windswept dunes stretch a mile long and hundreds of feet wide and shelter native grasses and shrubs, as well as nesting endangered green sea turtles. See p. 230.

3 THE BEST MODERATE HIKES

- **Honolulu Mauka Trail System** (Oahu): With its trail head adjacent to the offices of Na Ala Hele, the state's trails and access department, the Honolulu Mauka Trail System is, predictably, the best maintained trail system on the island. See p. 52.
- **Aiea Loop Trail** (Oahu): With its moderate distance, gentle rolling hills, and abundant natural beauty, Aiea Loop is considered an old reliable among local hiking enthusiasts. See p. 64.
- **Kaloko-Honokohau National Historical Park** (Big Island): A network of trails here crosses both loose sand along the shore and follows cinder paths through a tortured *a'alava* desert. You'll see lots of remnants of ancient Hawaii, including house sites, *heiau* (religious sites), petroglyphs, and the enormous seawall of a fishpond that modern Hawaiians are painstakingly restoring, rock by rock. See p. 109.
- **Kilauea Iki Trail** (Big Island): Located in Hawaii Volcanoes National Park, this gem of a hike crosses the floor of a 400-foot deep crater, the site of a spectacular 1959 eruption that blasted a fountain of lava nearly a half-mile into the sky. The crater floor is an otherworldly land of lava formations and sulfury steam vents. See p. 119.
- **Sleeping Giant Trail (Nounou Mountain East)** (Kauai): Hike the Sleeping Giant's chest! This trail is one of three that snake up the sides of Nounou Mountain, known as the Sleeping Giant, for its unmistakable ridgeline formation. You'll zigzag through the Nounou Forest Reserve and have great views of the Wailua River, the Kauai coastline, and—if the weather cooperates—the summit of Mount Wai'ale'ale. See p. 195.
- **Pepeopae Trail** (Molokai): This exquisite trail is located in Kamakou Preserve, in a remote mountainous region of northeast Molokai. The boardwalk trail climbs through dense native cloud forest to a fragile bog ecosystem. It ends at a stunning overlook into Pelekunu Valley. See p. 224.

4 THE BEST STRENUOUS HIKES

- **Mount Olomana** (Oahu): The three towering peaks of Mount Olomana have captured the imaginations of generations of adventurous hikers. The out-and-back trail that links the trio of peaks is a stout challenge that rewards skilled, careful hikers with thrilling climbs and descents and an amazing 360-degree view from the first peak. See p. 75.
- **Mauna Kea** (Big Island): The trail to the highest peak in the Pacific begins at the visitor center at 9,620 feet and ends at the 13,796-foot summit. The mountain is revered by native Hawaiians, who have erected a simple wood altar at the top, and prized by astronomers, who've built an international telescope complex. The trail passes through an ancient quarry and passes an alpine lake fed by the gradual melt of permafrost left over from the last ice age. And the views! See p. 136.
- **Sliding Sands Trail** (Maui): This is one of two trails leading into the Haleakala National Park wilderness and arguably one of the top hikes on Maui. You'll start on Maui's highest peak and descend into a nearly barren, eerie landscape of cinder cones and lava flows.

The trail drops to the massive crater floor, and then travels through native shrublands and rugged, exposed cliffs overlooking a cloud forest. See p. 144.

- **Halemau'u Trail** (Maui): This must-do hike is one of two treks leading into the Haleakala National Park wilderness. (Sliding Sands Trail, above, is the other.) Steep switchbacks descend the rim of the odd-shaped Haleakala basin to its valley floor. Along the way: neck-snapping views of Koolau Gap, Keanae Valley, and the eerie cinder cone and lava-rock landscape. See p. 148.

- **Kalalau Trail** (Kauai): This spectacular trail hugs the rugged and remote Na Pali coastline, providing the only land access to legendary Kalalau Valley.

Known the world over, the Na Pali Coast stretches from Ke'e Beach in the north to Polihale State Park in the west. For the rugged outdoors person, the rewards are worth the grueling effort: sweeping ocean vistas, tropical forests, sea caves, sugar-white beaches, and lush valleys rippled with waterfalls. See p. 185.

- **Pihea & Alakai Swamp Trails** (Kauai): There is no other place quite like this eerie swamp, located on an old caldera floor, created some 6 million years ago. The not-to-be-missed hike travels through the world's highest rainforest and open muddy bogs. Along the way, there's opportunity to see rare native plants and birds. See p. 203.

5 THE BEST COASTAL WALKS

- **Punaluu Coastal Trail** (Big Island): The hike starts out on a popular black-sand beach, passes World War II gun emplacements and a Hawaiian *heiau,* travels for a quarter of a mile on smooth cobble set in place by ancient Hawaiian hands, follows a jeep trail for a bit through dwarf kiawe trees, and ends up at a secluded point with dramatic views. See p. 116.

- **Hana-Waianapanapa Coastal Trail** (Maui): Coastal cliffs, stone arches, lava fields, black beaches, blowholes, and ancient temples are part of the highlights of this stunning coastal route, just north of Hana. The trail follows portions of the ancient King's Highway from Waianapanapa State Park to Hana Bay. See p. 158.

- **Hoapili & La Perouse Bay** (Maui): This is an enchanting walk through recent lava fields along the southern coastline, with picturesque coves, secluded beaches, and high surf. Along the way, you'll see remnants of old Hawaiian foundations and *heiau*

(religious sites), and have views of the inland foothills of Haleakala and the Pacific Ocean. See p. 176.

- **Polihale Beach Trail** (Kauai): Stand on the sweeping dunes of this vast, expansive beach, looking out into the wild surf, and you'll think you've been transported in time. You'll see miles of golden sand and rugged dunes—and no crowds. The isolated beach, in the shadows of the Na Pali cliffs, stretches for 17 miles, and is the state's longest and one of its most serene and picturesque. According to ancient Hawaiian mythology, Polihale was the gateway to the afterworld. See p. 213.

- **Mahaulepu Heritage Trail** (Kauai): Rugged sea cliffs, secluded coves, dunes, tidepools, sculpted lava formations, native plants, and petroglyphs are found along this ancient coastal route. The beach was also site of a legendary battle during the 1300s, has prime whale-watching in the winter, and is a favorite hangout for endangered monk seals. See p. 216.

6 THE BEST CULTURAL WALKS

- **Moanalua Valley Trail** (Oahu): First developed during a period of great social and political upheaval in Hawaii, the Moanalua Valley Trail, also known as the Kamananui Valley Trail, is as much a journey into the island's history as it is an exploration of its natural environment. See p. 66.

- **Puukohola Heiau Trail** (Big Island): This National Park Service trail leads around the base of an enormous war *heiau,* or temple, built by King Kamehameha between 1790 and 1791 before completing his conquest of the Hawaiian Islands. Located on the dry North Kohala coast, the trail passes other archaeological sites and leads to a shady palm grove that was once the site of a Hawaiian royal compound. See p. 96.

- **Iao Needle & Ethnobotanical Loop** (Maui): Arguably, Iao Valley is one of the prettiest and most sacred sites on Maui. A paved .6-mile walk provides a scenic viewpoint of Kuka'emoku (Iao Needle), rising 1,200 feet from the valley floor. It's believed that the lava-rock formation, surrounded by the forested walls of the Pu'u Kukui Crater, was once used as a natural altar. The valley is also the site of the battle of Kepaniwai where the forces of Kamehameha I conquered the Maui army in 1790. See p. 163.

- **Kalaupapa Trail** (Molokai): This dramatic trail on a remote peninsula drops nearly 2,000 feet over soaring sea cliffs, before reaching Kalaupapa National Historic Park, home to the infamous Molokai leper colony. It was here that Father Damien de Veuster helped people afflicted with Hansen's disease (leprosy), who were banished to the remote and isolated peninsula. See p. 227.

- **Halawa Valley Trail** (Molokai): Hike into a steep cathedral valley through dense forest and past ancient settlement sites, before reaching the 250-foot-tall Mo'oula Falls. Ancient Polynesians settled in lush Halawa Valley as early as A.D. 650, and archaeologists say it is one of the most culturally significant places in all of Hawaii. The sacred valley is home to 12 of Molokai's 19 ancient temples. See p. 233.

7 THE BEST WATERFALL HIKES

- **Manoa Falls Trail** (Oahu): Marrying easy access with a host of natural attractions, Manoa Falls is Oahu's most popular public trail. A photo of the roaring 150-foot waterfall is a must-have for many Oahu visitors. See p. 55.

- **Maunawili Falls Trail** (Oahu): Maunawili Falls Trail is perhaps the most popular hike on the Windward Coast, and for good reason. It's short, easy (except for a steep section of man-made stairs near the end), and, most of all, it features a 20-foot waterfall that feeds a deep, wide swimming hole. See p. 78.

- **Akaka Falls Trail** (Big Island): Located near Hilo on the island's lush windward side, the paved trail circles through a lowland rainforest thick with bamboo, banana, bird of paradise, azalea, gardenia, hibiscus, and so much more you could fill the index of a field guide to tropical botany with it. The trail brings you to two waterfalls: 100-foot Kahuna Falls, and even more impressive 442-foot Akaka Falls. See p. 127.

- **Pipiwai Trail** (Maui): This wonderfully scenic trail follows a stream through Oheo Gulch, passing through sweet-smelling guava and dark bamboo forests before reaching 400-foot Waimoku Falls, a truly breathtaking waterfall—and one of the largest on Maui. See p. 155.

- **Hanakapi'ai Falls Trail** (Kauai): This is the stuff of movies and fantasies: a tromp through a wet, tropical rainforest, dotted with sweet-smelling guava and mango trees, ending at a towering 300-foot waterfall. The misty cloud forest and rushing falls make for a very surreal, jungle atmosphere. Plus, there's a fine swimming hole at the base of the falls. See p. 188.

8 THE BEST HIKES FOR SEEING WILDLIFE

- **Ala Kahakai Trail** (Big Island): This segment of the traditional circle-island trail links pre-contact and contemporary Hawaii, passing through both ancient settlements and gleaming modern resorts. It hugs the North Kohala shoreline, aka The Gold Coast, crossing beaches, rocky cliffs, posh hotel grounds, and more. The hike offers plenty of opportunities to see migrating whales during the winter months. See p. 102.

- **Lahaina Pali Trail** (Maui): During the winter whale-watching season you'll have birds-eye views of migrating pods on this lofty trail. It's hot, dry, and rough-going, walking on sharp lava rocks. But don't let that stop you! This ancient highway, built more than 200 years ago for horses and foot traffic, zigzags up and over the Kealaloloa Ridge in the West Maui Mountains, with panoramic views of the Pacific Ocean, as well as Kahoolawe and Lanai islands. See p. 173.

- **Pihea & Alakai Swamp Trails** (Kauai): Take a magical, mystical journey through Old Hawaii! There is no other place quite like this eerie swamp, located on an old caldera floor, created some 6 million years ago. There's opportunity to see rare native plants and birds. See p. 203.

- **Mahaulepu Heritage Trail** (Kauai): Rugged sea cliffs, secluded coves, dunes, tide pools, sculpted lava formations, native plants, and petroglyphs are found along this ancient coastal route. The beach has prime whale-watching in the winter, and is a favorite hangout for endangered monk seals. See p. 216.

- **Mo'omomi Preserve Trail** (Molokai): Walk along the most intact beach and sand dune area in the main Hawaiian Islands. Wild, remote, windswept dunes stretch a mile long and hundreds of feet wide and shelter native grasses and shrubs, as well as nesting endangered green sea turtles. The 921-acre preserve is also home to 22 native Hawaiian plant species and birds. The Hawaiian owl, sanderlings, plovers, and the great frigate bird can all be spotted here. See p. 230.

9 THE BEST UNIQUELY HAWAIIAN RESTAURANTS

- **Kapahulu Poi Shop** (Oahu; ℭ **808/737-8014**): In the great tradition of family-owned Hawaiian restaurants, the Poi Shop induces smiles, belly slaps, and naps in almost equal proportion. Order your *lau lau, lomi* salmon, squid *luau, kalua* pig, or dried *aku* a la carte or as part of a combination plate. See p. 89.

- **Ken's House of Pancakes** (Big Island; © 808/935-8711): The menu here has page after page of American and local classics, from pork chops with applesauce to *loco moco* (two scoops of rice, one hamburger patty, fried egg, and gravy). Breakfast is served around the clock. See p. 141.

- **Rainbow's Drive-In** (Oahu; © 808/737-0177): An after-beach staple for nearly 50 years, Rainbow's is the plate-lunch spot of choice for thousands of long-time residents. The traditional two scoops of rice and one scoop of macaroni salad anchor overloaded plates of teriyaki beef, breaded cutlets, deep-fried mahimahi, chili franks, and other local comfort foods. Two hands required. See p. 90.

- **KJ's Local Grindz** (Oahu; © 808/235-5799): At KJ's, just do as the locals do and go with the chicken. The Windward Oahu cheap-eat favorite specializes in *mochiko* chicken, which is coated with rice flour and deep fried. Portions can be daunting to the uninitiated. See p. 89.

- **Restaurant Matsu** (Maui; © 808/871-0822): The deep-fried *katsu* pork and chicken are specialties of this casual eatery. California rolls, cold *saimin,* and bento platters are also popular. The daily specials are a changing lineup of home-cooked classics: oxtail soup, roast pork with gravy, teriyaki ahi, and miso butterfish. See p. 181.

10 THE BEST OVERALL RESTAURANTS

- **Hoku's** (Oahu; © 808/739-8888): Located in the Kahala Hotel and Resort, this comfortably elegant beachside restaurant offers what just might be the best dining experience on Oahu. The ever-changing, but consistently excellent, menu mixes Polynesian, Asian, and European influences with an emphasis on locally grown ingredients. See p. 89.

- **Island Lava Java** (Big Island; © 808/327-2161): Casual, creative, organic, and affordable—what's not to love about Island Lava Java? Oh, right—the line you have to stand in to order. It's longest in the morning, before everyone's had their Kona coffee. Evenings are tamer, and lit by tiki torch. See p. 141.

- **Kilauea Lodge** (Big Island; © 808/967-7366): A Depression-era YMCA in the rainforest near Hawaii Volcanoes National Park is now the setting for the island's most exotic fine-dining establishment, which serves a mix of German, French, and Cajun cuisine. See p. 141.

- **The Banyan Tree** (Maui; © 808/669-6200): It's hard to top this romantic, oceanfront restaurant for a special night out. The distinctive menu includes dishes like the sautéed Kona *kampachi* with mustard greens and poached-shrimp salad and roasted duck with snake beans and *enoki* mushrooms. Make reservations for sunset. See p. 180.

- **Sansei Seafood Restaurant & Sushi Bar** (Maui; © 808/669-6286): Perpetual award-winner Sansei offers an extensive menu of Japanese and East-West delicacies, like the mango/crab-salad rolls, panko-crusted ahi sashimi, ahi carpaccio, noodle dishes, Asian shrimp cakes, and creative sauces like ginger-lime chile butter and cilantro pesto. See p. 181.

- **Tidepools** (Kauai; © 808/742-1234): Splurge-worthy and romantic, a cluster of thatched bungalows overlooks a

8

lagoon in this dreamy open-air restaurant. The atmosphere would be reason enough to book a table, but the cuisine—especially the fresh fish—is just as outstanding. See p. 221.

11 THE BEST EXPENSIVE ACCOMMODATIONS

- **JW Marriott Ihilani Resort and Spa** (Oahu; ✆ **808/679-0079**): This luxury resort is just 17 miles from Honolulu International Airport, but you'll feel like you're on another island. The average room here is a spacious 640 square feet, and the private lanai makes it easy to pretend that all those miles of white sand are yours alone. The golf course, restaurants, and spa are all top notch. See p. 87.

- **Turtle Bay Resort** (Oahu; ✆ **808/293-6000**): With two landscaped pools, a pair of world-class golf courses, horseback riding paths, hiking and mountain-biking trails, and 5 miles of pristine beach, this is a luxury hotel best enjoyed by the most active-minded guests. Or not. The Luana Spa offers coconut body scrubs, noni wraps, pineapple pedicures, and other delectable services. See p. 88.

- **Hilton Waikoloa** (Big Island; ✆ **800/ HILTONS** [445-8667] or 808/886-1234): Boredom is not an option at the most action-packed and family-friendly of the Gold Coast resort hotels. Among the highlights are a 175-foot-long waterslide, a mile-long artwalk, and a pool where you can swim with dolphins. Canal boats and a light-rail system carry guests around the sprawling grounds. See p. 140.

- **Four Seasons Resort Maui at Wailea** (Maui; ✆ **800/334-MAUI** [6284] or 808/874-8000): If money's no object, this is the place to stay. This Hawaiian palace by the sea, in a ritzy neighborhood with great restaurants and shopping, may also be the most family-friendly hotel on the island. See p. 179.

- **Outrigger Waipouli Beach Resort & Spa** (Kauai; ✆ **800/OUTRIGGER** [688-7444] or 808/823-8300): Nestled on 13 acres between Wailua and Kapaa, this luxurious beach resort features spacious, high-end condos, furnished with top-of-the-line accoutrements (think granite counters, Sub-Zero and Wolf appliances, and flatscreen TVs). There's also an Aveda spa, a fitness center, and a saltwater fantasy pool, and you're in walking distance to shops and restaurants. See p. 219.

12 THE BEST BUDGET ACCOMMODATIONS

- **Aqua Bamboo** (Oahu; ✆ **808/922-7777**): A recent $2.5-million upgrade has only added to the intimate charm of this surprisingly affordable gem. The saltwater swimming pool (with waterfall) is a nice touch. See p. 87.

- **Hilo Bay Hostel** (Big Island; ✆ **808/ 933-2771**): The most centrally located lodging in Hilo is also one of the most affordable places on the island. This backpackers' roost occupies the top half of a nicely restored turn-of-the-20th-century hotel, smack in the heart of old downtown. Rooms are tiny, but airy and clean. See p. 140.

8

- **Namakanipaio Campground** (Big Island; © 808/967-7321): You can't beat the prices at Hawaii Volcanoes National Park's drive-up campgrounds. The tiny, rustic cabins are dirt cheap, and the tent sites are free! Be ready to bundle up at night. It gets cold at 6,000 feet—even in Hawaii. See p. 140.

- **Napili Bay** (Maui; © 877/782-5642): One of Maui's best bargains is this small complex on Napili's beach, one of the finest on the coast for swimming and snorkeling. The studio apartments are small, but they pack in everything you need, from a full kitchen to a roomy lanai that's great for watching sunsets over the Pacific. See p. 179.

- **Waiananpanapa State Park Cabins** (Maui; © 808/984-8109): These 12 rustic cabins, overlooking Pailoa Bay, are the best lodging deal on Maui. The cabins come complete with kitchen, living room, bedroom, and bathroom with hot shower; furnishings include linens, towels, dishes, and basic cooking and eating utensils See p. 179.

- **Kokee Lodge** (Kauai; © 808/335-6061): If you plan to spend time hiking Kokee State Park and Waimea Canyon trails (and you should!), consider staying in one of these cabins. Older cabins have dormitory-style sleeping arrangements, while the new ones have two separate bedrooms each. See p. 220.

THE BEST OF HIKING IN HAWAII

1

THE BEST BUDGET ACCOMMODATIONS

Planning Your Trip to Hawaii

Ahh, yes . . . warm, sunny Hawaii. All you need is a pair of hiking shorts, bathing suit, and an aloha shirt and you're good to go. Nope! It's true that the islands are very informal. Shorts, T-shirts, and tennis shoes will get you by at most restaurants and attractions; a casual dress or a polo shirt and khakis are fine even in the most expensive places. But if you're hitting the trail, you'll need a lot more. It really can get cold in Hawaii. If you plan to see the sunrise from the top of Maui's Haleakala Crater, venture into the Big Island's Hawaii Volcanoes National Park, or spend time in Kokee State Park on Kauai, you'll need a warm jacket; 40°F (4°C) upcountry temperatures, even in summer when it's 80°F (27°C) at the beach, are not uncommon. If you're taking a rainforest hike—and of course you will—be sure to toss some rain gear into your suitcase, especially if you'll be in Hawaii between November and March. Many trails are slippery and muddy, requiring sturdy, good gripping boots. Finally, while Hawaii is an outdoor lover's paradise, you won't find many stores selling camping or hiking gear; it's best to bring all your hiking and camping supplies with you.

One last thing: You can easily dehydrate in the tropical heat, so figure on carrying 2 quarts of water per day on any hike. Campers should bring water-purification tablets or devices. For additional tips, see "What to Bring: The Hiker's Checklist," later in this chapter; visit our website at www.frommers.com/go/hiking; and turn to the "Fast Facts, Toll-Free Numbers & Websites" appendix on p. 238.

1 BEFORE YOU GO

VISITOR INFORMATION

For information about traveling in Hawaii, contact the **Hawaii Visitors & Convention Bureau (HVCB),** Waikiki Business Plaza, 2270 Kalakaua Ave., Ste. 801, Honolulu, HI 96815 (© **800/GOHA-WAII** [464-2924] or 808/923-1811; www.gohawaii.com). The bureau publishes the helpful "Accommodations and Car Rental Guide" and *Islands of Aloha* magazine, the official HVCB magazine, as well as supplying free brochures and maps.

Individual Island Visitor Bureaus

Oahu Visitors Bureau, 733 Bishop St., Ste. 1875, Honolulu, HI 96813 (© **808/524-0722;** www.visit-oahu.com).

Big Island Visitors Bureau East Office, 250 Keawe St. Hilo, HI 96720 (© **808/961-5797;** www.bigisland.org). **Big Island Visitors Bureau West Office,** 65-1158 Mamalahoa Hwy, Ste. 27B, Kamuela, HI, 96743 (© **808/885-1655;** www.bigisland.org).

Maui Visitors Bureau, 1727 Wili Pa Loop, Wailuku, HI 96793 (© **808/244-3530;** www.visitmaui.com).

Kauai Visitors Bureau, 4334 Rice St., Ste. 101, Lihue, HI 96766 (© **808/245-3971** or 800/262-1400; www.kauaidiscovery. com).

Molokai Visitor Association, Moore Center, 2 Kamoi St., Ste. 200, Kaunakakai, HI 96748 (© **800/800-6367;** www. molokai-hawaii.com).

HAWAII'S PARKS

Hawaii has several national parks and historical sites—four on the Big Island and one each on Maui, Oahu, and Molokai. The following offices can supply you with hiking and camping information (or check online at www.nps.gov).

On the Big Island: Hawaii Volcanoes National Park, P.O. Box 52, Hawaii National Park, HI 96718 (© 808/985-6000); Puuhonua O Honaunau National Historical Park, P.O. Box 129, Honaunau, HI 96726 (© 808/328-2326); Puukohola Heiau National Historic Site, P.O. Box 44340, Kawaihae, HI 96743 (© 808/882-7218); and Kaloko-Honokohau National Historical Park, 72–4786 Kanalani St., Kailua-Kona, HI 96740 (© 808/329-6881).

On Maui: Haleakala National Park, P.O. Box 369, Makawao, HI 96768 (© 808/572-9306).

On Molokai: Kalaupapa National Historical Park, P.O. Box 2222, Kalaupapa, HI 96742 (© 808/567-6802).

On Oahu: USS *Arizona* Memorial at Pearl Harbor (© 808/422-0561).

To find out more about Hawaii's state parks, contact the Hawaii State Department of Land and Natural Resources, 1151 Punchbowl St., No. 130, Honolulu, HI 96813 (© **808/587-0300;** www.hawaii. gov). The office can provide you with information on hiking and camping at the parks and will send you free topographic trail maps. NaAlaHele (www.hawaiitrails.org) is

a state-sponsored organization that supplies information and maps on hiking trails throughout the islands. Also, specific trail maps are recommended for each hike featured in this guide.

General driving maps are readily available from island visitor centers and car-rental companies.

PASSPORTS

Every foreign traveler entering the U.S. must show a passport, including all persons traveling by air or entering at land and seaports. A passport is not required for U.S. citizens. For information on how to obtain a passport, see "Passports" in the appendix.

Visas

The U.S. State Department has a Visa Waiver Program (VWP) allowing citizens of the following countries to enter the United States without a visa for stays of up to 90 days: Andorra, Australia, Austria, Belgium, Brunei, Denmark, Finland, France, Germany, Iceland, Ireland, Italy, Japan, Liechtenstein, Luxembourg, Monaco, the Netherlands, New Zealand, Norway, Portugal, San Marino, Singapore, Slovenia, Spain, Sweden, Switzerland, and the United Kingdom. (*Note:* This list was accurate at press time; for the most up-to-date list of countries in the VWP, consult www.travel.state.gov/visa.)

Canadian citizens may enter the United States without visas; they will need to show passports and proof of residence, however. *Note:* Any passport issued on or after October 26, 2006, by a VWP country must be an e-Passport for VWP travelers to be eligible to enter the U.S. without a visa. Citizens of these nations also need to present a round-trip air or cruise ticket upon arrival. E-Passports contain computer chips capable of storing biometric information, such as the required digital photograph of the holder. (You can identify an e-Passport by the symbol on the bottom center cover of your passport.) If your passport doesn't have this feature, you

Plan Before You Hike at Frommers.com

Want to make your walking vacation as smooth and enjoyable as possible? We've added lots of valuable information about how to plan the perfect trip on our website at www.frommers.com/go/hiking. You'll find tips on how to get fit before your trip, suggestions on how best to plan your route, and useful packing tips.

can still travel without a visa if it is a valid passport issued before October 26, 2005, and includes a machine-readable zone, or between October 26, 2005 and October 25, 2006, and includes a digital photograph. For more information, go to www.travel.state.gov/visa.

Citizens of all other countries must have (1) a valid passport that expires at least 6 months later than the scheduled end of their visit to the U.S., and (2) a tourist visa, which may be obtained without charge from any U.S. consulate.

Many international visitors traveling on visas to the United States will be photographed and fingerprinted on arrival at Customs in airports and on cruise ships in a program created by the Department of Homeland Security called US-VISIT. Exempt from the extra scrutiny are visitors entering by land or those (mostly in Europe; see above) that don't require a visa for short-term visits. For more information, go to the Homeland Security website at www.dhs.gov/dhspublic.

MEDICAL REQUIREMENTS

Unless you're arriving from an area known to be suffering from an epidemic (particularly cholera or yellow fever), inoculations or vaccinations are not required for entry into the United States.

CUSTOMS
What You Can Bring into the U.S.

Every visitor more than 21 years of age may bring in, free of duty, the following:

(1) 1 liter of wine or hard liquor; (2) 200 cigarettes, 100 cigars (but not from Cuba), or 3 pounds of smoking tobacco; and (3) $100 worth of gifts. These exemptions are offered to travelers who spend at least 72 hours in the United States and who have not claimed them within the preceding 6 months. It is forbidden to bring into the country almost any meat products (including canned, fresh, and dried meat products such as bouillon, soup mixes, etc.). Generally, condiments including vinegars, oils, spices, coffee, tea, and some cheeses and baked goods are permitted. Avoid rice products, as rice can often harbor insects. Bringing fruits and vegetables is not advised, though not prohibited. Customs will allow produce depending on where you got it and where you're going after you arrive in the U.S. Foreign tourists may carry in or out up to $10,000 in U.S. or foreign currency with no formalities; larger sums must be declared to U.S. Customs on entering or leaving, which includes filing form CM 4790. For details regarding U.S. Customs and Border Protection, consult your nearest U.S. embassy or consulate, or **U.S. Customs** (www.cbp.gov).

What You Can Take Home from Hawaii

Canadian Citizens: For a clear summary of Canadian rules, write for the booklet *I Declare,* issued by the Canada Border Services Agency (© **800/461-9999** in Canada, or 204/983-3500; www.cbsa-asfc.gc.ca).

U.K. Citizens: For information, contact **HM Customs & Excise** at ☏ **0845/010-9000** (from outside the U.K., 020/8929-0152), or consult their website at www.hmce.gov.uk.

Australian Citizens: A helpful brochure available from Australian consulates or Customs offices is *Know Before You Go.* For more information, call the **Australian Customs Service** at ☏ **1300/363-263,** or log on to www.customs.gov.au.

New Zealand Citizens: Most questions are answered in a free pamphlet available at New Zealand consulates and Customs offices: *New Zealand Customs Guide for Travellers, Notice no. 4.* For more information, contact **New Zealand Customs,** The Customhouse, 17–21 Whitmore St., Box 2218, Wellington (☏ **04/473-6099** or 0800/428-786; www.customs.govt.nz).

2 WHEN TO GO

Hawaii is a year-round destination, sunny and warm throughout the year, with little variation in temperatures. It's not so much when you visit the islands as where you visit, as weather can vary greatly from one end of an island to another. That said, winter, from late November through March, is Hawaii's rainy season—and its busiest (as tourist flee colder climates). Trails are often muddy and slippery, but hikers are rewarded with views of spectacular waterfalls, rippling streams, and tumbling cascades. It's also the best time for whale-watching.

The off season, when the best rates are available and the islands are less crowded, is spring (mid-Apr to mid-June) and fall (Sept to mid-Dec)—a paradox because these are the best seasons to be in Hawaii, in terms of reliably great weather. If you're looking to save money, or if you just want to avoid the crowds, this is the time to visit. Hotel rates and airfares tend to be significantly lower, and good packages are often available.

Due to the large number of families traveling in summer (June–Aug), you won't get the fantastic bargains of spring and fall. However, you'll still do much better on packages, airfare, and accommodations than you will in the winter months.

The last 2 weeks of December, in particular, are the prime time for travel to Hawaii. If you're planning a holiday trip, make your reservations as early as possible, expect crowds, and prepare to pay top dollar for accommodations, car rentals, and airfare.

Also, if you plan to come to Hawaii between the last week in April and early May, be sure you book your accommodations, interisland air reservations, and car rentals in advance. In Japan, the last week of April is called Golden Week because three Japanese holidays take place one after the other. Waikiki is especially busy with Japanese tourists during this time, but the neighboring islands also see dramatic increases.

Average Temperature

	Jan	Feb	Mar	Apr	May	June	July	Aug	Sept	Oct	Nov	Dec
°F	73	73	74	76	77	79	80	81	81	80	77	74
°C	22	23	23	24	25	26	27	27	27	27	25	23

Average Precipitation

	Year	Jan	Feb	Mar	Apr	May	June	July	Aug	Sept	Oct	Nov	Dec
in.	21.6	3.4	2.6	2.8	1.3	1	.4	.6	.6	.7	2	2.6	3.5

(Tips) What to Bring: The Hiker's Checklist

- Day pack or overnight backpack
- Boots
- Socks
- Underwear
- Pants and shorts
- Sun visor or hat
- Long-sleeved shirt or sweater
- Outerwear: parka or windbreaker
- Waterproof jacket and pants
- Warm fleece or sweater
- Gloves, warm hat for high-altitude hiking

- Tent and sleeping bag
- Cooking gear and utensils
- Water bottle
- Water purifier
- Food
- First aid kit
- Map and compass
- Sunglasses
- Sun block
- Insect repellant
- Matches and fire starter
- Plastic bags

Also consider these items:

Camera, battery charger, extra memory card

Binoculars for wildlife-viewing

Snorkeling gear for underwater viewing

Trekking pole(s), the collapsible, telescoping variety

A bandana has many uses. Soak one in water and tie around your neck for an instant pick-me-up in hot weather; tie around your head for a sweatband; or use as a mask tied below your eyes to protect from wind and dust.

Heart-rate monitor to wear on wrist to track target heart rate, particularly if you have any physical infirmities that would require paying particular attention to over-exertion, especially on strenuous walks at altitude or in extreme weather.

A good book for after the walk, or to enjoy during a break on the trail. A paperback is lighter to carry around.

Complete information on what to bring on your walking vacation can be found at www.frommers.com/go/hiking, including tips on day packs, clothing, and equipment to pack, and recommendations for other things to bring with you.

When Hawaii observes holidays (especially those over a long weekend), travel between the islands increases, interisland airline seats are fully booked, rental cars are at a premium, and hotels and restaurants are busier.

Federal, state, and county government offices are closed on all federal holidays; for a list, go to "Holidays" in the appendix.

State and county offices are also closed on local holidays, including Prince Kuhio

Day (Mar 26), honoring the birthday of Hawaii's first delegate to the U.S. Congress; King Kamehameha Day (June 11), a statewide holiday commemorating Kamehameha the Great, who united the islands and ruled from 1795 to 1819; and Admissions Day (third Fri in Aug), which honors the admittance of Hawaii as the 50th state on August 21, 1959.

Other special days celebrated in Hawaii by many people, but which involve no closing of federal, state, and county offices are the Chinese New Year (which can fall in Jan or Feb), Girls' Day (Mar 3), Buddha's Birthday (Apr 8), Father Damien's Day (Apr 15), Boys' Day (May 5), Samoan Flag Day (in Aug), Aloha Festivals (Sept–Oct), and Pearl Harbor Day (Dec 7).

---

3 GETTING THERE & GETTING AROUND

BY PLANE

Most major U.S. and many international carriers fly to Honolulu International Airport (HNL), on Oahu. Some also offer direct flights to Kona International Airport (KOA), near Kailua-Kona on the Big Island; Kahului Airport (OGG), on Maui; and Lihue Airport (LIH), on Kauai. If you can fly directly to the island of your choice, you'll be spared a 2-hour layover in Honolulu and another plane ride. If you're heading to Molokai or Lanai, you'll have the easiest connections if you fly into Honolulu.

United Airlines offers the most frequent service from the U.S. mainland, with flights to Honolulu as well as nonstop service from Los Angeles and San Francisco to the Big Island, Maui, and Kauai. American Airlines offers flights from Dallas, Chicago, San Francisco, San Jose, Los Angeles, and St. Louis to Honolulu, plus several direct flights to Maui and Kona. Continental Airlines offers the only daily nonstop from the New York area (Newark) to Honolulu. Delta Air Lines flies nonstop from the West Coast and from Houston and Cincinnati. Hawaiian Airlines offers nonstop flights to Honolulu from several West Coast cities (including new service from San Diego), plus nonstop service from Los Angeles to Maui.

For complete airline contact information, see the appendix.

Overseas visitors can take advantage of the APEX (Advance Purchase Excursion) reductions offered by all major U.S. and European carriers. In addition, some large airlines offer transatlantic or transpacific passengers special discount tickets under the name **Visit USA,** which allows mostly one-way travel from one U.S. destination to another at very low prices. Unavailable in the U.S., these discount tickets must be purchased abroad in conjunction with your international fare. This system is the easiest, fastest, cheapest way to see the country.

Inter-island flights are offered by **Hawaiian Airlines** (© 800/367-5320; www.hawaiianair.com); **go!** (© 888/I-FLY-GO-2 [435-9462]; www.iflygo.com); **Pacific Wings** (© 888/866-5022 or 808/ 873-0877; www.flypwx.com); and **Island Air** (© 800/323-3345 or 808/484-2222; www.islandair.com).

Getting into Town from the Airport

Some major hotels on the Big Island, Oahu, Kauai, and Maui offer shuttle services to and from the airport. Cabs are also available at airports. But hikers will need a car to get around, and to access trails. You'll get the best deal if you rent a vehicle at the airport. For a list of major rental-car companies and toll-free phone numbers, see the appendix on p. 246.

Long-Haul Flights: How to Stay Comfortable

- Your choice of airline and airplane will definitely affect your legroom. Find more details about U.S. airlines at **www.seatguru.com**. For international airlines, the research firm Skytrax has posted a list of average seat pitches at **www.airlinequality.com**.

- Emergency exit seats and bulkhead seats typically have the most legroom. Emergency exit seats are usually left unassigned until the day of a flight (to ensure that someone able-bodied fills the seats); it's worth checking in online at home (if the airline offers that option) or getting to the ticket counter early to snag one of these spots for a long flight. Many passengers find that bulkhead seating offers more legroom, but keep in mind that bulkhead seats have no storage space on the floor in front of you.

- To have two seats for yourself in a three-seat row, try for an aisle seat in a center section toward the back of coach. If you're traveling with a companion, book an aisle and a window seat. Middle seats are usually booked last, so chances are good you'll end up with three seats to yourselves. And in the event that a third passenger is assigned the middle seat, he or she will probably be more than happy to trade for a window or an aisle.

- To sleep, avoid the last row of any section or the row in front of an emergency exit, as these seats are the least likely to recline. Avoid seats near highly trafficked toilet areas. Avoid seats in the back of many jets—these can be narrower than those in the rest of coach. Or reserve a window seat so you can rest your head and avoid being bumped in the aisle.

- Get up, walk around, and stretch every 60 to 90 minutes to keep your blood flowing. This helps avoid **deep vein thrombosis,** or "economy-class syndrome."

- Drink water before, during, and after your flight to combat the lack of humidity in airplane cabins. Avoid caffeine and alcohol, which will dehydrate you.

BY FERRY

The **Hawaii Super Ferry** (© 877/443-3779; www.hawaiisuperferry.com) offers service from Oahu to Maui. The ferry departs several times a day (schedules vary depending on time of year) and the trip takes about 3 to 4 hours.

BY CAR
Car Rentals

First off: Hikers will need a car to get around. Good news: Hawaii has some of the lowest car-rental rates in the country. (An exception is the island of Lanai, where they're very expensive.) At Honolulu International Airport and most neighbor-island airports, you'll find most major car-rental agencies, including: Alamo, Avis, Budget, Dollar, Enterprise, Hertz, National, and Thrifty. For complete rental-agency contact information, see the appendix. It's almost always cheaper to rent a car at the airport than in island cities or through your hotel (unless there's one already included in your package).

Rental cars are usually at a premium on Kauai, Molokai, and Lanai, and may be sold out on the neighboring islands on holiday weekends, so be sure to book well ahead.

A wide variety of cars is offered, including sports cars, convertibles, jeeps, and an assortment of four-wheel-drive vehicles. Generally, major roads are well maintained, though secondary roads may be muddy and pot-holed. Many rental-car agencies will prohibit you from traveling specific roads that are known to be in rough shape. For the most part, you can get around without a four-wheel-drive vehicle, except on Molokai where they're an absolute must to reach some of the trails.

Generally, roads are well marked, and getting around the islands is relatively easy. Gas is available in all major cities and towns throughout the islands. Hikers will find small parking lots or off-road spaces at most trail heads.

Distances

Remember to leave adequate time to travel from one end of an island to another (and—alas—traffic can be a problem during peak commuting hours on Maui, Kauai, and the Big Island). Here are some general guidelines to follow when calculating travel time:

On the Big Island, from Hilo allow 50 minutes to reach Hawaii Volcanoes National Park, 2 hours and 45 minutes to Kailua-Kona, 1 hour and 25 minutes to Waipio Valley, and 1 hour and 30 minutes to Waimea. On Maui, from Kahului Airport allow 45 minutes to reach Lahaina, 30 minutes to Wailea, 60 minutes to Kapalua, 50 minutes to Kaanapali, 3 hours and 30 minutes to Hana, and 2 hours and 30 minutes to Haleakala National Park. On Kauai, from Lihue allow 35 minutes to reach Poipu, 40 minutes to Hanalei, 15 minutes to Kapa'a, 35 minutes to Princeville, 55 minutes to Waimea, and 75 minutes to Waimea Canyon. On Oahu, from Honolulu allow 15 minutes to reach Waikiki, 25 minutes to reach Hanauma Bay, 25 minutes to Diamond Head, 40 minutes to Kailua, 45 minutes to Waimea Bay, and 55 minutes to Kawela Bay. On Molokai, from the airport, allow 15 minutes to reach Maunaloa, 10 minutes to Kaunakakai, 35 minutes to Mapulehu, and 2 hours to Halawa Valley.

Car-Rental Rules

To rent a car in Hawaii, you must be at least 25 years of age and have a valid driver's license and credit card. *Note:* If you're visiting from abroad and plan to rent a car in the United States, keep in mind that foreign driver's licenses are usually recognized in the U.S., but you should get an international one if your home license is not in English.

Insurance

Hawaii is a no-fault state, which means that if you don't have collision-damage insurance, you are required to pay for all damages before you leave the state, whether or not the accident was your fault. Your personal car insurance may provide rental-car

coverage; check before you leave home. Bring your insurance identification card if you decline the optional insurance, which usually costs from $12 to $20 a day. Obtain the name of your company's local claim representative before you go. Some credit card companies also provide collision-damage insurance for their customers; check with yours before you rent.

Rules of the Road

Hawaii state law mandates that all car passengers must wear a seat belt and all infants must be strapped into a car seat. You'll pay a $50 fine if you don't buckle up. Pedestrians always have the right of way, even if they're not in the crosswalk. You can turn right on red after a full and complete stop, unless otherwise posted.

Road Maps

The best and most detailed maps for activities are published by Franko Maps (www.frankosmaps.com); they feature a host of island maps, plus a terrific "Hawaiian Reef Creatures Guide" for snorkelers curious about the fish they spot underwater. Free road maps are published by *This Week Magazine,* a visitor publication available on Oahu, the Big Island, Maui, and Kauai. For even greater detail, check out Odyssey Publishing (© **888/729-1074;** www.hawaiimapsource.com), which has very detailed maps of East and West Hawaii, Maui, and Kauai.

Another good source is the University of Hawaii Press maps, which include a detailed network of island roads, large-scale insets of towns, historical and contemporary points of interest, parks, beaches, and hiking trails. If you can't find them in a bookstore near you, contact University of Hawaii Press, 2840 Kolowalu St., Honolulu, HI 96822 (© **888/847-7737;** www.uhpress.hawaii.edu). For topographic and other maps of the islands, go to the Hawaii Geographic Society, 49 S. Hotel St., Honolulu, or contact P.O. Box 1698, Honolulu, HI 96806 (© **800/538-3950** or 808/538-3952).

BY BUS

The only public bus transportation in the islands is on Oahu. TheBus (© **808/848-5555**; www.thebus.org) has 90 routes throughout Honolulu and major points on the island. Hikers will find it difficult to access trails via public bus transportation.

4 CHOOSING A HIKE

Hawaii is a rich and diverse hiking destination, and there are obviously thousands of different trails you could take. So what makes these hikes the best? While any choice is going to be subjective, we've used our years of experience hiking in the area to choose the best hikes for all kinds of interests: the best hikes for spectacular views, the best to see wildlife, the best forest walks, the best coastal routes, the best challenges, and the best to see places to explore the culture while you walk. Above all, we've strived to provide hikes that show you something unique about Hawaii that you won't likely find where you've come from.

To do this, we've consulted with experts such as park rangers, naturalists, outings-club group leaders, nature-center directors, and many local hikers. Of course, we'd love to hear from you: If you think something doesn't deserve to be among our selections—or you know of a route that deserves to be included—get in touch through www.frommers.com/contact_us.

ELEMENTS OF A FROMMER'S "BEST HIKING TRIP"

At the beginning of each hike review, we provide lots of information to help you decide if a particular hike is right for you. Keeping in mind what kind of vacation experience you want, use these tools to help you plan your hike and get the most out of your vacation.

Star Ratings and Icons

Located in the title bar at the beginning of the hike review, these ratings are the quickest way to see what we believe are "the best of the best."

All hikes in this book have been carefully recommended and make for an excellent hiking experience; however, a few routes are so exceptional that they deserve special attention. For these hikes, we've awarded a star (or two, or three stars) for easy identification.

Likewise, some hikes have special qualities that deserve recognition:

- **Finds** Are lesser-known hikes that don't have the crowds of some of the more popular routes—the hidden treasures.
- **Kids** These hikes are ones best suited for doing with young families, with easier terrain and lots to see and do to keep children engaged.
- **Moments** These routes contain experiences that are so special they will leave lasting memories—something you may never have seen before, but will never forget.

Difficulty Rating

A trail's degree of difficulty greatly affects hiking time. Park agencies and guidebook writers rate the degree of challenge a trail presents to the average hiker. Of course the "average" hiker varies widely, as do the average hiker's skills, experience, and conditioning; assessing "degree of difficulty" is inevitably subjective.

A path's elevation gain and loss, exposure to elements, steepness, climatic conditions, and the natural obstacles a hiker encounters along the way (for example, a boulder field or several creek crossings would increase the difficulty rating) figure prominently in determining the hike's difficulty rating.

In this book, hikes are rated with an Easy-Moderate-Strenuous system. The hike rating in brief is:

Easy: A hike that is 2 hours or less and covers relatively flat, even terrain. It's accessible for people of modest fitness or people bringing small children; no hiking boots or other special equipment should be necessary.

Moderate: A hike that can take up to 5 hours to complete. It can be completed without significant difficulty by people of moderate fitness or by older children. There may be significant changes in elevation or difficult terrain for portions of the route, but not for the majority of the hike. It does not contain any sections of excessive difficulty or areas that require navigational skill.

Strenuous: Day hikes in excess of 6 hours, multi-day hikes, or shorter hikes that feature particularly challenging terrain or require skilled navigation. The trails may have some difficult features such as scree, dense vegetation, swampy sections, boulders to traverse, or ladders; however, they do not require special equipment or climbing knowledge, or feature sections of significant danger.

Distance

Distance is expressed in miles for a round-trip hike beginning at the trail head. The hikes in this guide range from 2 to 16 miles round-trip, whether the hike is a loop trail, out-and-back route, or point-to-point (one-way) path.

Estimated Time

Estimated times needed to complete the hikes in this guidebook are based on the expected performance of a person in average physical and aerobic condition, traveling at a moderate pace. Age, fitness, and trail experience vary widely among hikers, and the estimated time may be far too long for some hikers, far too short for others. The estimate also includes recommended amounts of time for taking breaks along the route.

Elevation Gain

Elevation gain measures the net gain from the trail head to the hike's highest point. Overall gain (or gross gain) on a trail with rolling terrain that climbs and loses elevation could be substantially more. The elevation chart that appears with the trail map for each hike will show the route's topography.

Costs & Permits

Expect an admission fee (usually collected per vehicle entry rather than per person) at national parks described in this guide. Some backcountry cabins and campsites require reservations and permits; these are noted. Also, a few hikes require permits or local guides. These are also noted.

Pet-Friendly

Hawaiian citizens love their pets, but getting your furry friend into the state may be difficult. Hawaii has very stringent rules regarding entering pets. Dogs and cats must meet pre- and post-arrival requirements to qualify for a 5-day-or-less quarantine program. If they do not meet the requirements, pets are subject to 120-day quarantine. For information, contact the Department of Agriculture at www.hawaii.gov/hdoa/ai/aqs/info.

In national parks, pets are not allowed on trails. Generally, dogs should be kept on a leash. We've included specific pet rules for each hike.

Best Time to Go

We have suggested the months—or, where we can, time of day—that are best to take a particular hike. Hawaii offers four-season hiking, but some trails may be closed due to mudslides, lava flows, and road conditions. Websites for more trail information and up-to-date conditions have been provided for each hike, where available.

The suggested times are intended to show the best time for maximum enjoyment of the trail, but the trail may also be accessible outside of the suggested time period.

Websites

The suggested website is the best place to go to get further information on the trail and surrounding area.

Recommended Map

We've listed our favorite trail maps, those that are reasonably easy for the traveler to obtain. These will likely provide additional detail to the map provided in this guide.

Trail Head GPS

We've listed the latitude and longitude coordinates for where the recommended trail begins. The intent is to get you to the start of the trail easily, by entering the coordinates into a handheld or automotive GPS device, GPS-enabled cellphone, or online mapping program.

Trail Head Directions

Directions to the hike starting point are given from the nearest highway or major road to the parking area for the trail head. For trails having two desirable trail heads, directions to both are given. A few trails can be hiked one-way with the possibility of a car shuttle. Suggested car shuttle points are noted.

NAVIGATION ASSISTANCE
Maps

Each trail in this guide has a map. Before setting out, familiarize yourself with the map legend. To follow the map easily, first look for the north. Then find the trail

head and follow the directions given to each waypoint.

Reading GPS Coordinates

Every spot on the Earth can be numbered by the coordinates on a GPS unit. Latitude is noted in north or south; in the case of Hawaii destinations, it's north. Longitude is shown as east or west; in Hawaii, the location is west. For example, the trail head for the Sliding Sands trail in Haleakala National Park is located at N 20 42.866 W 156 15.051. Latitude and longitude are measured in "degrees," which translate into distance from the 0 line (longitude) in England or the equator (latitude).

Hikes can be broken up with waypoints, or stops along the way. These waypoints can guide you back to the trail head if you are lost, by checking the coordinates for where you are and aiming yourself towards the coordinates of the nearest waypoint.

Having a GPS reading of the trail head and of certain trail waypoints can be both helpful and confusing. Such readings can be particularly helpful as a supplement to a map for finding obscure trail heads, unsigned junctions, or going off-trail—situations you will rarely encounter while hiking any of the high-quality trails in this guide.

Where a GPS reading can be confusing to the less experienced hiker and GPS user has to do with the fact that a GPS device only shows direction or gives distance "as the crow flies," or, in a straight line. But hikers are not crows! Most trails don't take a straight line from Point A to Point B, so be sure to consult the map included with the hike description along with your GPS readings.

---

5 HEALTH, SAFETY & TRAIL HAZARDS

STAYING HEALTHY

In general, Hawaii is a very safe and healthy place. Food hygiene standards are

very high, so you shouldn't have many problems. Also, Hawaii tap water is excellent (although you'll find bottled waters in convenience and grocery stores throughout the islands). Ice cubes and drinking water supplied in restaurants and bars are safe. *Note:* **Do not drink from streams or lakes.**

The biggest health risks in the islands are excessive sun exposure, dehydration, and water hazards (see "Ocean Safety," below).

GENERAL AVAILABILITY OF HEALTH CARE

You'll find major hospitals and a variety of walk-in clinics easily accessible throughout the islands. Drugstores, with full-service pharmacies, are plentiful. Be sure to bring any prescribed medications with you, but common, over-the-counter medicines, like pain relievers, cough and cold remedies, and more, are readily available.

COMMON AILMENTS
Vog

The volcanic haze dubbed *vog* is caused by gases released when molten lava—from the continuous eruption of Kilauea Volcano on the Big Island—pours into the ocean. Some people claim that long-term exposure to the hazy, smoglike air has caused bronchial ailments, but it's highly unlikely to cause you any harm in the course of your visit.

There actually is a vog season in Hawaii: the fall and winter months, when the trade winds that blow the fumes out to sea die down. The vog is felt not only on the Big Island, but also as far away as Maui and Oahu.

One more word of caution: If you're pregnant or have heart or breathing problems, you should avoid exposure to the sulfuric fumes that are ever present in and around the Big Island's Hawaii Volcanoes National Park.

Sun Exposure

Hawaii's Caucasian population has the highest incidence of malignant melanoma (deadly skin cancer) in the world. And nobody is completely safe from the sun's harmful rays: All skin types and races can burn. To ensure that your vacation won't be ruined by painful sunburn, be sure to wear a strong sunscreen that protects against both UVA and UVB rays at all times (look for zinc oxide, benzophenone, oxybenzone, sulisobenzone, titanium dioxide, or avobenzone in the list of ingredients). Wear a wide-brimmed hat and sunglasses. Keep infants under 6 months out of the sun completely, and slather older babies and children with strong sunscreen frequently.

If you do get a burn, aloe vera, cool compresses, cold baths, and benzocaine can help with the pain. Stay out of the sun until the burn is completely gone.

Bugs

Like any tropical climate, Hawaii is home to lots of bugs. Most of them won't harm you. However, watch out for mosquitoes, centipedes, and scorpions, which do sting and may cause anything from mild annoyance to severe swelling and pain.

MOSQUITOES These pesky insects are not native to Hawaii, but arrived as larvae stowed away in water barrels on the ship *Wellington* in 1826, when it anchored in Lahaina. There's not a whole lot you can do about them, except to apply commercial repellent, which you can pick up at any drugstore.

CENTIPEDES Segmented crawling bugs with a jillion legs that come in two varieties: 6- to 8-inch-long brown ones and 2- to 3-inch-long blue guys. Both can really pack a wallop with their sting. Centipedes are generally found in damp, wet places, such as under wood piles or compost heaps; wearing closed-toe shoes can help prevent stings. If you're stung, apply ice at once to prevent swelling. See a doctor if you experience extreme pain, swelling, nausea, or any other severe reaction.

SCORPIONS Rarely seen, scorpions are found in arid, warm regions; their stings can be serious. Campers in dry areas should always check their boots before putting them on and shake out sleeping bags and bedrolls. Symptoms of a scorpion sting include shortness of breath, hives, swelling, and nausea. In the unlikely event that you're stung, apply diluted household ammonia and cold compresses to the area of the sting and seek medical help immediately.

HIKING SAFETY

In addition to taking the appropriate precautions regarding Hawaii's bug population, hikers should always let someone know where they're heading, when they're going, and when they plan to return; too many hikers get lost in Hawaii because they don't let others know their basic plans.

Before you head out, always check weather conditions with the **National Weather Service** (© **808/973-4381** on Oahu; see individual island chapters for local weather information). Hike with a pal, never alone. Wear hiking boots, a sun hat, clothes to protect you from the sun and from getting scratches, and high-SPF sunscreen on all exposed areas of skin.

Take water. Stay on the trail. Watch your step. It's easy to slip off precipitous trails and into steep canyons. Many experienced hikers and boaters today pack a cellphone in case of emergency; just dial © **911.**

OCEAN SAFETY

Because most people coming to Hawaii are unfamiliar with the ocean environment, they're often unaware of the natural hazards it holds. With just a few precautions, your ocean experience can be a safe and happy one. First, always heed warning signs and flags that indicate unsafe swimming conditions. A yellow flag means there's a lifeguard on duty; a blue flag means swimming is dangerous; a red flag: Don't even think about going in! Riptides, breaking surf, and currents can be very

strong in the waters surrounding the islands.

If no flags are flying, it doesn't mean it's safe. For up-to-date information, visit http://oceansafety.soest.hawaii.edu. The Pacific Whale Foundation has a free brochure called "Enjoying Maui's Unique Ocean Environment," that introduces visitors to Hawaii's ocean, beaches, tide pools, and reefs. Although written for Maui (with maps showing Maui's beaches), it's a great general resource on how to stay safe around the ocean, with hints on how to assess weather before you jump into the water and the best ways to view marine wildlife. To get the brochure, call © **808/ 244-8390** or visit www.pacificwhale.org.

SHARKS   Note that sharks are not a big problem in Hawaii; in fact, they appear so infrequently that locals look forward to seeing them. Since records have been kept, starting in 1779, there have been only about 100 shark attacks in Hawaii, of which 40% have been fatal. Most attacks occurred after someone fell into the ocean from the shore or from a boat; in these cases, the sharks probably attacked after the person was dead. Just in case though, the general rules for avoiding sharks are: Don't swim at sunrise, at sunset, or where the water is murky due to stream runoff—sharks may mistake you for one of their usual meals.

And don't swim where there are bloody fish in the water, as sharks become aggressive around blood. The Hawaii State Department of Land and Natural Resources has launched a website, www. hawaiisharks.com, which covers the biology, history, and culture of these carnivores. It also provides safety information and data on shark bites in Hawaii.

SEASICKNESS   The waters in Hawaii can range from as calm as glass (off the Kona Coast on the Big Island) to downright frightening (in storm conditions); they usually fall somewhere in between.

In general, expect rougher conditions in winter than in summer. Some 90% of the population tends toward seasickness. If you've never been out on a boat, or if you've been seasick in the past, you might want to heed the following suggestions:

- The day before you go out on the boat, avoid alcohol, caffeine, citrus and other acidic juices, and greasy, spicy, or hard-to-digest foods.
- Get a good night's sleep the night before.
- Take or use whatever seasickness prevention works best for you—medication, an acupressure wristband, gingerroot tea or capsules, or any combination. But do it before you board; once you set sail, it's generally too late.
- While you're on the boat, stay as low and as near the center of the boat as possible. Avoid the fumes (especially if it's a diesel boat); stay out in the fresh air and watch the horizon. Do not read.
- If you start to feel queasy, drink clear fluids like water, and eat something bland, such as a soda cracker.

STINGS The most common stings in Hawaii come from jellyfish, particularly Portuguese man-of-war and box jellyfish. Since the poisons they inject are very different, you need to treat each type of sting differently.

A bluish-purple floating bubble with a long tail, the Portuguese man-of-war is responsible for some 6,500 stings a year on Oahu alone. These stings, although painful and a nuisance, are rarely harmful; fewer than 1 in 1,000 requires medical treatment. The best prevention is to watch for these floating bubbles as you snorkel (look for the hanging tentacles below the surface). Get out of the water if anyone near you spots these jellyfish.

Reactions to stings range from mild burning and reddening to severe welts and blisters. The book *All Stings Considered* (Latitude 20 Books) recommends the following treatment: First, pick off any visible tentacles with a gloved hand, a stick, or anything handy; then rinse the sting with salt- or freshwater, and apply ice to prevent swelling and to help control pain. Avoid folk remedies like vinegar, baking soda, or urinating on the wound, which may actually cause further damage. Most Portuguese man-of-war stings will disappear by themselves within 15 to 20 minutes if you do nothing at all to treat them. Still, be sure to see a doctor if pain persists or a rash or other symptoms develop.

Transparent, square-shaped box jellyfish are nearly impossible to see in the water. Fortunately, they seem to follow a monthly cycle: 8 to 10 days after the full moon they appear in the waters on the leeward side of each island and hang around for about 3 days. Also, they seem to sting more in the morning hours, when they're on or near the surface.

The stings can cause anything from no visible marks to hivelike welts, blisters, and pain lasting from 10 minutes to 8 hours. *All Stings Considered* recommends the following treatment: First, pour regular household vinegar on the sting; this will stop additional burning. Do not rub the area. Pick off any vinegar-soaked tentacles with a stick. For pain, apply an ice pack. Seek additional medical treatment if you experience shortness of breath, weakness, palpitations, muscle cramps, or any other severe symptoms. Most box-jellyfish stings disappear by themselves without any treatment.

PUNCTURES Most sea-related punctures come from stepping on or brushing against the needlelike spines of sea urchins (known locally as *wana*). Be careful when you're in the water; don't put your foot down (even if you have booties or fins on) if you can't clearly see the bottom. Waves can push you into *wana* in a surge zone in shallow water. The spines can even puncture a wet suit.

A sea-urchin puncture can result in burning, aching, swelling, and discoloration (black or purple) around the area where the spines entered your skin. The best thing to do is to pull any protruding spines out and consult with a local doctor. The body will absorb the spines within 24 hours to 3 weeks, or the remainder of the spines will work themselves out. Again, contrary to popular wisdom, do not urinate or pour vinegar on the embedded spines—this will not help.

CUTS All cuts obtained in the marine environment must be taken seriously because the high level of bacteria present in the water can quickly cause the cut to become infected. The best way to prevent cuts is to wear a wet suit, gloves, and reef shoes. Never touch coral; not only can you get cut, but you can also damage a living organism that took decades to grow.

The symptoms of a coral cut can range from a slight scratch to severe welts and blisters. *All Stings Considered* recommends gently pulling the edges of the skin open and removing any embedded coral or grains of sand with tweezers.

Next, scrub the cut well with fresh water. If pressing a clean cloth against the wound doesn't stop the bleeding, or the edges of the injury are jagged or gaping, seek medical treatment.

WHAT TO DO IF YOU GET SICK AWAY FROM HOME
See the list of major **hospitals** and **emergency numbers** in the "Fast Facts, Toll-Free Numbers & Websites" appendix, p. 238.

STAYING SAFE
Although tourist areas on the islands are generally safe, visitors should always stay alert, even in laid-back Hawaii (and especially in Waikiki). It's wise to ask the island tourist office if you're in doubt about which neighborhoods are safe. Avoid deserted areas, especially at night. Don't go into any city park at night unless there's an event that attracts crowds—for example, the Waikiki Shell concerts in Kapiolani Park. Generally speaking, you can feel safe in areas where there are many people and open establishments.

Avoid carrying valuables with you on the street, and don't display expensive cameras or electronic equipment. Hold on to your pocketbook, and place your billfold in an inside pocket. In theaters, restaurants, and other public places, keep your possessions in sight.

Oahu has seen a series of purse-snatching incidents, in which thieves in slow-moving cars or on foot have snatched handbags from female pedestrians. The

---

Really Lost Hikers Should:

- S.T.O.P. (Stop, Think, Observe, Plan).
- Blow a whistle to signal you need assistance.
- Stay put. Most likely, if you've informed friends and authorities of your itinerary, a rescue effort will be launched quickly on your behalf after you fail to show up at the appointed time.
- Drink enough water.
- Put on your extra clothing. Avoid getting cold or hypothermic.
- If appropriate, build a fire for warmth and as a locator. Make sure to build a simple fire pit so you don't set the woods on fire with your blaze.

Tips for Better Hiking Photos

Don't center your subject in the frame. Allow the terrain, trail, and surroundings to help tell the story.

Don't fight the light—use it. Silhouettes add an offbeat dimension to the usual buddies-on-the-trail shots. By all means, take good advantage of bad weather and shoot in rain and fog.

A sign to remember. Include a sign in your coverage: a trail sign, wilderness, mileage. Signs are useful as little inserts in a publication or to help you remember a great day on the trail.

Details, please. One or two flowers are often more compelling than a long shot of a flower-dotted meadow.

Get some emotion. Sure a winsome grin is nice, but how about showing some fatigue, grime, sweat, tears?

Use your camera's delayed shutter release to good effect. Put yourself in the picture.

Don't be shy about asking someone to photograph you. You'll get a picture to remember, and it's a great way to get to meet people.

Honolulu police department advises women to carry purses on the shoulder away from the street or, better yet, to wear the strap across the chest instead of on one shoulder. Women with clutch bags should hold them close to their chests.

Remember also that hotels are open to the public and that at a large property, security may not be able to screen everyone entering. Always lock your room door—don't assume that once inside your hotel, you're automatically safe. And keep valuables in an in-room safe if one's available.

STAYING ON THE TRAIL

When you're on the trail, keep your eyes open. If you're hiking so fast that all you see is your boots, you're not attentive to passing terrain—its charms or its layout. *Stop* once in awhile. Sniff wildflowers, splash your face in a spring. *Listen.* Maybe the trail is paralleling a stream. Listen to the sound of mountain water. On your left? On your right? Look up at that fire lookout on the nearby ridge. Are you heading toward it or away from it? *Look around.* That's the best insurance against getting lost.

Watch for way-marks. Parks are marked with basic trail mileage signs and in many other ways, including blazes, disks, posts, and cairns.

Be aware of your surroundings. Note passing landmarks and natural features. Use the east-rising, west-setting sun and its respective position to the trail to help you in your orientation. Stop now and then to compare your progress on the ground to the route on the map. Look behind you frequently. Knowing where you come from always gives you a better feel for where you're going and prepares you for the return trip.

It's important, for your sake, to stay on the trail. Getting lost is usually the result of taking a "shortcut" off an established trail. Most of the park and forest trails described in this guide are well-signed, well-maintained, and easy to follow.

It's also important, for the environment's sake, to stay on the trail. Staying on the trail protects certain fragile terrain and is essential when hiking through sensitive bird habitats.

(Tips) It's Easy Being Green

Here are a few simple ways you can help conserve fuel and energy when you travel:

- Each time you take a flight or drive a car, greenhouse gases release into the atmosphere. You can help neutralize this danger to the planet through "carbon offsetting"—paying someone to invest your money in programs that reduce your greenhouse gas emissions by the same amount you've added. Before buying carbon offset credits, just make sure that you're using a reputable company, one with a proven program that invests in renewable energy. Reliable carbon offset companies include **Carbonfund** (www.carbonfund.org), **TerraPass** (www.terrapass.org), and **Carbon Neutral** (www.carbonneutral.org).

- Whenever possible, choose nonstop flights; they generally require less fuel than indirect flights that stop and take off again. Try to fly during the day—some scientists estimate that nighttime flights are twice as harmful to the environment. And pack light—each 15 pounds of luggage on a 5,000-mile flight adds up to 50 pounds of carbon dioxide emitted.

- Hikers should always stay on the trail to avoid damage to native plants—often endangered species—and to reduce erosion. Respect all NO TRESPASSING signs and stay off private property unless you have permission. Do not take plants, trimmings, flowers, or rocks. Wipe your boots off before and after all hikes to avoid spreading pests and invasive seedlings. Do not disturb wildlife.

- Where you stay during your travels can have a major environmental impact. To determine the green credentials of a property, ask about trash disposal and recycling, water conservation, and energy use; also question if sustainable

TRAIL HEAD SAFETY & PARKING PRECAUTIONS

Returning to the trail head after a joyful day on the trail to find a car window smashed and valuables missing can ruin your hiking vacation. Almost all the featured hikes in this guide begin at what land managers characterize as "developed trail heads"—which is to say they're usually safer and better patrolled than undeveloped trail heads, such as pullouts and dirt lots hidden far from the highway.

Statistics suggest that after three decades of LOCK YOUR CAR AND TAKE YOUR VALUABLES WITH YOU signs and campaigns in North America, hikers are finally heeding this safety advice, resulting in fewer reported car break-ins.

A few simple steps can minimize the likelihood of your car being broken into: Don't leave valuables in the car, and leave the car open; this way thieves will not cause damage breaking into the vehicle looking for goods (best idea). Lock valuables in the trunk (second best idea). Always bring your wallet and keys with you rather than hiding them in your vehicle.

materials were used in the construction of the property. The website **www. greenhotels.com** recommends green-rated member hotels around the world that fulfill the company's stringent environmental requirements. Also consult **www.environmentallyfriendlyhotels.com** for more green accommodations ratings.

- The Hawaii Department of Business, Economic Development & Tourism's Green Business Program recognizes businesses, including hotels and resorts that operate in an environmentally responsible way. For more information visit http://hawaii.gov/dbedt/info/energy/resource/greenbusiness.

- At hotels, request that your sheets and towels not be changed daily. (Many hotels already have programs like this in place.) Turn off the lights and air-conditioner (or heater) when you leave your room.

- Use public transportation where possible—even taxis are more energy-efficient than driving. Even better is to walk or cycle; you'll produce zero emissions and stay fit and healthy on your travels.

- If renting a car is necessary, ask the rental agent for a hybrid, or rent the most fuel-efficient car available. You'll use less gas and save money at the tank.

- Eat at locally owned and operated restaurants that use produce grown in the area. This contributes to the local economy and cuts down on greenhouse gas emissions by supporting restaurants where the food is not flown or trucked in across long distances. Visit **Sustain Lane** (www.sustainlane. org) to find sustainable eating and drinking choices around the U.S.; also check out **www.eatwellguide.org** for tips on eating sustainably in the U.S. and Canada.

6 PACKAGES FOR THE INDEPENDENT TRAVELER

There are several tour companies that offer guided hikes on the islands. On Maui, you can't go wrong with these two top-notch outfitters: **Hike Maui** (© **866/324-MAUI** [6284] or 808/879-5270; www. hikemaui.com) and **Maui Eco-Adventures** (© **877/661-7720** or 808/661-772; www.ecomaui.com). On the Big Island, consider **Hawaiian Walkways** (© **800/457-7759** or 808/775-0372; www.hawaiian walkways.com) and **Hawaii Forest & Trails** (© **800/464-1993** or 808/331-8505; www.hawaii-forest.com). The well-regarded **Country Walkers** (© **800/464-9255;** www.countrywalkers.com), known for its full-service guided walking tours throughout the world, offers an all-inclusive hiking tour of the Big Island. The itinerary includes daily scheduled hikes, optional cultural tours and outdoor

Frommers.com: The Complete Travel Resource

Planning a trip or just returned? Head to **Frommers.com,** voted Best Travel Site by *PC Magazine*. We think you'll find our site indispensable before, during, and after your travels—with expert advice and tips; independent reviews of hotels, restaurants, attractions, and preferred shopping and nightlife venues; vacation giveaways; and an online booking tool. We publish the complete contents of over 135 travel guides in our **Destinations** section, covering over 4,000 places worldwide. Each weekday, we publish original articles that report on **Deals and News** via our free **Frommers.com Newsletters.** What's more, **Arthur Frommer** himself blogs 5 days a week, with cutting opinions about the state of travel in the modern world. We're betting you'll find our **Events** listings an invaluable resource; it's an up-to-the-minute roster of what's happening in cities everywhere—including concerts, festivals, lectures, and more. We've also added weekly **podcasts, interactive maps,** and hundreds of new images across the site. Finally, don't forget to visit our **Message Boards,** where you can join in conversations with thousands of fellow Frommer's travelers and post your trip report once you return.

activities, and meals and accommodations at top-quality inns and oceanfront resorts.

On Oahu, a top choice is **Oahu Nature Tours** (© 808/924-2473; www.oahu naturetours.com). On Kauai, there are two great tour companies: **Kauai Eco-Tours** (© 877/538-4453; www.kauaieco-tours. com) and **Kayak Kauai** (© 800/437-3507 or 808/826-9844; www.kayakkauai. com). All companies offer insider, local guides who are knowledgeable about island flora, fauna, and culture; most

provide transportation from major hotels and resorts to and from the trail head. On Molokai, join **The Nature Conservancy's** (© 808/553-5236; www.nature.org) monthly tours of Kamakou and Mo'omomi preserves. Also on Molokai are cultural tours of Halawa Valley run by the **Hotel Molokai** (© 808/553-5347; www.hotel molokai.com).

For more information on Package Tours and for tips on booking your trip, see www.frommers.com/planning.

Suggested Itineraries

We've included 60 hikes in this book, covering five of the major Hawaiian Islands: Oahu, the Big Island, Kauai, Maui, and Molokai. Ideally, you would spend at least a couple weeks on each island, and still you wouldn't be able to see and do it all. We realize few vacationers have that much time to devote to their Hawaii hiking getaway. So, instead, we've suggested four abbreviated itineraries that feature the not-to-be-missed trails. You can always come back for more!

1 KAUAI IN 6 DAYS

The Garden Isle, measuring 33 miles long and 25 miles across, is a nature-lover's paradise. It's nearly impossible to get lost; one main road travels the perimeter of the island, and services, lodgings, and restaurants are readily available. Tourists cluster around three major resort areas: Coconut Coast, including Lihue, Wailua and Kapa'a; sunny Poipu on the south shore; and Princeville and Hanalei Bay on the north shore. Hikers will also want to spend time near Waimea Canyon and Kokee State Park on the west-northwest corner of the island. If you plan on hiking the strenuous Kalalua Trail along the Na Pali Coast, allow at least an additional 2 days.

Day ❶: Poipu

For a fabulous overview of the island, splurge for an early-morning helicopter ride. More than 90% of Kauai's wild landscape is inaccessible, and the best way to see it all is from the air. Now you'll know where you're headed. Spend the afternoon hiking the **Mahaulepu Heritage Trail.** Rugged sea cliffs, secluded coves, dunes, tide pools, sculpted lava formations, native plants, and petroglyphs are all found along this ancient coastal route. Nearby is Sprouting Horn, where the surf rushes through a lava tube and erupts 50 feet into the air through a blowhole. You can also visit Poipu Beach Park, a popular string of crescent-shaped beaches. Surf lessons anyone?

Day ❷: Waimea Canyon

Drive to the "Grand Canyon of the Pacific," the 10-mile-long, more than 3,500-foot-deep canyon with rugged cliffs, multi-hued folds, and rippling waterfalls.

For great canyon views, walk the **Iliau Nature Loop,** located off Waimea Canyon Drive. If you're up for a more strenuous hike, continue on the **Kukui Trail,** making a switchbacked descent into the canyon. Go as far as you like, but remember you have to climb back out! In the afternoon, visit **Polihale State Park,** with miles of luscious beach, 100-foot dunes, and dramatic surf. It's also a great place for sunset-viewing and stargazing. Stay in the area—Waimea Plantation Cottages and Kokee Lodge are good choices—so you'll be close to the next day's hike in Kokee State Park.

Day ❸: Kokee State Park

Get going early for the trip up Waimea Canyon Drive to **Kokee State Park.** It'll take about 30 minutes from Waimea town. You'll pass the visitor center and small museum and then drive to the end of the road. Spend a few moments, soaking in the views of the Na Pali Coast and

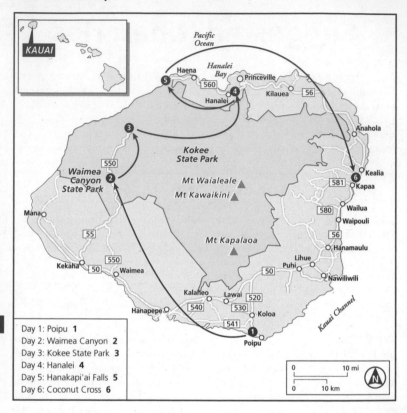

Pacific
Ocean

KAUAI

Haena
Hanalei
Bay
5
560
Princeville
Hanalei
4
Kilauea
56
Anahola

3

Kokee
State Park

Kealia
6
Kapaa

Waimea
Canyon
State Park
2
550

Mt Waialeale
Mt Kawaikini
581

580
Wailua
Waipouli
56
Hanamaulu

Mana

Mt Kapalaoa

55

550
Kekaha
50
Waimea

Lihue
Puhi
50
Nawiliwili

Kalaheo
Lawai
520

Kauai Channel

Hanapepe
540
530
Koloa

541

Poipu
1

Day 1: Poipu **1**
Day 2: Waimea Canyon **2**
Day 3: Kokee State Park **3**
Day 4: Hanalei **4**
Day 5: Hanakapi'ai Falls **5**
Day 6: Coconut Cross **6**

| 0 | | 10 mi |
| 0 | | 10 km |

N

the Pacific Ocean at the Pu'u O Kila Lookout. Then hit trail! Allow at least 6 hours to hike the **Pihea and Alakai Swamp trails.** This 7.4-mile, out-and-back trek takes you through an eerie swamp located on an old caldera floor created some 6 million years ago. The not-to-be-missed hike travels through dense rainforest and open muddy bogs—the world's highest rainforest and swampland. At the end of the day, stop by the Shrimp Station in Waimea for a well-earned basket of coconut battered shrimp or spicy shrimp tacos.

Days **4** & **5**: North Shore

It's time to head to the other side of the island. Pass through busy Kapa'a (you'll be

back) and continue north, driving the narrow, twisting road and crossing the one-lane bridges of Kauai's pristine north shore. There are several beaches to visit along the way, including Hanalei Bay, Lumahai Beach, Tunnels Beach, and Haena Beach Park. Carve out time in the day to hike one of two Hanalei area trails: **Hanalei 'Okolehao Trail** or the **Hanalei River Trail.** Or, consider a guided kayak trip along the Na Pali Coast. The town of Hanalei is a nice place to stop for a bite to eat, and the Hanalei Bay Resort & Suites, overlooking Bali Hai Cliffs and Hanalei Bay, is a splurge-worthy place to stay for the night.

The next morning, drive to the end of Hwy. 56 to the Kalalua trail head. Allow 6 to 8 hours to hike the stunning **Hanakapi'ai Falls Trail,** a tromp through a wet, tropical rainforest, dotted with sweet-smelling guava and mango trees, ending at a towering 300-foot waterfall.

Day ❻: Coconut Coast

Spend your last day near Kapa'a, one of the popular resort areas on Kauai. In the morning, hike the **Sleeping Giant Trail** for lofty island views. In the afternoon, visit Lydgate State Park for a swim (there's good snorkeling, too), or take a guided kayak trip along the Wailua River to visit Fern Grotto, a lava-rock cave draped in tropical foliage. Before heading home, pick up souvenirs at the open-air Coconut Marketplace in Kapa'a; with more than 70 shops, it's the largest on Kauai.

---

2 MAUI & MOLOKAI IN 10 DAYS

This jam-packed itinerary takes in the best hiking on Maui, along with a 3-day side trip to Molokai. If you plan to hike the entire Sliding Sands Trail in Haleakala National Park on Maui, with an overnight stay at a backcountry cabin or campsite, you'll need to add an additional day or two. You'll also need a car on both islands to get around (a four-wheel-drive is essential on Molokai).

Days ❶ & ❷: Waihee Valley & Kapalua

Stay in the resort town of Lahaina or Kaanapali, where you'll find a slew of lodgings, restaurants, shops, and services. The first day, hike the **Waihee Valley Swinging Bridge Trail,** a walk through a lush rainforest, across two swinging bridges, ending at a waterfall swimming hole. Consider joining a guided trip (p. 27); guides provide detailed information about Maui's flora and fauna and cultural history, a good base of knowledge to have for the rest of the week. The trek takes about half a day, leaving plenty of time to stop at the **Iao Valley State Park** in the afternoon. The Valley is one of the prettiest and most sacred sites on the island. A paved .6-mile walk provides a scenic viewpoint of Kuka'emoku (Iao Needle), rising 1,200 feet from the valley floor. After a long hot day, take a swim at Kaanapali Beach, where you'll also find a large number of nearby restaurants and vendors.

The next day, take the winding, scenic road around Maui's northern tip to see the **Nakalele Blowhole,** where water surges through a hole in the lava shelf, erupting like a geyser. Walking trails weave through the lava-rock landscape. Nearby, visit the upscale resort community of Kapalua to hike the **Honolua Ridge and Maunalei Arboretum trails,** for sweeping views into the Pu' u Kukui Watershed Preserve, the largest private preserve in Hawaii. If you've timed it right, you can stop for dinner at Sansei in Kapalua for the island's best sushi. Get to bed early; tomorrow's a long day.

Day ❸: Haleakala National Park

Plan to reach the summit of Haleakala before sunrise (trust us—it's worth it!). Park at the Halemau'u trail head and follow the path leading to a hiker's pullout, where you'll hitch a ride to the upper visitor center. Watch the sunrise as you begin the 11-mile trek down **Sliding Sands Trail** and out **Halemau'u Trail.** Lava fields; cinder cones; blooming silversword; and steep, forested crater walls are some of the eye-candy rewards on this long day hike.

Day ❹: Wailea

Today, head south to explore **Hoapili Trail and La Perouse Bay,** with picturesque coves, secluded beaches, and high surf. Along the way, you'll see remnants of old Hawaiian foundations and *heiau* (religious sites), and have views of the inland foothills of Haleakala and the Pacific Ocean. After your hike, you should have time to relax at Wailea Beach, one of Maui's top beaches for snorkeling and swimming. If money is no object, stay at the Four Seasons Resort in Wailea, a fine reward for all your hard work on the trail!

Day ❺: Molokai's Kamakou Preserve

Take an early-morning ferry (departing from Lahaina) or a small plane (from the Kahalui Airport) to Molokai. Pick up your rental car and follow Hwy. 460, heading west out of Kaunakakai, Molokai's main town. The road to the Pepeopae trail head is rough going and can take up to 2 hours, if it's passable at all. But the reward is well worth the bumpy ride. The **Pepeopae** boardwalk trail in the Kamakou Preserve climbs through dense native cloud forest to Pepeopae Bog, a fragile bog ecosystem. It ends at a stunning overlook into Pelekunu Valley. The best way to see the preserve is on a guided Nature Conservancy hike, offered once a month (p. 28), but you can go it alone if you have a four-wheel-drive vehicle to access the trail head. Be sure to pack a picnic lunch to enjoy at the outlook, one of the best seats on the island. Return to Kaunakakai to check into the Hotel Molokai, one of the liveliest—and few—places to stay on the island.

Day ❻: Kalaupapa National Park

Today, you'll visit **Kalaupapa National Historic Park,** home to the infamous Molokai leper colony. Father Damien de Veuster came here in the late 1800s to aid the Hansen's disease (leprosy) sufferers who were banished to this remote and isolated peninsula. You've booked a tour with Damien Tours, right? That's required to access the trail (p. 227). This dramatic and strenuous trail drops nearly 2,000 feet, switchbacking 26 times over soaring sea cliffs. The hike down takes less than 2 hours, but the required tour is almost 4 hours long, and then you'll need to hike back up to your car. Allow a full day for this adventure; a dinner at the Kualapuu Cook House is a fine way to end the day.

Day ❼: Halawa Valley

Have an early breakfast at Kanemitsu's Bakery, a local standout, and then take Hwy. 450 to Halawa. The 30-mile—very scenic—drive takes about 90 minutes from Kaunakakai. Access to the **Halawa Valley Trail** crosses private property, so you must hire a local guide (p. 28). Allow about 4 hours to hike the steep cathedral valley, which some say is one of the most culturally significant places in Hawaii. You'll walk through dense forest and past ancient settlement sites before reaching the 250-foot-tall Mo'oula Falls.

Catch a late-afternoon flight or ferry back to Maui. On your way back from Halawa Valley, stop by Mana'e Goods & Grindz for snacks to enjoy on the trip.

Day ❽: Road to Hana

Today, take the famously scenic and slow road to Hana. The twisting, narrow, barely two-lane road flanks dense tropical forests and lush slopes dotted with cascades and waterfalls. Take your time to stop and ogle the landscape at the many pullouts, and, of course, to take a hike. The **Waikamoi Forest Ridge Trail,** off Hana Highway, is a short jaunt through a thick bamboo and fern forest with valley-to-ocean views of the Keanae Peninsula.

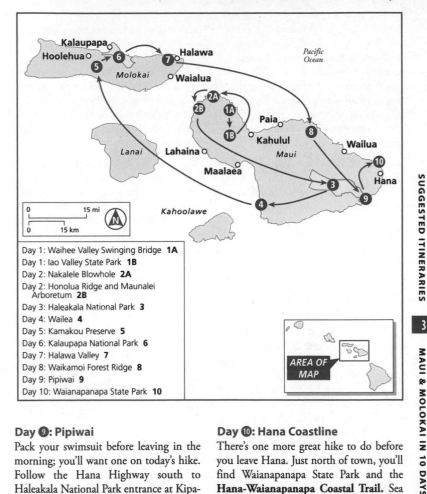

Day 1: Waihee Valley Swinging Bridge **1A**
Day 1: Iao Valley State Park **1B**
Day 2: Nakalele Blowhole **2A**
Day 2: Honolua Ridge and Maunalei Arboretum **2B**
Day 3: Haleakala National Park **3**
Day 4: Wailea **4**
Day 5: Kamakou Preserve **5**
Day 6: Kalaupapa National Park **6**
Day 7: Halawa Valley **7**
Day 8: Waikamoi Forest Ridge **8**
Day 9: Pipiwai **9**
Day 10: Waianapanapa State Park **10**

Day ❾: Pipiwai

Pack your swimsuit before leaving in the morning; you'll want one on today's hike. Follow the Hana Highway south to Haleakala National Park entrance at Kipahulu (10 miles south of Hana) to hike the 4-mile round-trip **Pipiwai Trail.** The scenic trail follows a stream through Oheo Gulch traversing sweet-smelling guava and dark bamboo forests before reaching 400-foot Waimoku Falls, a truly breathtaking waterfall—and one of the largest on Maui. This is a great place for a small picnic and a refreshing swim. Stop by one of the roadside stands to grab a fish taco and cold drink on your way back to Hana.

Day ❿: Hana Coastline

There's one more great hike to do before you leave Hana. Just north of town, you'll find Waianapanapa State Park and the **Hana-Waianapanapa Coastal Trail.** Sea cliffs, stone arches, lava fields, black beaches, blowholes, and ancient temples are part of the highlights of this stunning coastal route. The trail follows portions of the ancient King's Highway from Waianapanapa State Park to Hana Bay. If this is your last day in Hana, be sure to leave plenty of time for the ride back on Hana Highway.

Oahu, measuring 44 miles long and only 30 miles wide at its broadest point, is the most bustling and developed of the islands. It's home to more than 1.2 million people, a sizzling nightlife, and scores of restaurants, hotels, museums, and shopping venues. Most of the action is centered around Honolulu and Waikiki Beach. The popular resort area serves as a good base for exploring the island and accessing many of the trails, but you'll also want to spend a day on the island's laid-back and ultra scenic North Shore, where the surf culture is alive and well. If you plan on visiting Oahu's top attractions, including Pearl Harbor and the USS *Arizona* Memorial, Iolani Palace, the Bishop Museum, and the Polynesian Cultural Center, allow at least 3 to 4 additional days.

Day ❶: Waikiki Beach Area
Begin your visit to Oahu by hiking the island's two most popular trails: **Diamond Head Trail,** leading to the top of the dramatic volcanic crater at the end of Waikiki beach, remains the most popular trail on the island. The easy 2-hour round-trip hike culminates in the lookouts at the top of the crater ridge where you'll get one of the finest views there is of East Honolulu. From the uppermost point, you can see nearly all of the south shore as well as the eastern end of the Koolau Mountain Range and much of East Honolulu

In the afternoon, hike the **Manoa Falls Trail.** The trail head is located near the old Paradise Park in Manoa Valley, a quick 10-minute drive from downtown Honolulu. The short, 1.6-mile round-trip hike ends at a roaring 150-foot waterfall. Finish your day with a stroll along people-packed Waikiki Beach, where you can rent a canoe, take a surfing lesson, swim, snorkel, or just relax and watch the world go by.

Day ❷: Keaiwa State Park
Start the day early, around 8am, at Hanauma Bay (they turn away people when the parking lot is full) to snorkel the crystal-clear waters of the protected marine conservation area. In the afternoon, visit Keaiwa State Park to hike the **Aiea Loop Trail.** With its moderate distance, gently rolling hills, and abundant natural beauty, Aiea Loop is considered an old reliable among local hiking enthusiasts and takes

about 3.5 hours round-trip. Also check out Keaiwa Heiau, located just after the entrance to the park. The original *heiau* (temple) consisted of a large thatched hut surrounded by rock walls. Today, you can still see some of the original rock walls.

Day ❸: North Shore
No visit to Oahu is complete without a drive to the North Shore. The region is famous worldwide for its huge surf and beautiful beaches, including Waimea Bay, Sunset Beach, and the infamous Banzai Pipeline. Spend the morning on the beach, or, if you're an experienced hiker, definitely carve out time (about 5 hours) to hike the strenuous **Puu Manamana Trail** in Kaaawa. This is one of the most challenging, and most exhilarating, day hikes to be found in the state.

To celebrate your hike, or just to fuel up after a morning of surf, grab a burger at the Crouching Lion Inn, a Kaaawa landmark since 1927. Replenished, continue your drive to one of the North Shore beaches to chill out. It's a long day, but worth the effort.

If you didn't hike Puu Manamana this morning, in the afternoon spend about 2 hours hiking and spending some leisure time on the easy **Maunawili Falls Trail,** which leads to a 20-foot waterfall and deep swimming hole.

At night, consider staying on the North Shore; for a real treat, check in to the plush Turtle Bay Resort.

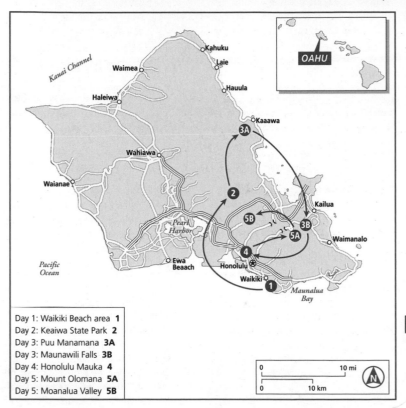

Day 1: Waikiki Beach area **1**
Day 2: Keaiwa State Park **2**
Day 3: Puu Manamana **3A**
Day 3: Maunawili Falls **3B**
Day 4: Honolulu Mauka **4**
Day 5: Mount Olomana **5A**
Day 5: Moanalua Valley **5B**

Day **4**: Honolulu

It's an easy day today—if you wish! Just 5 minutes from downtown Honolulu (15 min. from Waikiki), you can access the **Honolulu Mauka Trail System.** The well-maintained network of trails is perfect for a quick immersion into nature. Pick and choose your trails, allotting as much time as you wish. To do the entire trail network, it'll take close to 5 hours, with plenty of time left in the day to enjoy the beach. Stop by the Kapahulu Poi Shop, an Oahu mainstay, for traditional Hawaiian dishes such as *lau lau, lomi* salmon, squid *luau, kalua* pig, or dried *aku.*

Day **5**: Valleys & Summits

You have two choices today for hikes. If you're up for a serious challenge, hike the three towering peaks of **Mount Olomana.** The out-and-back trail that links the trio of peaks is a serious challenge that takes about 5 hours and rewards hikers with thrilling climbs and descents and an amazing 360-degree view from the first peak. Facing the ocean, you'll see the Windward Coast from Makapuu to Kualoa. Turn around and you can see Maunawili Valley and the major peaks of the Koolau Mountain Range, including Konahuanui, Puu o Kona, Lanipo, and Mount Olympus.

If you prefer less of a challenge, take the historic **Moanalua Valley Trail.** First developed during a period of great social and political upheaval in Hawaii, the Moanalua Valley Trail is as much a journey into the island's history as it is an exploration of its natural environment.

4 THE BIG ISLAND IN 6 DAYS

There's a reason they call it the Big Island. It's the biggest of the chain, measuring 4,028 square miles, nearly twice as large as the rest of the Hawaiian Islands combined. You'll want to see both sides of the island, including the sunny west coast (think beaches, sea cliffs, and ancient sites) and the wetter east coast (think waterfalls and tropical gardens). This itinerary includes 3 days on each side (book accommodations accordingly), including 2 days exploring Hawaii Volcanoes National Park.

Day ❶: Kohala Coast

You'll find plenty of services, restaurants, and lodging options along the Big Island's west coast, dubbed the Gold Coast. Several large, upscale resorts are located here, just north of Kailui-Kona and the Kona International Airport. Make this area your base for the next 3 days.

On your first morning, get up early with the sun! Pack your swimsuit and snorkeling gear for today's adventures along the Big Island's sunny west coast. If you have binoculars, bring those, too. From Kailui-Kona, travel north to Holoholokai Beach Park, where you can hike a short, 1.4-mile round-trip trail to the **Puako petroglyph field,** one of the world's largest collections of prehistoric rock carvings. There are 2,717 petroglyphs clustered on a sloping patch of smooth, reddish lava about 400 feet wide. On your way out, stop by Holoholokai Beach Park, a lovely spot for a post-petroglyph picnic.

Spend the afternoon at pretty **Kiholo Bay.** The trail traverses a pebbly black-sand beach on its way to a cold freshwater pond set in a raw, black lava field. Then it backtracks to an enchanting blue lagoon, filled with turtles. The hike will take about 3 hours, in and out, but you'll want to spend time exploring the Queen's Bath lava tube, swimming in Lauhinewai, and snorkeling at the Blue Lagoon, a favorite hangout for sea turtles.

Day ❷: Kona Coast

This morning, stop by Island Lava Java in Kona for a hot cup of locally grown coffee and homemade pastries. Then, head north to **Kaloko-Honkohau National Historic Park** and take a hike through Hawaii's prehistoric past. You'll loop through the network of trails passing ancient fishponds and several archeological sites including *heiau,* petroglyphs, and a massive seawall. Honokohau Beach, where you'll start and end, is a perfect perch for watching surfers and sea turtles just off shore.

Ready to relax? Take the afternoon off and visit one of the popular Gold Coast beaches, such as Kaunaoa Beach or Hapuna Beach State Recreation Area. Another more ambitious option: Travel south, about 10 miles from Kailui-Kona, to the **Captain Cook Monument Trail.** It's a steep, 1,325-foot descent—and climb back up—but you'll have fabulous views along the way. The trail ends at the Captain Cook Monument at the edge of Kealakekua Bay, one of the best snorkeling spots in Hawaii.

Day ❸: North Kohala

Drive north to the end of the road today, and be rewarded with scenic views galore and two short hikes. First stop is the Puukohola Heiau National Historic Site. The 1.5-mile round-trip **Puukohola Trail** leads past the base of an enormous temple, built by King Kamehameha the Great.

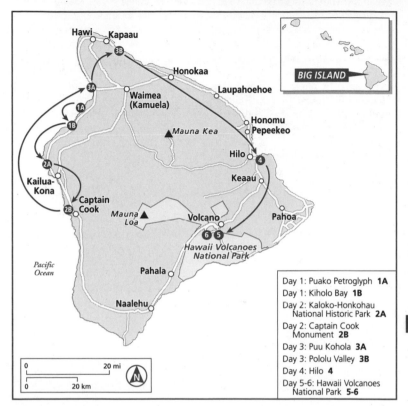

Day 1: Puako Petroglyph **1A**
Day 1: Kiholo Bay **1B**
Day 2: Kaloko-Honkohau
       National Historic Park **2A**
Day 2: Captain Cook
       Monument **2B**
Day 3: Puu Kohola **3A**
Day 3: Pololu Valley **3B**
Day 4: Hilo **4**
Day 5-6: Hawaii Volcanoes
         National Park **5-6**

SUGGESTED ITINERARIES

3

THE BIG ISLAND IN 6 DAYS

Back on the coastal highway, continue north until you reach Pololu Lookout at the end of the road. You'll have lots of sea cliff and ocean views along the way; if you're here during the winter months, look for migrating humpback whales. The **Pololu Valley Trail** leads to a windswept beach at the mouth of a lush valley.

Day ❹: Hilo

Time to leave the Gold Coast for the Big Island's wet east side! Take your time getting to Hilo, perhaps visiting Hawaii Tropical Botanical Gardens and driving the scenic Pepeekeo Loop. The 4-mile detour offers views of the rocky coastline on one side and tropical forests and waterfalls on the other.

Be sure to visit Akaka Falls State Park, located on the island's rainy Hamakua Coast. The paved **Akaka Falls Trail** circles through a steamy rainforest thick with tropical plants. The hike ends at two waterfalls: 100-foot Kahuna Falls and 442-foot Akaka Falls.

Consider spending the night at Hilo Bay Hostel, one of the most affordable places to stay on the island and very popular with hikers.

Days ❺ & ❻: Hawaii Volcanoes National Park

Before heading to the park, stop by Ken's House of Pancakes in Hilo for *loco moco* (two scoops of rice, one hamburger patty, a fried egg, and gravy). It will take about

45 minutes to reach the park entrance; stop in the visitor center to get up-to-date information on trails and road conditions. Take the 11-mile Crater Rim Drive, with plenty of outlooks and opportunities to stare into craters, steaming vents, and lava-rock hillsides. The drive will take at least 3 hours—more for lingering. Allow another 3 hours to hike the **Kilauea Iki Trail.** The 4-mile round-trip loop explores 400-foot-deep Kilauea Iki Crater, passing through lush rainforest at the edge of the crater, then across an otherworldly land of lava formations and sulfur steam vents on the crater floor.

Consider staying in one of the park's drive-up campgrounds (cabins are super cheap; tent sites are free).

The next day, wake up early for a long and strenuous volcano adventure. Drive the spectacular 38-mile Chain of Craters Road, twisting through lava fields and ending at the coast. Along the way, stop to hike **Napau Crater Trail.** The trek is a 14-mile round-trip huff and puff, following a line of craters and cones that has formed along the volcano's fiery seam. It's a fine ending to your Big Island hiking trip.

Oahu Hikes

by Michael Tsai

To the first-time visitor, the island of Oahu and its metropolitan center Honolulu can present quite a stir of contradictions. A 15-minute taxi ride from Honolulu International Airport to Waikiki, the congested tourist center many locals avoid like e-mails from deposed Nigerian ministers, is sometimes all it takes to strip away the popular image of Hawaii marketed by the local tourism authority: a sultry, tropical paradise where the living is easy and the famous aloha spirit is extended without social obligation or expectation. And it is true that Oahu has a number of social issues: a squeezed-tight population of more than 1 million people struggling to cope with a cost of living more than one-third higher than the national average and a native population still waiting for redress more than a century after its kingdom was illegally overthrown are just some of them.

But leave Waikiki for the island's natural environment, and you'll witness marketing hype and dew-slick reality converging along hundreds of miles of public-access trails stunning in their natural beauty, rich ecological and geographical diversity, and deep historical and cultural significance.

Each trail is a journey into history. Just as modern sustainability movements now find meaningful lessons in the sophisticated agricultural systems that fed and clothed the island's displaced host culture for centuries, the Depression-era work crews that constructed most of the island's trail systems relied heavily on pathways blazed long before western contact. On Oahu, a single trail may transition through sections of lush rainforest, rocky ridgeline, dry steppe, and soft grassland while at the same time crossing the physical remnants of a long and complicated Hawaiian history: ancient *heiau* (temples), 19th-century estates, World War II–era bunkers, and modern satellite towers.

Most public-access hikes on Oahu are well maintained, relatively short, and easy to navigate. However, those unfamiliar with island terrain should proceed with caution. Each year, scores of tourists are rescued off of trails after encountering problems with crumbly lava rock, slick clay, or thick vegetation. Also, while the elevation gain on most trails is relatively minimal (the highest point on the island is just 4,200 ft.), steep ascents and descents can appear suddenly and on decidedly difficult footing. High heat and humidity can also waylay nature lovers from cooler climates who are not accustomed to the hydration demands of tropical hiking.

Still, for true nature lovers, there are few hiking destinations that have as much to offer as Oahu. Whether your preference is climbing through clouds on jagged peaks or cooling your feet in waterfall pools, the island is uniquely suited to accommodate hikers of all stripes. And, best of all, no matter where you are on Oahu, you're never more than a few minutes' drive from a stirring descent into nature.

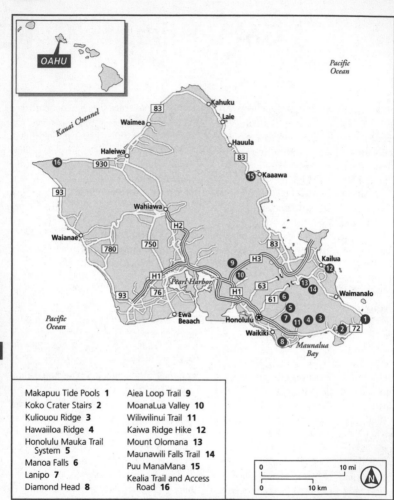

Makapuu Tide Pools **1**
Koko Crater Stairs **2**
Kuliouou Ridge **3**
Hawaiiloa Ridge **4**
Honolulu Mauka Trail
    System **5**
Manoa Falls **6**
Lanipo **7**
Diamond Head **8**

Aiea Loop Trail **9**
MoanaLua Valley **10**
Wiliwilinui Trail **11**
Kaiwa Ridge Hike **12**
Mount Olomana **13**
Maunawili Falls Trail **14**
Puu ManaMana **15**
Kealia Trail and Access
    Road **16**

OAHU HIKES

4

ESSENTIALS

ESSENTIALS

GETTING THERE

The Honolulu International Airport (HNL; www.honoluluairport.com) is the major hub for all flights in and out of the state. The airport is located just 7 miles from Waikiki, where most hotels are located. Expect to spend about $20 for a taxi, or take advantage of one of the hotel shuttles that run continuously back and forth. If you're traveling light, the city bus service also provides cheap ($2 for adults) and reliable transportation.

GETTING AROUND
By Car

Oahu residents own 600,000 registered vehicles, but they have only 1,500 miles of mostly two-lane roads. That's 400 cars for every mile, a fact that becomes abundantly clear during morning and evening rush hours. You can avoid the gridlock by driving between 9am and 3pm or after 6pm.

ORIENTATION

Oahu, nicknamed "the Gathering Place," is the second-oldest of Hawaii's eight major islands. Waikiki, on the south shore, is the major center of tourist activity, with an array of hotels, restaurants, and stores. Downtown Honolulu is home to Iolani Palace; the state capital; historic Chinatown; and scores of museums, galleries, and restaurants. Twenty minutes to the northeast, the Windward Coast boasts a wide range of ocean activities along some of the island's most scenic beaches. The North Shore, birthplace of the modern big-wave surfing scene, is a scenic wonder with a laid-back, country feel.

VISITOR INFORMATION

Unlike many tourist destinations, Oahu does not have official visitor information centers. However, most major hotels are well equipped to provide the same information on services, restaurants, activities, transportation, and other essentials. You can also get up-to-date information by visiting the official websites of the Oahu Visitors Bureau (www.visit-oahu.com), or the Hawaii Visitors and Convention Bureau (www.gohawaii.com).

MAKAPUU TIDE POOLS ★★

Difficulty rating: Moderate/strenuous

Distance: 2.5 miles round-trip

Estimated time: 2.5 hr.

Elevation gain: 500 feet

Costs/permits: None

Best time to go: 8 to 10am

Recommended map: "Koko Head" (www.hawaiitrails.org)

Trail head GPS: N21 18.312 W157 39.304

Trail head directions: Heading east on Kalanianaole Highway, drive straight past Koko Marina, Hanauma Bay, and Sea Life Park. Turn right at a break in the guardrail and enter a gated parking area. The trail follows the paved road to the right.

The Makapuu Tide Pools have long been a secret treasure for local hikers, many of whom still remain mum about their access points. And while increased attention in the media has let that secret out somewhat, the daunting descent helps to ensure that the pools are almost never crowded. The shoreline path is safer but underused because it's a long, boring approach through dry, barren fields. If you decide to take either route, bring plenty of water and be sure to liberally apply and reapply the sunscreen; aside from a cave on the side of the mountain, there's no shade anywhere.

The trail starts at Makapuu Point State Wayside Park with a walk up Makapuu Point Lighthouse Road. The road is broad and evenly paved, and it offers increasingly stunning views of the jagged coastline below.

❶ Path to the Tide Pools Roughly 1 mile up is a designated whale-watching lookout, and just beyond that, to the right, lies the unmarked path toward the tide pools. You'll need to venture out to the rock ledge at the side of the road to locate the pools; a powerful blowhole about 50 yards to the left is a good landmark if you're unsure. Simply wait for a large enough wave to activate the roaring, white plume and you'll know for sure that you're in the right spot. Depending on the amount of hydraulic pressure exerted on the hard lava fissure, the resulting explosion of seawater can reach up to 30 feet or more.

It doesn't matter precisely where you begin your descent, since the initial band of jagged black rock leads to several improvised paths to the shoreline. The rocky cliff it descends is in layers, and you'll need to make it all the way down to each successive narrow plateau to plot your next downward route.

Though difficult to spot and hold, a thin trail of switchbacks can be discerned from the plunging mass of loose rocks and boulders. Even on this path, you will need to step with extreme caution and be prepared for abrupt turns and drops.

❷ Blowhole The safest routes down will deposit you about midway between the blowhole and the main cluster of tide pools.

Be extremely cautious if you intend to approach the blowhole, and never put any part of your body over the exposed fissure. At least two tourists have been seriously injured by the explosive release in recent years, and another was killed at a similar spot.

❸ Tide Pools The largest of the pools is wide and deep enough for a couple of swim strokes; at least two other smaller pools are suitable for a Jacuzzi-like dip

(and can get almost as warm under the midday sun).

Just don't expect to swim alone. The tide pools are home to a wide variety of sea life, including *haukeuke* (shingle urchin), *aama* (rock crab), *pipipi* (sea snails), and at least three species of sea cucumber.

The crashing waves in the background can make for spectacular vacation photos, but they also require constant attention. Most waves will disperse in a harmless blast of spray as they hit the flat face of the facing cliff, but the force from larger waves can easily knock you over if you are unaware.

While the tide pools are a relaxing way to spend an afternoon, keep in mind as you bask in the sun that you still need to return up that steep, rocky slope to the road. Expect the return scramble to take twice as long as the descent. Hikers have painted arrows on some of the larger rocks to indicate the best routes back to the top, but these are only general guides, as erosion and rockslides continuously alter the face of the slope.

Your other option is to take a right on the shoreline and work your way toward a long dirt road leading back to the parking lot. On the way, you'll pass a vertical rock formation known as Pele's Chair. (*Note:* This path is more circuitous. It's also quite boring for long stretches as it meanders through a barren field. The coastal portions can also be dangerous depending on wave and tide conditions.)

❹ Lighthouse If your legs are still working after regaining the main road, you can hang a right and continue uphill, past the point where the pavement gives way to dirt road, to the lighthouse at Makapuu Point.

The site served as a lookout during World War II, and later operated as a nautical navigational lighthouse under the

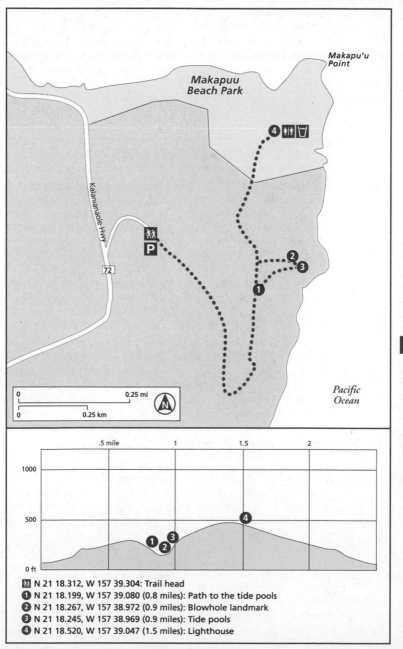

OAHU HIKES

4

MAKAPUU TIDE POOLS

🏃 N 21 18.312, W 157 39.304: Trail head
1 N 21 18.199, W 157 39.080 (0.8 miles): Path to the tide pools
2 N 21 18.267, W 157 38.972 (0.9 miles): Blowhole landmark
3 N 21 18.245, W 157 38.969 (0.9 miles): Tide pools
4 N 21 18.520, W 157 39.047 (1.5 miles): Lighthouse

Coast Guard. Now maintained by the state, the automated lighthouse continues to shine for passing ships. The area also includes several dilapidated World War II pillboxes, a remembrance plaque, and a series of lookouts that offer excellent views of Koko Crater, Sandy Beach, and parts of Kailua.

Just down the highway from the Makapuu Lighthouse Trail is Makapuu Beach Park, considered one of the best body-surfing and body-boarding spots on the island. If the surf is too rough for you to jump in on the action, take a seat on the large rock at the middle of the bay and watch how the local semi-pros handle themselves.

KOKO CRATER STAIRS ★

Difficulty rating: Moderate

Distance: 1 mile round-trip

Estimated time: 2 hr.

Elevation gain: 1,200 feet

Costs/permits: None

Best time to go: Before 9am or after 3pm

Recommended map: USGS' "Koko Head Quadrangle" map

Trail head GPS: N21 16.824 W157 41.513

Trail head directions: Traveling east on the Kalanianaole Highway, turn left on Lunalilo Home Road, the right on Kaumakani Street. Follow the road until you reach Anapalau Street; then turn right and continue to Koko Head District Park. Park in the back lot next to Mike Goes Field. Follow the short dirt path to the right to reach the unmarked trail head.

For better or worse, there are no surprises on this trail. Koko Crater towers over its otherwise flat surroundings and is visible from miles away. The trail, which follows an abandoned tramway to the summit, rises straight up. There are no switchbacks, and no relief from an ascent that only gets steeper as it reaches the top. Marathoners, athletes, and even boxers flock to the trail because it offers a powerful cardiovascular and muscular workout that can be completed in as little as 45 minutes. However, you don't need to be a high-level endurance athlete to make it up the more than 1,000 railroad ties that lead to the 1,208-foot summit, just patient and a tad daring.

The trail is hot, dry, and entirely exposed, so plan on bringing more water than normal for a hike of this distance. Strong quadriceps and sure-footedness are also required to properly navigate the aging ties and the crumbly, uneven ground around them.

From the parking lot, follow the paved pathway that curves toward the crater. The trail head is unmarked, so keep an eye out for a steep, narrow dirt trail on the right that curls left toward the base of the tracks.

The ties were laid as part of a World War II–era incline tram system that transported soldiers to a now-defunct radar station. Most are still in excellent condition, but caution is required for a few that have rotted or split. Concrete slabs support or replace a few with significant damage.

The trail begins at a significant incline that only grows steeper as you progress. Many first-timers make the mistake of starting off too quickly, a folly that becomes evident soon enough as hips and quads begin to fatigue.

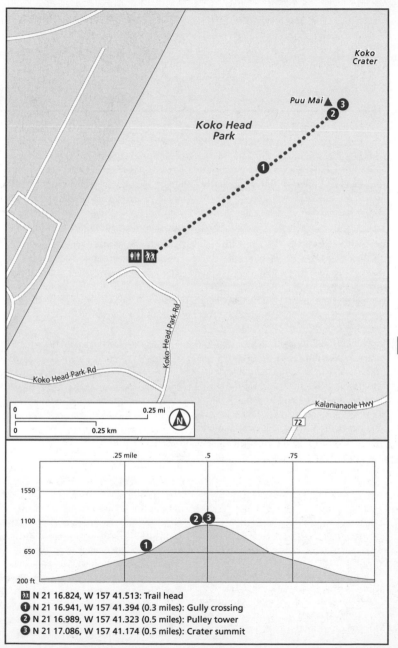

N 21 16.824, W 157 41.513: Trail head
1 N 21 16.941, W 157 41.394 (0.3 miles): Gully crossing
2 N 21 16.989, W 157 41.323 (0.5 miles): Pulley tower
3 N 21 17.086, W 157 41.174 (0.5 miles): Crater summit

46

Fun Facts   **The Legend of Koko Crater**

The Hawaiian name for Koko Crater is Kohelele, literally "winged vagina." According to legend, the goddess Kapo flung her sexual organ across the sky to distract the pig-god Kamapuaa as he attempted to force himself on Kapo's sister, the volcano god Pele. The phantom organ landed on the southeastern point of Oahu. Kamapuaa gave chase, launching himself upon on the earth where it lay, thus creating Koko Crater.

The terrain here is arid and crumbly, with just a smattering of scrub and kiawe at the fringes. Where broad enough, the dirt shoulders offer a gentler means of ascent and can save your major muscle groups the exertion of high-stepping from tie to tie.

❶ Gully Crossing   Roughly halfway up the crater lies a 70-track expanse that spans a 15-foot-deep gully. Given the incline, the crossing can be treacherous, especially in the three or four spots where the ties have splintered or worn away. The space between the tracks isn't wide enough for you to fall through, though serious injury could still occur if you misstep. In general, the section to the right of the rails offers the best footing, provided the sheer drop-off doesn't make you dizzy. Whichever tack you choose to take, it's best to try and maintain your momentum through the entire expanse. Acrophobic hikers can also opt to descend beneath the bridge via the rough, rocky gully and rejoin the trail on the other side.

Beyond the bridge, the trail gets significantly steeper, and it's a good idea to take careful inventory of your muscles, joints, and lungs before continuing.

❷ Pulley Tower   You can clearly see the top of the tram's pulley system as you make the final, long climb—no false peaks here—although that certainly can make your progress seem all the more glacial. Most repeat visitors take a brief stop for

water at the shady clearing beneath the pulley tower before heading back down. However, first timers will want to continue along the dirt path to the right, which takes you about 50 yards farther (and not much higher) to Puu Mai, the true summit of the crater.

❸ Crater Summit   The spot is marked by an old concrete powerhouse and a steel-grated lookout area that offers fantastic views of Hawaii Kai, Hanauma Bay, the eastern tip of the island, as well as the inside of the crater.

Puu Mai offers a welcome escape from the pinched, narrow trail and is a unique vantage point from which to view the serene waters of Hanauma.

Again, the hike back to the trail head requires caution, especially if you're attempting to descend the steep, at times unstable, trail on tired legs. Hopping down from track to track can be difficult for those with knee or joint problems, yet walking down the slopes of the shoulders can be dangerous given the loose dirt and rocks. Some hikers find it easiest to crab-crawl down the steepest sections. Fitter hikers may find it tempting to jog down the path. If you do, be sure to scan ahead for missing or eroded ties; given the angle of descent and the relatively narrow spaces between ties, stopping can be difficult.

OAHU HIKES

4

KOKO CRATER STAIRS

Note: In February 2008, the state attempted to close the trail in response to safety and liability concerns. The state also cited the trail's proximity to a popular shooting range, although there have been no reported incidents relating to this. Ultimately, the ban lasted just a day thanks to hundreds of complaints from regular visitors to the stairs.

An ad hoc committee of hikers has been working with the state to alleviate the concerns and has recommended regular maintenance and increased signage warning of potential hazards. Although the trail is expected to remain open, a final official determination has yet to be made.

KULIOUOU RIDGE TRAIL

Difficulty rating: Moderate

Distance: 5 miles round-trip

Estimated time: 4 hr.

Elevation gain: 1,900 feet

Costs/permits: None

Best time to go: After 3pm

Website: http://www.hawaiitrails.org/trail. php?TrailID=OA+15+016&island=Oahu

Recommended map: "Kuliouou Ridge Trail" (www.hawaiitrails.org)

Trail head GPS: N21 18.223 W157 43.466

Trail head directions: Heading east on Kalanianaole, turn left onto Elelupe Street and proceed to Kuliouou Road. Follow the road left, then right, and turn right on Kalaau Place. Street parking is available just before the cul-de-sac. Pass the Board of Water Supply gate and take the right side of the fork. The trail head is located to the right; continuing straight on the path will take you to the Kuliouou Valley Trail.

Kuliouou is widely considered the best ridge hike on the island, and for good reason. With turnaround points to accommodate hikers of all levels, ever-changing terrain, and great views of the windward and leeward coasts, the 5-mile link to the Koolaus offers a unique experience with every visit.

To start, take the short paved trail beyond the chain fence. Straight ahead is the Kuliouou Valley Trail, but keep an eye out for a sign on the right, next to a boot scrub, that marks the trail head to the ridge trail.

The hike begins gently with a series of rolling hills that lead to a long succession of koa-lined switchbacks overlooking the south shore. The trail appears to fork at least twice early on, but stick to the broader, more clearly defined path. The turns are often sharp, and careful footing is needed to safely negotiate a few steep, rocky elbows. The trail meanders in and out of the grooves of the mountain, providing good views of the valley interior.

❶ Ironwood Grove About .8 mile up, the trail steepens as it passes through the first of two ironwood groves. After a brief return to open trail, you'll hit a second, longer ironwood grove. Here the thick carpet of fallen needles covers everything in sight, including the trail. Still, observant hikers will be able to discern the shape of the path beneath the needles as they cross over a broad clearing. Just to be safe, aim for the open space beyond the stand of Norfolk Island pines.

❷ Picnic Table Shelter After making a narrow turn and climbing a short but slippery hill, you'll come to a pair of picnic tables beneath a simple but well-maintained shelter. For novice hikers, or if

> ### (Fun Facts) Iron Willed Ironwood
>
> Gentle, even mournful, in appearance, ironwoods are nonetheless unscrupulous competitors in the natural environment. The pine-like trees were introduced to Hawaii in 1882 and were widely used for watershed protection, soil and sand binding, and as windbreaks for housing and crops. They continue to thrive because their fine, brittle needles (actually branchlets) carpet the earth around them, suffocating competing vegetation and acidifying the soil as they decompose.

you're simply looking for a short, easy hike, this is a good place to turn around. Before you go, take a look at the exposed root system of a tall tree growing on an eroded hill to the side.

From here, the trail gets steeper and much more slippery, though not too difficult for intermediate hikers in decent physical condition. A short climb leads to a broad clearing within a Norfolk pine forest. Though camping is not permitted, there are usually signs of illegal campfires and tent stakes in the area.

❸ **Hawaii Kai Lookout** The lookout to the left overlooks the Hawaii Kai and its neighboring communities. If you need a break, this is a perfect spot to linger and enjoy the steady crosswind that flows through the line of towering pines.

A longer uphill stretch up a twisting, rocky path rises through a dense ohia forest. The footing here is tenuous at best, but the ohia provide ample support. The path eventually leads to a plastic-lumber bench at a small clearing on the summit ridge. A portal formed by crossing tree trunks marks the beginning of a small patch of protected Native Hawaiian forest made up of uluhe, koa, ohia, and lama.

The final 200 feet of elevation is gained in a series of lung-burning ascents up loose dirt and man-made steps. Be careful of the badly eroded areas around the steps, which can be especially treacherous when wet.

❹ **Steps to the Summit** A second, longer series of steps comprises the steepest sustained climb on the trail and ultimately leads to the exposed summit. The stairs themselves are badly worn and can be especially dangerous when rain fills the ruts left by erosion; in some spots, only the plastic lumber and metal stakes meant to shape the step are left. The side alleys are mainly smooth slopes of loose dirt and small rock.

The official end point is located at a dry, windswept plateau overlooking the Windward Coast. Be careful of strong gusts, especially when walking near the sheer drops on either side of the plateau. Novice hikers should turn around here and follow the route back to the trail head.

❺ **Puu o Kona** Experienced hikers can continue on the path to the left to reach Puu o Kona, a flat peak on the windward side. The approach is difficult, as you'll have to skirt three large rock faces, descend sharply to a narrow saddle, and climb through two heavily eroded spots.

The downhill return can be treacherous given the steep grade of the uppermost sections, loose rock and soil along the summit ridge, and the exposed metal spikes intended to secure the man-made steps. Farther down, the exposed roots of the ohia forest can easily send a quick-descending hiker sprawling.

Despite these concerns, the Kuliouou Ridge Trail attracts a steady flow of local and visiting hikers—an estimated 2,000 per year—because of its easy accessibility and abundant rewards.

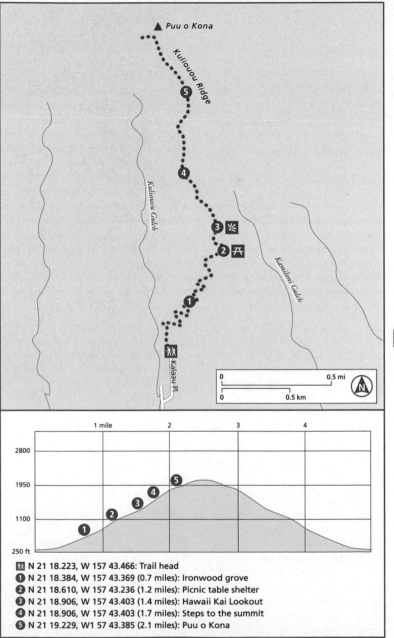

N 21 18.223, W 157 43.466: Trail head
1 N 21 18.384, W 157 43.369 (0.7 miles): Ironwood grove
2 N 21 18.610, W 157 43.236 (1.2 miles): Picnic table shelter
3 N 21 18.906, W 157 43.403 (1.4 miles): Hawaii Kai Lookout
4 N 21 18.906, W 157 43.403 (1.7 miles): Steps to the summit
5 N 21 19.229, W1 57 43.385 (2.1 miles): Puu o Kona

HAWAIILOA RIDGE ★★

Difficulty rating: Moderate/strenuous

Distance: 5 miles round-trip

Estimated time: 3.5 hr.

Elevation gain: 1,400 feet

Costs/permits: None

Best time to go: 8 to 10am

Website: http://www.hawaiitrails.org/trail.
php?TrailID=OA+15+010&island=Oahu

Recommended map: "Hawaiiloa Ridge"
(www.hawaiitrails.com)

Trail head GPS: N21 17.845 W157.44.766

Trail head directions: From the H-1 east, proceed to Kalanianaole Highway heading toward Hawaii Kai. At Kawaikui Beach Park, turn right onto a roundabout and cross the highway on Puu Ikena Drive heading into the gated Hawaiiloa Ridge subdivision. Stop at a guard station, where you will need to present identification and sign in. Proceed up the steep, winding road until it ends near a water tank. Park in the lot.

Hawaiiloa Ridge is not nearly as heavily trafficked as the neighboring Kuliouou Ridge, despite its relatively easy access, stunning views, and straight path to the Koolau summit. The check-in is a minor inconvenience, since you theoretically need to hike with someone who has a local ID. Hotels have been known to call ahead for their guests, but how effective that is depends on who's manning the guard shack. Usually, local hikers are willing to let visitors join their party to get through the gate. The tradeoff is that you get a free tour of one of the island's most exclusive neighborhoods, with multimillion-dollar homes around every bend.

OAHU HIKES

4

HAWAIILOA RIDGE

From the parking lot, walk north along a gravel jogging path that leads to a dirt road along the ridge. You'll pass through a rocky, deeply rutted stretch before arriving at an ironwood forest with a lookout point to the right.

Proceed along an open ridge path past a second stand of ironwoods and through a shady forest of eucalyptus. As the canopy clears, look to the right for a great view of the interior valley.

❶ Fork in the Trail A third stand of ironwoods gives way to a long, mostly level stretch of dry forest crowded with guava, *ilima,* and patches of vibrant uluhe fern that burn bright green even in overcast conditions. (The trail forks at two junctions; keep to the broader, marked trail that follows the main ridge.)

❷ Guava Tree Tunnel Along the way, you'll pass a rather eerie tunnel of guava trees that appears perpetually bathed in blue-gray light regardless of conditions

outside. Locals sometimes refer to this stretch as "the bouncing forest" because of the soft, spongy carpet of vegetation that lends a distinct bounce to your step as you make your way through.

The trail rises and falls, narrows and widens as it progresses toward a moss-covered knob and the first daunting glimpse of the summit ridge. Here, the surrounding foliage gently transitions from guava and *ilima* to a native forest of ohia, koa, and akia as the trail turns along the exposed ridge. Still, many hikers have a hard time diverting their eyes from the skyward-arcing trail in the distance

❸ Steps and Rope Ascent After a few rolling hills, the trail rises toward the summit with a half-mile of enervating ascents where you'll find steps and climbing ropes.

Steps shaped by recycled plastic lumber were constructed by the Department of Land and Natural Resources to aid with

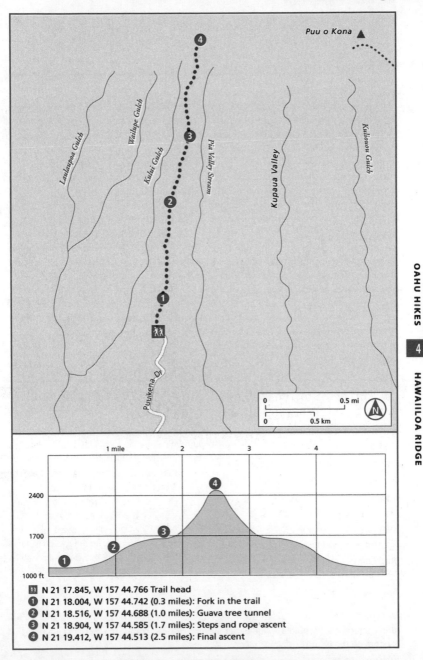

🏃 N 21 17.845, W 157 44.766 Trail head

1 N 21 18.004, W 157 44.742 (0.3 miles): Fork in the trail

2 N 21 18.516, W 157 44.688 (1.0 miles): Guava tree tunnel

3 N 21 18.904, W 157 44.585 (1.7 miles): Steps and rope ascent

4 N 21 19.412, W 157 44.513 (2.5 miles): Final ascent

> **Tips** **Camp Out**
>
> Hawaiiloa Ridge is one of only 10 public trails on Oahu on which camping is allowed. Download an application for a permit at http://www.state.hi.us/dlnr/ dofaw/pubs/oahu_colllect_camp_hike.pdf.

the climb, but many have been hollowed by erosion—some stick up on their metal posts like real estate signs—making it safer at certain points to walk along the still-firm shoulders of the trail.

In other areas, climbing ropes have been installed by private groups and citizens to assist with steep climbs over loose dirt and gravel. As always, make sure the ropes are securely anchored, and use them only as complementary support. (Using the ropes as a primary weight-bearing device can leave you vulnerable to a serious fall should the rope break or detach from its anchor.)

Stretches of loose red dirt along this portion add to the challenge, particularly where the vegetation thins, but slow, careful steps will eventually lead you to firmer rock climbs.

❹ Final Ascent The final ascent along a very steep, at times very narrow path will test your legs and lungs, but the view from the summit is spectacular, with a clear, continuous view of Diamond Head, Koko Crater, Waimanalo, and the three rising peaks of Olomana.

The initial descent back toward the trail head can be tricky, particularly with tired legs. Winter rains can make the nearly vertical upper section even more dangerous, turning the eroded dirt inclines into treacherous mud slicks.

While the first two-thirds of the hike is relatively mild, the final third poses a stiff physical challenge. It is certainly not recommended for anyone with a fear of heights.

HONOLULU MAUKA TRAIL SYSTEM ★★★

Difficulty rating: Moderate
Distance: 9 miles (loop)
Estimated time: 5 hr.
Elevation gain: 1,300 feet
Costs/permits: None
Best time to go: 7 to 10am
Website: http://www.state.hi.us/dlnr/dofaw/ nah/HonoluluMaukaTrailsSystem.pdf
Recommended map: "Honolulu Mauka Trail System" (www.hawaiitrails.com)
Trail head GPS: N21 18.999 W157 49.664

Trail head directions: From H-1 east, take the Punahou exit and turn left onto Punahou Street. Turn left on Nehoa Street; then take the second right onto Makiki Street. Follow the fork left onto Makiki Heights Drive and proceed through the gate into the Makiki Forest Recreation Area. Public parking is located on the left as you enter. Walk up the paved road to the Hawaii Nature Center and turn right at the restroom area.

With its trail head adjacent to the offices of Na Ala Hele, the state's trails and access department, the Honolulu Mauka Trail System is, predictably, the best maintained trail system on the island.

Honolulu Mauka Trail System 53

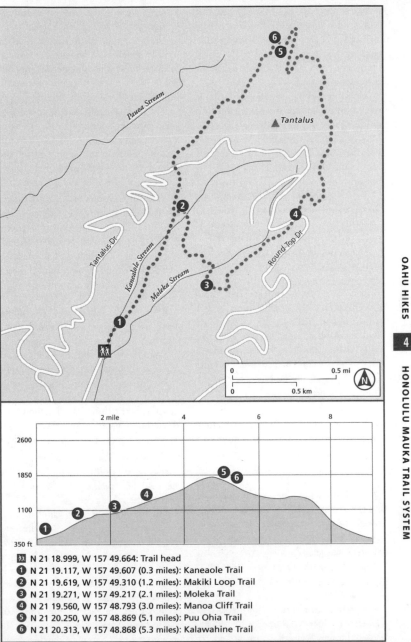

OAHU HIKES

4

HONOLULU MAUKA TRAIL SYSTEM

🚶 N 21 18.999, W 157 49.664: Trail head
1 N 21 19.117, W 157 49.607 (0.3 miles): Kaneaole Trail
2 N 21 19.619, W 157 49.310 (1.2 miles): Makiki Loop Trail
3 N 21 19.271, W 157 49.217 (2.1 miles): Moleka Trail
4 N 21 19.560, W 157 48.793 (3.0 miles): Manoa Cliff Trail
5 N 21 20.250, W 157 48.869 (5.1 miles): Puu Ohia Trail
6 N 21 20.313, W 157 48.868 (5.3 miles): Kalawahine Trail

Just 5 minutes from downtown Honolulu (15 minutes from Waikiki) with access points throughout the Makiki, Tantalus, and Round Top areas, this trail is a favorite among local hikers who find its individual components ideally situated for a quick immersion into nature during lunch or before or after work.

The interlocking system of trails is composed of the Tantalus-Arboretum (.25 mile), Kaneaole (.7), Maunalaha (.7), Makiki Loop (2.5), Makiki Valley (1.1), Ualakaa (.5), Moleka (.75), Manoa Cliff (3.4), Puu Ohia (.75), Pauoa Flats (.75), Nuuanu (1.5), Judd (.75), Aihualama (1.3), Manoa Falls (.8), Kolowalu (1), Waahila (2.4), and Puu Pia (.5) trails.

Each section has its own unique features, and most are suitable for novice hikers.

This particular assemblage is a modified version of the figure-eight loop popularized by the Hawaiian Ultra Running Team's old Tantalus Tropical Trek trail-running event. The original route ended with a second pass over the Manoa Cliff Trail and a treacherous descent down the rooty Maunalaha, also known as Hog's Back. This version cuts the mileage (and the risk of injury) just a bit with a return down the Kaneaole Trail.

❶ Kaneaole Trail The hike begins just behind the Hawaii Nature Center with a gentle stroll on a dirt-and-gravel path that passes a *loi kalo* (taro pond). At a junction, take the Kaneaole Trail to the left (the right goes to Maunalaha) through a native forest restoration area that includes indigenous plants such as ti, akia, wiliwili, *noni, aulu, ape,* lama, *hoawa, 'uki'uki, ulu, palapa kepau,* and *kului,* each clearly identified by signage. Along the way, you'll also pass over dry-packed stone walls that once supported a bridge leading to the old J. M. Herring estate.

❷ Makiki Loop Trail This pathway connects to the Makiki Loop Trail, which passes through a clearing surrounded by towering native Hawaiian trees overrun by

invasive vines and continues up a steep, rocky passage that runs parallel to Kaneaole Stream. This is the steepest continuous section of trail you will encounter.

Near the top, you'll pass two plastic-lumber benches. As you emerge from the forest canopy, you come upon a junction. Follow the path to the right over a short bridge spanning a narrow stream.

The trail ascends and descends three times over the course of a mile. There are a few sections where you will need to scale boulders on the ascent and high-step protruding roots on the descent, but the path here in general is wide and flat enough for easy passage.

❸ Moleka Trail The trail eventually rises to a four-way junction. The trail to the right is Maunalaha; straight ahead is Ualakaa. Take the rising path to the left to Makiki Valley and follow it until you reach a V-turn to the left, which will take you up the Moleka Trail.

After a brief climb, the trail rises and falls gently along a narrow path, eventually climbing again along two steep switchbacks.

From there, you will enter a long corridor of bamboo so beautiful you may not even notice the steep, muddy climb required to make it through. It's worth stopping here to listen to tall, hollow stalks knock in the breeze.

❹ Manoa Cliff Trail Emerging from the bamboo forest, you'll come upon an intersection with Round Top Road. Cross the road and pick up the Manoa Cliff Trail on the other side.

After a short but steep climb through cool, dark forest, you'll reach the open ridgeline facing Manoa Valley. You'll pass patches of strawberry guava and another small stand of bamboo as you meander along the ridgeline. In the winter, this section becomes a miserable mud bog, with puddles thick and deep enough to pry the boot off your foot.

Working your way along the ridge, you'll come to a thin, two-slat bench with a great

Terrific Taro

From ancient times through the early 20th century, *loi kalo,* or irrigated taro flats, were a fundamental part of the traditional Hawaiian sustainable lifestyle, providing Hawaiian families a primary source of nutrition. Taro root was boiled and pounded into poi, while the vitamin-rich leaves of the plant were used in a variety of every-day dishes.

view of Manoa Valley. This is a nice spot to sit, catch your breath, and rehydrate. During the rainy season, you should be able to spot several waterfalls across the valley.

With the most strenuous climbing behind you, it would be a crime not to spend a few recuperative minutes on the elevated bench and enjoy your first expansive view of Manoa Cliffs and the cascading waterfalls that streak its lush, overgrown face.

❺ **Puu Ohia Trail**   Continue along the ridge, passing Puu Ohia Trail on the left, until you come to a junction. Keep to the left (the path to the right leads to Pauoa Flats), and continue down a series of descending switchbacks. As the trail levels, you'll pass a series of large boulders, patches of white ginger, and a few grassy pathways.

❻ **Kalawahine Trail**   At the next fork, take a left along Kalawahine Trail, where you'll pass a protected snail habitat. Farther down, a long, uphill stretch will lead to an intersection with Tantalus Road. Turn right along the paved roadway, pass a bridge, and connect on the left side with the Nahuina Trail.

Work your way along muddy, rutted switchbacks and a large mango grove until you reconnect with the Makiki Valley Trail. Follow this winding pathway down to the initial junction you passed a few hours earlier. Take a right to return back down Kaneaole.

The Honolulu Mauka Trail System offers a myriad of hiking possibilities through terrain that is richly varied and easily accessible. The trees are filled with native birds, and the streams are home to a wide variety of marine life, including Tahitian prawns, mosquito fish, sword-tails, thiarid snails, and bufo toads.

OAHU HIKES

4

MANOA FALLS

MANOA FALLS ★

Difficulty rating: Easy

Distance: 1.6 miles round-trip

Estimated time: 1.5 hr.

Elevation gain: 425 feet

Costs/permits: $5 parking in lot

Best time to go: June to September

Website: http://www.hawaiitrails.org/trail. php?TrailID=OA+19+007&island=Oahu

Recommended map: "Manoa Falls Trail" from www.hawaiitrails.org

Trail head GPS: N21 19.953 W157 48.071

Trail head directions: From Punahou Street, head north toward Manoa Valley. Stay left as Punahou turns into Manoa Road, and continue on until it terminates at the Paradise Park parking lot near the Lyon Arboretum. Parking is available in the lot (fee), or the neighborhood below (free).

Marrying easy access with a host of natural attractions, Manoa Falls is the island's most popular public trail. The trail is relatively short and aggressively managed to appeal to hikers of all ages and skill levels.

The trail head is located near the old Paradise Park in Manoa Valley, a quick 10-minute drive from downtown Honolulu. The area is known for its frequent rainfall, so bring rain gear or at least a change of clothes. Mosquito repellent is also highly recommended.

❶ **Aihualama & Waihi Streams** The trail begins on broad, flat ground and proceeds past a grassy meadow and over a small bridge. The path continues left alongside a second waterway that eventually splits into Aihualama and Waihi streams. A barely noticeable side trail crosses the stream and leads to Luaalaea Falls.

While the path here is wide and relatively even, loose, slippery rock and veiny, toe-trapping roots demand attention, especially from novice hikers.

❷ **Steps to the Falls** The trail continues along Waihi Stream, past a towering bamboo grove, and rises gently along a narrow, rocky path. The trail steepens on the approach to the falls, but a series of steps shaped with plastic lumber and gravel fill eases the climb.

Along the way, the trail cuts through a dense forest of fragrant wild ginger, guava, eucalyptus, African tulip, kukui nut, and lawae fern. And, if you listen closely, you can hear the trills of a half-dozen species of native birds, and maybe the squawk of a feral parrot or two, in the treetops.

Due to the year-round high traffic to the falls, Na Ala Hele, the state's trails and access program, has had to take an aggressive approach to addressing wear and tear. Much of the first half of the trail is reinforced with gravel fill and lumber bracketing.

While some regular hikers avoid the trail because of this conspicuous mainte-

nance, many others visit frequently precisely because it allows hikers of any age and skill level the opportunity to enjoy a true rainforest environment quickly and safely.

The trail turns and narrows on the final, brief climb to the viewing area. You'll hear the falls before they appear, suddenly and dramatically, around the bend.

❸ **Falls Viewing Area** The viewing area itself is rather small, and it's not unusual for hikers to have to wait in line for a spot around the pool. Still, the roaring 150-foot waterfall is worth the inconvenience. For many visiting hikers, it's a must-have photo.

In 2002, a major rockslide deposited some 30 tons of rock and debris from the upper slopes to the valley below. You can still see large boulders piled in the gully to the right of the trail. There are several signs posted in the area warning of the danger (loose rocks continue to fall during heavy rains).

Visitors to the falls should be aware of another potential danger: leptospirosis, a debilitating disease caused by bacteria present in many inland bodies of water on the island. Still, many ignore posted signs to take a dip in the pool, some even stealing a massage from the pummeling cascade.

The state has removed a long rope that adventurous hikers once used to scale the cliff face next to the falls. However, if you want to continue exploring this lush valley, retrace your steps to a small outcropping of trees and pick up the Aihualama Trail off to the right. From there, you can reach the Manoa Valley ridgeline via 14 switchbacks with options to visit Pauoa Flats, the Judd Trail, or the Manoa Cliff Trail.

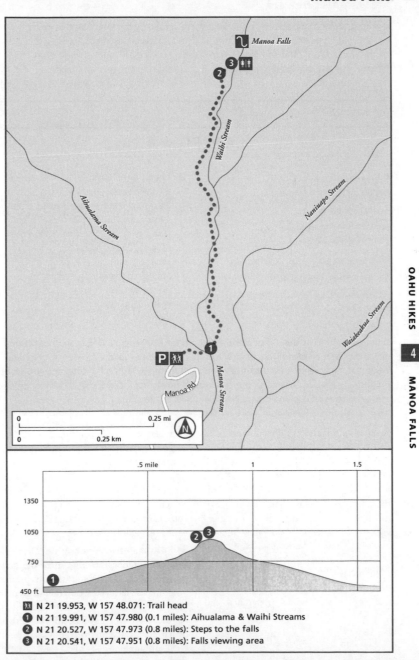

Manoa Falls

Waihi Stream

Naniuapo Stream

Aihualama Stream

Waiakeakua Stream

Manoa Stream

Manoa Rd.

| 0 | | 0.25 mi |
| 0 | | 0.25 km |

N

.5 mile   1   1.5

1350

1050

750

450 ft

N 21 19.953, W 157 48.071: Trail head
1 N 21 19.991, W 157 47.980 (0.1 miles): Aihualama & Waihi Streams
2 N 21 20.527, W 157 47.973 (0.8 miles): Steps to the falls
3 N 21 20.541, W 157 47.951 (0.8 miles): Falls viewing area

Swimmers Beware

Leptospirosis is a potentially deadly disease caused by bacteria found in many freshwater streams and pools in Hawaii. The bacteria are commonly released through animal urine, so hikers should be especially wary of low-lying waterways. The risk of exposure is minimal in quick-moving streams, and higher in standing water.

LANIPO ★★

Difficulty rating: Strenuous

Distance: 7 miles round-trip

Estimated time: 5 hr.

Elevation gain: 1,700 feet

Costs/permits: None

Best time to go: August to October

Recommended map: USGS' "Honolulu Quad" map

Trail head GPS: N21 17.845 W157 47.131

Trail head directions: From H-1 E., take the Koko Head Avenue exit and turn left onto Koko Head Avenue. Cross Waialae Avenue and turn right at the second stop sign onto Sierra Drive. Follow the winding road up Maunalani Heights until you reach the end, and then turn right onto Maunalani Circle. Park on the right side of the street next to a Board of Water Supply tank. The trail head is located to the left of a chain-link fence.

Often recognized as the quintessential Oahu ridge hike, Lanipo Trail in southeast Honolulu makes demands of hikers in direct proportion to the sublime pleasures it provides. While first-time visitors tend to fixate on the breath-seizing rock climbs and the stout climb to the Koolau Summit at the turnaround point, there are a host of subtler enjoyments all along the up-and-down, 7-mile journey.

Lanipo is a ridge-lover's dream, with all of the positive and negative connotations that follow. Best undertaken under cool, overcast conditions, particularly after a few good weeks of rain, the trail rewards those who can meet the hardy challenge of its numerous rises and falls with great views of Waimanalo, Palolo Valley (including Kaau Crater), the Koolaus, and much of East Honolulu.

In the thick of summer, however, the direct sunlight and surrounding humidity can leave hikers feeling as parched and shriveled as the dead, gray scrub that lines the exposed ridge.

The trail head is located just off Maunalani Circle and is accessible via a narrow alley between two chain-link fences. The trail begins right on Mauumae Ridge with a series of moderate descents along the ridgeline. After a short but steep climb, the trail descends sharply along a narrow stretch of exposed rock. The first lookout appears on the right, offering a clear view of Waimanalo.

❶ **Palolo Valley Overlook** Descend to a brief saddle; then dig in for the first significant climb as you pass a telephone pole on the left via a canyonlike trench along the ridge. At the top of the hill is another lookout, this one equipped with a bench (dedicated to late Hawaiian Trail and Mountain Club hike leader Steve Becker) that overlooks Palolo Valley.

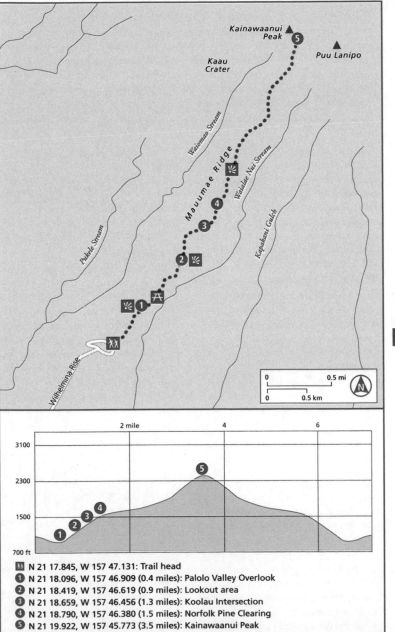

N 21 17.845, W 157 47.131: Trail head
1 N 21 18.096, W 157 46.909 (0.4 miles): Palolo Valley Overlook
2 N 21 18.419, W 157 46.619 (0.9 miles): Lookout area
3 N 21 18.659, W 157 46.456 (1.3 miles): Koolau Intersection
4 N 21 18.790, W 157 46.380 (1.5 miles): Norfolk Pine Clearing
5 N 21 19.922, W 157 45.773 (3.5 miles): Kainawaanui Peak

Fun Facts Guava Invaders

Strawberry guava (*Psidium littorale*) holds the dubious distinction of being the most popular invasive species in the islands. Originating from Brazil, the aggressive plant was introduced to Hawaii more than 200 years ago. Environmentalists have documented its devastating impact on native flora (and, indirectly, fauna), but hikers look forward to the summer months when the plants bear their tangy fruit. For a taste, pluck a dark-red fruit straight from the branch and nibble at the soft, strawberry-flavored rind.

Advancing along the ridge, up and down a series of large and small knobs, you can also spot Kaau Crater and a small waterfall. The trail alternates from broad and secure to very narrow and unstable as it climbs and falls. Small groves of ironwood and eucalyptus provide shady respite along the way, but most of the trail is wide open and exposed.

2 Lookout Area Another large lookout area (which some hikers apparently use for camping) lies to the right of a juncture along a long, uphill stretch of trail.

The lookout area is wide, flat, and grassy, making it an ideal spot to sit and rest (maybe even sneak a quick nap). Abundant strawberry guava plants, which overflow with fruit in the late summer, offer a quick energy boost as you regain your breath.

While the sight of the misty Koolau Mountain Range rising in the distance is a strong lure for hikers determined to make it to the summit, it's worth taking the approach slowly to preserve energy and to fully appreciate the clusters of 'ohia lehua, fiddlewoods, koa, and other flora along the way.

3 Koolau Intersection The second half of the approach to the Koolau intersection is typically overgrown with tall grass and thick, scratchy uluhe fern. Hikers with sensitive skin will want to be sure

to have lightweight long pants for this stretch.

The trail along this latter section is deeply rutted in places, and the ferns and moss at the edges obscure several treacherous sections of eroded trail, making each wide, errant step the potential start of a long, lacerating slide down the gully.

4 Norfolk Pine Clearing Continue uphill to a broad clearing that offers a 360-degree view of Palolo Valley, Mauumae, and Waialaenui, then on to another tall knob marked by three towering Norfolk pines. Beyond that is a narrow path to a third knob, this one marked by a lone, bald pine.

The trail rises and falls several times along a narrow, muddy path before rising steeply up an uluhe-fringed approach to a large clearing from which you can clearly see the long, rising trail to the Koolau summit. This is a good point at which to take inventory of your physical condition. Quaking quads, prolonged shortness of breath, or general fatigue are all strong signs that you should turn around. Remember, every downhill on the approach represents a climb on the return.

5 Kainawaanui Peak The final run to the summit crosses long expanses of windy, exposed ridge. The trail narrows as it rises steeply along jagged, slippery terrain leading to the turnaround point at Kainawaanui Peak. From the top, you can see all the way from Diamond Head to

Waimanalo Bay to Mount Olomana. Most hikers turn around here, but you can also elect to continue on to the true Lanipo Peak via a steep, narrow path to the right.

Unlike other out-and-back trails, Lanipo is often more taxing on its return than it is on its approach, particularly in the last mile where a series of three false peaks obscures the final, rocky climb.

Technically, the trail climbs just 1,700 feet from trail head to turnaround, but you should expect to climb (and descend) at least twice that as the ridge rises and falls more than a dozen times on each leg. Still, for well-conditioned hikers, Lanipo offers a roller coaster of quality hiking experiences.

DIAMOND HEAD (LEAHI) ★

Difficulty rating: Easy

Distance: 1.7 miles round-trip

Estimated time: 2 hr.

Elevation gain: 520 feet

Cost: $5 parking in lot ($1 walk-in)

Best time to go: Before 9am or after 4pm

Recommended map: "Diamond Head State Monument" official map (free at trail head)

Trail head GPS: N21 15.807 W157 48.333

Trail head directions: From Waikiki, take Kalakaua Avenue heading southeast; then bear left onto Monsarrat Avenue. Follow Monsarrat as it becomes Diamond Head Road. The entrance to Diamond Head State Monument will be on your right. Follow the winding road uphill and through a tunnel, which will lead directly to the parking lot. The trail head is located to the left of the back of the lot.

When locals give directions, they don't speak in terms of north and south, east and west, but rather mauka (mountain side) or makai (toward the sea), Ewa (toward the Ewa Plains), or Diamond Head. Such is the significance of Oahu's most prominent and recognizable geographic landmark to the Hawaiian sense of place.

While visitors tend to overrate the physical challenge presented by this rather mild hike (it wasn't long ago that the state shooed away vendors hawking "I Survived the Diamond Head Trail" T-shirts), the trail leading to the top of the volcanic crater remains the most popular trail on the island.

The current trail to the summit follows the same route as the government's 1908 mule trail, but was furbished with railings and handholds on steeper sections as part of a massive renovation project in the 1990s.

The trail is occasionally rocky and uneven but well maintained, perhaps too well for the tastes of some hardcore hikers.

Local runners take advantage of the light early-morning and late-afternoon traffic to use the trail portions of the hike as part of the Diamond Head–area circuit.

The trail head is located toward the back of the parking lot, next to a visitor information center and a cluster of mobile food vendors. Starting at an elevation of about 200 feet, the trail rises gently along a concrete path that was recently installed to reduce erosion. From here you can still see the earthen berms that mark the site of an old pistol range.

❶ Mule Path The concrete pathway eventually gives way to a dirt trail that overlays the original 1908 mule path.

All About Leahi (Diamond Head)

Leahi was formed roughly 300,000 years ago during a single, brief eruption. The crater measures about 350 acres, and its width is greater than its height. The southwestern rim is higher than the rest because winds blew ash in that direction during the eruption.

According to legend, the Hawaiian goddess Hiiaka named the crater Leahi because it resembled the forehead (*lae*) of the ahi fish. The name is also translated as "fire headland," and may refer to the navigational fires that were once lit at its summit to guide canoes along the island's southern shoreline.

In the late 1700s, Western explorers mistook the calcite crystals contained in rocks on the slope for diamonds and thereby dubbed the crater Diamond Head.

In 1904, the federal government purchased the site, valued for its panoramic view of the island, for military use. The original trail to the summit was constructed as a mule trail to assist in moving materials to Fire Control Station Diamond Head, part of the U.S. Army's Coastal Artillery defense system. Five artillery batteries were later constructed along the crater rim.

Follow the trail up a series of switchbacks along the steep interior slope. Though rocky in spots, the trail is broad enough in most sections to walk three abreast.

Roughly midway to the top, you will come across a concrete landing on the left that once held a winch and cable used to deliver building materials to the crater floor. Today, it's a good place to take a quick water break and scan the south shore.

❷ **Concrete Steps** From there, a short switchback leads to a steep stairwell of 74 concrete steps leading to a narrow 225-foot tunnel. During peak hours, traffic is likely to bottleneck here as first-time hikers stop abruptly to catch their breath.

The tunnel ends at the bottom of a steep, 99-step stairwell leading to the bottom level of the Fire Control Station. To break the monotony, take a look up at the crossbeams and try to imagine the layers of camouflage they once supported.

❸ **Fire Control Station** Within the station itself, you'll see a long, dark corridor. Take the narrow, winding metal staircase to the third level of the structure, where mounts for the original observation

equipment are still in place. The area is likely to be congested as visitors wait their turn to ascend and descend.

At the top of the stairs is a narrow slit, once secured with metal shutters, that serves as an exit to the concrete lookout and the next phase of the hike. From here, a short walkway rises to the top level of the station and a pair of prime lookouts.

Though a bit crowded at peak hours, the two cement lookouts at the top of the crater ridge offer one of the finest views you'll find of East Honolulu. From the uppermost point, you can see nearly all of the south shore as well as the eastern end of the Koolau Mountain Range and much of East Honolulu.

Though rich in history, the trail offers little for those interested in observing Hawaiian flora and fauna. The dry, rocky slopes are covered primarily with non-indigenous kiawe and koa haole, which were first brought to Hawaii as cattle feed and thrive in hot, dry environments. From here, turn around and walk back the same way you came to get to the trail head.

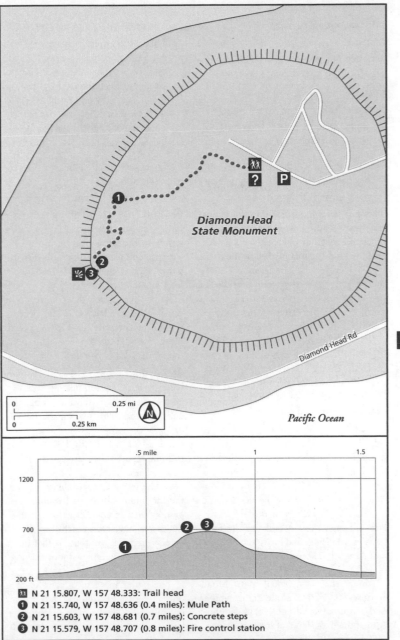

Diamond Head
State Monument

Diamond Head Rd

Pacific Ocean

0   0.25 mi
0   0.25 km

.5 mile   1   1.5

1200

700

200 ft

N 21 15.807, W 157 48.333: Trail head
1   N 21 15.740, W 157 48.636 (0.4 miles): Mule Path
2   N 21 15.603, W 157 48.681 (0.7 miles): Concrete steps
3   N 21 15.579, W 157 48.707 (0.8 miles): Fire control station

AIEA LOOP TRAIL ★★

Difficulty rating: Moderate

Distance: 4.5 miles (loop)

Estimated time: 3.5 hr.

Elevation gain: 800 feet

Costs/permits: None

Best time to go: May to August

Recommended map: "Aiea Loop Trail" (www.hawaiitrails.org)

Trail head GPS: N21 23.916 W157 54.020

Trail head directions: Heading west on the H-1 freeway, keep left on Hwy. 78 and take the Stadium-Halawa exit. Continue on Ulune Street; then turn right on Aiea Heights Drive. Head straight to Keaiwa State Park and follow the road to the upper parking lot. The trail head is located to the left and is clearly marked.

With its moderate distance, gentle rolling hills, and abundant natural beauty, Aiea Loop is considered an old reliable among local hiking enthusiasts.

OAHU HIKES

4

AIEA LOOP TRAIL

The trail starts in a thick grove of lemon eucalyptus and Norfolk pines. Foresters replanted much of the area in the 1920s, and the bright, piquant smell of the eucalyptus is especially strong in the early morning. For those who skip breakfast, a cluster of strawberry guava trees, which overflow with fruit during the summer months, can provide a tasty energy boost.

The trail arcs upward to a rocky clearing that offers a good view of the city, then proceeds through a stand of ironwood trees whose long, soft needles provide safe, cushiony footing as you wend along the gentle contours of the mountain.

❶ Puu Uau After crossing the exposed ridgeline, you'll pass a pair of electricity towers before reaching another small clearing from which you can scan almost the entire Waianae Mountain Range. Continuing on, you'll follow the ridgeline up to Puu Uau, which is marked by native koa and ohia trees. A path on the right leads to Aiea Ridge and the Koolau Mountain Range, but keep going along the main trail.

Along the way, you'll pass broad expanses of native uluhe fern, which, under normal conditions, glow brightly against the dark slopes of the mountain.

❷ Ohia Tree A tall ohia tree marks the farthest point of the trail. Halawa Valley is visible to the left as you begin the return leg, providing, according to your taste, either a great or awful view of the H-3 freeway cutting through Halawa Valley. (The 16-mile freeway that connects Windward Oahu to Halawa was for decades a symbol of the state's inefficiency, costing more than $1 billion and taking more than 2 decades to complete.)

❸ Cargo Plane The trail then dips beneath a thick, sun-defying canopy of eucalyptus and koa toward a long, broad gully. To the right, just off the trail, you can spot the wing section of a cargo plane that crashed in the early 1940s. Contrary to some reports, these are not the remains of a Japanese bomber.

As the trail meanders along the side of the mountain, you'll need to duck below or hop over several fallen trees. Some of the trunks have been notched to allow for an easy step over, but be sure that the tree can bear your weight without shifting or slipping.

The path forks after a corridor of tall pines. The trail to the left ends at Camp Smith (and a likely military escort off the base), so continue down the wider path to the right.

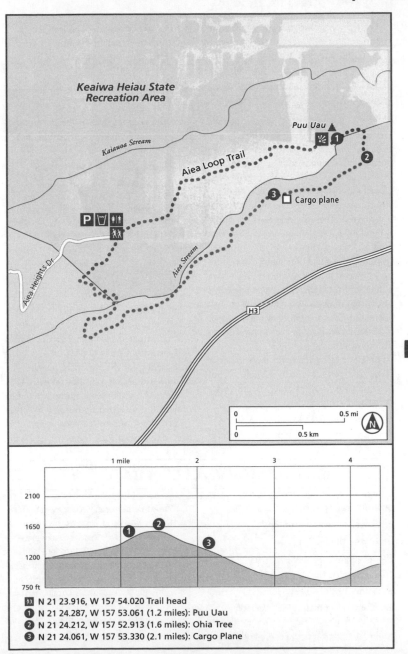

N 21 23.916, W 157 54.020 Trail head
1 N 21 24.287, W 157 53.061 (1.2 miles): Puu Uau
2 N 21 24.212, W 157 52.913 (1.6 miles): Ohia Tree
3 N 21 24.061, W 157 53.330 (2.1 miles): Cargo Plane

(Fun Facts   **Trees for Thought**

The Norfolk Island pines that grace the start and end of the Aiea Loop Trail are the botanical progeny of the original pines brought to Hawaii from Norfolk Island by Capt. James Cook. Cook, a dubious figure in Hawaiian history, also brought a similar looking pine that bears his name.

The trail dips briefly before quickly ascending up three steep switchbacks and across a small, mostly dry stream. This portion of the trail requires careful footing to scale slippery rocks and exposed roots, as well as a bit of stamina to complete the climb to the top. However, it should not be overly difficult for hikers of moderate fitness.

While easily passable in the summer, the long, root-filled path along the switchbacks can be miserably muddy in the wet winter months. Tamped grass on the edges of the trail may provide surer footing, but be careful not to step on rotted wood or moss that can give way to a precipitous drop down the slope.

An electrical tower marks the end of the climb and your return to daylight. From there, it's just a short walk to the park's designated camping area.

Unfortunately, Aiea Loop isn't a true loop trail. To complete the route, you need to cross the camping area to the steep, winding road leading back to the parking lots.

While the final march back to the upper lot is a grind, the lot does adjoin a nice grassy area with faucets to rinse the mud from your boots and ample seating areas from which to enjoy either a quick lunch or a long nap.

Also check out Keaiwa Heiau, located just after the entrance to the park. The original *heiau* (temple) consisted of a large thatched hut surrounded by rock walls. It was constructed sometime in the 1500s and served as a place of physical and spiritual healing for the Hawaiian people. The *heiau* was desecrated in the 1940s by U.S. soldiers who took sacred stones for a road project, but was partially restored in 1951. Today, the 1,600-square-foot *heiau* consists of just short rock walls.

MOANALUA VALLEY TRAIL ★★

Difficulty rating: Moderate

Distance: 3.6 miles round-trip

Estimated time: 3.5 hr.

Elevation gain: 350 feet

Costs/permits: None

Best time to go: Noon to 3pm

Recommended map: USGS' "Kaneohe Quad" map

Trail head GPS: N21 22.444 W157 52.769

Trail head directions: Heading west on the H-1 freeway, go straight as the freeway merges with H-78 west and take exit 2 for Moanalua-Red Hill. Turn right onto Ala Aolani Street and head straight back into Moanalua Valley. The road ends at Moanalua Valley Park. The trail head is located at the top of a dirt road on the far side of a small playground.

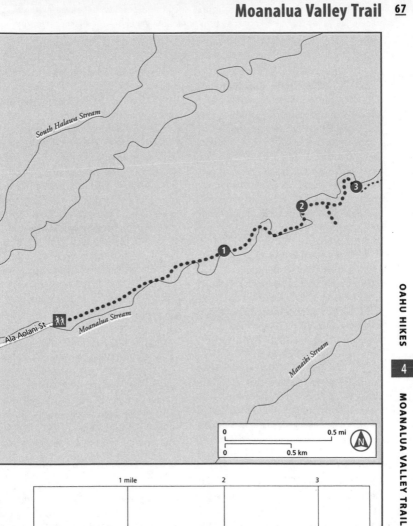

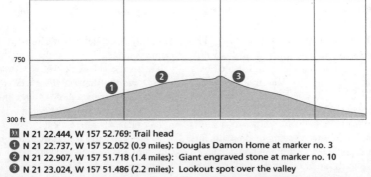

N 21 22.444, W 157 52.769: Trail head
1 N 21 22.737, W 157 52.052 (0.9 miles): Douglas Damon Home at marker no. 3
2 N 21 22.907, W 157 51.718 (1.4 miles): Giant engraved stone at marker no. 10
3 N 21 23.024, W 157 51.486 (2.2 miles): Lookout spot over the valley

First developed during a period of great social and political upheaval in Hawaii, the Moanalua Valley Trail, also known as the Kamananui Valley Trail, is as much a journey into the island's history as it is an exploration of its natural environment.

The *ahupuaa* (land) of Moanalua was originally held by Kamehameha the Great. Over the course of more than 100 years, it passed through a succession of owners, including Prince Lot (Kamehameha IV), Princess Ruth Keelikolani, and Princess Bernice Pauahi Bishop, who at last bestowed it to her husband's business partner Samuel Damon in 1884. Damon was the minister of finance under Queen Liliuokalani (Hawaii's last reigning monarch) and was one of the first trustees of Kamehameha Schools.

Damon's son Douglas built a palatial estate on the grounds and linked it, via a carriage road made of lava-rock cobbles, to a smaller home built for his sister, Mary. This route constitutes the main portion of the Moanalua Valley Trail, which is now administered by the state's Department of Land and Natural Resources.

The first part of the trail crosses seven turn-of-the-19th-century bridges. Side trails lead to the vegetation-covered remnants of both Douglas and Mary Damon's homes: The Moanalua Gardens Foundation, which successfully fought against the routing of the H-3 freeway through Moanalua Valley in the 1970s, set up numbered markers along the trail to highlight these and other special features and side trails.

❶ The Douglas Damon Home The trail begins at the back of Moanalua Valley Park on a broad, rolling path shaded by a thick forest canopy. After passing a brush of vibrant red hibiscus and a giant, century-old monkeypod tree, keep an eye out for marker no. 3, which indicates a short, muddy driveway leading to the remnants of the old Douglas Damon home.

Shortly after, you'll cross the first of the seven bridges. At most of these crossings, you can walk on the bridge itself or across

the dry streambed to the right or left. The side routes are preferable if you want to get a good look at the elegant, arching structure of the cement bridges.

The rest of the bridges follow in rather quick succession as you follow the mostly level path toward the back of the valley. Although the trail is regularly maintained, long, shallow puddles can accumulate in the wheel ruts along the way. These can be easily avoided by switching sides or walking along the grassy shoulders.

Swamp mahoganies and eucalyptus dominate the surrounding forest, although you can also spot mountain apple trees, hau, uluhe and lawae ferns, guava, and koa.

❷ Pohaku Luahine At the seventh bridge (marker no. 10) you'll find a giant, oval stone on a rock pile to the right. The stone, dubbed Pohaku Luahine, is engraved with Hawaiian petroglyphs. Natural weathering has rendered many of the glyphs shallow, so you may need to traverse the tiny ravine in between to get a good look. To the right of the stone is an old papamu konane, an engraved stone board used for a Hawaiian game similar to checkers.

The trail continues with a series of smaller stream crossings. At marker no. 11, turn right up a side trail to view an old brick fireplace left over from Mary Damon's home.

The trail loops back to the main road, where, shortly after, another side trail (indicated by marker no. 12 and three pink trail ribbons) rises steeply toward the nearest ridge.

The climb starts off gently through a stretch of overgrown grass and uluhe fern. After a series of clearly marked twists and turns, the trail shoots upward along a slick, muddy path crowded by thick

(Fun Facts) The Ghosts of Moanalua

Huaka 'I po, the spectral "night marchers" of Hawaiian legend, are said to frequent Moanalua Valley. The Huaka 'I po are the ghosts of ancient Hawaiian warriors and their appearance is heralded by loud drums and chanting. To avoid death, unlucky bystanders are supposed to strip naked, lie on the ground, and avoid eye contact at all costs: just one more reason to get out of the park before the parking lot closes.

eucalyptus trees. You may need to grab the dense, resilient stalks to mitigate the unstable ground and pull yourself up the increasingly steep slope.

❸ **Valley Views** Eventually the trail leads you to a prime lookout spot on the ridge, from which you can see almost the entire valley.

 While the climb to the valley view lookout is stout, the payoff is sublime, with clear views of the summit ridgeline and the interior of the valley.

Make sure you have recovered sufficiently from the climb before attempting the hazardous descent back to the main road. Experienced hikers can continue on to another side trail to the ridge or follow the main trail another mile or so to the upper valley.

Be sure to keep track of the time. The thick canopy that shelters much of the trail can make even midday seem like early evening, in turn making it difficult to notice when the sun is actually setting.

Because of the abundant plant life all along the trail, Moanalua Valley is also a favorite stomping ground for wild pigs. They're harmless unless protecting their young or cornered. If you happen upon one, give it a wide berth and keep on walking.

For more information about the hike, including an explanation of each of the marker points, you can pick up a brochure at Moanalua Gardens.

OAHU HIKES

4

WILIWILINUI TRAIL

WILIWILINUI TRAIL ★

Difficulty rating: Moderate

Distance: 4.6 miles round-trip

Estimated time: 4 hr.

Elevation gain: 1,200 feet

Costs/permits: Permission from the security guard (bring ID)

Pet-friendly: Yes, but dogs must be on leash.

Best time to go: Avoid if rainy, but 2 days after rain the trail should be in good shape.

Website: http://www.oahuhiking.com/wiliwilinui.htm

Recommended map: "Wiliwilinui Trail" map (available at above website)

Trail head GPS: N21 18.157 W157 45.737

Trail head directions: Take the Kalanianaole Highway eastbound and turn left onto Laukahi Street, past the Kalani High School. Near the top of Laukahi Street is the security guard booth. Check in, and continue on up to Okoa Street, turn right, and park in the small lot at the trail head. Alternatively, take bus no. 22/23/24 from Kuhio Street toward Hamuamu Bay; get off at the stop closest to the country club. Follow Laukahi Street as above.

There are several ridge hikes on Oahu, especially just outside of Honolulu, but you'll likely have this one all to yourself. Explore the Koolau Mountain Range, overlooking the Kapakahi Gulch, not only for the amazing views back at Honolulu, Diamond Head, and Koko Crater, but also for the view of the windward side's white sand beaches at Waimanalo Bay. Also you'll enjoy the native flora, hiking up through the ironwood, koa, and ohia forests, with an opportunity to taste strawberry guava straight from the tree.

You can drive all the way up to the trail head, but if you prefer to use local transit you'll have to then walk up an additional 1,200 feet of altitude gain through the subdivision on Laukahi Street. However, it's a worthwhile add-on, with spectacular views along the way of the million-dollar cliffside mansions and beautifully landscaped gardens. You will still need to check in with the security guard to continue up Laukahi through the gated community. As Laukahi Street ends, you turn right onto Okoa Street and follow it until the paved road ends.

A brown-and-yellow painted post indicates the Wiliwilinui trail head in front of you. Wiliwili, the trail's namesake, is a tree *(Erythrina sandwicensis)* found throughout the Hawaiian Islands that can grow up to 4 or 5 feet, with reddish bark and yellow-orange or red blossoms. Nui means "lots of" in Hawaiian, so naturally you can expect to see several specimens on this hike.

The first mile or so follows an old service road of red earth. As you walk up through the koa and ironwood forest, keep an eye out for ripe and ready-for-the-picking strawberry guava to sample. The trail in this section has portions that are completely covered by the canopy, making it hard to believe you're just an hour or so out of the downtown hustle and bustle.

❶ **Out of the Woods** As you leave the cover of ironwood and koa, the trail opens up a bit; if it's not too cloudy, look back (to the leeward side of the island) to see right down into Diamond Head Crater. There are several Cook pine trees nearby, and small purple flowers line the trail. The

power lines to and from the radio-transmitting utility station near the summit make for ominous company along the trail. On a windy day their deep hum in the breeze can be rather haunting.

❷ **Viewpoint** Looking back on the trail now, the city of Honolulu and Waikiki Beach come into view. Below in the green gulches are stands of Norfolk pine, koa, and the strawberry guava in between. There are lighter-shade leaves that can be seen down in the valley; these are the kukui (or candlenut) trees. Designated the state's official tree, candlenuts provided the oil Hawaiians once used to fuel their lamps. *Note:* The open road on this section of the trail can get very muddy and slippery with rain, so proper hiking footwear is important.

❸ **Bench Marker** At this point, another trail marker appears on the left, and the trail itself changes from open road to windy path. A small park bench suggests a snack break before starting the steep part of the trail. The taller trees now give way to lower shrubs including fern and ohia (with beautiful bright red blooms). Most of the ascent is terraced with a staircase made of lava, mud, and wooden boards. On other sections, ropes are helpful for negotiating footholds on the steep ascent. You can't help but stop to take in the 360 degrees of breathtaking views with every step as you hike along the narrow ridge.

❹ **Radio Tower** The trail levels off and widens for this relay station that transmits TV and radio signals all over Oahu. It would be a fine place to stop and have

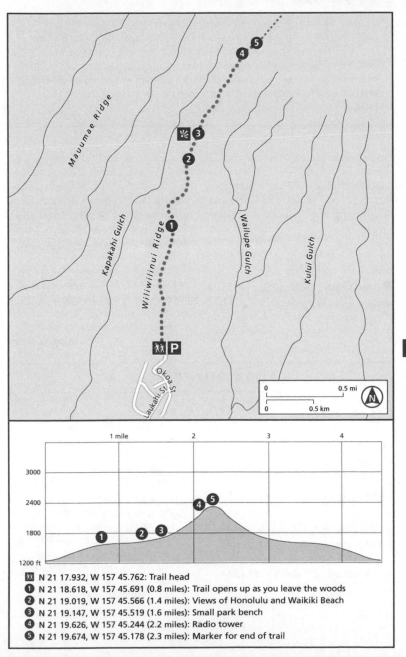

N 21 17.932, W 157 45.762: Trail head
1 N 21 18.618, W 157 45.691 (0.8 miles): Trail opens up as you leave the woods
2 N 21 19.019, W 157 45.566 (1.4 miles): Views of Honolulu and Waikiki Beach
3 N 21 19.147, W 157 45.519 (1.6 miles): Small park bench
4 N 21 19.626, W 157 45.244 (2.2 miles): Radio tower
5 N 21 19.674, W 157 45.178 (2.3 miles): Marker for end of trail

A Valley Home

It's interesting to reflect on what these gulches and ridges would have looked like in the days of the ancient Hawaiians. Centuries ago, families were allotted land, with the ridges providing the boundaries. In the valley between, a family had all they needed to sustain a healthy existence: access to the oceans for fish, mountain streams for fresh water, hillsides for planting and growing their crops, and the forest for hunting and to source materials for building their modest shelters.

lunch, but the summit is only another 20 minutes or so away. With lush green valleys all around, the trail continues behind the station and down a saddle stretch before rising again through two shorter exposed ascents to the final summit of Koolau. Koko Crater and Hamuamu Bay, the popular snorkeling site, can be seen back and to the left from here.

⑤ Trail's End   Only 200 to 300 feet to go, and then the windward side of Oahu comes into view, including the two rocky outcrop islands that mark Lanikai Beach,

and the white sands of Waimanalo Bay. For experienced hikers, the trail continues on in two directions, joining with other trails in the ridgeline network. A marker indicating the end of Wiliwilinui Trail is to the left, and there is enough vegetation cleared here to make for a nice spot for lunch before heading back down. *Mauna* is the word for mountain in Hawaiian, and the view from here offers you views of many in the Koolau Mountain Range; to the left Olomana, with the airfield behind it, and to the right, Hawaii Loa.

—Kari Romaniuk

KAIWA RIDGE HIKE ★

Difficulty rating: Easy/moderate

Distance: 2 miles round-trip

Estimated time: 1.5 hr.

Elevation gain: 550 feet

Costs/permits: None

Best time to go: 6am to 10pm

Website: http://www.hawaiitrails.org/trail. php?TrailID=OA+14+001&island=Oahu

Recommended map: "Kaiwa Ridge Trail" (www.hawaiitrails.org)

Trail head GPS: N21 23.405 W157 43.141

Trail head directions: Heading north on Kalanianaole Highway, turn right on Kailua Road into Kailua town (the highway turns into Kuulei St.). At a T-intersection and traffic light, turn right onto Kalaheo Road; continue past Kailua Beach Park. Heading into Lanikai, follow the right fork onto Aalapapa Drive and take a right onto Kaelepulu Drive. Park on the right side of the road just after the entrance to Mid-Pacific Country Club. Across the street from the golf course, you'll find the unofficial trail head at the start of a narrow dirt path.

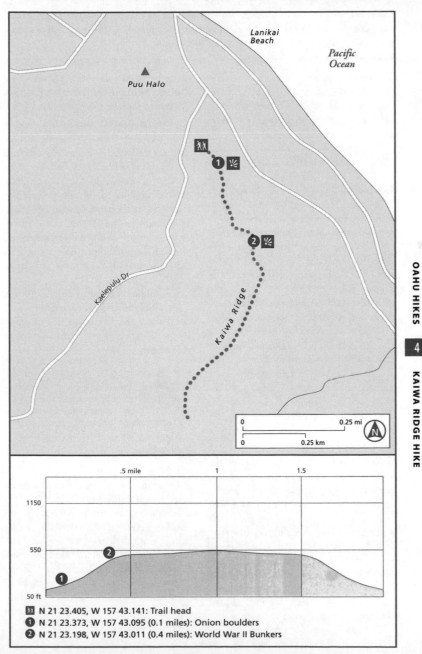

OAHU HIKES

4

KAIWA RIDGE HIKE

N 21 23.405, W 157 43.141: Trail head
1 N 21 23.373, W 157 43.095 (0.1 miles): Onion boulders
2 N 21 23.198, W 157 43.011 (0.4 miles): World War II Bunkers

Though it's one of the most active and attractive recreational areas on Oahu, Lanikai is not commonly associated with great hiking. Yet, if you turn your attention from the white sands and blue waters of Kailua Beach Park and Lanikai Beach, past the enclave of million-dollar homes, and toward the rising peaks in the near background, you'll find a short but challenging gem of a hike in the Kaiwa Ridge Trail.

The trail is popular with local hikers but is not officially maintained by the state. Because of this, several sections are badly eroded and others overgrown with native and non-native plants.

The unmarked trail head is located along a chain-link fence across the street from the Mid-Pacific Golf Course. The steep uphill climb begins immediately along a slick, eroded rut bordered by scrub brush and bristly *koa haole*. The vegetation can be useful as handholds to maintain your balance; just remember that every other hiker has the same idea and some plants are no longer as strongly rooted as they once were.

Roughly 100 yards up the red-dirt path, the trail opens up along the exposed ridgeline and you get your first stirring views of the Lanikai and the Mokulua to the southeast and Kaneohe to the north.

The trail continues to rise steeply as you negotiate a faint pathway through crumbling rock and loose gravel. You'll have to do some rock scrambling and boulder hopping, but there are usually alternate paths around the largest rock faces.

❶ **Onion Boulders** Take note of the weathered boulders with circular patterns of erosion. These "onion boulders" are the result of an unusual process in which water absorbed by the boulders causes the outer layers to separate and peel away.

After an extended climb up the southern face of the mountain, you'll come upon a pair of junctions. Either will advance you to the next short plateau, but you'll find the surest footing on the broader, less graded paths to the right.

The climb is relatively simple in dry conditions, but even a little rain can turn

the red dirt into slick wet clay and cause the long shelves of black lava to become as slippery as they are sharp.

❷ **World War II Bunkers** After a skinny, eroded section bordering a sheer drop on the ocean side, veer right around a large mass of black rock and ascend to the first of two World War II–era pillbox bunkers established to help protect the southeastern shoreline in case of attack. The interior of the concrete box is empty except for assorted debris. Most hikers opt to climb atop the roof (though it is officially discouraged) to enjoy the 360-degree view of the area.

Continuing on, the trail rises and falls along a ridgeline partially overgrown with tall native grass. Eventually, after gaining about 100 feet in elevation, you'll come to the second pillbox.

This is an excellent vantage point to enjoy truly spectacular panoramic views of Mokapu Point, Kailua Bay, the Koolau Mountain Range, and Bellows Beach from up high.

Many hikers take an extended break here before heading back down. However, if you aren't quite ready to call it a day, you can always continue on the trail for another half-mile to reach the true summit. The otherwise clearly defined route is interrupted by a bulging knob, but a short, descending pathway allows you to avoid the sheer drop on the other side by arcing slightly to the south and then back onto the main trail.

The Pull of Kaiwi

Kaiwi Ridge is named for the chieftess Kaiwi who once lived in the area. She was beloved by Ahiki, the official guardian of Kawainui and Kaelepulu fishponds. According to legend, Ahiki became the third of the three famous peaks of Mount Olomana. Ahiki is located the farthest south, it is said, because he pulled himself away from the others to be closer to Kaiwi.

The trail is not regularly maintained, so it is very likely that you will complete the final leg to another concrete structure in increasingly thick *koa haole*.

As you will likely deduce coming up, the return trip can be a bit hairy, especially as you try to find traction on the banking rocks and slopes of loose dirt. Your patience in navigating the descent is worth it; one trip and you could be in for a long and unpleasant tumble down the trail or off the sides to the koa-snarled embankments.

The beauty of this hike is that you can get a good workout and enjoy a fantastic 360-degree view of the island while still leaving plenty of time to enjoy the myriad of ocean activities available immediately below.

Lanikai and nearby Kailua Beach are immensely popular spots for swimming, waterskiing, sail-boarding, snorkeling, kayaking, and wakeboarding, and there is no shortage of affordable rental companies within a mile radius to outfit you with anything you might need. The parks also feature wide expanses of soft grass shaded by ironwoods and other coastal trees, a perfect setting for a picnic.

OAHU HIKES

4

MOUNT OLOMANA ★★★

MOUNT OLOMANA

Difficulty rating: Strenuous
Distance: 5 miles round-trip
Estimated time: 5 hr.
Elevation gain: 1,300 feet
Costs/permits: None
Best time to go: May to September
Recommended map: USGS' "Koko Head Quad" map
Trail head GPS: N21 22.104 W157 45.655

Trail head directions: From H-1 W., take the Pali exit and proceed through Nuuanu and the Pali tunnels. Pali Highway becomes Kalanianaole Highway. Turn right at the second Auloa Road turn; then take an immediate left onto an unnamed road parallel to the highway. Park on the left side of the road, just before a small bridge. The trail head is located exactly a half-mile up the road on the left side.

While Diamond Head might cut the most recognizable figure in the Oahu skyline, it is the three towering peaks of Mount Olomana that have captured the imaginations of generations of adventurous hikers. The out-and-back trail that links the trio of peaks is a stout challenge that rewards skilled, careful hikers with thrilling climbs and descents and an amazing 360-degree view from the first peak. Still, with its steep ascents; narrow, rocky pathways; and windswept ridgeline, the complete 5-mile, out-and-back trail presents as many perils as any day hike on the island, and only experienced hikers in strong physical condition should venture past the first peak.

The hike starts beneath a thick canopy of trees along a short zigzag of switchbacks before steadily ascending past short, rocky climbs and even shorter flat, grassy respites. The initial section is typically very muddy. Just resign yourself to the fact that you're going to get dirty and step right in; the quickest way through is to walk straight across the mud-filled ruts.

The footing gets firmer as you reach a grove of ironwood trees and walk through an open grassy ridge. Next comes a short, steep climb up a badly eroded hill of hard-packed red dirt, then a second ironwood grove.

❶ Rope-Assisted Climb The climb intensifies as you ascend a deeply rutted path up a red-dirt hill and continue on past a long stretch of Christmas berry. The first real challenge comes with a near-vertical rock climb assisted by three sections of well-anchored rope. To gain the top of this climb, you'll need to work your way around a jutting mass of rock using a horizontal rope for support. Try not to look down at the 30 feet of open air behind you.

Continue climbing along an increasingly narrow trail as it skirts the right side of the mountain. Another set of ropes is in place to help you regain the narrow, rocky ridgeline.

❷ Fifteen-Foot Rock Face Just before the first peak stands a 15-foot rock face, a wise turnaround point for novice hikers. There are two ways to get up, both indicated by thick climbing ropes. The handholds are small and far apart on either route, so you will need to rely on the ropes to pull yourself up (be sure to straddle the rope for the surest footing).

Upon reaching the top, you will need to climb over a very narrow ridge of brittle rock then bear right to work your way around a tall, jagged rock outcropping. You'll regain the ridge on the other side then climb steeply to finally reach the first peak.

The view doesn't get any better than from here. Facing the ocean, you can see the Windward Coast from Makapuu to Kualoa. Turn around and you can see Maunawili Valley and the major peaks of the Koolau Mountain Range, including Konahuanui, Puu o Kona, Lanipo, and Mount Olympus. The area is small but more than suitable for an extended break.

Depending on your disposition, the looming presence of the knobby second peak and the spire-like third, both seemingly so close, can be either irresistibly attractive or a final confirmation that some challenges are best left unexplored.

To many experienced local hikers, the hike to Olomana's second and third peaks marks a sort of graduation from one level of hiking ability and experience to the next. And it's a crossing that must be earned.

❸ Second Peak To get to the second peak, descend steeply along a crumbly path then rappel down a sheer incline with the help of ropes. The saddle between the first and second peak is narrow and very crumbly (watch out for a section midway through where overgrown grass obscures a portion of the trail that has dropped away). The climb to the second peak is brief but rocky.

From the second peak, bear right to descend to the second saddle. The drop is once again sheer and you will need to use a single, long, climbing rope to make it to the bottom. Be sure to take careful inventory of your strength and energy before committing yourself to what will be a difficult return leg.

❹ Third Summit The approach to the third summit is the most dangerous. The path climbs sporadically around large clusters of rocks and boulders. As the ridge narrows, you'll need to evaluate the available paths to the peak. Climbing directly

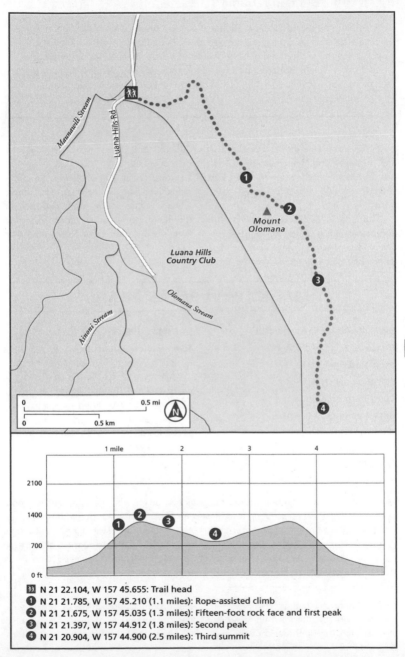

👣 N 21 22.104, W 157 45.655: Trail head
❶ N 21 21.785, W 157 45.210 (1.1 miles): Rope-assisted climb
❷ N 21 21.675, W 157 45.035 (1.3 miles): Fifteen-foot rock face and first peak
❸ N 21 21.397, W 157 44.912 (1.8 miles): Second peak
❹ N 21 20.904, W 157 44.900 (2.5 miles): Third summit

> **Fun Facts** **Olomana Drama**
>
> According to Hawaiian legend, Olomana was a powerful warrior who stood some 30 feet tall and ruled the lands between Makapuu and Kualoa. Olomana fell into conflict with the then king of Oahu, Ahuapau, who sent Palila, his best warrior, to confront the giant. Bolstered by supernatural power, Palila cleaved Olomana in half. The top half flew into the sea; the bottom remained where it stood and became Mount Olomana.

over rock formations may seem expedient, but it leaves you vulnerable to sudden wind gusts; often there are narrow paths around the sides that have already been roped.

The summit itself is unspectacular, but its achievement is something worth savoring with a deep chug of Gatorade. Just remember that the return will be more difficult than the approach, especially on tired arms and legs.

However far you choose to go, Olomana is a worthy challenge with ample rewards. Once you've conquered each of the three peaks, you'll never view the Windward Coast skyline the same way again.

MAUNAWILI FALLS TRAIL

Difficulty rating: Easy/moderate

Distance: 2.5 miles round-trip

Estimated time: 2.5 hr.

Elevation gain: 300 feet

Costs/permits: None

Best time to go: 2 to 4pm

Website: http://www.hawaiitrails.org/trail. php?TrailID=OA+15+092&island=Oahu

Recommended map: "Maunawili Falls Trail" (www.hawaiitrails.org)

Trail head GPS: N21 21.536 W157 45.807

Trail head directions: On H-1 W., take the Pali Highway exit, proceed past the Pali Tunnels, and take the second of two Auloa Road turns to the right. Veer left on Maunawili Road and follow it to the end. Park in the residential area to the right. The trail head is on the left of Maunawili Road.

Maunawili Falls Trail is perhaps the most popular hike on the windward side, and for good reason. It's short, easy (except for a steep section of man-made stairs near the end), and, most of all, it features a 20-foot waterfall that feeds a deep, wide swimming hole. Though relatively short, the Maunawili Falls Trail can be difficult to navigate because of its many side trails. However, because it is so popular with area residents, all you need to do if you get confused is wait for the next pack of hikers to pass by.

Like most of the island's trail-accessible waterfall areas, Maunawili Falls is subject to heavy foot traffic throughout the year. Still, the trail is well maintained, with gravel fill and mostly unobtrusive lumber reinforcements preventing the sort of serious erosion present on many Oahu trails.

The trail head is located to the right of a dirt path opposite the start of Kelewina Street. To begin, follow a narrow pathway

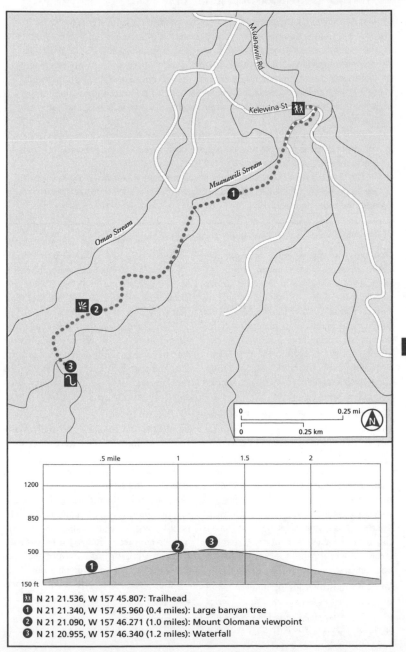

N 21 21.536, W 157 45.807: Trailhead
① N 21 21.340, W 157 45.960 (0.4 miles): Large banyan tree
② N 21 21.090, W 157 46.271 (1.0 miles): Mount Olomana viewpoint
③ N 21 20.955, W 157 46.340 (1.2 miles): Waterfall

The Rich Landscape of Maunawili

Maunawili was an integral part of the complex farming system that fed ancient Hawaiians in the Koolau Poko *ahupuaa* (traditional land divisions that cut from the mountains to the ocean). Prior to modern commercial and residential development of the area, Maunawili's land bore a wide variety of fruit and nuts, and its waterways bore abundant fish (especially mullet) and fed loi kalo. It is believed that Kamehameha the Great's warriors even fed on the nutrient-rich mud of the area (then the consistency of poi) when food was scarce following the Battle of the Pali.

Coffee and banana plants along the trail are floral holdovers from repeated attempts by Westerners to take advantage of the area's abundant water and rich soil with profit-yielding crops.

The terraces near the start of the trail surround what was once the Kukapoki Heiau (temple). The area is believed to contain several ancient burial sites, which are now protected by law.

that cuts through a grove of mountain apple trees and coffee plants until you come to the first stream crossing. Under normal conditions, you should be able to hop across three or four medium-size boulders to get to the other side. If the stream is running high and fast, test the strength of the flow from the side before venturing across. If the flow is too strong for you to maintain your balance should you fall in, turn around.

❶ Large Banyan Tree Continue along a rooty trail lined with giant torch ginger. The next stream intersection appears soon after, marked by a large banyan tree. After crossing, follow the narrow trail to the right to yet another crossing; then bear left.

After a gradual uphill walk, you'll reach a large intersection. Look for the sign on the left and follow the path away from the stream.

❷ Mount Olomana Viewpoint You'll do most of your climbing over the next quarter-mile stretch, aided by a series of man-made steps. After a brief but strenuous ascent, you'll reach a lookout

with a bench and a fine view of Mount Olomana. Straight ahead is a path leading to an intersection with the Maunawili Trail. Bear left down a long flight of stairs that terminates back at the stream.

Many hikers lose their way at the next stream intersection. When you reach the stream, cross carefully over a series of boulders and then bear left—the more obvious trail to the right leads nowhere—walk along the stream, and cross back over at the next clearing.

❸ Waterfall Follow the trail over a gentle, rolling trail that leads directly to the falls.

The falls area is an ideal spot for an extended break. The 20-foot cataract provides a moderate but steady flow, minimizing the chance of leptospirosis. The pool it feeds is wide and deep, and you may be tempted to follow the lead of local teens in jumping into it from the rock ledge above. Just be sure you scout a safe landing area; many would-be jumpers have been injured on the large boulders beneath the surface.

If the pool is too crowded for your taste, check out the smaller pool just above it, which is accessible via a short, vertical rock climb.

The multiple stream crossings and junctions and shifting terrain can make the return trip a bit confusing. As with any trail, it's a good idea to look backwards on the way in so you'll know what to look for on your return.

If you'd prefer not to get wet, you can grab a seat on one of the smooth, sun-warmed boulders downstream and settle in for a quick lunch or even a few Zs. In the quieter early morning and late afternoon hours, you can close your eyes and enjoy the clacking of bamboo from the ridge above and the polyphonic birdsong from the surrounding forest.

PUU MANAMANA ★★

Difficulty rating: Strenuous

Distance: 4.5 miles (horseshoe)

Estimated time: 5 hr.

Elevation gain: 2,100 feet

Costs/permits: None

Best time to go: March to September

Recommended map: USGS' "Kahana Quad" map

Trail head GPS: N21 33.421 W157 52.034

Trail head directions: From H-1 W., take the Likelike Highway exit through Kalihi Valley and the Wilson Tunnel and follow as it becomes Kamehameha Highway. Continue past Kahaluu, Waiahole, and Kaaawa and park on the right shoulder of the highway by Kahana Bay just before the road turns right and crosses Kahana Stream. Backtrack along Kamehameha Highway. Look for a short guardrail on the right and a Route 83 sign; at the next utility pole, turn right onto an unmarked pathway into the forest.

Among local hikers, Puu Manamana has been referred to as "Devil's Horseshoe," "Death Ridge," "Crouching Lion Death Plunge," and other similarly melodramatic monikers. Venerable hiking expert Stuart Ball famously wrote of the trail, "It becomes difficult right at the start and then gets worse." Simply put, Puu Manamana is one of, if not the, most dangerous hiking trails on the island. For hardcore hikers, it is also one of the most challenging and exhilarating day hikes to be found in the state.

It goes without saying (though we'll say it), only expert hikers should attempt this trail—and only with a healthy surplus of caution. The trail gains most of its 2,100 feet in the first mile and a half, with most of it coming along incredibly narrow, rocky ridgeline, with sheer drops of several hundred feet on each side. Complicating matters are a series of fatigue-inducing knobs in the middle section and a very steep, very narrow descent on a root-encumbered ridge riddled with plunge-inducing patches of moss and rot.

The trail begins at an unmarked clearing roughly a quarter-mile from the Crouching Lion Inn on Kamehameha Highway. From the start, it is clear that the trail is deserving of its daunting reputation. A steep climb through Christmas berry and scattered ti plants delivers you to a clearing fronted by a series of towering rock faces that you must climb with the help of ample if not totally reliable handholds.

① Crouching Lion The trail briefly levels on a rocky plateau. To the left is a small side trail crowded by *hao* brush that leads to the famous Crouching Lion rock formation. For some hikers, getting a photograph atop the head of the lion is a souvenir too tempting to pass up. It probably isn't worth the risk of falling several hundred rocky feet.

The ascent continues up five successively taller and more dangerous peaks, each completely obscured by the one before. Even in dry, windless conditions, the climb up the razor-like ridge is perilous (at a couple of spots, the path is no wider than an average adult male's thigh).

To the right, you can clearly see the tree-lined ridge you will descend on the way back to the highway. It seems much, much closer than it really is.

② Rock Mound and Belt Cable Near the 2,000-foot mark, the path narrows and arcs around a massive mound of rock. A short belt-like cable is there to help you maintain your balance as you sidestep around the protrusion, but at last test, its anchor was less than secure. If that's still the case when you visit, it's best to hug the rock and inch your way to the ohia brush on the other side.

The middle portion of the trail is an odd cobbling of slick, muddy stretches and dry, crumbly patches overlaid on a series of jutting knobs along the ridgeline. Like swimming in high surf, it may sometimes feel as though you are moving more up and down than forward.

Here the vegetation grows thick and constricting. The trail is infrequently maintained, meaning it is often overgrown with prickly brush and scratchy ohia branches. Fallen trees soften and rot at several points and light-green moss carpets several long stretches.

③ Turnover Knob You'll eventually reach a sixth knob, called Turnover, and shortly thereafter a clearing where you can enjoy hard-earned views of Kaaawa Valley, Puu Ohulehule, and Punaluu Valley.

The small Christmas berry clearing just beyond Turnover is your last chance to stand on broad, solid ground. While you rest, look to the left for a stunning view of Kaaawa Valley, then scan to the right for look at Punaluu Valley.

From there, backtrack a few steps and take the side trail leading to the return ridge. The descent is every bit as hairy as the initial climb, perhaps more so because you now have gravity pulling in the same direction. And, whereas the approach to the summit unfurled along narrow, exposed, windswept rock, the return to sea level can only be accomplished by carefully navigating down an equally narrow ridge of wet, crumbly rock, mud, moss, and exposed roots.

As the ridge narrows, the footing gets even worse. There are stretches, mostly at the top of small, downward-tilting hills, where all you have to step on are intertwining roots elevated inches off heavily eroded trail.

④ Hala Grove The path drops into a grove of hala and then into a bumpy slalom of more rocks and more roots. Thin tree trunks on either side provide a bit of stability, but be careful that your momentum doesn't spin you around as you reach for them.

The trail terminates in surreal fashion, broadening into an increasingly indistinct path before finally leveling at a small Mormon cemetery, the final resting place for victims of a 1946 tidal wave.

Finishing Puu Manamana can be deeply satisfying, especially considering the sustained tension you have to endure to safely negotiate each challenging yard of the

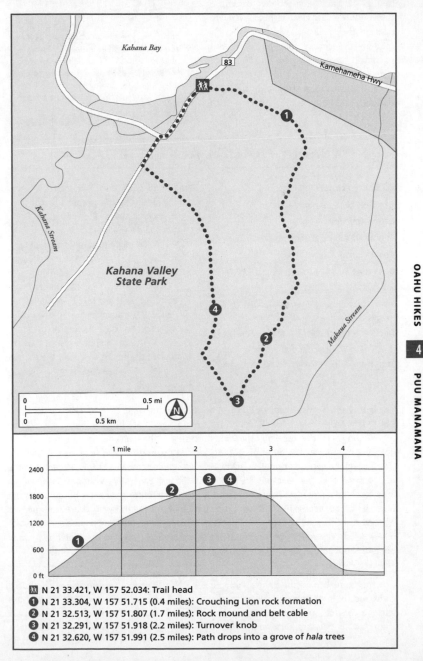

N 21 33.421, W 157 52.034: Trail head
1 N 21 33.304, W 157 51.715 (0.4 miles): Crouching Lion rock formation
2 N 21 32.513, W 157 51.807 (1.7 miles): Rock mound and belt cable
3 N 21 32.291, W 157 51.918 (2.2 miles): Turnover knob
4 N 21 32.620, W 157 51.991 (2.5 miles): Path drops into a grove of *hala* trees

trail. Again, this trail requires advanced hiking skill and tremendous concentration. While relatively few hikers dare to take on the challenge—there is a better-than-average chance that you and your party will be the only ones on the mountain—there have been a disproportionate number of fatalities, serious injuries, and rescues over the years. Proceed with extreme caution.

There's no better way to celebrate a successful ascent of Puu Manamana than good burger and a cold beer. You can find both at the nearby **Crouching Lion Inn** (51-666 Kamehameha Hwy.; ℭ **808/237-8981**), a Kaaawa landmark since 1927. The inn takes its name from the famous rock formation on the ridge above.

KEALIA TRAIL & ACCESS ROAD ★

Difficulty rating: Moderate

Distance: 6 miles round-trip

Estimated time: 4 hr.

Elevation gain: 1,900 feet

Costs/permits: None

Best time to go: 8 to 11am April, May, and August

Website: http://www.hawaiitrails.org/trail.php?TrailID=OA+01+006&island=Oahu

Recommended map: "Kealia Trail and Access Road" (www.hawaiitrails.org)

Trail head GPS: N21 34.582 W158 12.4.51

Trail head directions: Take the H-2 freeway toward Wahiawa and continue straight on to Route 99 north (Wilikina Dr.). Pass Schofield Barracks and continue on to a fork; go straight toward Waialua and on to Farrington Highway. At a roundabout, head left to Mokuleia and continue on to Dillingham Airfield and Glider Port. Pass the Glider Port and take the next left. Follow the road in, arcing left toward a parking lot next to the control tower. Park in the lot and head straight back toward the mountain. Follow the road to the left, passing a concrete building on your right.

Kealia Trail and Access Road is a bit of an oddball among Oahu trails. Located just behind Dillingham Airfield and Glider Port and traversing a wide fire break and popular pig and bird hunting area, the trail along the windward side of the Waianae mountain range does not offer the typical illusion of ascending into untouched nature. Because much of the trail follows the exposed ridgeline, hiking in midsummer can be a burner. Winter months offer a break from the heat, but the wide, flat dirt trail can get very slippery with even a little bit of rain. (Whenever you decide to go, be sure to bring an extra bottle of water.) Given its broad, accessible pathways, the trail is popular with North Shore trail runners who like their courses clear of rocks, roots, and other ankle-buckling obstacles. Mountain bikers also occasionally use the trail, although humping a bike up the switchbacks may be more trouble than it's ultimately worth.

The trail starts behind the airfield, along a wide, mostly level, gravel pathway to the left of a concrete structure and just past a scattering of old airplanes and airplane parts.

While certain sections along the initial switchbacks are narrow and rocky, and others near the upper path eroded or deeply rutted, Kealia does not require any technical skill. Still, the constant climbing

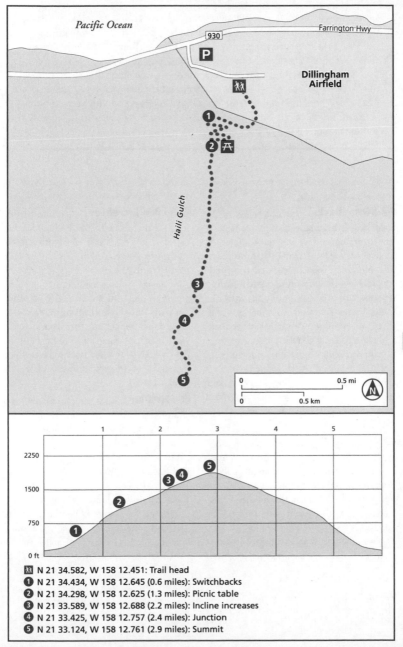

🥾 N 21 34.582, W 158 12.451: Trail head
❶ N 21 34.434, W 158 12.645 (0.6 miles): Switchbacks
❷ N 21 34.298, W 158 12.625 (1.3 miles): Picnic table
❸ N 21 33.589, W 158 12.688 (2.2 miles): Incline increases
❹ N 21 33.425, W 158 12.757 (2.4 miles): Junction
❺ N 21 33.124, W 158 12.761 (2.9 miles): Summit

OAHU HIKES

4

KEALIA TRAIL & ACCESS ROAD

(Fun Facts) Lost Airport

Dillingham Airfield, a former military facility, serves as a regional airport, primarily for recreational use. The ABC television series "Lost," which films nearby, has used the airfield in several episodes, and the fuselage from the fictional Oceanic Airlines Flight 815 is stored at the facility.

Dillingham Air Field is also a great place to take advantage of the numerous deals offered by local glider operations. **Honolulu Soaring Club** (© **808/637-0207**; www.honolulusoaring.com) for example, offers everything from scenic and aerobatic rides in a bubble-topped sailplane to initial flight instruction at rates starting around $80.

and descending does require a bit of strength and stamina.

❶ **Switchbacks** An accordion of 14 switchbacks gradually elevates you along the towering cliff facing the airfield. As you wend your way along the contours of the mountain, you can see fixed-wing gliders taking off and landing, even gliding parallel to your line of vision with the North Shore coastline in the background. In good conditions, you may also see parachuters and hang gliders.

The switchbacks are long but not very steep, and gaining the ridgeline is simply a matter of patience. Along the way, take note of the abundant wiliwili trees, with their thick, gnarled trunks and orange flowers.

❷ **Picnic Table** This slightly monotonous climb ends at a small grove of ironwood trees that descends a small gully. A small, covered picnic table about 1.5 miles up offers shelter from the heat (or rain) and is a good turnaround point for novice hikers.

From there, you will pick up a wide dirt path lined with silk oaks and Christmas berry shrubs.

The trail rises and falls—sometimes steeply—as you walk along the ridgeline. To the left is an elevated water tower; far-

ther ahead, to the right, is a wire fence and weathered gate.

❸ **Incline increases** At around 1,600 feet, the trail ascends steeply though a forest of Cook pine and eucalyptus before reaching a clearing that offers a great view of the North Shore.

The road splits at several junctions, but continue along the straightest, most obvious path—usually just off to the left.

As you approach the turnaround point, you'll pass the Kuaokala Public Hunting Area, which is marked by a bullet-riddled sign and—in the past, at least—a large pig skull.

❹ **Junction** After a steep descent and climb, you'll come to a junction: To the right is a road leading to the Kaena Point Satellite Tracking Station, but you should continue to the left along the Mokuleia firebreak road heading toward Makua Valley.

At a four-way junction, you will continue straight ahead while the firebreak road splits off to the left. At yet another junction, follow the steep path to the right, which leads to the Kuaokala Trail and the summit.

❺ **Summit** From the top, you'll enjoy a panoramic view of Makua Valley, Ohikilolo Ridge, and the Waianae mountain range.

SLEEPING & EATING

ACCOMMODATIONS

★ **Aqua Bamboo**   A recent $2.5-million upgrade has only added to the intimate charm of this surprisingly affordable gem. From the aromatherapy candles in the reception area to the feng shui–friendly design of the rooms, there's no mistaking Bamboo's goal of total tranquillity. The saltwater swimming pool (with waterfall) is a nice touch.

2425 Kuhio Ave., Waikiki Beach, HI 96815. © 808/922-7777. www.aquaresorts.com. 80 units. $110–$207 double; suites from $365. AE, DC, DISC, MC, V. **Close to:** Diamond Head.

★ **Hotel Renew**   Here's another recently renovated boutique that has positioned itself nicely to attract visitors who seek tasteful, serene sanctuary from the cheesy, noisy mess that is Waikiki. We're not sure what to make of the complimentary Red Bull available in one booking package, but we'll take the free Wi-Fi, yoga classes, and gourmet breakfast.

129 Paoakalani Ave., Honolulu, HI 96815. © 808/687-7700 or 888/485-7639. www.hotelrenew.com. 70 units. $169–$209 double; suites from $595. Rates include breakfast. AE, DC, MC, V. **Close to:** Diamond Head.

★★ **Hyatt Regency Waikiki**   This daunting hotel complex is composed of a pair of 40-floor towers that occupy nearly an entire city block. Though not exactly cozy, rooms are well furnished, dining options are excellent, and the location (a couple of minutes from the beach, the Honolulu Zoo, and Kapiolani Park) is as good as it gets in Waikiki.

2424 Kalakaua Ave., Honolulu, HI 96815. © **808/923-1234.** http://waikiki.hyatt.com/hyatt/hotels. 1,230 units. $257–$529 double; suites from $785. AE, DC, DISC, MC, V. **Close to:** Diamond Head.

★★★ **JW Marriott Ihilani Resort and Spa**   This luxury resort is just 17 miles from Honolulu International Airport, but you'll feel like you're on another island. The average room here is a spacious 640 square feet, and the private lanai makes it easy to pretend that all those miles of white sand are yours alone. The golf course, restaurants, and spa are all top notch.

92-1001 Olani St., Kapolei, HI 96707. © **808/679-0079.** www.ihilani.com. 387 units. $299–$659 double; suites from $850. AE, DC, MC, V. **Close to:** Aiea Loop, Moanalua Valley.

★★ **Kahala Hotel and Resort**   Nestled amidst the multimillion-dollar homes of exclusive Kahala, this luxury hotel built its reputation as the default lodging of celebrities who like their privacy in proximity to the action of Waikiki. Enjoy the star treatment at the spa, swim with one of the resident dolphins, or simply sit back and enjoy the sunset.

5000 Kahala Ave., Honolulu, HI 96816. © **808/739-8888** or 800/367-2525. www.kahalaresort.com. 338 units. $455–$820 double; suites from $1,600. AE, DC, DISC, MC, V. **Close to:** Diamond Head, Hawaiiloa Ridge, Lanipo.

Ke Iki Beach Bungalows   You don't have to worry about tracking your muddy boots across any plush-carpeted lobby here. This complex of cottages invites you to make yourself at home along the most famous stretch of beach in the surfing universe. All units have full kitchens and private barbecue areas.

59-579 Ke Iki Rd., Sunset Beach, HI 96712. ✆ **808/638-8828.** www.keikibeach.com. 11 rooms. $145–$185 double. AE, MC, V. **Close to:** Kealia.

Lanikai Bed and Breakfast   Cool, comfortable, and meticulously maintained, this B&B provides ample space to stretch out and relax. There's complimentary use of just about anything you need to enjoy enchanting Lanikai Beach, located just 100 yards away.

1277 Mokulua Dr., Kailua, HI 96734. ✆ **808/261-7895.** www.lanikaibeachrentals.com. 2 units. $145–$195 double. MC, V. **Close to:** Kaiwa Ridge, Olomana, Maunawili Falls.

Manoa Valley Inn   Located in lush, quiet Manoa Valley, this historic inn makes good on its promise of peace and tranquillity with old Hawaii charm. The rooms and cottage are relatively small, but elegantly decorated. If only they weren't named for the annexationists who facilitated the illegal overthrow of the Hawaiian monarchy.

2001 Vancouver Dr., Honolulu, HI 96822. ✆ **808/947-6019.** www.manoavalleyinn.com. 10 units. $99–$125 double w/shared bathroom; $140–$170 double w/private bathroom (shower only); $150 cottage double. Rates include continental breakfast. MC, V. **Close to:** Manoa Falls.

★★ **Royal Hawaiian**   Honolulu's most storied hotel was immortalized in Joni Mitchell's "Big Yellow Taxi" as the pink hotel for which paradise was paved. And while the hotel's flamingo-pink paint may not suit every sensibility, you'll surely find something to love, either in the gorgeously preserved historic wing (built in 1927) or the more modern oceanfront towers.

2259 Kalakaua Ave., Honolulu, HI 96815. ✆ **808/923-7311** or 866/716-8110. www.royal-hawaiian.com. 527 units. $370–$570 double; suites from $925. AE, MC, V. **Close to:** Diamond Head, Honolulu Mauka Trail System.

Schrader's Windward Country Inn   "Country inn" might be a stretch, but this collection of charming, if weathered, cottages offers a nice, low-key alternative to Waikiki, with Kaneohe Bay and an ancient Hawaiian fishpond just steps away and the lovely Koolau Mountain Range rising in the distance.

47-039 Lihikai Dr., Kaneohe, HI 96744. ✆ **808/239-5711** or 800/735-5071. www.schradersinn.com. 20 units. $72–$143 1 bedroom. AE, DC, DISC, MC, V. **Close to:** Mount Olomana, Maunawili Falls.

★★★ **Turtle Bay Resort**   With two landscaped pools, a pair of world-class golf courses, horseback riding paths, hiking and mountain biking trails, and 5 miles of pristine beach, this is a luxury hotel best enjoyed by the most active-minded guests. Or not. The Luana Spa offers coconut body scrubs, noni wraps, pineapple pedicures, and other delectable services.

57-091 Kamehameha Hwy., Kahuku, HI 96731. ✆ **808/293-6000.** www.turtlebayresort.com. 443 units. $440–$520 double; $900–$1,300 cottages. AE, DC, DISC, MC, V. **Close to:** Kealia.

★ **Waikiki Parc**   Close enough to the beach that you can smell the seawater, yet exclusive enough to keep the masses at bay, the Parc boasts great service and finely appointed rooms designed to meet all your high-tech needs. Their comfortable yet sophisticated wine gatherings are a great excuse to stay in.

2233 Helumoa Rd., Honolulu, HI, 96815. ✆ **808/921-7272** or 800/422-0450. www.waikikiparc.com. 297 units. $229–$415 double. AE, DC, MC, V. **Close to:** Diamond Head, Honolulu Mauka Trail System.

★ **Assaggio's Ristorante Italiano** (Hawaii Kai) ITALIAN This popular Italian restaurant chain serves up an impressive menu, from chicken saltimbocca to catch-of-the-day piccatta to succulent osso bucco, all in small or regular portions.

7192 Kalanianaole Hwy., Honolulu. ℂ **808/296-0756.** www.kokomarinacenter.com/stores/asssaggios_ristorante.php. Main courses $10–$25. Lunch Mon–Fri 11:30am–2:30pm; dinner daily 5:30–9:30pm. Reservations recommended. **Close to:** Makapuu Tide Pools, Koko Crater, Kuliouou Ridge.

★ **Buzz's Original Steakhouse** (Kailua) STEAKHOUSE Beachgoers flock to this island favorite, located between Lanikai and Kailua beaches, for its famous kiawe-grilled steaks, fresh mahi mahi, artichoke surprise, and salad bar. Grab a table outside, order a cold one, and watch the paddle-boarders cruise nearby Kailua Beach.

413 Kawailoa Rd., Kailua. ℂ **808/261-4661.** www.buzzssteakhouse.com. Main courses $11–$25. Daily 11 am–10pm Reservations required. No credit cards. **Close to:** Kaiwa Ridge, Olomana, Maunawili Falls.

★ **Crouching Lion Inn** (Kaaawa) CONTINENTAL Located just beneath the landmark rock formation from which it takes its names, this historic restaurant got a much needed renovation in 2008. The salmon kabobs and crab cakes are great, but don't leave without sampling from one of the best pupu menus on the island.

51-666 Kamehameha Hwy., Kaaawa. ℂ **808/237-8981.** www.crouchinglionhawaii.com. Main courses $10–$25. Lunch and dinner daily. **Close to:** Puu Manamana.

Hog Island (Kaimuki) SOUTHERN BARBECUE Trying to find great barbecue on Oahu is a bit like looking for really good Samoan *pulasami* in Tennessee. Yet, the Memphis-style ribs, brisket, pulled pork, and other saucy delicacies at tiny Hog Island make up in quality what the island lacks in quantity. And you can't go wrong with any of the tasty sides.

1132 11th Ave., Honolulu. ℂ **808/388-7784.** Main courses $5–$25. Lunch and dinner Tues–Sun. **Close to:** Diamond Head, Lanipo.

★★★ **Hoku's** (Kahala) EUROPEAN/ASIAN/POLYNESIAN Located in the Kahala Hotel and Resort, this comfortably elegant beachside restaurant offers what just might be the best dining experience on the island. The ever-changing, but consistently excellent, menu mixes Polynesian, Asian, and European influences with an emphasis on locally grown ingredients.

5000 Kahala Ave., Honolulu. ℂ **808/739-8888.** Main courses $20–$60. Lunch and dinner Tues–Sat 5:30–10pm; brunch Sun. **Close to:** Diamond Head, Lanipo, Kuliouou Ridge.

Kapahulu Poi Shop (Kapahulu) HAWAIIAN In the great tradition of family-owned Hawaiian restaurants, the Poi Shop induces smiles, belly slaps, and naps in almost equal proportion. Order your *lau lau, lomi* salmon, squid *luau, kalua* pig, or dried *aku* a la carte or as part of a combination plate.

3110 Winam Ave., Honolulu. ℂ **808/737-8014.** Main courses $5–$9. Breakfast, lunch, and dinner Mon–Sat. **Close to:** Diamond Head, Honolulu Mauka Trail System.

KJ's Local Grindz (Kaneohe) LOCAL At KJ's, just do as the locals do and go with the chicken. The Windward Oahu cheap-eat favorite specializes in *mochiko* chicken, which is coated with rice flour and deep fried, but the *furikake* chicken, crusted with a traditional Japanese dry-seaweed mix, is a close second. The portions can be daunting to the uninitiated.

Windward City Shopping Center (45-481 Kaneohe Bay Dr.), Kaneohe. 𝒞 **808/235-5799.** Main courses $5–$7. Breakfast, lunch, and dinner daily. **Close to:** Olomana, Maunawili Falls.

★ **Kua Aina** (Haleiwa) BURGERS/SANDWICHES   A top contender for best burger joint on the island, the original Kua Aina location is a must-stop for North Shore visitors, particularly after a day in the surf. Get yours topped with bacon, avocado, or *ortega* pepper. A basket of thinner-than-shoestring fries is also required eating. Lines are always long, and the dining area is always crowded, so patience is a virtue.

66-160 Kamehameha Hwy., Haleiwa. 𝒞 **808/637-6067.** Burgers/sandwiches $5–$7.50. Lunch and dinner daily from 10:30am. No credit cards. **Close to:** Kealia.

★★ **Pavilion Café** (Downtown) EUROPEAN/ASIAN   Island gourmands know there's no shame in visiting the Honolulu Academy of Arts simply for the piadina or mahimahi-and-soba salad. Like the museum itself, the indoor-outdoor cafe offers an eclectic mix of international flavors. Tables fill quickly, and patrons like to linger amidst the garden, waterfall, and sculptures, so be sure to make a reservation.

900 S. Beretania St., Honolulu. 𝒞 **808/532-8700.** www.honoluluacademy.org. Main courses $12–$20. Lunch Tues–Sat. Reservations suggested. **Close to:** Honolulu Mauka Trail System.

Rainbow's Drive-In (Waikiki/Kapahulu) LOCAL   An after-beach staple for nearly 50 years, Rainbow's is the plate-lunch spot of choice for thousands of long-time residents. The traditional two scoops of rice and one scoop of macaroni salad anchor overloaded plates of teriyaki beef, breaded cutlets, deep-fried mahimahi, chili franks, and other local comfort foods. Two hands required.

3308 Kanaina Ave., Honolulu. 𝒞 **808/737-0177.** www.rainbowdrivein.com. Main courses $5–$7. Breakfast, lunch, and dinner daily. **Close to:** Diamond Head.

★★ Ⓕⓘⓝⓓⓢ **Tokkuri-Tei** (Kapahulu) JAPANESE   A true hidden gem, this hole-in-the-wall Japanese restaurant features a huge menu of sushi and *izakaya* (tapas-style) a la carte items, including squid pancakes, wasabi chicken, ahi-cheese salad, and miso butterfish. The tables are uncomfortably close, but the service is quick and friendly. Chug the "snake juice" at your own risk.

611 Kapahulu Ave., Honolulu. 𝒞 **808/739-2800.** A la carte items $2–$10. Lunch and dinner daily. **Close to:** Diamond Head.

★★ **Town** (Kaimuki) AMERICAN/ITALIAN   Actors from the ABC drama "Lost" love this place, and for good reason. The creative menu, heavy on locally grown ingredients, is especially good at lunch, and the restaurant's fresh, hip design has helped set the tone for the newly gentrified neighborhood.

3435 Kaimuki Ave., Honolulu. 𝒞 **808/735-5900.** www.townkaimuki.com. Main courses $10–$30. Reservations required. Lunch and dinner Mon–Sat. Reservations required. **Close to:** Lanipo, Diamond Head.

The Big Island Hikes

by David Thompson

It hasn't quite been a million years since the first of the five overlapping volcanoes that make up the Big Island rose out of the boiling sea. Since then, the island has grown to become the largest, tallest, and most geographically diverse of all the Hawaiian Islands. It is also, I believe, the island most likely to get your heart pounding in awe.

The Big Island is Hawaii's youngest island, and the one that's still growing. It's the place where lava still burns forests and houses, devours beaches and bays, and adds to the terra firma. The youngest of the five volcanoes, Kilauea, has been erupting almost nonstop since 1983. Its landscape is blackened, tortured, and darkly beautiful. When you are there you very much know you are in the realm of Pele, the volcano goddess, whose dual powers as creator and destroyer charge the land with an energy that's both terrifying and exhilarating.

As Kilauea builds on the southeast side of the island, the island's only genuinely extinct volcano, Kohala, becomes increasingly graceful with age. It is so old and weathered that it's completely lost its volcano-like appearance. It's not even called a volcano, going by the name "Kohala Mountains" instead. Forming the northernmost part of the island, the Kohala region's emerald sea cliffs, deep valleys, and velvety green ranchlands are some of the most picturesque places in Hawaii.

On the island's dry west side, the cone-shaped Hualalai Volcano rises to 8,271 feet above the city of Kailua-Kona. It hasn't erupted since 1801, but it's by no means extinct. Roughly half of the island's 200,000 residents live on or around Hualalai's slopes. When the Hualalai does rumble back to life—probably within the next 100 years, scientists say—it won't be pretty.

Most of the Big Island is comprised by Mauna Loa, which is absolutely massive. From seafloor to summit it takes up 10,000 cubic miles. One geologist described it as "the largest projected land mass between Mars and the Sun." When Mauna Loa last erupted in 1984, the lava flow that crept down its flank stopped just 3 miles short of the Hilo city limits. Smaller than Mauna Loa, but a wee bit taller, is Mauna Kea. Dormant for the last 4,500 years, it has an international astronomical complex on its summit. It's the highest peak in the Pacific, and the view from the top will take your breath away. If it doesn't, hiking in the thin air there certainly will.

Both Mauna Loa and Mauna Kea rise more than 13,000 feet above sea level, and snow sometimes caps their peaks. There are days every winter when it's possible to build sandcastles on the beach and snowmen on the mountains. The sharp spike in elevation gives the Big Island an astounding range of climates, including "arid," "wet tropical," and even "polar tundra." The island has vast stretches of lava desert, Hawaii's largest swaths of rainforest, and even a few spots where permafrost has been found.

At 4,028 square miles, the Big Island really is big. It could hold all of the other Hawaiian Islands and then some. If you've got a few days to explore, spend at least

THE BIG ISLAND HIKES

5

ESSENTIALS

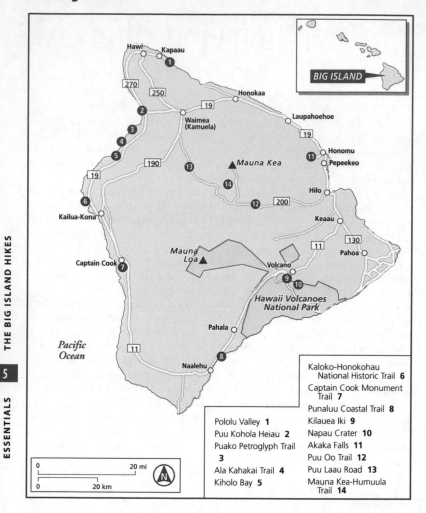

Pololu Valley **1**
Puu Kohola Heiau **2**
Puako Petroglyph Trail **3**
Ala Kahakai Trail **4**
Kiholo Bay **5**

Kaloko-Honokohau National Historic Trail **6**
Captain Cook Monument Trail **7**
Punaluu Coastal Trail **8**
Kilauea Iki **9**
Napau Crater **10**
Akaka Falls **11**
Puu Oo Trail **12**
Puu Laau Road **13**
Mauna Kea-Humuula Trail **14**

1 night on the east side and another on the west side. That will save you a lot of driving, and put you in proximity to Hawaii Volcanoes National Park on the east side and the sunny coastal trails on the west side.

ESSENTIALS

GETTING THERE

The Big Island is so big it has two airports. Most visitors land at **Kona International Airport at Keahole (KOA)** (© **808/329-3423**) in West Hawaii, which has several daily inter-island flights, and regular direct flights from the mainland. Located about 7 miles north of Kailua-Kona, the airport sits in the lava desert at Keahole Point. Don't worry when you land—the entire island isn't so desolate. **Hilo International Airport (ITO)** (✆ **808/934-5801**) is on the lush east side of the island, 10 minutes from downtown Hilo. Daily flights connect Hilo International to Honolulu. Hawaiian Airlines, go!, Island Air, and Mokulele are the four inter-island carriers. It takes about 35 minutes to fly from Honolulu to Kona and 40 minutes to Hilo.

VISITOR INFORMATION

The **Big Island Visitors Bureau** (✆ 800/648-2441; www.bigisland.org) is the local branch of the state-run Hawaii Visitors and Convention Bureau. It has offices in Waimea (aka Kamuela) at 65-1158 Mamalahoa Hwy., Ste. 27B (✆ **808/885-1655**), and in downtown Hilo at 250 Keawe St. (✆ **808/961-5797**). Both are open Monday through Friday from 8am to 4:30pm. For general information about **Hawaii Volcanoes National Park,** and for the daily eruption update, call ✆ **808/985-6000** or visit www.nps.gov/havo.

LAY OF THE LAND

The Big Island is roughly divided into East Hawaii and West Hawaii, separated by Mauna Loa and Mauna Kea. Visitors favor the sunny west side, while the island's largest city and the seat of local government, Hilo, is on the rainy east side. Three roads link east and west: Hwy. 11 is the southern route, Hwy. 19 is the northern route, and Hwy. 200, also known as Saddle Road, runs across the mid-section, in the saddle between Mauna Loa and Mauna Kea. Hawaii Volcanoes National Park is located on the southeast side of the island. It's a 45-minute drive from Hilo, and about a 2.5-hour drive from Kailua-Kona, on Hwy. 11.

GETTING AROUND

You really need a car to get around the Big Island. The island's very limited public transportation is geared primarily for hotel workers commuting from their east-side homes to the west-side resorts. Alamo, Avis, Budget, Dollar, Hertz, National, and Thrifty have rental cars at the Hilo and Kona airports. **Harpers Car and Truck Rental** in Hilo (✆ **800/852-9993** or 808/969-1478; www.harpershawaii.com) is located near the Hilo airport. It's the only rental car company on the island with four-wheel-drive vehicles, and the only one that allows customers to drive on the unpaved roads to the summit of Mauna Kea and to South Point.

POLOLU VALLEY TRAIL ★★

Difficulty rating: Moderate

Distance: 1 mile round-trip

Estimated time: 1.5 hr.

Elevation gain: 420 feet

Costs/permits: None

Best time to go: Year-round. Mornings offer the best chances of sunny, clear weather. Afternoons along this stretch of coast are typically cloudy.

Recommended Map: USGS' "Honokane Quadrangle"

Trail head GPS: N20 12.221 W155 44.030

Trail head directions: In the North Kohala District, drive north on Hwy. 270 until you reach Pololu Lookout at the end of the road. The drive is quite scenic, so leave time for sightseeing along the way.

Near the northern tip of the island, this short but sharply inclined trail leads to a wind-swept beach at the mouth of a lush valley on the island's windward shore. The riveting views of the cliff-lined coast along the way are an extra treat. The beach is too hazardous for swimming on most days, but the beachcombing is fantastic.

The trail begins at the edge of Pololu Lookout's tiny parking lot, and it wastes no time in beginning its descent—a quick, steep drop to the valley floor 420 feet below. The hike down is easy. The climb back up is an aerobic workout. The trail is wide, well worn, and deeply cut into the cliff face. The hard-packed dirt can be slippery sometimes, but there are roots and branches along the edges that double as handholds. At a few key points, ancient cobblestones—polished smooth by centuries of foot traffic—help with footing.

❶ First Switchback About halfway to the bottom, the trail hits the first of three switchbacks, and the best vista of the hike.

Pololu is the northernmost valley in a series of seven valleys along this rugged, roadless stretch of North Kohala coast. North Kohala is the oldest part of this volcanic island, and the deep valleys are the result of several hundred thousand years of weathering. But the gradual process of erosion tells only part of the story. About 110,000 years ago, a massive landslide tore off a huge chunk of the island and dumped it into the sea. The cliffs along this coast mark the fault line, the snapping point along which the landslide occurred.

The view from the green cliffs of North Kohala is picture-postcard-perfect. You can, in fact, see it on postcards in gift shops all over the island. It looks across the mouth of the valley, past three near-shore islets, and down the coast's emerald wall of sea cliffs.

❷ Pololu Stream The trail comes to the valley floor just behind the shoreline and near Pololu Stream. Sometimes the stream flows; other times it's trapped behind a sand berm that builds up on the beach. You might find a few stepping stones or a strategically placed log to help keep your feet dry. Or you might be able to walk across the berm on dry sand. Otherwise, you'll have to wade through the shallow water.

From the stream the trail runs behind the black-sand beach, through an iron-wood forest growing atop tall sand dunes. I prefer to leave the trail and walk the beach from here, coming back through the ironwoods. The waves along this wild stretch of coast are typically too crazy to risk swimming (think deadly currents, no lifeguards), but the flotsam that washes up can make for brilliant beachcombing.

Fun Facts   The Straight (Long) and Narrow

Pololu Valley is more than 2 miles long, but just ⅓ mile wide at most. It's shaped like a javelin, and indeed "long spear" is exactly what *pololu* means in Hawaiian. The valley is private property, and public access is limited to the beach area, I'm sorry to say.

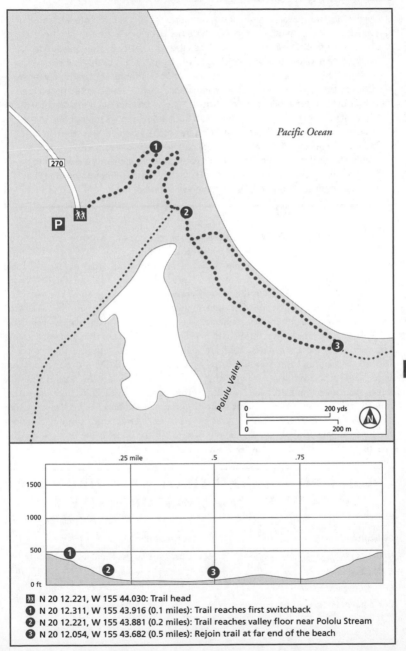

THE BIG ISLAND HIKES

5

POLOLU VALLEY TRAIL

Pacific Ocean

270

P

Polulu Valley

| 0 | 200 yds |
| 0 | 200 m |

.25 mile   .5   .75

1500

1000

500

0 ft

N 20 12.221, W 155 44.030: Trail head
1 N 20 12.311, W 155 43.916 (0.1 miles): Trail reaches first switchback
2 N 20 12.221, W 155 43.881 (0.2 miles): Trail reaches valley floor near Pololu Stream
3 N 20 12.054, W 155 43.682 (0.5 miles): Rejoin trail at far end of the beach

A Hideaway for the Boy Who Would be King

Even in ancient Hawaiian times, this mountainous coast was remote—the kind of wild place where a mother might, say, hide her baby boy to protect him from a ruler with infanticidal intent. That was the case with the child who grew up to become King Kamehameha, according to the legend of his birth. A prophecy foretold that the infant Kamehameha, born under a strange light in the sky (now believed to have been the 1758 appearance of Haley's Comet), would become a powerful king, and a killer of chiefs. Not wishing to test his luck, King Alapai sent out a hit team to take out the little threat. But Kamehameha's mother had him spirited him away to a hiding place along this coast, where he was raised in hiding until around age 5. Eventually Alapai had a change of heart and invited the child to be raised, safe from harm, in his royal court. Kamehameha went on to become the first king to unite all of the Hawaiian Islands. Although he did kill a fair share of rivals along the way, Alapai was not one of them.

③ Ironwoods in the Dunes   You can pick up the trail easily here at the far end of the beach. You'll see that it climbs the south wall of the valley, and, as you might surmise, it does continue down the coast. But beyond Pololu Valley it crosses private land, not open to the public. So from here, head back across the valley through the ironwood trees and sand dunes. You can stick to the path, but it's more fun to go rogue and pick your way through the dunes. You might find driftwood shacks, rope swings, campers, and even some remnants of World War II. The Army practiced amphibious landings on this beach, and rising out of the sand in at least one spot are some of the rusting landing tracks it left behind.

The ironwoods aren't native; they were introduced to Hawaii in the 1880s for windbreaks and erosion control, and they've been thriving on the windward coasts of all the main islands ever since. These dunes used to shift around, as dunes are wont to do, but the thick matt of needles dropped by the ironwoods has locked them in place. Ironwoods also shed tiny cones, which look like miniature pineapples and hurt like heck to step on in bare feet. Ordinarily, running barefoot through the dunes is the thing to do. But not here.

PUUKOHOLA HEIAU TRAIL AT PUUKOHOLA HEIAU NATIONAL HISTORIC SITE ★

Difficulty rating: Easy
Distance: 1.5 miles (loop)
Estimated time: 1 hr.
Elevation gain: 100 feet
Costs/permits: None

Pet-friendly: No
Best time to go: February is the height of whale-watching. *Note:* Park open from 7:45am to 4:55pm daily (hr. are subject to change—double check on park website).

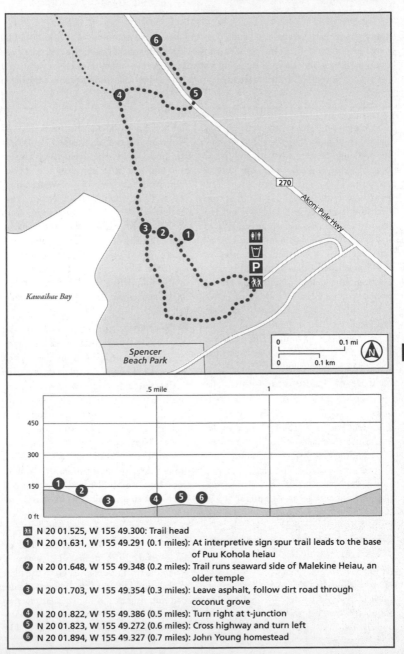

N 20 01.525, W 155 49.300: Trail head

1 N 20 01.631, W 155 49.291 (0.1 miles): At interpretive sign spur trail leads to the base of Puu Kohola heiau

2 N 20 01.648, W 155 49.348 (0.2 miles): Trail runs seaward side of Malekine Heiau, an older temple

3 N 20 01.703, W 155 49.354 (0.3 miles): Leave asphalt, follow dirt road through coconut grove

4 N 20 01.822, W 155 49.386 (0.5 miles): Turn right at t-junction

5 N 20 01.823, W 155 49.272 (0.6 miles): Cross highway and turn left

6 N 20 01.894, W 155 49.327 (0.7 miles): John Young homestead

Website: www.nps.gov/puhe

Recommended map: "Exploring Pu'ukohola Heiau," available at park visitor center

Trail head GPS: N20 01.525 W155 49.300

Trail head directions: One mile south of Kawaihae in North Kohala, along Hwy. 270.

This National Park Service trail leads past the base of an enormous war *heiau* built by King Kamehameha the Great. Located on the dry North Kohala Coast, the trail takes you to other historic sites as well, including a shady palm grove where Hawaiian royalty once lived, and the ruins of the homestead of a stranded British sailor who became a Hawaiian royal.

The trail head, which branches left and right, begins at the visitor center, a graceful building of native wood and stone nestled unobtrusively into the rolling landscape. Go right, toward the *heiau*, looming atop the nearby hill. But first stop in at the visitor center, which lays out the story of how the *heiau* played a central role in Kamehameha's conquest of the Hawaiian Islands. In a nutshell: A soothsayer told Kamehameha that to succeed in conquering all of the islands, something nobody had ever done, he would first have to build a war *heiau* on a hill over Kawaihae Bay and sacrifice a high-ranking chief there. Kamehameha built the *heiau*, made the offering, and eventually became king of the entire island chain.

❶ Base of Puukohola Heiau The trail, paved with asphalt initially, soon arrives at an interpretive sign, where a short spur leads to the **base of the temple.** You're not allowed to go onto the *heiau*, but from the base you get a close-up look at the un-mortared, perfectly stacked stones that make up its walls. Construction was a massive Stone Age public works project requiring thousands of laborers. Even Kamehameha himself participated. The tiered structure is 224 feet long by 100 feet wide, with thick walls on three sides and the ocean side left open.

❷ Mailekini Heiau An older temple, **Mailekini Heiau,** sits on the hillside about 200 feet below Puukohola Heiau, and the trail runs right in front of it. Not much is known about this *heiau,* though historians believe that, after Puukohola was built, it was transformed into a fort and outfitted with some of the canons Kamehameha acquired from Western traders. A third *heiau,* Hale o Kepuni, lies underwater in ruins just offshore from Mailekini. It was dedicated to sharks, whose offering of choice was human flesh. Hale o Kepuni was last seen above water in the 1950s. Black-tipped reef sharks abound in the waters here to this day, and you might spot them in the water if you're lucky.

❸ Pelekane At the bottom of the hill, the paved trail loops back toward the starting point. Break away from the asphalt here and follow the dirt path through the shady, beachside coconut grove. This is Pelekane, site of an ancient royal compound. Kamehameha's residence, and probably housing for his royal court, were located here, and a few stone features remain. The peninsula adjoining Pelekane did not exist in ancient times. It was built from coral rubble dredged from the reef when modern Kawaihae Harbor was created.

❹ Service Road Junction From Pelekane, the trail becomes an unpaved service road cutting through kiawe woods. When the road reaches a T, go to the right and hike uphill toward the highway. As the road approaches the highway, it emerges from the trees, giving you a great side view of Puukohola Heiau in the distance. The

Fun Facts **Hill of the Whale**

Puukohola means "hill of the whale," and this area is indeed a good place for whale-watching. Look for humpbacks between mid-December and mid-March. February is peak season.

heiau has swooping, curvy lines that blend with the contours of the hillside, and the farther away you get from it, the better you can see this.

⑤ Hwy. 270 When you come to the highway, cross it, turn left, and walk about 600 feet to an unmarked but well-worn path into the kiawe on the right, just after the bridge over Makeahua Gulch. The short path leads to John Young's homestead.

⑥ John Young's Homestead John Young was an English sailor who became stranded on the island in 1790. He and another Brit became advisors to Kamehameha; the king prized the foreigners' insight into the ways of the West and their skills with cannons and muskets. Young married Kamehameha's niece and built a home on the little ridge between two seasonal streams here. The two stone houses

he constructed were the first Western structures in Hawaii. He mixed burnt coral and sand with animal hair and poi for mortar, and finished the walls with plaster made from coral lime. The houses are in ruins, but enough of the walls remain for you to see where the windows and doors were. Young's wife, children, and servants lived in traditional grass houses, and the stone terraces of these also remain. This is a very fragile archeological site, so tread lightly and please don't remove a thing.

Retrace your steps back to the asphalt path and complete the loop back to the parking lot. From here you get fresh angles on Puukohola Heiau, and you pass a stone "leaning post" where Chief Alapai Kupalupalu Mano used to sit and watch sharks devour the cadavers left as offering at the *heiau*.

PUAKO PETROGLYPH TRAIL
(AKA MALAMA TRAIL)

Difficulty rating: Easy

Distance: 1.4 miles round-trip

Estimated time: 30 minutes if you don't linger, much longer if you hunt for rock carvings.

Costs/permits: None

Pet-friendly: No

Best time to go: Late afternoon or early morning, when the shadows are long and the petroglyphs stand out most clearly. The parking area is open from 6:30am to 6:30pm, and it's gated, so be careful not to get locked in.

Recommended map: USGS' "Puu Hinai Quadrangle"

Trail head GPS: N19 57.305 W155 51.564

Trail head directions: From Kailua-Kona drive about 25 miles north on Hwy. 19. Turn left on Mauna Lani Drive, at the Mauna Lani Resort. At the traffic roundabout, bear right onto North Kaniku Drive. Watch for a sign reading Holoholokai Beach Park & Puako Petroglyph Park.

This short, often hot, hike through a dry-land kiawe forest leads to the Puako petroglyph field, one of the world's largest collections of prehistoric rock carvings. Note: To really get a good look at the petroglyphs near the middle of the main enclosure, bring binoculars.

The trail head is located at the parking lot of Holoholokai Beach Park, just north of the elegant Fairmont Orchid Hotel. The park is the primary public-access point for the shoreline at the Mauna Lani Resort. The trail kicks off along a short asphalt path snaking through a field of jagged lava.

❶ Rubbing Area The pavement ends at the edge of the lava, where the trail enters an old kiawe forest. Reproductions of the Puako petroglyphs have been set out here in the official rubbing area. Petroglyphs may seem indelible, but they're actually fading away, ever so slowly, all the time. This unstoppable process is hastened when people take rubbings, so the state has outlawed the practice. It's okay to take rubbings of the reproductions, though. If you bring paper, chalk, and tape, you can create your own handmade Hawaiian gifts or souvenirs just two steps removed from the handiwork of the ancients.

While the petroglyph trail can be a scorcher, Holoholokai Beach Park, where the trail begins, is a little seaside oasis. It has green grass, shady trees, tide pools, picnic tables, barbecue grills, restrooms, and a shower—a lovely spot for a post-petroglyph picnic.

❷ Lava Cave The asphalt turns to a well-tread, root-and-rock-laced dirt trail once it enters the kiawe. These dusty woods offer welcome shade on the Kohala Coast's sweltering days, but there's a downside. The kiawe tree, known in the American Southwest as mesquite, has wicked thorns that can puncture a rubber sole like a wooden skewer through a slice of pineapple. So keep an eye out. Kiawe was

introduced to the islands in the 1820s, so it's not native or endemic, despite the Hawaiian name. The ancient Hawaiians who walked this way to leave their marks in the stone didn't have to watch their step like you do.

About halfway down the trail, a low-ceilinged lava cave appears on your right. If claustrophobia or the cobwebs don't stop you, and you wriggle to what looks like the back of the cave, you'll find the entrance to a larger, hidden chamber. It's roomy enough for a dozen people. Quite possibly this cave was used as refuge by women and children during times of war. Any intruder trying to squeeze into the inner chamber could have been easily thwarted with a spear to the face or a rock to the skull.

Outside of the cave is where the first petroglyphs come into view. A few of them are obvious, though there are undoubtedly more lost beneath the forest debris. But these are nothing compared to the mother load of carvings up ahead.

❸ Firebreak When the trail crosses what seems like a four-wheel-drive road, you know you're getting close. This isn't really a road. It's a firebreak. Brush fires are common on this part of the island during the dry summer months.

❹ Viewing Area A few minutes beyond the firebreak, the trail comes to the main attraction: the greatest grouping of rock carvings in the Pacific. There are 2,717 petroglyphs clustered on a sloping patch of smooth, reddish lava about 400 feet wide. Among them are women, men, warriors, paddlers, dancers, fishermen, fish, dogs, chickens, turtles, sails, and mysterious symbols we can only guess at. The area is so thick with rock art that you can't walk across it without stepping on some, which is why it's fenced off like a corral.

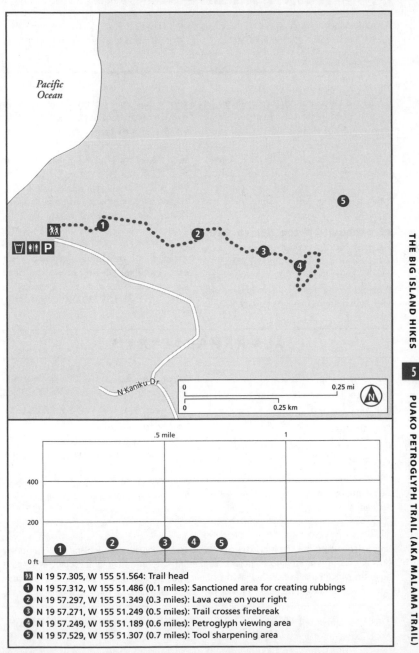

Pacific Ocean

N Kaniku Dr

0   0.25 mi
0   0.25 km

.5 mile   1

400

200

0 ft

🚶 N 19 57.305, W 155 51.564: Trail head
❶ N 19 57.312, W 155 51.486 (0.1 miles): Sanctioned area for creating rubbings
❷ N 19 57.297, W 155 51.349 (0.3 miles): Lava cave on your right
❸ N 19 57.271, W 155 51.249 (0.5 miles): Trail crosses firebreak
❹ N 19 57.249, W 155 51.189 (0.6 miles): Petroglyph viewing area
❺ N 19 57.529, W 155 51.307 (0.7 miles): Tool sharpening area

Fun Facts What's in a Name?

Malama (the actual official name of this trail) is Hawaiian for "take care of," "care for," and "preserve," among other things. It's a good word to keep in mind when visiting the slowly weathering petroglyphs.

Take a walk around the perimeter to take them all in. The lava here dates back to around A.D. 1300, and the first carvings came about a century later and were added to until around 1800. A change in styles is noticeable in the human forms. The stick figures are the earliest carvings, and the figures with triangular bodies came later.

⑤ Striking Off the Beaten Path
Another 1,112 petroglyphs have been recorded in the surrounding area. They're more widely dispersed than the swarm of carvings in the petroglyph enclosure, and it's fun to hunt for them. Just tread carefully

so you don't trample any. An arrow spray-painted on the rock at the north end of the viewing area suggests a marked route into the greater petroglyph field, but you'll need better tracking skills than I have to find all of the faded arrows. The rolling lava landscape and clumps of brush make it easy to lose your way out there, so a GPS device can come in real handy. Look for clusters of deep grooves in the rock that aren't petroglyphs but are clearly man-made. These are the abrader areas, where the petroglyph carvers sharpened their stone tools. One such area is located at N19 57.529 W155 51.307.

ALA KAHAKAI TRAIL

Difficulty rating: Moderate/Strenuous

Distance: 11.5 miles one-way

Estimated time: 7 hr.

Elevation gain: 140 feet

Cost/permits: About $40 for taxi back to trail head

Pet-friendly: No

Best time to go: February, when whale-watching season peaks.

Website: www.hawaiitrails.org

Recommended map: USGS's Kiholo Quadrangle

Trail head GPS: N19 54.843 W155 53.237

Trail head directions: Head north of Kailua-Kona about 22 miles on Hwy. 19. Turn left on Waikoloa Beach Drive, just before mile marker 76. Drive .6 miles then turn left on Kuualii Place, and park in the Anaehoomalu Beach Park at the end of the road.

This segment of the traditional circle-island trail links pre-contact and contemporary Hawaii, passing through both ancient settlement sites and gleaming modern resorts. It hugs the North Kohala shoreline, aka the Gold Coast, crossing beaches, rocky cliffs, posh hotel grounds, and more. Have a friend or a cab pick you up at the end.

This hike starts out along the beach at Anaehoomalu Bay, aka A-Bay, which fronts a palm grove, a pair of enormous

ancient royal fishponds, and the Waikoloa Beach Marriott. The trail starts at the public showers. Turn right as you face the

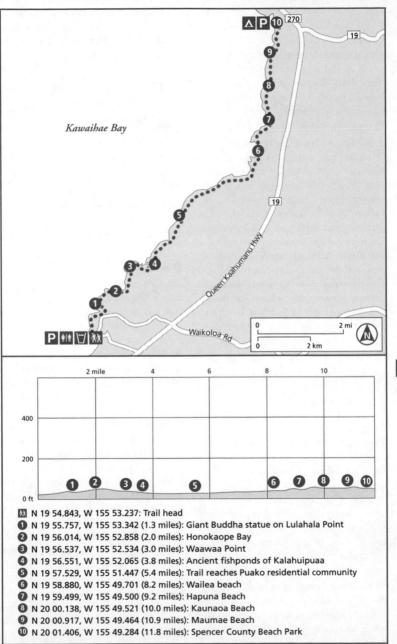

🚶 N 19 54.843, W 155 53.237: Trail head

1 N 19 55.757, W 155 53.342 (1.3 miles): Giant Buddha statue on Lulahala Point

2 N 19 56.014, W 155 52.858 (2.0 miles): Honokaope Bay

3 N 19 56.537, W 155 52.534 (3.0 miles): Waawaa Point

4 N 19 56.551, W 155 52.065 (3.8 miles): Ancient fishponds of Kalahuipuaa

5 N 19 57.529, W 155 51.447 (5.4 miles): Trail reaches Puako residential community

6 N 19 58.880, W 155 49.701 (8.2 miles): Wailea beach

7 N 19 59.499, W 155 49.500 (9.2 miles): Hapuna Beach

8 N 20 00.138, W 155 49.521 (10.0 miles): Kaunaoa Beach

9 N 20 00.917, W 155 49.464 (10.9 miles): Maumae Beach

10 N 20 01.406, W 155 49.284 (11.8 miles): Spencer County Beach Park

ocean and head to the north end of the beach, past the sunbathers and catamarans.

The fish that the ancient Hawaiians raised in the ponds at Anaehoomalu Bay were reserved for royal travelers sailing by canoe up and down the coast. Mullet was the primary fish farmed there, and therein lies the name of Anaehoomalu which means "restricted mullet."

❶ **Buddha Point**   At the end of idyllic Anaehoomalu Beach, the trail runs along a storm beach of white sand and coral rubble on a lava bench loaded with tide pools. Not quite a mile from the trail head it rounds Kaauau Point and comes to the Hilton Waikoloa Village hotel, the most sprawling (62 acres) and family-oriented (with the coolest swimming pools on the Big Island, including one filled with dolphins) of the Gold Coast hotels. The trail cuts through the hotel grounds, passes the dolphin pool, rounds narrow Wailua Bay, and finally comes to Lulahala Point, aka Buddha Point, on account of the giant Buddha statue sitting there.

❷ **Honokaope Bay**   Beyond the Buddha the trail skirts the edge of a golf course then peels away from the greens and passes a small cluster of ancient Hawaiian housing platforms perched atop rugged lava cliffs. Along these cliffs the trail traverses loose, sharp lava, where you'll want to watch your footing. Another golf course waits just up ahead, and the trail follows the cart path for a while then drops down through a swanky resort neighborhood onto a lovely little salt-and-pepper beach on deep, cliff-lined Honokaope Bay. Stairs lead from the beach back up to the top of the crumbly cliffs along the bay where, again, you'll want to watch your footing.

❸ **Waawaa Point**   The trail then skirts the edge of another golf course, marches through more jagged lava, then rejoins the golf course along the cart path. Along the way it passes: an anchailine pond, home to a tiny red native shrimp called *opaeula*;

and an ancient Hawaiian housing platform on a patch of raw lava on the emerald green fairway. At the edge of the course the trail turns to a concrete thoroughfare popular with rollerbladers and joggers, and then rounds the corner of Waawaa Point, which you've been trekking across since leaving Honokaope Bay.

> You'll catch a great view here looking north over Makaiwa Bay, with the green North Kohala Mountains and, on a clear day, Maui looming in the distance. Kawaihae Harbor, near the end-point of this hike, is visible at the foot of the Kohala range, 6.5 miles away as the crow flies. The ziggurat by the sea, just across the bay, is the Manu Lani Bay Hotel.

❹ **Kalahuipuaa**   As the trail traces the shoreline of Makaiwa Bay it runs along a short white crescent of sand usually lined with cabana chairs, then travels along the seawall of one of the ancient fishponds of Kalahuipuaa, a 27-acre tract of ancient Hawaiian archaeological sites preserved amid the golf courses and condominiums of the Manu Lani Resort. An asphalt trail runs through Kalahuipuaa, which, in addition to seven ancient fishponds, has shelter caves, petroglyphs, a stone tool making area, and early footpaths. Kalahuipuaa is open to the public, but don't let that fool you into thinking this is an ordinary quasi-public place. It is hallowed ground, alive with the spirit of the ancient Hawaii, and an area to approach with care and maybe even a touch of awe.

The trail then works its way along the beach at the foot of the Mauna Lani Bay Hotel, skirts yet another golf course, travels along a lonely salt-and-pepper beach popular with green sea turtles (I almost tripped over one basking in the sun), then runs along the shore of the grand and ultra-ritzy Fairmont Orchid hotel.

⑤ Puako Beyond the Fairmont Orchid the trail passes Holoholokai Beach Park (see Puako Petroglyph Trail, page 99), runs along a low stretch of rocky white sand beach 1/3 mile, then comes to Puako, beachside residential community that stretches for almost two miles along the sea. This is a nice stretch of coast—a wide, wave-washed lava bench with lots of inlets, coves, small points, tide pools, and beach houses.

You can either stick to the coast here, or you can save a bit of time by cutting over to Puako Beach Drive via one of the six public-access points along the way. Pick up the trail again at the Puako Boat Ramp, at the north end of the neighborhood.

⑥ Wailea Beach After a few short stretches through the kiawe trees, the trail comes to Puako Boat Ramp, where you may find local fishermen coming or going. Next it crosses a barren point, cuts through another little beachside neighborhood, then emerges on Wailea Beach, which has calm waters and lots of shade. The trail picks up again at the north end of the beach, where it climbs a hill and strikes out across a half mile of hot, scrubby landscape criss-crossed with 4-wheel-drive tracks. Stone cairns mark the trail you're hiking.

⑦ Hapuna Beach The reward at the end of the dry stretch is a big one: Hapuna Beach. This broad swath of white sand beach, a third of a mile long, is one of the loveliest and most popular beaches on the island. Take off your shoes and walk from

the county beach park at the south end past the luxurious Hapuna Beach Prince Hotel at the north end. The trail resumes there and climbs a small cliff, where an archaeological complex consisting of nine ancient Hawaiian house sites, plus some walls, terraces, and middens. Artifacts like a bone pendant found by archaeologists here suggest the houses were occupied by high-ranking people. A few hundred yards down the trail you'll pass some of the poshest vacation homes on the planet, suggesting that the low cliffs along this stretch of coast are still favored by if not high ranking, at least very well-heeled, people.

⑧ Kaunaoa Beach The next beach you hit is a long, gorgeous crescent of sand dominated by the Mauna Kea Beach Hotel. It's a fine beach in its own right, and one made all the more perfect by ice-cold beer poured at a little open-air bar on the sand. At the end of the beach the trail resumes as an asphalt path running through the hotel grounds across Kaaha Point. It then cuts through a golf course, runs through a strange cluster of thatched-roof, storybook-like vacation rentals, drops into a dry gully, pops out on a pocket beach, and rounds a rocky little point.

⑨ Maumae Beach From the point the trail ducks behind an oceanfront estate, drops down a hill, and comes out on Maumae Beach, one of the jewels of the North Kohala Coast. If you're ready for another dip, this is the place to do it. It's lovely and rarely crowded.

ⓘ Tips Take a Swim

Wailea Beach is a great place for a dip, and it's well protected from the big winter surf. Hapuna Beach is a great swimming beach when the waves are down, which you can usually count on in the summer. But in the winter, the surf might be too intimidating to go in. Kaunaoa Beach gets more waves than Wailea Beach, but it's better protected than Hapuna Beach.

⑩ Spencer County Beach Park The trail becomes its old hot and dusty self for a while before ducking into a shady old kiawe forest for its final quarter mile run to the end-point, Spencer County Beach Park. This is a favorite hang-out for locals, where native Hawaiians pitch tents beneath awnings and camp for long stretches. If you're taking a cab back to your starting point, there's a big, cool stone pavilion with picnic tables and a great ocean view where you can wait. If the trail hasn't completely worn you out at by this point, take a walk over to Puu Kohola Heiau National Historic Park.

If you're just hiking one-way, you can arrange to have a cab meet you at Spencer County Beach Park and take you back to your car at Anaehoomalu Beach Park. There are several cab services, including **Air Taxi** (*©* **808/883-8262**). Fare is around $40.

KIHOLO BAY

Difficulty rating: Moderate
Distance: 5.5 miles round-trip
Estimated time: 3 hr.
Elevation gain: 150 feet
Costs/permits: None
Pet-friendly: No
Best time to go: Before 10am to beat the heat and hit the beach in its morning prime

Recommended map: USGS' "Kiholo Quadrangle"
Trail head GPS: N19 51.121 W155 54.796
Trail head directions: Take Hwy. 19 north about 17 miles from Kailua-Kona. Park on the ocean side of the road at the gravel pull-out just before mile marker 81. If all the spots are taken, you'll find additional parking ⅓ mile to the north, on the same side of the highway, at the end of a short gravel road.

A hot and dusty trek from the highway leads to the palm-fringed, turquoise waters of Kiholo Bay. The hike continues along a pebbly black-sand beach and passes a couple of notable beach houses on its way to a cold freshwater pond set in a raw, black lava field. Then it backtracks to an enchanting blue lagoon, filled with turtles.

The trail begins behind the boulders blocking the gravel road that runs parallel to the highway. It runs through dry scrubland and kiawe thickets for nearly a mile before reaching the beach. The rock walls you'll pass along the way are remnants of one of Hawaii's great ranches of old. The Puu Waawaa Ranch once stretched from high up the slopes of Hualalai Volcano down to the sea, taking in 6 miles of coastline including Kiholo Bay. The bay was a major shipping point for cattle, which were tied to lighter boats and made to swim out to waiting steamers.

❶ The Beach After passing two gated roads, you'll come to the well-marked public-access path to the beach. A hand-lettered sign spells out the Kiholo Bay ethos: "Take only pictures, leave only footprints." A short walk from there through coastal vegetation lands you on the beach, which is like coming to an oasis after crossing a desert.

❷ Bali House Turn left as you face the ocean, head south along the shore, and check out the funky little beach shack nestled in the naupaka. This is the caretaker's residence of the Bali House. Keep going and you'll see the Bali House itself, a weathered jewel among beach houses of the rich and famous in Hawaii. Hair-care mogul Paul Mitchell had this exquisitely

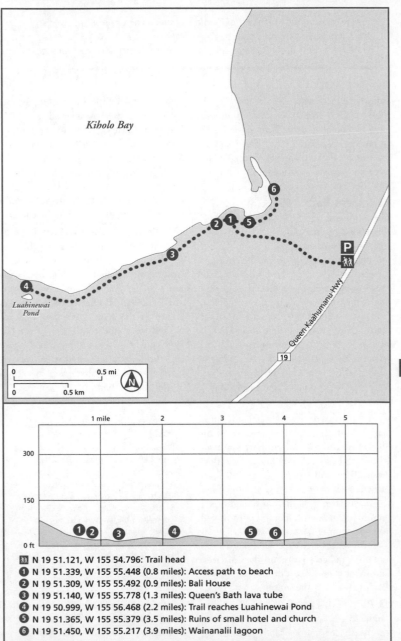

N 19 51.121, W 155 54.796: Trail head
1 N 19 51.339, W 155 55.448 (0.8 miles): Access path to beach
2 N 19 51.309, W 155 55.492 (0.9 miles): Bali House
3 N 19 51.140, W 155 55.778 (1.3 miles): Queen's Bath lava tube
4 N 19 50.999, W 155 56.468 (2.2 miles): Trail reaches Luahinewai Pond
5 N 19 51.365, W 155 55.379 (3.5 miles): Ruins of small hotel and church
6 N 19 51.450, W 155 55.217 (3.9 miles): Wainanalii lagoon

Fun Facts **Blue Fish Lagoon?**

The lava flow at the north end of Kiholo Bay filled in an enormous royal fish pond, 2 miles in diameter, built by King Kamehameha in 1810. The blue lagoon is possibly—I think likely—a remnant of that pond. But archaeologists aren't sure.

crafted home—with its eccentric multi-peaked roof—constructed in Indonesia and reassembled here. Next door is the sprawling mansion of Dr. Earl Bakken, inventor of the implantable pacemaker. It's a gaudy monstrosity in Holiday Inn yellow, but fun to see.

❸ Queens Bath The beach ends near the south end of the Bakken estate, where the hike continues on a gravel road along the shoreline. About 75 yards from the end of the beach, set back in the trees, is Queen's Bath, a lava tube filled with cold, pure spring water, plus a few fish. The ceiling of the tube has collapsed in two places, and there's a little ladder beneath one of the openings for people to climb in and out. If you go in, please wash off sunscreen in the ocean beforehand—the lava tube is a fragile ecological area, not really a bath. Better yet, keep your shoes on and continue hiking—there's a better swimming hole ahead.

❹ Lauhinewai Pond For the next half-mile, the hike follows the shoreline on the gravel road, then hits a short stretch of black sand before reaching a lava flow from 1859, still looking fresh 150-years later. Follow the trail across the flow for a quarter of a mile to the black-sand beach fronting Lauhinewai Pond, a spring-fed oasis of coconut trees and naupaka.

If the waves aren't too wild, take a dip in the ocean here to wash off the sunscreen and sweat. Then take a dip in Lauhinewai Pond to wash off the sea salt.

❺ Ruins Backtrack to the first waypoint; then continue northward along the beach for another 200 yards or so, where you'll round a point and enter an

embayment—a little bay within the bay. Kiholo Bay was a commercial hub in the late 19th century, thanks to the ranching operation, and in this embayment you'll find some ruins of the small settlement that formed. They include the crumbled lava-rock walls of a small hotel, sitting right at the point, and the fully-intact walls of a lava-rock church, just around the corner.

❻ Wainanalii, aka the Blue Lagoon Crunch along black sand and pebbles to the north end of the beach, and, after crossing the stubby foot bridge over a narrow seawater channel, you'll hit the edge of another vast lava field. This is a separate branch of the same 1859 flow that you trekked on at the south end of the bay. Here you'll find a sandy-bottomed lagoon with brilliant blue waters that seem to glow against the black lava backdrop. Turtles abound here.

If you packed your snorkel gear with you, you'll be glad when you get here. Turtles abound in these waters. You won't have any trouble spotting them from the shore, but you can get a better look if you go in with them. Brace yourselves though. Cold spring water seeps into the lagoon and sits in a chilly layer atop the warmer seawater. *Note:* State and federal law prohibits harassing the turtles in any way. So it's strictly look but don't touch.

When you find the will to tear yourself away from this lovely place, return to the first waypoint to get back to your car.

KALOKO-HONOKOHAU NATIONAL HISTORICAL PARK LOOP ★★★

Difficulty rating: Moderate

Distance: 4 miles (loop)

Estimated time: 2 hr.

Elevation gain: 160 feet

Costs/permits: None

Pet-friendly: No

Best time to go: To avoid roasting in the lava desert section of this hike, go before 10am or after 4pm.

Website: www.nps.gov/kaho

Recommended map: "Kaloko-Honokohau National Historical Park," brochure available at park visitor center.

Trail head GPS: N19 40.265 W156 01.415

Trail head directions: For the trail head at Honokohau Small Boat Harbor, drive 1 mile north of Kailua-Kona on Hwy. 19, turn left on Kealakehe Parkway, and turn right on the boat-ramp access road. Park in the big gravel lot near the end of the road. You could start this hike at the visitor center, a half mile farther up Hwy. 19, but don't do that unless you relish withering heat. The visitor center parking lot is locked from 5pm to 8am. The harbor parking lot is open 'round the clock, freeing you to hike in the cooler parts of the day.

This hike into Hawaii's prehistoric past loops through the network of trails in Kaloko-Honokohau National Historical Park. Despite the harsh lava landscape, the area supported thriving populations in the past, thanks to the large fishponds here and the sophisticated aquaculture practices of the ancient Hawaiians. Hundreds of archeological sites dot the area and the trail passes some of them, including *heiau*, petroglyphs, and a massive seawall.

A National Park Service sign marks the trail head, at the northeast corner of the harbor parking lot. The trail starts out briefly on old lava, ducks into shady kiawe woods (enjoy the shade while it lasts), and then gives you two opportunities to change your mind about hiking and go to the beach instead. Stick to the trail. You'll come back along the beach on the return trip.

1 Lava-Rock Foundation At the second beach cutoff, there's a 100-foot-long rectangle of lava rock. This is the foundation of a structure that park service archaeologists believe blended Western and traditional Hawaiian building styles. It's likely that a thatched grass roof covered its wood-framed walls. The composting toilets nearby are fully modern.

2 Petroglyphs A few minutes farther down the trail you'll come to a petroglyph field, an area of smooth lava adorned with hundreds of ancient rock carvings. Take a short detour along the boardwalk that arcs across the field to keep visitors from trampling the ancient artwork and includes several anatomically correct warriors. When you get back on the trail, keep your eyes peeled for a neat pile of stones hidden in the trees off to the right. This is one of the many *heiau*, or temples, found in the park, though one of only two the trail passes. Various thatched structures, including residences of the priests, would have stood atop these tall, broad platforms at one time. On the left side of the trail you'll spot some curiously shaped rock walls, which aren't as prehistoric as they look.

THE BIG ISLAND HIKES

5

KALOKO-HONOKOHAU PARK LOOP

(Fun Facts   There but for the Grace of the National Park Service . . .

Kaloko-Honokohau became a national historic landmark in 1962 and a historical park in 1978, saving scores of archaeological sites from the bulldozer. The deep zigzag grooves that you'll see scraped into the rock along early parts of the trail were actually left by bulldozers before the area was protected.

They're corrals, built when the area was owned by a cattle ranch. They probably once held goats.

❸ **Visitor Center**   When the trail emerges from the trees, it climbs a jagged lava flow from Hualalai, the 8,271-foot-tall volcano whose slopes make up this part of the island. The barren flow looks fairly recent, but it's actually 2,000 to 3,000 years old, a testament to how slowly vegetation returns with just 10 to 12 inches of rain a year. The visitor center was built on the flow, the trail runs right to it, and the rangers there are fun to talk to, if you're not too early or late to catch them.

❹ **Mamalahoa Trail**   The trail then resumes near the entrance to the visitor center parking area and quickly connects with the Mamalahoa Trail, an old mule highway that runs as straight as a spear. Built using convict labor between 1835 and 1855, the Mamalahoa connects Kailua-Kona with Kawaihae, 30 miles away. According to local lore, riders could set their mules in motion and then sleep in the saddle, so uneventful was the ride.

❺ **Ala Huehue Junction**   You'll be on the Mamalahoa Trail for about half a mile, through the hottest, most grueling segment of this hike. Scarcely a shrub grows on the tortured lava landscape, though—surprisingly—a few dwarfed noni trees planted along the trail somehow manage to survive. After a quarter of a mile, the trail intersects with the Ala Huehue Trail, which runs to the shore. Stick to the straight and narrow Mamalahoa for now.

❻ **Ala Nui Kaloko Junction**   Turn off the Mamalahoa toward the sea at the intersection of an unpaved service road, the **Ala Nui Kaloko Trail.** Surfers, fishermen, and local beachgoers walk this trail to the shoreline.

❼ **Stone Planters**   After .3 miles, the trail comes to a cluster of stone enclosures. Aha!—more goat corrals, you might think. But no, these are ancient Hawaiian planters. As arid as the land is here, the ancient Hawaiians still managed to grow a few things—probably sweet potatoes, gourds, and fibrous plants for nets—in planters like these. Coconut husks, soaked in water, protected the roots, while the tall planter walls supported vines and offered protection from the wind and the brunt of the afternoon sun. A spur trail runs from the planters to the north end of the park and a lovely stretch of beach; unfortunately, it was closed at press time.

❽ **Kaloko Fishpond**   The Ala Nui Kaloko Trail leads to **Kaloko Fishpond,** one of two major fishponds at the heart of the ancient Hawaiian settlements here. Eleven-acre Kaloko Fishpond is a natural inlet walled off from the ocean. The wall is a mortarless marvel of Hawaiian Stone Age engineering, 6½ feet tall and 40 feet wide, with a tapered shape that dissipates the energy of crashing waves. A team of native Hawaiian stone masons has been gradually reconstructing the wall, fitting the stones back together like an enormous jigsaw puzzle with very heavy pieces. The key, they say, is to listen to the stones,

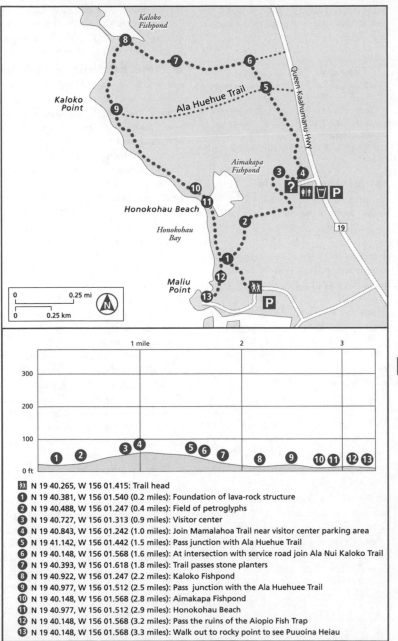

🏃 N 19 40.265, W 156 01.415: Trail head
1 N 19 40.381, W 156 01.540 (0.2 miles): Foundation of lava-rock structure
2 N 19 40.488, W 156 01.247 (0.4 miles): Field of petroglyphs
3 N 19 40.727, W 156 01.313 (0.9 miles): Visitor center
4 N 19 40.843, W 156 01.242 (1.0 miles): Join Mamalahoa Trail near visitor center parking area
5 N 19 41.142, W 156 01.442 (1.5 miles): Pass junction with Ala Huehue Trail
6 N 19 40.148, W 156 01.568 (1.6 miles): At intersection with service road join Ala Nui Kaloko Trail
7 N 19 40.393, W 156 01.618 (1.8 miles): Trail passes stone planters
8 N 19 40.922, W 156 01.247 (2.2 miles): Kaloko Fishpond
9 N 19 40.977, W 156 01.512 (2.5 miles): Pass junction with the Ala Huehuee Trail
10 N 19 40.148, W 156 01.568 (2.8 miles): Aimakapa Fishpond
11 N 19 40.977, W 156 01.512 (2.9 miles): Honokohau Beach
12 N 19 40.148, W 156 01.568 (3.2 miles): Pass the ruins of the Aiopio Fish Trap
13 N 19 40.148, W 156 01.568 (3.3 miles): Walk out to rocky point to see Puuoina Heiau

which tell the masons where to place them. It's an unrushed conversation. At press time, after 10 years of work, the restoration was about three-quarters complete.

> If you need to recharge after trekking through the lava desert, this is a good place to do it. It's got shade and picnic tables, as well as composting toilets. And you might get to watch the stone masons at work on the seawall.

9 Ala Huehue Again The trail becomes sandy, and much cooler, as it heads south along the shore. Initially it runs through a band of native coastal vegetation. Look for *ilima,* with its paper-thin blossoms in yellow, orange, or dull red. Also look for the puaapio vine, which has small white or pink flowers. Along the way you'll pass the seaward junction of **Ala Huehue Trail.** The trail roughly marks the boundary between two *ahupuaa,* the basic unit of land division in ancient Hawaii. *Ahupuaa* generally reached from the mountains to the sea and contained all or most of the resources the people living within them needed to survive. This historical park comprises the ocean ends of two mountain-to-sea *ahupuaa,* Kaloko to the north and Honokohau to the south. The coastal residents of these *ahupuaa* traded seafood for fruits and vegetables with the people who lived inland.

10 Aimakapa Fishpond After passing the seaward junction of the Ala Huehue Trail, your path finds its way to the ocean edge of a marsh. This is the north end of **Aimakapa Fishpond.** Originally it covered about 30 acres, but now half of it is marshland. During ancient times, fishponds were reserved for royalty, but commoners were

allowed to fish in some of them some of the time. Aimakapa Fishpond was one of these. Loosely translated, *aimakapa* means "what you can take with your hands," suggesting a handicap might have applied during open fishing season.

11 Honokohau Beach A natural barrier of sand separates Aimakapa Fishpond from the sea. For awhile the trail runs along a low seawall, a modern addition put in for erosion control. Stop at the end of the wall and take off your shoes. You've made it to **Honokohau Beach,** and it's time to feel some sand between your toes.

Plant yourselves anywhere along the beach and enjoy the ocean view. You may see turtles near shore, surfers on the outside reef, and fishing boats coming and going from nearby Honokohau Harbor. If you can time it right, this is a great place to catch the sunset.

12 Aiopio Fish Trap Farther down the coast, you'll come to the cutoff leading back to the 100-foot-long house foundation. Stay on the beach and head for the peaked grass roof in front of you. It's a reproduction of a canoe *hale,* a Hawaiian canoe shed. In the ocean fronting the *hale,* just beneath the surface but still visible in the clear Kona waters, lie the fallen walls of the **Aiopio Fish Trap.** Fish swam in at high tide but couldn't leave when the tide dropped. The four rectangular enclosures near the shore were probably holding tanks for the netted catch.

13 Puuoina Heiau The wall of the trap stretches out to a rocky point, where you'll find a large, terraced temple platform. This is **Puuoina Heiau.** Oral tradition says the *heiau* was both an operations headquarters and a living place for warrior priests. From the *heiau,* it's a short walk along the mouth of the boat harbor back to the parking lot.

Difficulty rating: Strenuous
Distance: 3.6 miles round-trip
Estimated time: 3 hr.
Elevation gain: 1,300 feet
Costs/permits: None
Pet-friendly: No
Best time to go: Before 10am, to beat the heat and catch the best snorkeling conditions.

Recommended map: USGS' "Honaunau Quadrangle"
Trail head GPS: N19 29.543 W155 55.085
Trail head directions: From Kailua-Kona, drive 10 miles south on Hwy. 11. After passing through the town of Captain Cook, turn right on Napo'opo'o Road. After the second telephone pole on the right, look for a wide spot on the shoulder. Park there, across the street from the residence at 81-6236 Napo'opo'o Rd.

There are two ways to get to the spot on Kealakekua Bay where Captain Cook died: by boat or by trail. The latter involves a steep, 1,325-foot descent (a real quad-burner on the way back up), with some unforgettable views along the way. Bring a mask and fins—one of the best snorkeling spots in Hawaii awaits at the bottom.

The start of the trail is often overgrown with elephant grass that towers overhead and leans into the trail. You may be thinking, "This can't possibly be right." Forge ahead. The grass will thin, and spectacular views will appear, but not for the first mile or so. That's just as well since this stretch of the trail is rugged and littered with ankle-twisting rocks that you need to keep an eye on. Horseback riders frequent the trail too, giving you other reasons to watch your step. The only real highlights at the outset are the fruit trees, which include mango, litchi, Brazilian cherry, and tamarind.

❶ First Peeks Gradually the elephant grass gives way to ekoa, a dryland shrub with dangling seed pods, and you get your first little glimpses of Kealakekua Bay. Mauna Loa Volcano's long, steep southwestern slope ends abruptly at the edge of the sheer cliffs above the bay. These cliffs hint at the gentle bay's violent geologic past. Somewhere between 100,000 and 200,000 years ago, a massive undersea slide ripped a huge chunk out of Mauna Loa's flank. Enormous pieces of the island—blocks up to 6 miles long—tumbled down Mauna Loa's steep underwater slopes toward the bottom of the ocean, creating a debris field that extends nearly 50 miles out to sea. The cliffs above the bay, known as Pali Kapu o Keoua, are part of the new shoreline that was left after the dust settled. Hidden within the many inaccessible caves that dot Pali Kapu o Keoua's face lie the bones of Hawaiian royals.

❷ First Vistas Keep hiking and suddenly the little glimpses of the bay will open into a broad look at the bay. Check to see if the spinner dolphins are out. Spinner dolphins go out to sea at night to hunt, and spend their days recharging in protected near-shore waters like this. You're most likely to see them in the morning or late afternoon, when they mark their comings and goings with the flashy aerial acrobatics from whence they got their name. Through the midday they go on auto-pilot, breathing and diving in sync, and swimming in quiet formations along the bottom for long periods. If they're splashing about, you'll be able to see them from here.

The Death of Captain Cook

Captain James Cook, the British explorer who literally put Hawaii on the map, anchored his ships in Kealakekua Bay in January 1779. The Hawaiians treated Cook and his officers as if they were the highest-ranking *alii*, and may have even suspected at first that Cook was the god Lono.

When they pulled anchor after 3 weeks, relations with the Hawaiians were good overall; but when Cook limped back to Kealakekua Bay a week later with a broken mast, things went bad. Someone stole a boat's cutter, and Cook went ashore to get it back. He planned to kidnap King Kalaniopuu and hold him for ransom until the boat was returned. Kalaniopuu initially went along willingly, but when his wife and some chiefs caught him at the waterline and implored him to stay ashore, he sat down and refused to budge. The drama, naturally, drew a large crowd.

Meanwhile, a chief paddling a canoe near one of Cook's ships was shot and killed. News reached the shore and the crowd exploded. Cook tried to retreat. Someone went at him with a dagger, and Cook shot and killed the man. When Cook turned his back on the crowd, he was knocked into the shallow water with a club to the head. He tried to rise but was stuck in the back with a dagger and fell back into the water. Whether he died of his wounds or drowned is unknown.

Four of Cook's marines were also killed, and, during that melee and in the several days of British reprisals that followed, more than 20 Hawaiians were killed.

The Hawaiians carried Cook's body up the trail here to a *heiau*, where he was ritually dismembered in a ceremony reserved for royalty.

③ Kaawaloa Peninsula As the trail emerges from the brush, it sidles up to the edge of an old lava flow. The barren flow looks fairly recent, but it's actually more than 400 years old. Both the trail and the lava run down the steep grade, side by side, until they reach the top of a high bluff. There the trail makes a 90-degree turn and begins its final descent to the sea. The lava just kept going, pouring over the edge of the bluff and into the ocean, forming a broad delta known as **Kaawaloa Peninsula.** To the south of the peninsula you can see the whole of Kealakekua Bay, and across the bay you can see Palemano Point, the little shoreline community of Keei, and idyllic palm-fringed Keei Beach.

This is the best view on the entire hike. To the right, at the apex of the lava delta, is Keawekaheka Point. If there's any kind of wave action, you'll see the blow hole there—a surf-powered geyser that blasts seawater through the lava rock.

④ Old Government Road The trail's final descent to the sea is steep and rocky, but pretty short, less than a quarter-mile. Near the bottom the trail intersects with Old Government Road, though "road" may seem like an overstatement for this rocky track across the peninsula. If you're really focused on your footing, you might

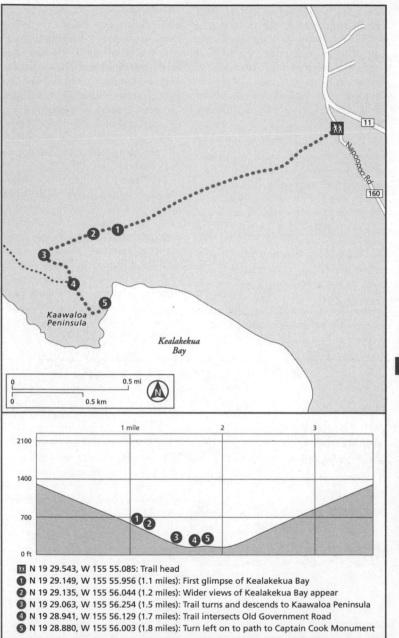

THE BIG ISLAND HIKES

5

CAPTAIN COOK MONUMENT TRAIL

N 19 29.543, W 155 55.085: Trail head
1 N 19 29.149, W 155 55.956 (1.1 miles): First glimpse of Kealakekua Bay
2 N 19 29.135, W 155 56.044 (1.2 miles): Wider views of Kealakekua Bay appear
3 N 19 29.063, W 155 56.254 (1.5 miles): Trail turns and descends to Kaawaloa Peninsula
4 N 19 28.941, W 155 56.129 (1.7 miles): Trail intersects Old Government Road
5 N 19 28.880, W 155 56.003 (1.8 miles): Turn left on to path to Captain Cook Monument

miss the intersection entirely. Just make sure that you don't accidentally stray onto Old Government Road on your way back up. It can happen. As the trail begins to level out near the shore, lava-rock walls appear up on either side. You are now entering the ancient Hawaiian village of Kaawaloa. Extensive remnants of the village exist, but most of them are locked away in impenetrable thickets of thorny kiawe.

❺ **Captain Cook Monument** The trail runs through the kiawe to the rocky shore. Just before you reach the water's edge you'll see a cut-off to the left. Follow it a few hundred feet to the Captain Cook Monument. Cook was killed near this spot in a skirmish with Hawaiians in 1779. In 1874 British sailors erected an obelisk here in Cook's honor, forming a fence around the monument by planting a dozen cannons in the ground and stringing them together with anchor chain. Nearby, a plaque in the water that appears at low tide marks the exact spot where Cook is believed to have fallen.

If you find other people here, they probably kayaked across the bay or came with one of the early morning or late afternoon snorkel tour boats. It's definitely worth your while to pack snorkeling gear with you on this hike. The clear water, nearly pristine coral reef, and abundance of marine life make Kealakekua Bay one of the Big Island's premier snorkeling spots.

Since this trail is no place to be in the heat of the day, a good strategy is to hike down early, spend some time snorkeling and picnicking, then hike back up when things cool off a bit.

The water just off the monument plunges straight to 60 feet, and fish love the coral ledge there. Be careful not to touch the coral. It's super sensitive and even brushing a coral head with your fin can kill scores of the tiny coral polyps that form reefs. As for dolphin encounters, keep in mind that it's illegal to approach them. Your best bet is to swim a bit offshore and think friendly thoughts. Maybe they'll come to you. If not, at least you'll know you didn't disturb anyone's much needed rest.

PUNALUU COASTAL TRAIL

Difficulty rating: Moderate

Distance: 2 miles round-trip

Estimated time: 1½ hr.

Elevation gain: 90 feet

Costs/permits: None

Pet-friendly: No

Best time to go: Whale-watching season, mid-December to mid-March

Recommended map: USGS' "Pahala Quadrangle" map

Trail head GPS: N19 08.036 W155 30.196

Trail head directions: From Hilo, drive south on Hwy. 11 for about an hour. Turn right on Punaluu Road, after the 56-mile marker. Park at Punaluu Beach Park.

Starting along a popular black-sand beach, this trail passes the ruins of a sugar port, cuts through a Hawaiian *heiau,* travels through a jagged lava landscape on smooth cobbles set in place by ancient hands, and ends up on a secluded point with a sweeping view.

The hike really begins as soon as you get out of the car at Punaluu Beach Park, on the rocky point at the south end of the beach. Take a few minutes there to find the park's petroglyphs. They're in an unmarked walled enclosure near the pavilion.

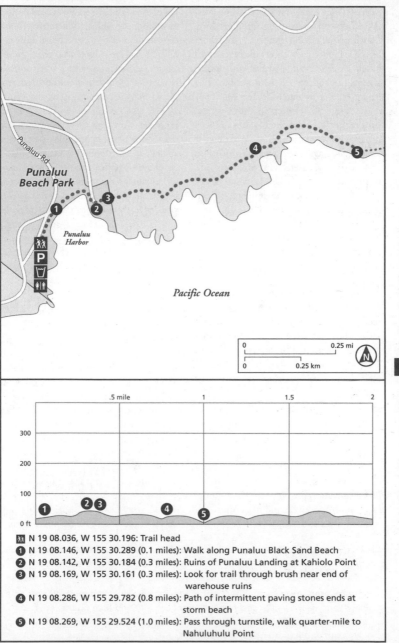

N 19 08.036, W 155 30.196: Trail head
1 N 19 08.146, W 155 30.289 (0.1 miles): Walk along Punaluu Black Sand Beach
2 N 19 08.142, W 155 30.184 (0.3 miles): Ruins of Punaluu Landing at Kahiolo Point
3 N 19 08.169, W 155 30.161 (0.3 miles): Look for trail through brush near end of
    warehouse ruins
4 N 19 08.286, W 155 29.782 (0.8 miles): Path of intermittent paving stones ends at
    storm beach
5 N 19 08.269, W 155 29.524 (1.0 miles): Pass through turnstile, walk quarter-mile to
    Nahuluhulu Point

① Punaluu Black Sand Beach Ordinarily, you lace up your boots before setting off on a hike, but for this one, you take them off so you can crunch along Punaluu Black Sand Beach in your bare feet. This is the most accessible black-sand beach on the island, popular with locals, visitors, and green sea turtles alike. The turtles love it as much as anyone. They feed on the red seaweed in the bay then haul themselves onto the beach to bask in the sun. If they're sunbathing, give them at least 15 feet of leeway, and keep in mind that state and federal law prohibits you from touching them. Unlike some of the Big Island's black-sand beaches, which were formed by silt and are really gray-sand beaches, this is the real thing. Molten lava poured into the sea here and exploded into the tiny particles that are now polishing the soles of your feet. Unlike some beaches, this one has a strictly finite amount of sand to work with. Tsunamis periodically wash it all away (tidal waves scoured the coast in 1868, 1960, and 1975), but the same oceanic forces that originally deposited it always return it. That's not the case when people carry it off, which, like harassing the turtles, is illegal.

② Punaluu Landing Behind the low sand dune at the north end of the beach, you'll pass a funky souvenir stand and a placid spring-fed pond. Then you'll come to rocky Kahiolo Point, where locals hang out in their trucks and fishermen launch boats from an impossibly steep boat ramp. Lace up your footwear and head out to the ruins of **Punaluu Landing,** just beyond

the boat ramp. The sugar plantations and mills that began springing up on this corner of the island in the 1860s used Punaluu as a shipping point. Nineteenth-century tourists coming to see the eruption of Kilauea Volcano used the port as well. Visitor traffic plummeted when a paved road from Hilo to the volcano was completed in 1893, and shipping died by the 1940s, when sugar could be trucked to Hilo on the new road. The decaying remains of the concrete quay where boats landed, and the foundation of the adjacent warehouse, are just about all that remains of Punaluu's heyday as a bustling port village.

③ Punaluu Nui Heiau Look for the trail running up the side of a brush-covered ledge on the boat-ramp end of the warehouse. At the top of the ledge, the brush clears and you'll find the long, low walls of a huge (nearly two football fields long) *heiau,* or Hawaiian temple. There are three *heiau* around Punaluu, and each served a specific purpose. This one, **Punaluu Nui Heiau,** was used for human sacrifice in ancient times. A large slab along the south wall is known as *Pohaku Mohai,* the sacrificial stone. Follow the trail across the northern end of the *heiau* and out onto the barren, jagged lava field. Look closely at the lava and you'll see housing platforms and remnants of other ancient structures there. How on earth did the Hawaiians adapt to a landscape as unfriendly to the feet as this one? They did what we would do—they paved it. Except they did it Hawaiian style, setting large, smooth sea stones into the hostile ground.

⒯ips Swim with Care

Rough waters and treacherous currents generally make swimming at Punaluu Black Sand Beach a bad idea, but you might luck out and hit it on the rare calm day. If that's the case, the north end of the beach is the best place to take a dip. The south end has too much exposed rock.

Many of those stones remain firmly in place today, and your feet will appreciate each one they meet.

❹ Storm Beach The paving stones come and go for about a quarter of a mile as the trail runs along sea cliffs and across the lava field. The last paved segment ends at a curious little **storm beach,** a steeply sloped pocket of sand set behind a high wall of lava and almost entirely blocked from the sea. It takes some ferocious surf to crash over this wall and blast through its one narrow opening to make the black-sand deposits that created the beach. This would be a great place to stop for a bit of secluded beach time, except with nothing but a big wall of lava to stare at, you might feel a little claustrophobic.

❺ Nahuluhulu Point Just beyond the storm beach, at the edge of the lava flow, you'll pass through a turnstile. That's right, a turnstile. It gets you through the barbed-wire fence that keeps the cattle, which you may or may not see but will most likely smell, on their side of the line. You'll now hike along a rutted jeep trail, which runs through tall brush and dwarf kiawe trees for about a quarter of a mile to **Nahuluhulu Point,** your turn-around point. If you exit the brush and find yourself on a massive black lava flow, you've gone too far.

On a clear day, the view from Nahuluhulu Point stretches from South Point, the southernmost tip of both the island and the United States, to the 13,680-foot summit of Mauna Loa. Just offshore you may see whales from mid-December to mid-March.

KILAUEA IKI TRAIL IN HAWAII VOLCANOES NATIONAL PARK ★★★

Difficulty rating: Moderate

Distance: 3 miles (loop)

Estimated time: 3 hr.

Elevation gain: 470 feet

Costs/permits: $10 per car. All National Park Service passes accepted

Pet-friendly: No

Best time to go: On one of the two or three Tuesdays each month when "After Dark in the Park," an evening lecture series focused on natural and cultural history, takes place

Website: www.nps.gov/havo

Recommended map: "Kilauea Iki Trail Guide," available at the trail head

Trail head GPS: N19 24.985 W155 14.575

Trail head directions: Enter Hawaii Volcanoes National Park; turn right on Crater Rim Drive. Continue about 2 miles to Kilauea Iki Overlook.

Located in Hawaii Volcanoes National Park, this gem of a hike explores 400-foot-deep Kilauea Iki Crater, site of a spectacular 1959 eruption that featured lava fountains blasting nearly a mile into the sky. The hike passes through lush rainforest at the edge of the crater, then across an otherworldly land of lava formations and sulfur steam vents on the crater floor.

The twin trail heads sit at either end of the Kilauea Iki Overlook parking lot, perched on the rim of the crater. Start on the trail head to the right as you face the crater. This takes you out along the rim and back through the crater, giving you a thorough survey of the lava landscape from above before you plunge into it.

The trail head is at the crater rim's highest point, 400 feet above the crater floor. The view from there is like the view from the penthouse of a 40-story building, but the scale is hard to fathom until you spot people at the bottom of the crater. From here, they look like ants in colorful hiking outfits.

❶ First Overlook   The first half of the trail runs through the rainforest along the crater rim, passing several overlooks along the way. It hits the first one after just a few minutes of hiking. Kilauea Iki's last eruption began on the crater wall directly across from this overlook on November 14, 1959, when a half-mile-long horizontal crack opened up on the wall and a curtain of lava poured out. Within a day the broad curtain pulled back to a single vent near the back of the crater. The eruption went on for the next 5 weeks in 17 separate episodes. Some lasted hours; some lasted days. Sometimes lava poured out of the vent in a rolling boil. Other times it blasted skyward in towering fountains of fire. The tallest lava eruption shot 1,900 feet into the air; a record for Hawaiian lava fountains. You can't see the crack that opened up in the wall any longer because

it's below the surface of the solidified lava lake that formed in the crater.

❷ Fourth Overlook   After passing two other overlooks, the trail reaches a junction with a trail to the visitor center (bear left). The overlook here has a particularly good view.

Iki means "little" in Hawaiian. So Kilauea Iki is Little Kilauea. It sits right beside Kilauea Volcano's huge summit caldera, which you might call Big Kilauea. From this overlook you can see across the tree-lined Byron Ridge separating the two. On the caldera's edge you can see the building housing the USGS Hawaiian Volcano Observatory and Jaggar Museum. Within the caldera you can see Halemaumau Crater, once believed to be the home of Pele, the volcano goddess. On a clear day, you can see Mauna Loa rising behind it all.

❸ Rock Slide   Two big earthquakes—a 7.2 in 1975 and a 6.8 in 1983—shook loose a stream of boulders that ripped a hole in the ohia forest here. The scar offers an eye-level view of the forest canopy from the trail—an irresistible stop for birdwatchers.

❹ First Byron Ridge Cutoff   The trail bears left at a well-marked junction with a Byron Ridge Trail connector, then continues onward through an area thick with kahili ginger, which blooms fragrantly in late summer. Lovely as the ginger may be, it is an exotic species that the park service wants to eradicate. So don't feel bad about picking the flowers.

THE BIG ISLAND HIKES

5

KILAUEA IKI TRAIL

Fun Facts   How Deep is the Lava Lake?

A 1988 drilling project found the bottom of the lava lake at 440 feet—deeper than scientists originally thought. Apparently, the original floor of the crater melted away into the chamber of magma beneath it, creating a single extra-deep pool of molten rock.

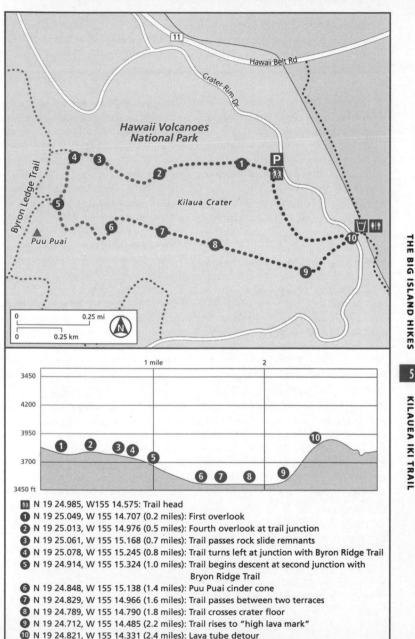

N 19 24.985, W155 14.575: Trail head
1. N 19 25.049, W 155 14.707 (0.2 miles): First overlook
2. N 19 25.013, W 155 14.976 (0.5 miles): Fourth overlook at trail junction
3. N 19 25.061, W 155 15.168 (0.7 miles): Trail passes rock slide remnants
4. N 19 25.078, W 155 15.245 (0.8 miles): Trail turns left at junction with Byron Ridge Trail
5. N 19 24.914, W 155 15.324 (1.0 miles): Trail begins descent at second junction with
   Bryon Ridge Trail
6. N 19 24.848, W 155 15.138 (1.4 miles): Puu Puai cinder cone
7. N 19 24.829, W 155 14.966 (1.6 miles): Trail passes between two terraces
8. N 19 24.789, W 155 14.790 (1.8 miles): Trail crosses crater floor
9. N 19 24.712, W 155 14.485 (2.2 miles): Trail rises to "high lava mark"
10. N 19 24.821, W 155 14.331 (2.4 miles): Lava tube detour

Fun Facts Hot Rocks

It took about 35 years for all of the molten rock trapped beneath the solidified surface of the lava lake to crystallize. But even now, the rocks down there are still piping hot, as the steam vents all over the crater floor reveal.

5 Second Byron Ridge Cutoff Kilauea Iki Trail begins its descent into the crater at a second marked cutoff to Byron Ridge Trail. Since it's been gradually working its way downhill since it left the parking lot, the trail's final drop to the crater floor is only about 200 feet.

6 Lip of Puu Puai This end of the crater floor is a chaotic jumble of jagged lava, the spattery fallout from the lava fountains. The half-domed, half-crumbled hillside rising out of the crater on the right is **Puu Puai,** the cinder cone that formed around the base of the fountaining lava. Half of Puu Puai is missing, which provides a cross-section look into the anatomy of a cinder cone. At its closest point to the cone, the trail skirts the lip of Puu Puai's vent, now covered with rock, like the jammed barrel of an exploded canon.

7 Twin Terraces As the trail leaves the tumultuous lava fountain fallout zone and moves onto the smooth, now-solid surface of the lava lake, it passes between two curious terraces. These are pieces of Puu Puai's missing half. They broke off and floated on the surface of the lava lake to where they are now.

8 Lava Lake From the twin terraces, the trail makes a half-mile beeline across the crater floor. During the eruption, the surface of the lava lake was capped by a thin black crust that fragmented into plates 10 to 20 feet across. Periodically a few of the plates would overturn and sink, knocking the plates next to them over and setting off a chain reaction of flipping plates that swept across the surface of the lake. Within minutes, the entire crust would overturn and sink, and a new crust would form. This happened several times over the course of the eruption, and for about a week afterward. The trail cuts across the final crust that formed, which looks like the cracked top of an impossibly large brownie. About 175 feet to the north of this waypoint, you can see the bore holes scientists drilled to measure the cooling rate of the molten lava trapped below the lake's solidified surface.

9 Bathtub Ring Before the trail begins climbing back up the side of the crater, it steps up on the lava lake's subsidence terrace, also known as the bathtub ring. The lava lake rose and fell as the eruption surged. The bathtub ring, about 50 feet above the crater floor, is the high water mark—or rather, high lava mark.

10 Lava Tube Detour The steep 400-foot climb through the rainforest back up to the crater rim is the most challenging part of the hike. Benches, mercifully, have been placed at some of the half-dozen switchbacks if you need to catch your breath. When you don't see your car at the top, don't freak out—this is a different parking lot, the one for Thurston Lava Tube. Take a detour if you want and check out the tube, an artery of the volcano big enough to drive a bus through. Kilauea Iki trail resumes on the north end of the lava tube parking area, and runs a half-mile along the crater rim back to your starting point.

NAPAU CRATER TRAIL IN HAWAII VOLCANOES NATIONAL PARK

Difficulty rating: Strenuous

Distance: 14 miles round-trip

Estimated time: 5 to 6 hr.

Elevation gain: 700 feet

Costs/permits: $10 per car; National Park Service passes accepted. Hikers and campers must register and get permit at the Kilauea Visitor Center, open 7:45am to 4:45pm daily. Permits are free and issued on first-come-first-served basis no earlier than the day before the hike.

Pet-friendly: No

Best time to go: On one of the two or three Tuesdays each month when "After Dark in the Park," an evening lecture series focused on natural and cultural history, happens. Check park website for schedule.

Recommended map: "Visiting Hawaii Volcanoes," in brochure available at park entrance.

Website: www.nps.gov/havo/planyourvisit/hike_napau.html

Trail head GPS: N19 21.893 W155 12.911

Trail head directions: Drive to Hawaii Volcanoes National Park, register at the visitor center, and then head back toward park entrance and turn right on Crater Rim Drive. Turn left on Chain of Craters Road and drive about 3.5 miles to Mauna Ulu parking area, marked by a sign on the left.

This trail runs along Kilauea's East Rift Zone, following a line of craters and cones that has formed along the volcano's fiery seam. It offers a broad sampler of the vastly varied features and terrain within Hawaii Volcanoes National Park, including steam vents, lava trees, hornitos, and panoramic vistas. The route traverses a bleak, blackened landscape as well as a lush rainforest filled with giant tree ferns.

A 12-mile stretch of the original Chain of Craters Road was buried in lava between 1969 and 1974, and the trail head for this hike is located on a segment of the old highway, a few hundred feet before it dead-ends at the lava field. The trail starts out briefly through low ohia trees, then pops out onto a 1973 lava flow from nearby Pauhi Crater, the figure-eight-shaped hole in the earth that you passed driving to the trail head. As the flow ran through an ohia forest, lava piled up around the trunks of trees. The trees burned down, but the piled-up lava remained, forming "lava trees," with molds of the original trees inside. You'll see

plenty of them along this stretch, along with hornitos—stubby pillars formed when lava spattered or squirted through openings in the solid crust above a lava tube or crusted-over flow.

❶ **Puu Huluhulu** As the trail nears thickly-forested **Puu Huluhulu,** it crosses onto the blacker, smoother lava from a 1974 Mauna Ulu flow. Three- to four-hundred years ago, this hill was born as cinders and spatter fell around the base of an exploding and fountaining volcanic vent. A spur trail leads to the top, and it's well worth the short climb to survey the lay of the land. A weathered compass at the summit identifies all the major features

THE BIG ISLAND HIKES

5

NAPAU CRATER TRAIL

Hawaiian Berries: U-Pick, or Maybe Not

Among the handful of hardy pioneer plants that start the long process of natural reforestation on fresh lava are two types of native berry. One is pukiawe, which has small, narrow leaves and tiny red, white, or pink berries. Ancient Hawaiians used the non-edible berries to make leis and dye. They also used the leaves to treat headaches and colds. The other berry is ohelo, which has rounded leaves and red or yellow fruit the size of blueberries. Although ohelo berries are tasty, there are three good reasons to pause before picking them: First, they're a food source for the nene, the endangered Hawaiian goose. Two, they are believed to be the embodiment of Hiiaka, sister of Pele, the powerful and temperamental volcano goddess to whom they are sacred. And last, but certainly not least, they are easily confused with non-edible akia berries, which contain a poison Hawaiians used to stun fish in tide pools.

of the landscape before you. It's right next to an old hitching post, left from the days when visitors to the volcano came by horseback.

From Puu Huluhulu on a clear day you can see the Big Island's two dominant mountains: Mauna Loa, which looms massively above you, and Mauna Kea, which—although it's the tallest peak in the Pacific—appears tiny in the distance. To the east, 6 miles away, is Puu Oo, the cinder cone at the heart of the current eruption. In the foreground before it is gaping Makaopuhi Crater, which you'll get a much closer look at farther down the trail. Right beside Puu Huluhulu stands Mauna Ulu, which began its 5-year eruption on May 24, 1969, with fountains of lava up to 1,800 feet high. After the dramatic kickoff, the eruption shifted into a more low-key mode, with lava spilling out in flows that eventually covered 18 square miles. The flows reached all the way to the sea and added 230 acres of new land to the island.

❷ **Lava Channel** As the main trail threads between the forested edge of Puu Huluhulu and the blackened foot of Mauna Ulu, it passes beneath a "perch pond" on Mauna Ulu's flank. This self-formed, Olympic-swimming-pool-sized, above-ground lava pond is one of the many strange forms that occur when millions of cubic gallons of lava pour from the earth. From here the trail wraps around the northern flank of Mauna Ulu, setting off across the raw lava landscape. Stone carins, or *ahu* in Hawaiian, mark the way. But shortly after Puu Huluhulu the trail runs along the bed of a **lava channel.** Hiking through the channel is like traveling along the bottom of a dry streambed with overhead banks. Molten lava once coursed through this channel like a river.

❸ **Alae Shield** Before the 1969–74 eruption swallowed the old Chain of Craters Road, a popular stop along the way was Alae Crater, a 450-foot-deep pit crater right beside Mauna Ulu. The crater rumbled back to life during the eruption; filled with lava; and then grew to become a little shield cone, **Alae Shield.** The trail runs to the top of this mini version of Mauna Ulu and runs near the crumbling edge of the summit crater. Steam vents there give the impression that Alae Shield only just wrapped up its business, like the barrel of a smoking gun.

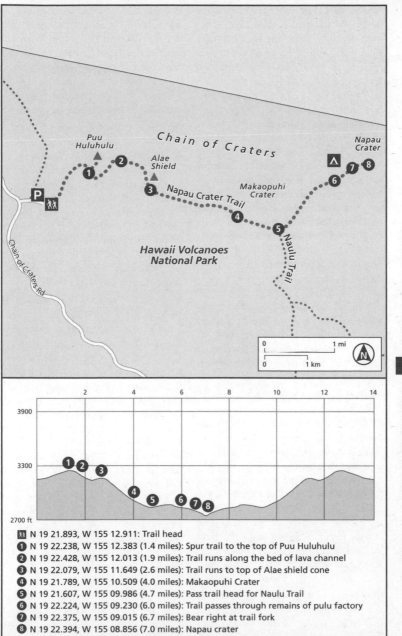

N 19 21.893, W 155 12.911: Trail head
1 N 19 22.238, W 155 12.383 (1.4 miles): Spur trail to the top of Puu Huluhulu
2 N 19 22.428, W 155 12.013 (1.9 miles): Trail runs along the bed of lava channel
3 N 19 22.079, W 155 11.649 (2.6 miles): Trail runs to top of Alae shield cone
4 N 19 21.789, W 155 10.509 (4.0 miles): Makaopuhi Crater
5 N 19 21.607, W 155 09.986 (4.7 miles): Pass trail head for Naulu Trail
6 N 19 22.224, W 155 09.230 (6.0 miles): Trail passes through remains of pulu factory
7 N 19 22.375, W 155 09.015 (6.7 miles): Bear right at trail fork
8 N 19 22.394, W 155 08.856 (7.0 miles): Napau crater

❹ Makaopuhi Crater The trail follows the cairns down the gentle slope of Alae Shield and across the black landscape toward **Makaopuhi Crater.** The enormous chasm, a mile long by a half-mile wide, was the site of a scientifically famous eruption in 1965. The crater filled with lava, giving volcanologists the best chance they've had before or since to study how lava circulates in a lava lake. One phenomenon they observed was the way the crust on a lava lake breaks up, sinks, and immediately reforms. Gas bubbles collecting beneath the floating plates of the crust would periodically lead the plates to tip on end and sink like ships. Waves of overturning plates would sweep across the lake like dominoes. The scientists were still doing experiments and taking measurements in the crater when the eruption of Mauna Ulu a few years later sent lava pouring over the rim of the crater, bringing the scientific fun to a halt.

This is a natural spot for a break, and maybe a picnic. While looking for a comfy rock to sit on, you might even find the remains of the overlook where travelers on the old Chain of Craters Road stopped to peer into chasm, that is before lava swallowed the road, along with most of the overlook.

❺ Trail head of Naulu Trail From Makaopuhi Crater onward, this hike changes from a trek across a lava field to a trip through a rainforest. For awhile the trail traces the southern edge of Makaopuhi Crater, but you'll only find a few breaks in the thick foliage where you can peer across the enormous chasm. About half a mile into the forest you'll come to the trail head for Naulu Trail, which leads 3.2 miles to the new Chain of Craters Road, several miles away from where you parked.

❻ Pulu Factory This rainforest is dominated by ohia trees and hapuu, or tree ferns. Young hapuu fronds unfurl from a coil covered with reddish-brown or golden fiber called pulu. Soft as down, pulu was popular as a mattress and pillow stuffing in the 19th century. The Big Island had a booming pulu export industry, and this trail runs right through the remains of a factory where the silky fiber was dried and bagged. Give yourself some time to poke around the site. The low lava-rock walls are beautiful examples of traditional Hawaiian dry masonry, with perfectly fitted stones and not a dab of mortar.

❼ Campgrounds or Crater? The rainforest opens up a few times where it hasn't yet grown back fully over fingers of an old lava flow that burned through the trees. Near the end of the trail, about .3 miles from the pulu factory, the trail forks. To the left: a primitive campground, which is nothing more than a few clearings in the brush and an outhouse. To the right: Napau Crater, the end of the line.

❽ Napau Crater Well, actually the trail continues from here for 2 miles to Puu Oo, the smoldering volcanic cone in the distance; but that stretch has been closed due to volcanic hazard. Puu Oo is the center of Kilauea's current eruption. It began rising from the rainforest in 1983 with a spectacular series of lava fountains that reached as high as 1,500 feet. Ash and lava spatter from these eruptions built Puu Oo into a perfectly shaped cone 835 feet tall. The peak of the cone has since collapsed, reducing Puu Oo to a lopsided 600 feet or so. As of press time, Puu Oo was still at the heart of Kilauea's eruption, the volcano's longest ongoing eruption in more than 600 years. A plume of volcanic gas typically streams from the top. It often glows orange at night, illuminated by incandescence within the crater. Although you can't hike to Puu Oo, you can (practically) peer into the crater in real time, thanks to a webcam set up on the rim by Hawaii Volcanoes Observatory (http://hvo.wr.usgs.gov/cam).

Difficulty rating: Easy

Distance: .4 miles (loop)

Estimated time: 30 min.

Elevation gain: 100 feet

Costs/permits: None

Pet-friendly: No

Best time to go: When it comes to water-falls, the more rain the better. October through April is rainy season in Hawaii.

Website: www.hawaiistateparks.org

Recommended map: USGS' "Akaka Falls Quadrangle"

Trail head GPS: N19 51.241 W155 09.136

Trail head directions: From Hilo, drive 13 miles north on Hwy. 19, turn left at Honomu, drive into town, and then turn right on Akaka Falls Road and drive 3.5 miles to Akaka Falls State Park.

Located on the island's rainy Hamakua Coast, the paved trail circles through a steamy rainforest thick with azalea, gardenia, hibiscus, ti leaf, tree ferns, ohia lehua, bird of paradise, banana, and so many other tropical species you could fill the index of a botanical field guide with them. This part of the island is chock-full of waterfalls, and the trail takes you to two of them: 100-foot Kahuna Falls and 442-foot Akaka Falls.

The loop trail starts at the edge of the parking lot, drops down a short flight of steps, then immediately presents you with a choice: go left or go right? Go right. That way you'll come to relatively shrimpy Kahuna Falls first, building drama as you approach the marquee attraction.

① Bamboo Grove The trail is paved the whole way and lined with handrails to help with the drops and climbs. It soon descends a second flight of steps, then enters a grove of giant bamboo. Take a moment on the bridge over the little stream there to enjoy the towering walls of bamboo. The perspective isn't unlike what an ant in the grass might experience. I'm not suggesting that you're ant-like, but bamboo is the largest member the grass family, not to mention the fastest growing woody plant on the planet.

② Kahuna Falls A few minutes further along the trail and you'll come to a little spur that dead-ends at the edge of a gorge. Across the gorge is Kahuna Falls, which drops 100 feet into Kolekole Stream. Akaka Falls is located on Kolekole Stream. Kahuna Falls has a different source. From this point though, water from both falls courses through Kolekole Stream to the ocean, 3 miles away.

③ Akaka Falls From Kahuna Falls the trail climbs a small hill, passes beneath some banyan trees, and then comes to the Akaka Falls overlook, the climax of this quickie hike. The falls form where the bottom drops out of a mountain stream

Tips Beat the Crowd

Akaka Falls is one of the Big Island's iconic attractions. Every tour bus and rental car driving around the island seems to stop here. Get up early, though, and you may have the falls to yourselves.

Fun Facts   **The Blue-Black Locks Iwa'iwa**

Keep an eye out for *iwa'iwa,* the lacy fern growing from the rocky faces along the trail and around the falls. It's a fern with a legend. Back in Hawaii's mythological past, Iwa'iwa was a beautiful maiden from the nearby village of Honomu who had the most beautiful hair in Hawaii—hair coveted by creepy outcast named Molemole. Bald as a river rock, Molemole lived in a secret cave near Akaka Falls. The women of Honomu knew not to venture to the falls alone for fear of the coughing, wheezing old man, but one day Iaw'iwa went to the falls by herself anyway. As she swam in the mountain pool, her locks floated on the water like blue-black seaweed, driving the spying Molemole mad with desire.

As Iwa'iwa headed back up the steep trail from the falls, she took a shortcut that went right passed Molemole's cave. As she passed he grabbed her by the ankles and dragged her inside, commanding his cave entrance to slam shut for all time. But Iwa'iwa's hair got stuck in the entrance, and so Molemole was denied what he wanted most. The goddess of the forest, Laka, who witnessed the whole thing, transformed Iwa'iwa's hair into the lacy fern that still dangles from the crags around Akaka Falls to this day.

draining the rainforest on the lush Hamakua Coast. Thousands of gallons of water per minute pour over the edge of the cliff, plunging 442 feet in a single, spectacular drop, and crashing into the dark pool below in a fearsome ball of exploding white water. It's not the tallest waterfall in Hawaii (that would be 2,953-foot Oloupena Falls on the north shore of Molokai), but it is the tallest Hawaiian waterfall plunging from top to bottom in a single, unbroken drop, without cascading over ledges along the way.

Even during a drought, when Akaka Falls is merely trickling, it's an impressive sight. Catch it after a winter deluge, and the awesome force of this tower of white water will get your heart pounding.

There's a little shelter at the overlook where you can duck out of the rain, which can exceed 250 inches per year on this part of the island. Of course, the more it rains, the mightier the falls flow. Hit Akaka Falls after several days of rain, when the afternoon sun is behind the falls, and you may get the coveted waterfall double-whammy: fiercely pounding water with rainbows!

I've heard a couple different versions of the legend of Akaka Falls, but all involve a handsome young chief named Akaka, who had a lover named Lehua, another lover named Maile, a loyal dog, and a loving wife. One day, while Akaka's loving wife was visiting her parents in the distant village of Hilo, Akaka visited Lehua in her hut. Afterwards, he visited Maile in her hut. Akaka's wife returned home early, and when he heard her calling, he slipped out of Maile's hut and hurried home.

In one version of the legend, Akaka slips off the edge of a cliff in his haste. In another version, his cheating heart fills with remorse and he jumps. In either case, his crushed body turns into the red stone at the bottom of the falls, and his loyal dog turns into the jagged rock at the edge of the cliff. His wife shows up moments later, and she too turns to stone, but still weeping so uncontrollably that her tears pour over the precipice and create Akaka Falls. When Lehua and Maile hear the news, they too turn to stone. Their unstoppable tears formed two smaller waterfalls downstream of Akaka Falls, not visible from the trail.

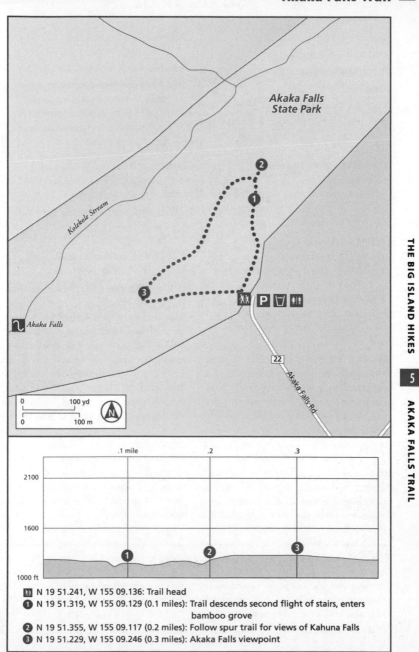

THE BIG ISLAND HIKES

5

AKAKA FALLS TRAIL

Akaka Falls State Park

Kolekole Stream

Akaka Falls

22

Akaka Falls Rd

| 0 | 100 yd |
| 0 | 100 m |

N

.1 mile   .2   .3

2100

1600

1000 ft

N 19 51.241, W 155 09.136: Trail head
1 N 19 51.319, W 155 09.129 (0.1 miles): Trail descends second flight of stairs, enters bamboo grove
2 N 19 51.355, W 155 09.117 (0.2 miles): Follow spur trail for views of Kahuna Falls
3 N 19 51.229, W 155 09.246 (0.3 miles): Akaka Falls viewpoint

PUU OO TRAIL

Difficulty rating: Moderate

Distance: 7.4 miles round-trip

Estimated time: 3 hr.

Elevation gain: 420 feet

Costs/permits: None

Best time to go: Early in the day to avoid rain and fog, which sets in around 2pm

Recommended map: USGS' "Puu Oo and Waikoloa Ponds Quadrangles"

Trail head GPS: N19 40.622 W155 23.069

Trail head directions: From either East Hawaii or West Hawaii, take Saddle Road. Look for gravel parking area on south side of road, halfway between mile markers 22 and 23.

Located at about 6,000 feet, in the saddle between Mauna Loa and Mauna Kea, this trail runs through a crazy quilt of old native forest, emerging forest, and grassland, all streaked with lava flows of various ages. A variety of rare native birds can be seen and heard along the way. If you bring a flashlight, and you're not claustrophobic, there's a lava tube to explore.

The trail head is at the edge of the parking lot, marked with a sign reading PUU OO HORSE & FOOT TRAIL. It doesn't say Cattle Trail, but historically this was the trail Hawaiian cowboys used to drive cattle from upcountry ranches to ships in the harbor at Hilo.

❶ **Lava Channel** The trail soon enters a low ohia forest emerging atop a 400-year-old lava flow. It snakes through the trees, climbs over a ridge, winds around a bit, and then climbs over a second ridge. The ridges are actually the banks of a lava channel that formed as this flow coursed downslope like a river. If you could see this section of trail from the above (and with Google Earth you can), you'd see that the lava channel is very clearly defined. This waypoint marks the top of the second ridge, which has nice views of Mauna Kea and Mauna Loa on clear days.

❷ **First Kipuka** The trail drops down the second ridge and emerges from the ohia into a grassland flanked by old-growth ohia and koa forest on either side. Where the trail is not clearly defined, it's marked by cairns, or *ahu* in Hawaiian. They appear at several points during this hike. After traveling for a quarter of a mile over the grassland, the trail briefly skirts the edge of a small patch of koa trees, a native hardwood easily identifiable by its crescent-shaped leaves. This is the first *kipuka* of the hike, an island of old forest surrounded by lava flows on all sides. Of course, this *kipuka* is on lava too, but it's several thousand years old with a thick layer of soil on top.

(Tips) Hope for Sun, but Prepare for Rain

Bring rain gear and pack it along even if there's not a cloud in the sky. Weather conditions change fast up here. Fog and rain are common in the afternoon, so the earlier you start the better.

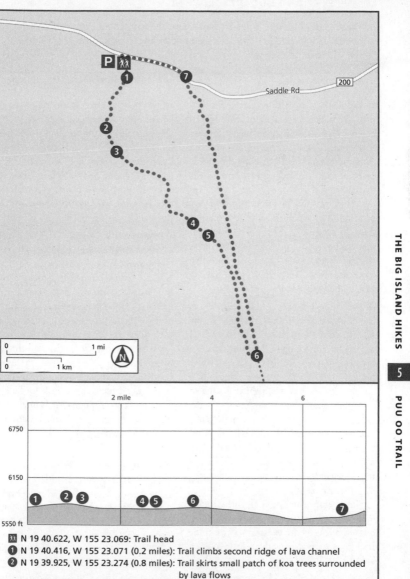

THE BIG ISLAND HIKES

5

PUU OO TRAIL

N 19 40.622, W 155 23.069: Trail head
1 N 19 40.416, W 155 23.071 (0.2 miles): Trail climbs second ridge of lava channel
2 N 19 39.925, W 155 23.274 (0.8 miles): Trail skirts small patch of koa trees surrounded by lava flows
3 N 19 39.664, W 155 23.158 (1.2 miles): Trail crosses lava flow of 1889
4 N 19 38.932, W 155 22.342 (2.4 miles): Tall Tree Kipuka
5 N 19 38.827, W 155 22.159 (2.6 miles): Trail crosses lava flow of 1881
6 N 19 37.605, W 155 21.660 (3.7 miles): Turn on to Powerline Road
7 N 19 40.402, W 155 22.426 (6.9 miles): Turn left on to Saddle Road

(Fun Facts) Bird Bonanza

This trail runs through prime bird-watching territory, where every remaining endemic forest bird in Hawaii can be found except for the palilla (for that one, see Puu Laau Rd., below).

3 Lava Flow of 1899 From the *kipuka*, the trail once again runs through an emergent ohia forest, then makes its way over another swath of grassland, crossing through two more *kipuka* along the way. It emerges from the second *kipuka* onto the barren, jagged lava flow from 1899. You may find sun-bleached bones of wild pigs or mufflon sheep on the lava, where hunters field-dressed their kills. The waypoint marks the high point across the flow; there's a good view of the surrounding landscape here, and, on a clear day, of Mauna Loa and Mauna Kea.

4 Tall Tree Kipuka At the edge of the lava flow, the trail slips through a tiny *kipuka;* comes out on a narrow branch of a lava flow from a big 1855 flow; crosses a broad stretch of ohia forest; crosses a wider branch of the 1855 lava flow; ducks into another *kipuka;* crosses a third branch of the 1855 flow; and finally comes to the tallest, oldest *kipuka* along the trail. When you see it you'll understand why I'm calling it Tall Tree Kipuka. Inside you'll find a canopy of enormous old-growth koa, a mid-story of large ohia, and an understory of giant tree ferns.

Just before entering Tall Tree Kipuka, look for the big lava tube just to the north of the trail. You have to step away from the trail to see it, but with a little poking around you'll find it.

5 Lava Flow of 1881 After emerging from Tall Tree Kipuka, the trail hits a fourth branch of the 1855 flow and soon comes to the lava flow of 1881. You'll

know you've crossed from one to the next because the texture and color of the rock changes. *Ahu* mark the way to the next kipuka, about half a mile away. It's easy to stray from the trail here without realizing it, so try to always keep at least one *ahu* in sight. If it's dark or foggy, you might not be able to see the *ahu,* so try to avoid getting caught out there then.

6 Powerline Road The trail passes through three more *kipuka* and crosses two more broad branches of the 1881 flow before reaching rough and rocky **Powerline Road.** After the first *kipuka,* a tremendous view opens up to the southwest of the patchwork of green forest streaked with black and gray lava flows on Mauna Loa's steep slopes. Ecologists call this area, which includes Puu Oo Trail, the Mauna Loa Kipuka Mosaic. Powerline Road offers a straight, if rocky, shot back to the highway, passing through the same mosaic terrain as the trail. Look for the stumps of chopped-down power poles lining the road.

7 Saddle Road When you finally reach Saddle Road, turn left and hike along the shoulder for ³/₄ mile back to your car. If you're not quite ready for the return to civilization that walking along a highway represents, a rugged utility road runs more or less parallel to the highway, and you can use that. But after 3.5 miles of uneven footing along Powerline Road, you'll probably welcome the smooth asphalt.

Difficulty rating: Moderate

Distance: 8.4 miles round-trip

Estimated time: 4½ hr.

Elevation gain: 1,760 feet

Costs/permits: Free. Permits required for hunters and ATV operators.

Pet-friendly: No

Best time to go: Weekdays to avoid the weekend hunters and ATV riders. Call the Division of Forestry and Wildlife to check on closures due to special hunts or fire: ℂ 808/887-6063. For birders, go near dawn or sunset, when birds are most active.

Website: www.hawaiitrails.org

Recommended map: USGS' "Keamuku and Ahumoa Quadrangles"

Trail head GPS: N19 48.437 W155 37.828

Trail head directions: Road begins at the Kilohana Hunter Check-In Station off of Saddle Road, aka Hwy. 200, between mile markers 43 and 44, about 15 miles from Waimea.

The high western slopes of Mauna Kea provide habitat for the palila, an endangered Hawaiian finch, and this hike climbs a steep 4×4 road through prime palila country. The area's mix of native dryland forest and grassland also provides a home for a variety of other Hawaiian forest birds as well as wild turkey and introduced game birds, moufflon sheep, and wild pigs.

Park beside the hunter check-in station and follow the road uphill. Along the way you'll pass seven marked roads and several unmarked roads and trails. Puu Laau Road is always the widest, so it's easy to identify. But just in case there any confusion, it's marked as road R-1 whenever it meets another marked road.

❶ **Fog Catcher** After a quarter of a mile you'll come to a curiously empty field enclosed on three sides by tall pines. I thought this must be a windbreak for some long-gone ranch structure, but after talking to one of the old-timers at the state's Department of Land and Natural Resources, I learned that it's actually a "fog interception device." The west side of Mauna Kea gets very little rain, but at this

elevation there's plenty of fog. When fog envelops the pines, moisture condenses on the needles and drips into the soil, irrigating the field. Soy beans, pigeon peas, and other crops were once grown there as a sort of outdoor buffet for game birds. Land managers now leave game birds, none of which are native or endemic to Hawaii, to fend for themselves. But the fog catcher's still catching fog.

❷ **Palila Zone Starts** This waypoint marks the 6,000-foot level, the beginning of the palila range, which stretches up to 9,000 feet.

The entire population of this endangered native Hawaiian honeycreeper, sometimes classified as a finch, numbers less than 5,000. Seventy-five percent of

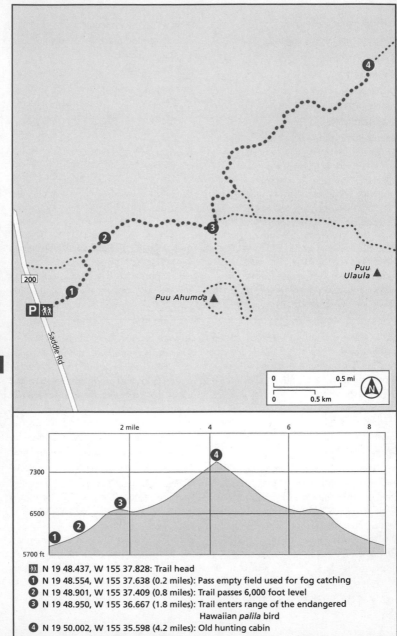

THE BIG ISLAND HIKES

5

PUU LAAU ROAD

200

P

Saddle Rd

Puu Ahumoa ▲

Puu Ulaula ▲

0   0.5 mi
0   0.5 km

N 19 48.437, W 155 37.828: Trail head
1 N 19 48.554, W 155 37.638 (0.2 miles): Pass empty field used for fog catching
2 N 19 48.901, W 155 37.409 (0.8 miles): Trail passes 6,000 foot level
3 N 19 48.950, W 155 36.667 (1.8 miles): Trail enters range of the endangered
                                                    Hawaiian *palila* bird
4 N 19 50.002, W 155 35.598 (4.2 miles): Old hunting cabin

ⓘ Tips   Dress Brightly

Some of the Big Island's 3,000 licensed hunters are known to shoot at anything that moves, and this is a hunting area. So be sure to wear brightly colored clothing, and don't stray from the road.

them live here on the western slope of Mauna Kea. They feed primarily from the seed pods of the native mamane tree. The loss of most of Hawaii's mamane forest to ranchland has left the palila on the brink of extinction. Look for a yellow-headed bird with a white belly, gray back, and olive-greenish wings. That's a palila. In the morning or afternoon you may hear its calls, a sharp, clear *chee-clee-o* or a *tee-cleet*. Among the more common Hawaiian forest birds you might spot along the road is the pueo, the Hawaiian owl, which likes to perch on fence posts, treetops, and rocky outcroppings. Wild turkey, pheasant, and a type of partridge called a francolin are among the game birds that were turned loose here for hunting. You may see them shuffling out of the road as you approach, or bursting out of the grass and fluttering off as you pass. Also keep your eyes peeled for wild pigs and mouflon sheep. If you don't spot any, you may still see their tracks and droppings on the road.

❸ **Road to Puu Ahumoa**   Fine views of the North Kohala Coast and the island of Maui to the west will come and go as you climb. To the east you'll spot a grassy cinder cone called Puu Ahumoa, and this is the 1¹/₂-mile road—marked as R-15—that

leads to its 7,042-foot summit. Cinder cones like this cover Mauna Kea like giant pimples, giving it a bumpier profile than its neighbor Mauna Loa, which has a shield volcano's dome shape. For the first several hundred thousand years of Mauna Kea's life, it too had the smooth lines of a volcanic shield. But somewhere around 200,000 years ago, near the end of its eruptive history, its smooth-flowing shield-stage eruptions transformed into explosive, post-shield eruptions, leaving it covered with cinder cones like Puu Ahumoa.

❹ **Cabin**   This hike starts at 5,800 feet and climbs to 7,500 feet, ending at an old hunting cabin beside a stand of enormous eucalyptus. The cabin is one of several that were built in the 1950s around Mauna Kea for hunters. The cabin's in good shape, but the outhouse has seen better days. At this point, the road splits to the left and to the right, and makes a 32-mile partial loop around the mountain. This is the turn-around point as far as the Puu Laau Road hike is concerned. On the way back down, you'll be better oriented to the views of the North Kohala Coast and Maui. To the south you'll see the long smooth slopes of Mauna Loa, which was hiding behind you on the way up.

MAUNA KEA-HUMUULA TRAIL
(AKA MAUNA KEA SUMMIT TRAIL)

Difficulty rating: Strenuous

Distance: 6 miles, one-way

Estimated time: 5 hr. up, 3 hr. down

Elevation gain: 4,300 feet

Costs/permits: Register at the Visitor Information Station so rangers know you're out there if you run into trouble and don't return.

Pet-friendly: No

Best time to go: April through October, when there's less chance of snow. Start as early as possible, not later than 8am, so you have time to get up and back before dark.

Website: www.ifa.hawaii.edu/info/vis

Recommended map: USGS' "Mauna Kea Quadrangle" map

Trail head GPS: N19 45.735 W155 27.385

Trail head directions: Drive west on Hwy. 200 (Saddle Rd.) from Hilo, or drive north on Hwy. 190 and then east on Hwy. 200 from Kona. Turn on Mauna Kea Access Road, near mile marker 28. Drive 6 miles up the access road to the Visitor Information Station and park there. The drive takes an hour from Hilo and 2 hr. from Kona. For road conditions on the mountain, which will give you some idea of trail conditions as well, call ℂ 808/935-6268.

This is the trail to the highest point in Hawaii, the tallest peak in the Pacific, and—according to the Guinness Book of World Records, measuring Mauna Kea from its submarine base—the tallest mountain in the world (33,476 ft. from seafloor to summit). The trail climbs from 9,300 feet to 13,000 feet, traversing an alpine desert where the air is thin, the temperatures hit freezing, and the views are astonishing. Highlights include an ancient Hawaiian adze quarry, an international astronomy complex, and a moon-like landscape shaped like fire and ice.

The trail head is a few hundred yards up the road from the Visitor Information Station, just across from the dormitories for the astronomical observatories on the summit. For the first .4 mile, you travel along an old jeep trail, the original road to the summit. Leave the jeep trail at the first switchback, picking up the footpath there that will lead you to the top of the mountain. For the first few miles, the grade is insanely steep, but it mellows out as you get closer to the summit.

❶ Mauna Kea Ice Age Natural Area Reserve Initially, the hike starts out in thin native mamane forest, where you may spot ring-necked pheasants and California quail. But the birds and trees soon

disappear, and it's just you and your hardworking lungs trudging up the steeply pitched rocky landscape. Around 10,200 feet, the trail meets the summit access road at a big horseshoe turn, where it crosses into the **Mauna Kea Ice Age Natural Area Reserve.** If you ever wondered how Hawaii fared during the ice ages of the Pleistocene epoch, then you're probably the type who can separate glacial outwash from glacial till at a glance. Your powers of forensic glaciology will come in handy all along the trail. For most of the last 200,000 years, Mauna Kea was capped with ice, which advanced and retreated four times, finally melting 11,000 years ago. During its last expansion, the ice cap covered 30

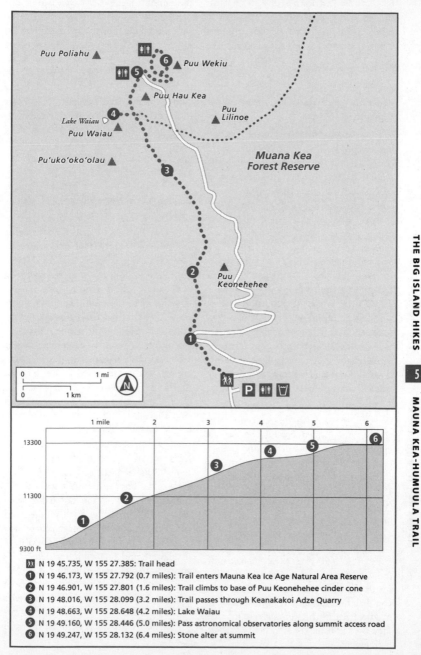

N 19 45.735, W 155 27.385: Trail head

1 N 19 46.173, W 155 27.792 (0.7 miles): Trail enters Mauna Kea Ice Age Natural Area Reserve

2 N 19 46.901, W 155 27.801 (1.6 miles): Trail climbs to base of Puu Keonehehee cinder cone

3 N 19 48.016, W 155 28.099 (3.2 miles): Trail passes through Keanakakoi Adze Quarry

4 N 19 48.663, W 155 28.648 (4.2 miles): Lake Waiau

5 N 19 49.160, W 155 28.446 (5.0 miles): Pass astronomical observatories along summit access road

6 N 19 49.247, W 155 28.132 (6.4 miles): Stone alter at summit

square miles, averaged 200 feet in thickness, and reached down to this level, leaving striated rock, moraines, and all sorts of other glacial evidence for you to either impress or irritate your hiking companions with. The glaciated terrain stretches all the way down to 9,000 feet, but within the reserve, which reaches to the summit, it's under the protective wing of state land managers.

❷ Puu Keonehehee   The trail continues steeply toward a prominent cinder cone named **Puu Keonehehee,** wraps around its base, then threads through a trio of smaller cones. Dozens of cinder cones like these dot the upper slopes of Mauna Kea. They are products of the explosive latter stage of in the volcano's evolution. In its younger days, Mauna Kea had the smooth profile of a classic shield volcano, just like dome-shaped Mauna Loa behind you. But around 200,000 to 250,000 years ago, it entered the post-shield stage of volcanic evolution with a series of explosive, fountaining eruptions that created the overlapping cinder cones that give the mountain its lumpy profile. Beyond Puu Keonehehee, a series of cairns and metal posts mark the way.

❸ Keanakakoi Adze Quarry   Lava that erupted beneath the ice cap cooled rapidly and formed basalt. The ancient Hawaiians prized this dense, fine-grained rock, which they made into adzes for chopping and carving wood. As early as the 15th century, they mined basalt at the **Keanakakoi Adze Quarry,** which the trail passes through between 11,000 and 12,500 feet. Piles of basalt chips and flakes can be found here, along with some partially completed adzes. It's all protected by state and federal law, so don't take or disturb a thing. If you stop here to explore, you may find shelter caves where the adze makers lived in the summer months that they worked here. You may even see some petroglyphs.

❹ Lake Waiau   As the trail closes in on the summit, it passes between two prominent cinder cones: Puu Hau Kea to the right and Puu Waiau to the left. In the saddle between the cones, take the short spur trail up Puu Waiau to visit little **Lake Waiau.** At 13,020 feet, it's one of the highest alpine lakes in the world. Ordinary cinder cones are too porous to hold water in their craters, but Puu Waiau is different. It has an impermeable floor, created when steam and hot water cooked the cinder and ash into clay. The lake is generally about $7^1/_2$ feet deep, and it's fed by snow melt. Occasionally, it overflows through the notch in the west side of the crater.

❺ Mauna Kea Observatories   From the cutoff to Lake Waiau, the trail wraps around the foot of Puu Hau Kea and meets the summit access road. From there it's a short walk uphill to the summit loop road, along which a dozen astronomical observatories are built. The summit is above 40% of the Earth's atmosphere and 90% of its water vapor, giving those peering into the cosmos an exceptionally clear view. At 19° north latitude, it's close enough to the equator to see much of the northern and southern skies, which are clear 300 nights a year. Astronomers worship the place. But so do native Hawaiians, many of whom lament the proliferation of telescopes and people here. In Hawaiian cosmology, the summit is the home of Poliahu, the goddess of snow, ice, and cold. The entire mountain is the domain of Wakea, the sky father, who mated with Papa, the earth mother, and got creation rolling. Management of the mountain is a perennial hot-button issue in Hawaii, and this land of sacred cinder cones and gleaming telescope domes is contested terrain in a culture clash between scientists trying to unlock the mysteries of the universe and Hawaiian activists trying to be true to their heritage. So tread gently.

(Tips) Climb with Care

This is a serious hike, one that needs to be prepared for carefully. At 13,000 feet, the weather can turn wintry at any time of year, and a pleasant sunny afternoon can turn to a blizzard without much warning. Bring the right clothes to survive the worst. Bring a compass, too, so you can find the road (it's to the east) if you need to scrub the hike mid-trail. The alpine desert climate will dry you out like a cracker, so drink plenty of water. A half-quart for each hour you hike is recommended. Given the chance, the high-altitude tropical sun will cook your face. Wear sunscreen, lip protection, sunglasses, and a broad-brimmed hat, as well as long sleeves and pants. If you're pregnant, or have heart, lung, or serious weight problems, talk to a doctor about this hike before getting too excited about it. If you've been scuba diving in the past 24 hours, do not hike to the summit, or you might get the bends. Go online to learn about the symptoms of Acute Mountain Sickness, High Altitude Pulmonary Edema, and High Altitude Cerebral Edema, which include headaches, nausea, dizziness, fatigue, loss of coordination, increasing anxiety, fainting, and an inability to catch your breath even after resting. If you experience one or more of these symptoms, descend to the Visitor Information Station. If symptoms persist, head for sea level. If they don't improve, head for the hospital.

⑥ Puu Wekiu, the Summit Walk counterclockwise along the summit loop for 1 mile, climbing until you reach a fork. You're now on the rim of a cinder cone called **Puu Wekiu,** the summit of Mauna Kea. To bag the peak, go right at the fork, hop over the guardrail across from the second observatory along the road, drop down into a saddle on the crater rim, and climb up the other side. A small *lele,* a Hawaiian stone altar, marks the exact spot where Hawaii comes closest to the heavens.

Complete the loop around the rim of the crater; then hike back down the trail or along the summit access road. You can also hitchhike back down (we won't tell anyone).

The view from 13,796 feet is, well, too sublime for me to describe. Let's just say it's next to impossible to shoot a bad picture up here.

SLEEPING & EATING

ACCOMMODATIONS
★★★ Hale Ohia Cottages A dash of rainforest whimsy leavens the simple elegance of Old Hawaii at this romantic hideaway near the volcano. Units range from a plush suite in the 1931-built main residence to a water tank converted into a surprisingly cozy cottage, with mahogany wainscoting and vintage lighting from the Royal Hawaiian Hotel.

Hale Ohia Rd., off Hwy. 11, near Hawaii Volcanoes National Park. © **808/455-3803** or 808/967-7986. www.haleohia.com. 4 cottages, 4 suites. $109–$189 double. Rates include continental breakfast. DC, DISC, MC, V. **Close to**: Kilauea Iki Trail, Napau Crater Trail.

Hilo Bay Hostel   The most centrally-located lodging in Hilo is also one of the most affordable places on the island. This backpackers' roost occupies the top half of a nicely restored turn-of-the-19th-century hotel, smack in the heart of old downtown. Rooms are tiny, but airy and clean.

102 Wainuenue Ave., Hilo, 96720. ℂ **808/933-2771.** www.hawaiihostel.net. 2 dorms, 12 private rooms. Dorms $25; private rooms $65–$75. MC, V. **Close to:** Akaka Falls, Puu Oo Trail.

★★ (Kids Hilton Waikoloa   Boredom is not an option at the most action-packed and family-friendly of the Gold Coast resort hotels. Among the highlights are a 175-foot-long waterslide, a mile-long artwalk, and a pool where you can swim with dolphins. Canal boats and a light-rail system carry guests around the sprawling grounds.

69-425 Waikoloa Beach Dr., Waikoloa, 96738. ℂ **800/HILTONS** (445-8667) or 808/886-1234. www.hilton waikoloavillage.com. 1,240 units, including 57 suites. Doubles start at $249; deals sometimes available. AE, DC, DISC, MC, V. **Close to:** Alakahakai Trail, Puu Kohola Heiau, Kiholo Bay.

(Finds Kona Tiki   This boutique budget hotel sits so close to the ocean that when the surf's up the lanais catch spray. The motel-basic rooms lack TVs, but who cares when you've got such a primo front-row seat for the glorious Kona sunset? The guests, prone to poolside potlucks and spontaneous ukulele jams, return year after year.

75-5968 Alii Dr., Kailua-Kona, HI 96740. ℂ **808/329-1425.** www.konatiki.com. 15 units. $66–$70 double, or $88 with kitchenette. 3-night minimum stay. Rates include continental breakfast. DC, DISC, MC, V. **Close to:** Captain Cook Monument Trail, Kaloko-Honokohau National Historical Park, Kiholo Bay.

★ **Maureen's B&B**   Baronial style comes at a budget price in this mansion built by a Japanese businessman in 1932 for his wife and seven kids. Restored to its original East-meets-West splendor, the place is loaded with tapestries, silk paintings, and cushy couches. There's no swimming pool, but there is a tearoom overlooking koi ponds and a beach park right across the street.

1896 Kalanianaole St., Hilo, 96720. ℂ **800/935-9018** or 808/935-9018. www.maureenbnb.com. 4 units. $90 double. Rate includes breakfast. AE, DISC, MC, V. **Close to:** Akaka Falls.

Namakanipaio Campground   You can't beat the prices at Hawaii Volcanoes National Park's drive-up campgrounds. The tiny, rustic cabins are dirt cheap, and the tent sites are free! Be ready to bundle up at night. It gets cold at 6,000 feet—even in Hawaii.

Hawaii Volcanoes National Park. Book cabins through Volcano House (P.O. Box 53, Hawaii Volcanoes National Park, HI 96718). ℂ **808/967-7321.** www.volcanohousehotel.com. 10 cabins. $55 double. No check-ins, reservations, or charge for camping. AE, DC, DISC, MC, V. **Close to:** Kilaueu Iki, Napau Crater.

RESTAURANTS

★ **Café Pesto** HAWAII REGIONAL CUISINE/PIZZA   With locations in downtown Hilo and on Kawaihae Harbor, Café Pesto catches you coming and going. Pesto puts Asian twists on its pasta and risotto, gourmet toppings on its pizzas, and fresh seafood all over the menu. The focaccia with rosemary and gorgonzola is a must, and the desserts are hard to resist.

308 Kamehameha Ave., Hilo. ℂ **808/969-6640.** Also at the Kawaihae Shopping Center in Kawaihae. ℂ **808/882-1071.** www.cafepesto.com. Pizza $8.95–$19; main courses $18–$25. AE, DC, DISC, MC, V. Sun–Thurs 11am–9pm; Fri–Sat 11am–10pm. **Close to:** Puukohola Heiau, Kiholo Bay Trail (Kawaihae location); Akaka Falls, Puu Oo Trail (Hilo location).

★ **Harbor House** PUB GRUB/SEAFOOD The only way to dine on fresher ono, ahi, or mahimahi is to eat it on the boat. Overlooking the sport-fishing fleet at Honoko-hau Harbor, this casual open-air bar-and-grill uses the daily catch to create grilled seafood plates, fish and chips, and towering fish sandwiches. It's right beside Kaloko-Honokohau National Historical Park.

74-425 Kealakehe Pkwy., Kona. 𝄢 **808/326-4166.** Main courses $7–$12. AE, MC, V. Lunch and dinner daily. **Close to:** Kaloko-Honokohau National Historical Park (right next door), Kiholo Bay.

★★★ **Island Lava Java** ISLAND COFFEE BISTRO Casual, creative, organic, and affordable—what's not to love about Island Lava Java? Oh, right—the line you have to stand in to order. It's longest in the morning, before everyone's had their Kona coffee. Evenings are tamer, and lit by tiki torch.

75-5799 Alii Dr., Kona. 𝄢 **808/327-2161.** http://islandlavajava.com. Most meals under $12. AE, DISC, MC, V. Daily 6am–10pm. **Close to:** Kaloko-Honokohau National Historical Park, Captain Cook Monument Trail.

★★ **Ken's House of Pancakes** 24-HOUR DINER The menu here has page after page of American and local classics, from pork chops with applesauce to *loco moco* (two scoops of rice, one hamburger patty, fried egg, and gravy). Sumo-size your moco and you get six scoops of rice, two hamburger patties, and three eggs! Breakfast is served around the clock.

1730 Kamehameha Ave., Hilo (corner of Hwy. 11 and Hwy 19). Most meals under $10. AE, DC, DISC, MC, V. Daily 24 hours. **Close to:** Akaka Falls Trail, Puu Oo Trail.

Kiawe Kitchen PIZZA/MEDITERRANEAN A wood-fired brick oven turns out pizzas with crispy, cracker-thin crusts and gourmet toppings like goat cheese and arti-choke hearts. If pizza isn't for you, there are pastas, sandwiches, and rack of lamb, all proportioned for hungry eaters. Kind of pricey, but options in Volcano are limited.

19-4005 Haunani Rd., Volcano Village, near Hawaii Volcanoes National Park. 𝄢 **808/967-7711.** Lunch $10–$13; dinner $16–$25. MC, V. Daily noon–2:30pm and 5:30–9:30pm. **Close to:** Kilauea Iki Trail, Napau Crater Trail.

★★★ **Kilauea Lodge** EUROPEAN A Depression-era YMCA in the rainforest near Hawaii Volcanoes National Park is now the setting for the island's most exotic fine-dining establishment. Traditional German dishes such as braised rabbit and French classics like *duck a l'orange* share the menu with ostrich, venison, and Cajun-style ahi.

19-3948 Old Volcano Rd., Volcano Village, near Hawaii Volcanoes National Park. 𝄢 **808/967-7366.** Reservations recommended. Main courses $20–$40. AE, MC, V. Breakfast 7:30–10am, dinner 5–9pm. Sunday brunch 10am–2pm. Reservations recommended. **Close to:** Kilauea Iki Trail, Napau Crater Trail, Puu Laau Road.

Maui Hikes

by Diane Bair & Pamela Wright

Grumble, grumble, grumble. You'll hear it: Maui isn't what it used to be (what is?). It's chock-a-block with fancy resorts, high-rise condos, overpriced shopping centers, and restaurants selling $20 burgers, not to mention the cruise ship hordes prowling Lahaina shops and boarding buses to top tourist sites. Oh, *pshaw,* we say. The truth is that more than 75% of Maui's 729 square miles is uninhabited! This means hikers who want to get off the beaten path will still find plenty of secluded, out-of-the-way, and unspoiled territory to explore. Added bonus: The variety of terrain on Maui is astounding. You can start the day with a cold sunrise hike to the top of a cinder cone jutting from a desolate and dry volcanic landscape and end it with a swim under a waterfall, deep in a moist, hot, tropical rainforest.

There is no denying Maui's visual charms. There are the surrounding blue, blue waters of the Pacific, of course (home to thousands of migrating endangered humpback whales during the winter), and long swaths of sand (the island boasts more miles of swimmable beaches than any other Hawaiian island). Maui, the second largest of the Hawaiian Islands, also has the largest dormant volcano in the world. Its 10,023-foot summit dominates the island, and is the star of Haleakala National Park, one of only two national parks in Hawaii. It's a top-visited site on

Maui, but hikers see the best of it on trails that descend to the basin floor, climb steep crater walls, and snake through lava fields on the way to cloud forests. Haleakala's basin measures more than 20 miles across and 4,000 feet deep, enough to hold Manhattan. You'll want to spend some time there. You'll also want to spend time at Oheo Gulch; it's part of the park, but in a totally different world of rainforests and waterfalls. Here, you can walk the Pipiwai Trail through the gulch to 400-foot Waimoku Falls, one of the largest on Maui.

In the West Maui Mountain Range, trails cross forested mountain slopes and drop into rainforests, dotted with rippling streams and waterfalls. Don't miss a visit to the luxuriant Iao Valley, one of the prettiest and most sacred sites on the island. It's home to "The Needle," a 1,200-foot lava-rock formation surrounded by the forested walls of the Pu' u Kukui Crater, that was once used as a natural altar.

On the east side of the island, near Hana, you'll find windswept black lava beaches, steep sea cliffs, blowholes, and sacred *heiau* (religious sites), as you walk in the footpaths of ancient Hawaiians.

At the end of the day, hunker down in a backcountry cabin, throw a tent on the beach, or check into a bustling, anything-you-want resort. Now, that's nothing to grumble about!

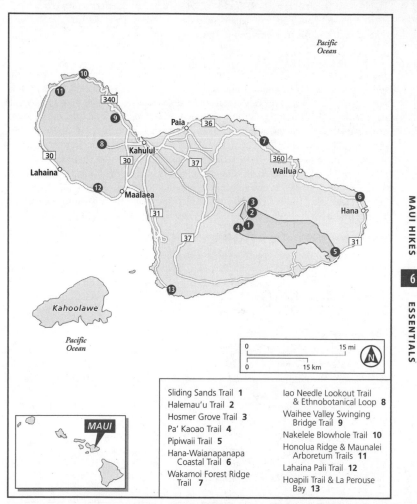

Pacific
Ocean

Paia

Kahulul

Lahaina

Maalaea

Wailua

Hana

Kahoolawe

Pacific
Ocean

MAUI

| 0 | | 15 mi |

| 0 | | 15 km |

MAUI HIKES

6

ESSENTIALS

Sliding Sands Trail **1**
Halemau'u Trail **2**
Hosmer Grove Trail **3**
Pa' Kaoao Trail **4**
Pipiwaii Trail **5**
Hana-Waianapanapa
Coastal Trail **6**
Wakamoi Forest Ridge
Trail **7**

Iao Needle Lookout Trail
& Ethnobotanical Loop **8**
Waihee Valley Swinging
Bridge Trail **9**
Nakelele Blowhole Trail **10**
Honolua Ridge & Maunalei
Arboretum Trails **11**
Lahaina Pali Trail **12**
Hoapili Trail & La Perouse
Bay **13**

ESSENTIALS

GETTING THERE
By Air
Several airlines fly directly from major cities to Maui's **Kahului Airport (OGG)** (© 808/872-3893; www.hawaii.gov/dot/airports/maui/ogg), located on the northern edge of the land bridge between Haleakala and the West Maui Mountain Range on Maui. **Hawaiian Airlines** (© 800/367-5320; www.hawaiianair.com) and **go!/Mesa** (© 888/435-9462; www.iflygo.com) offer inter-island flights.

The **Hawaii Super Ferry** (© **877/443-3779;** www.hawaiisuperferry.com) offers service from Oahu to Maui. The ferry departs several times a day (schedules vary depending on time of year) and the trip takes about 3 to 4 hours.

GETTING AROUND

Shuttle services, resorts, and taxis provide transportation to and from the airport. But, you'll need a car to get around the island and to be able to access trail heads. A four-wheel-drive vehicle is usually not necessary. Maui, measuring 48 miles long and 26 miles across at its widest point, is easy to get around. Major highways and decent secondary roads connect cities, towns, and resort areas. Top resort areas include Lahaina, Kaanapali, and Kapalua in the west; Makena and Wailea in the south; and Hana in the east. Hwys. 30 and 31 hug the west coast, connecting Kapalua, Lahaina, Wailea, and Makena. Hwys. 340 and 36 skirt the north coast, connecting with Hana Highway. The famed and spectacularly scenic Hana Highway connects Kahului to Hana. Several highways travel inland. Haleakala National Park sits in south-central Maui; from Kahului allow at least 90 minutes to reach the summit park headquarters.

VISITOR INFORMATION

There is no walk-in visitor center on the island, but you can get information from the **Maui Visitors Bureau** (1727 Wili Pa Loop, Wailuku, HI 96793; © **808/244-3530;** www.visitmaui.com). You can access a free vacation planning guide on the website or call © **800/525-6284;** allow at least 6 weeks for delivery. The www.mauivisitorinformation. com site also has good information on visiting the island.

WEATHER

The locals will tell you: If it's raining in one spot, just drive 5 miles and it'll be sunny and dry. It's no joke. The northeast, windward side of Maui gets the most rain, up to 300 inches a year. The southwest, leeward side, where most of the island's resorts are clustered, is sunny and dry, receiving very little rain.

The average temperature is 75° to 85°F (24°–29°C). But at the top of Haleakala, it might be 40°F (4°C); in January you might see snow! The wettest months are from November through March. It's a great time for waterfall viewing—and whale-watching. Humpback whales migrate between Hawaii and the Arctic Circle, stopping in Hawaii waters to breed, calve, and nurse their young. It's estimated that about 4,000 to 5,000 humpback whales come to Maui each year.

SLIDING SANDS TRAIL IN HALEAKALA NATIONAL PARK ★★★

Difficulty rating: Strenuous

Distance: 19 miles round-trip to Paliku Cabin

Estimated time: 1¹⁄₂ to 2 days

Elevation gain: 2,800 feet

Costs/permits: $10 per vehicle or $5 per person, valid for 3 consecutive days to enter the park (see "Accommodations," later in this chapter, for camping information).

Pet-friendly: No

Best time to go: Midweek when it's less crowded

Website: www.nps.gov/hale

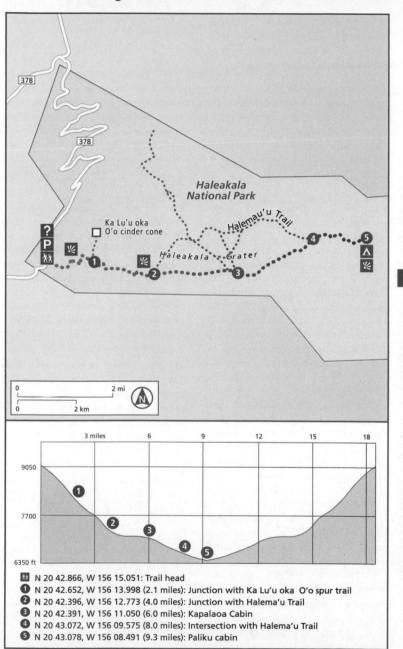

N 20 42.866, W 156 15.051: Trail head
1 N 20 42.652, W 156 13.998 (2.1 miles): Junction with Ka Lu'u oka O'o spur trail
2 N 20 42.396, W 156 12.773 (4.0 miles): Junction with Halema'u Trail
3 N 20 42.391, W 156 11.050 (6.0 miles): Kapalaoa Cabin
4 N 20 43.072, W 156 09.575 (8.0 miles): Intersection with Halema'u Trail
5 N 20 43.078, W 156 08.491 (9.3 miles): Paliku cabin

Trail head GPS: N 20 42.866 W 156 15.051

Trail head directions: From Kahului, take Route 37 to Route 377 to Route 378 to the entrance of the national park.

Continue to the Haleakala Visitor Center, just below the summit. The trail head is near the parking lot entrance and is well marked. Allow at least 1½ hours driving time to the summit headquarters from Kahului.

This is one of two trails leading into the Haleakala National Park wilderness and arguably one of the top hikes on Maui (Halemau'u Trail, described below, is the other). You'll start on Maui's highest peak and descend into a nearly barren, eerie landscape of cinder cones and lava flows. The trail drops to the massive crater floor, and then travels through native shrublands and rugged, exposed cliffs overlooking a cloud forest.

Did you wear your fleece layers, coat, hat, and gloves? You're starting this hike early in the morning, at nearly 10,000 feet, and it's likely to be cold. Temperatures at the summit are 30° to 50°F (–1° to 10°C), and it's often cloudy, wet, and windy. You'll be shedding layers later, but will be happy to have them at the beginning of this hike. *Note:* To hike the entire, up-and-back length of this trail, plan to stay overnight at the Paliku campsite. However, there are plenty of shorter options, too, which do not include an overnight stay, and still provide spectacular scenery. (See the sidebar "The Perfect Day Hike in Haleakala Wilderness," below.)

This trip begins in thin air; those unaccustomed to hiking in higher elevations are likely to feel it. Take your time. The trail starts with a bang—and an incredible view of the crater—as it slips down the rim of the crater. You'll see exactly where you're going; the trail is clearly visible in the wide, open landscape, switchbacking its way to the floor. To the north, you'll see the greener, forested slopes of Koolau Gap. You'll descend at a steady clip, down the sloping wall, into the dry, windy, barren landscape.

At about one mile in, there's a small promontory overlooking the giant depression, dotted with lava flows and cinder cones.

❶ **Ka Lu'uoka O'o Spur Trail** Continue down, down, down—and around—

getting closer to the floor. Notice the interesting-looking lava formations that flank the trail and the rolls of dried lava flows that make up the surrounding walls. Watch out for horse manure; this is a popular horseback riding trail, too. At 1.85 miles, you'll reach the junction with the Ka Lu'uoka O'o spur trail. Take the .6-mile, up-and-back side trail to the red-rimmed top of a cinder cone and an up-close look deep inside. Off in the distance, to the northeast, you'll see a larger cinder cone, called Puu o Pele, or "Hill of Pele."

❷ **Crater Floor & Halemau'u Trail Junction** Hike back to the main trail, turning left and following it as it parallels the lava flow working down the slopes of the crater wall. The trail gets a little rockier here and begins to narrow. Look for yellow-flowering kupaoa plants and the vivid green leaves of pukiawe plants that stand out against the stark, rocky, and ash-filled ground. You may also notice heat waves coming off the black rocks. Time to start shedding those layers of clothing as you descend to lower elevation and work up a sweat! To the right, you'll have views of black and red lava slides; to the left, you'll see the trail snaking down and across the floor. Continue into the crater for a final, steep slide before reaching an unnamed trail junction—this trail heads north (left) to link up with the Halemau'u Trail.

Ⓜ Moments   Dawn's Early Light

Watching the sun rise across the Haleakala Crater, spreading warm-lit hues across the lunar-like landscape, is an unforgettable experience. If you're up for it (set those alarm clocks and avoid the snooze buttons!), arrive at the trail head at dawn and watch the sun rise as you hike into the crater. It's worth it! (The easiest way to catch the sunrise and a few more winks is to camp (free) the night before at the Hosmer Grove campground; first-come, first-served.)

A lone mamane tree provides some shade, and is a good place to take a rest. Fields of ferns light up the ground, cinder cones poke up from the crater floor, and walls of red- and black-tinged lava surround you; it's a spectacular, surreal vista. Unfortunately, you probably can't stick around here for long—there are often swarms of hungry wasps in the area.

❸ Kapalaoa Cabin   The walk on to Kapalaoa cabin is another 1.9 miles, an easy, relatively flat traverse, across the valley floor. You'll pass two additional unnamed trails, both heading north to hook up with the Halemau'u Trail, before reaching the cabin. The modest cabin (reservations required) sits at 7,250 feet, at the base of a cliff. There's water (must be treated), a picnic area, and a pit toilet. You can poke around the cabin, or take well-trampled foot paths to explore the lava-carpeted valley. If you've made reservations, you can stay here for the night. Or, push on to the Paliku cabin and campsite.

❹ Halemau'u Junction   Continue on Sliding Sands Trail as it crosses a pebbly floor of lava. The going is tougher on this unstable, slip-out-from-under-you rock, but you'll begin to get a peek ahead at the rainforest and—what's that?—the ocean! The scrabble rock trail veers slightly left and meets up with the Halemau'u Trail. Look straight ahead for a view of this hike's destination: the Paliku cabin.

❺ Paliku Cabin & Campsite   The landscape begins to change quite noticeably from this point on. The air is moist; the landscape is greener. Keep your rain ponchos handy, as you're likely to need them. Mamane trees provide shade and canopy; ferns, pukiawe and pilo bushes decorate the lava fields. You're leaving the barren, lunarlike lava fields and entering a cool, lush rainforest. Head east over Kaupo Gap for an easy descent to Paliku Cabin (see Camping, below). The cabin sits at 6,380 feet at the base of a 1,000-foot-high rainforest cliff. It's nearly always cloud covered and wet, which provides the perfect environment for tropical plants.

MAUI HIKES

6

HALEMAU'U TRAIL IN HALEAKALA NATIONAL PARK

HALEMAU'U TRAIL IN HALEAKALA NATIONAL PARK ★★★

Difficulty rating: Strenuous

Distance: 21 miles round-trip to Paliku Cabin, up and back; there's a variety of shorter options, too.

Estimated time: 1½ to 2 days

Elevation gain: 1,500 feet

Costs/permits: $10 per vehicle or $5 per person to enter the National Park, valid for 3 consecutive days. Backcountry cabins require a reservation and cost $75 per night, per cabin, which sleeps up to 12 people. Permits are limited to one group (up to 12 people) and given through a monthly lottery. You must request a reservation in writing 2 months prior to the first day of the month in which you want the reservation. Primitive campsites are also available at Holua and Paliku. Permits are free at the Headquarters Visitor Center (open 8am–3pm) on the day you begin your trip.

Pet-friendly: No

Best time to go: June through July, which is the best time to see silversword in bloom, though winters are less crowded

Website: www.nps.gov/hale

Recommended map: The visitor center's free trail map

Trail head GPS: N 20 45.135 W 156 13.707

Trail head directions: From Kahului, take Route 37 to Route 377 to Route 378. The trail head begins at the 8,000-foot parking lot, 3½ miles above the Park Headquarters Visitor Center.

This must-do hike is one of two treks leading into the Haleakala National Park wilderness. (Sliding Sands Trail, described above, is the other.) Steep switchbacks descend the rim of the odd-shaped Haleakala basin to its valley floor. Along the way: neck-snapping views of Koolau Gap, Keanae Valley, and the eerie cinder cone and lava-rock landscape. This hike travels 10 miles for an overnight stay at Paliku cabin, but you can cut it short and still trek through magnificent scenery. Some options include an up-and-back 7.4-mile round-trip hike to Holua cabin and day hikes to Silversword Loop (8.2 miles round-trip) or Haalalii cinder cone (10 miles round-trip). You can also combine the Halemau'u Trail and Sliding Sands Trail for an incredible all-day hike (see "The Perfect Day Hike in the Haleakala Wilderness" sidebar below).

Piece of cake, you'll think as you begin this hike. The trail weaves easily through dryland shrubs and grasses for the first mile before it reaches the rim of Haleakala Crater. Now, the fun begins! It's a knee-crunching steep descent on switchbacks that hug the edge of the crater wall. But the eye-candy rewards are enough to keep you going.

You'll have far-reaching views into the 2-mile-wide Koolau Gap to the southeast and into the giant volcanic basin. Red-hued cones rise from the cinder and lava-rock floor of the crater. We like the contrast of the two environments: The wall is green with pines, ferns, and grasses; the basin ahead is dry and barren—a black, tan, and red colored tableau.

❶ **Holua Cabin** Climb down, down, down—some 1,400 feet—to the base of the wall and the bottom of the crater. Pass through the cattle gate and walk across the grassy meadow another mile to Holua

cabin. The cabin sits at 6,960 feet, at the foot of Leleiwi Pali (3,000 ft.) with views of Koolau Gap to the north and the surrounding walls and floor of the massive Haleakala basin.

There's a picnic table, pit toilet, water (must be treated), primitive camping sites, and likely a flock of nene birds looking for handouts. There's also a rustic horse corral, as this trail, along with the Sliding Sands Trail, is a popular equestrian route.

You're not afraid of the dark, are you? If not, think about grabbing your headlamps and exploring the 150-foot lava tube near Holua cabin. Just east of the cabin, you'll see an overgrown trail that heads right up a lava flow. The trail snakes over the flow a short distance—less than 100 yards—to a marked pit. Climb the ladder down into

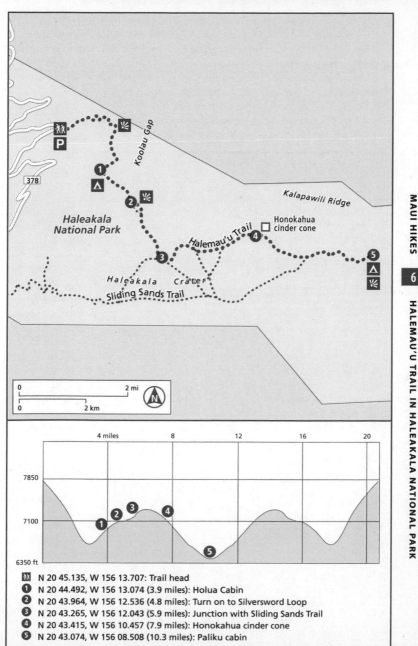

N 20 45.135, W 156 13.707: Trail head

1 N 20 44.492, W 156 13.074 (3.9 miles): Holua Cabin

2 N 20 43.964, W 156 12.536 (4.8 miles): Turn on to Silversword Loop

3 N 20 43.265, W 156 12.043 (5.9 miles): Junction with Sliding Sands Trail

4 N 20 43.415, W 156 10.457 (7.9 miles): Honokahua cinder cone

5 N 20 43.074, W 156 08.508 (10.3 miles): Paliku cabin

The Perfect Day Hike in the Haleakala Wilderness

The 11-mile trek down Sliding Sands Trail and out Halemau'u Trail is right up there on our best-day-hikes-in-the-country list. Arrive in the park early morning (how about catching sunrise?) and park at the Halemau'u trail head. There's a small path leading to a hiker's pullout where you'll hitch a ride to the upper visitor center. Hike down the extraordinary Sliding Sands Trail to the floor of the crater. An unnamed trail heads left across the basin to connect with the Halemau'u Trail. Hike the steep switchbacks up the crater wall, where your car will be waiting. Lava fields, cinder cones, steep, forested crater walls, and blooming silversword are some of the eye-candy rewards on this long day hike.

the dark, dank tube. It'll take about a half-hour to follow the uneven path as it squeezes through tight corners and opens to larger, murky areas.

❷ Silversword Loop From here, you get your next piece of cake, a near effortless, flat meander for a mile, across the cinder and lava-flow landscape. Follow it 9 miles to the Silversword Loop junction. Don't even think about skipping this short loop. It adds only steps more to the hike. The spectacular silversword plant—especially in bloom—is a sight not to be missed. This threatened plant can live 50 years but only flowers once in its lifetime, but what a final show it puts on! There are several plants along the trail, and hopefully some are in full bloom (plants flower most frequently in June–July).

❸ Halalii Cinder Cone Continue across the bleak and eerie landscape for another mile or so of flat walking to an unnamed junction, to the right. This trail heads south to connect with Sliding Sands Trail. Ahead is the towering Halalii cinder cone. On your right, you'll also see a large lava outcropping. Crawl in for a little shade and shelter before continuing on. Stay to the left as you skirt the cone.

❹ Honokahua Cinder Cone The trail continues at an easy pace, with wide-angle views of the basin. You'll pass several

prominent cinder cones along the way: Puu Kumu looms to your left; Puu Naue, Puu Nole, Na Mana o ke Akua (this sits very close to the trail); and finally, Honokahua cinder cone. You'll also pass several trail junctions along the way, all leading to Kapalaoa cabin on the Sliding Sands Trail.

❺ Paliku Cabin Views continue as you make your way across grassy shrublands. Be sure to look back; the wide-open panorama of the lunarlike basin and surrounding green-hued mountains is jarringly beautiful. Before you know it, in less than a mile from the Honokahua cinder cone, Halemau'u and Sliding Sands trails join on the final leg to Paliku Cabin. On the final push, heading east over Kaupo Gap, the environment begins to change drastically. The world around you becomes moist, lush, and green as you enter the rainforest. A final hump down brings you to Paliku Cabin, at the foot of a 1,000-foot cliff, overlooking a tropical rainforest.

If you're looking for an alternate route out of the Haleakala Wilderness from Paliku Cabin, consider the knee-crunching, 9.5-mile drop through eye-catching Kaupo Gap. The Kaupo Trail travels from the cabin to Kaupo Ranch. Walk the dirt road through the ranch and on to Kaupo Village, where you've arranged to get picked up.

Difficulty rating: Easy

Distance: .6 miles round-trip

Estimated time: 30 min.

Elevation gain: 120 feet

Costs/permits: $10 per vehicle or $5 per person, valid for 3 consecutive days

Pet-friendly: No pets on the trail. Pets must be kept on a leash at the campground.

Best time to go: Early morning when the birds are most active

Website: www.nps.gov/hale

Recommended map: The visitor center's free trail map

Trail head GPS: N 20 46.106 W 156 14.246

Trail head directions: From Kahului, take Route 37 to Route 377 to Route 378. To reach the trail head, make the first left above the park entrance station, following the signs to Hosmer Grove campground. Park in the campground lot.

This easy, perfect-for-families hike leads through alien and native forests to an overlook with pretty vistas into Keanae Valley and Waikamoi Gulch. Interpretive signs mark plants along the way. In the native forest, many of the plants are endemic to Hawaii and found nowhere else on earth.

Pick up the trail near the campground sign, at the north end of the parking lot. It's easy to find and the path is well-traveled. You'll enter a shady, mature grove of towering trees, almost immediately.

❶ Alien Forest We know the trees here are not native to Hawaii and that some have become invasive, crowding out the island's indigenous species. Still, what a fun fairyland this is!

During the early 1900s, Hawaii forester Ralph Hosmer introduced 86 different species of trees to Maui, bringing in trees from around the world to help with the island's erosion and also to develop a successful lumber industry. The results were mixed, but remnants of Hosmer's original grove are here. The path meanders through this old, alien forest, passing under a plantation of tall pines and eucalyptus. Take a deep sniff: You'll smell the crushed leaves of eucalyptus and the earthy scent of cedar. Signs point to incense cedar and deodar cedar trees, before you walk through impressive stand of tall, straight messmate eucalyptus trees and twisty black peppermint eucalyptus trees. Walk under the twisty branches and the sculpturelike tree trunks of fallen eucalyptus. Kids love it here in this enchanted forest. Other alien species include sugi pines, spruce, juniper, and fir. Hawaiian raspberries blanket the ground beneath the canopy.

❷ Mixed Forest Follow the trail up the gentle slope to an upper forest of alien and native plants. Look for 'ohia lehua trees, which are endemic to Hawaii. Monterey pines and lodgepole pines, native to the western U.S., stand guard overhead. You'll have a quick peek into the valley to your left as you climb to the overlook at 6,933 feet.

❸ Native Forest From here you'll have expansive views into Keanae Valley and Waikamoi Gulch. 'Iliahi, also known as Haleakala sandalwood, and native manane trees surround the overlook. Gnarled ohi'i trees fill the valley; their bright red flowers light up the green backdrop. This is a good place to look for the vermillion-colored i'iwi bird, or honeycreeper, that likes to feed on the nectar of the ohi'i flowers. Continue the loop through native shrublands, including pilo and ohei plants, both endemic to Hawaii.

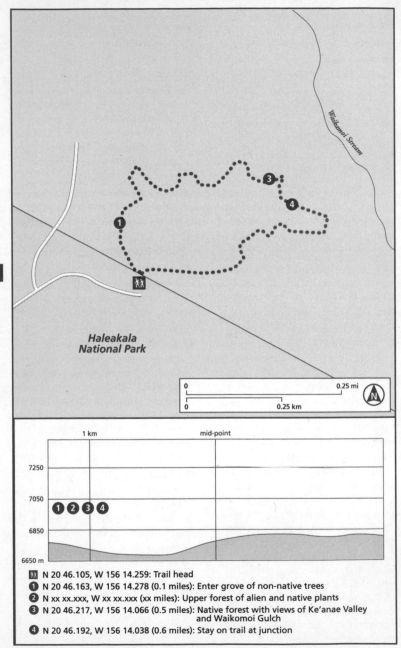

Haleakala
National Park

| 0 | | 0.25 mi |
| 0 | 0.25 km | |

1 km   mid-point

7250

7050 **1** **2** **3** **4**

6850

6650 m

🚶 N 20 46.105, W 156 14.259: Trail head
1 N 20 46.163, W 156 14.278 (0.1 miles): Enter grove of non-native trees
2 N xx xx.xxx, W xx xx.xxx (xx miles): Upper forest of alien and native plants
3 N 20 46.217, W 156 14.066 (0.5 miles): Native forest with views of Ke'anae Valley
　　　　　　　　　　　　　　　　　　　　and Waikomoi Gulch
4 N 20 46.192, W 156 14.038 (0.6 miles): Stay on trail at junction

Sunrise, Sunset

Sunrises and sunsets at the summit of Haleakala are breathtaking. It's also one of the best places in the world for nighttime sky watching. The park stays open 24 hours a day, but make it easier on yourself and stay at the Hosmer Campground, first-come, first-served.

Along the way, you'll have several more views into the valley.

❹ Nature Trail Junction There's a junction offering you the option of continuing on the nature trail or looping back to the first section of Hosmer Grove. Take the nature trail through native shrublands and then climb rock steps to another open outlook, where you'll have a clear view of the forests you just came through and a peek at the twisting road through Haleakala National Park. Continue down the trail to complete the loop and return to your car.

PA KAOAO TRAIL ⓚKids

Difficulty rating: Easy

Distance: .5 miles round-trip

Estimated time: 30 min.

Elevation gain: 300 feet

Costs/permits: $10 per vehicle or $5 per person, valid for 3 consecutive days

Pet-friendly: No

Best time to go: Sunrise or sunset

Website: www.nps.gov/hale

Recommended map: The visitor center's free trail map

Trail head GPS: N 20 42.890 W 156 14.992

Trail head directions: From Kahului, take Route 37 to Route 377 to Route 378. The trail starts at the Haleakala Visitor Center (second center), just below the summit.

Want to see the top of a small cinder cone—without a lot of effort? Take this short trail to the summit of Pa Kaoao, one of the highest view points in Haleakala National Park. Black cinder, ashes, and hardened lava flows make up the barren landscape. Cinder cones, the volcanic vents formed from smaller eruptions, dot the wilderness. You'll have great views of the stark Haleakala volcanic wilderness and, on clear days, neighboring Big Island's tallest peaks.

The short trail up one of Haleakala's distinctive cinder cones begins just a few steps from the visitor center.

❶ Climbing the Cone The lollipop-shaped trail begins with a gentle ascent up the side of the rocky cone, heading south. You'll have views of the summit observation center and Puu Ulaula cinder cone to the west (right). The rocky path is easy to follow as it skirts the bottom edge of the cone. The trail then veers left and you'll begin to climb the cone.

❷ Sliding Sands Trail To your right, looking south, you'll have a glimpse of the Sliding Sands Trail snaking down the sloped sides of Haleakala. The swath of trail is clearly visible in the stark, lunar-like landscape, as it heads to the crater floor. Continue climbing the rock-strewn path. The path loops again, tuning left, as it gains the top of the cone.

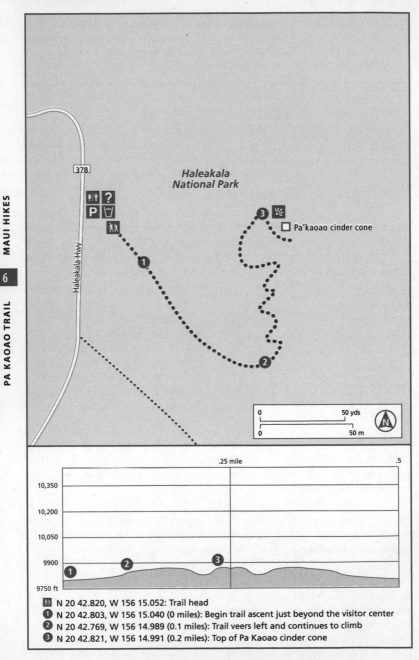

Haleakala
National Park

378

Pa'kaoao cinder cone

0   50 yds
0   50 m

N

.25 mile   .5

10,350
10,200
10,050
9900
9750 ft

N 20 42.820, W 156 15.052: Trail head
1 N 20 42.803, W 156 15.040 (0 miles): Begin trail ascent just beyond the visitor center
2 N 20 42.769, W 156 14.989 (0.1 miles): Trail veers left and continues to climb
3 N 20 42.821, W 156 14.991 (0.2 miles): Top of Pa Kaoao cinder cone

Kids Ranger-Led Hikes in Haleakala National Park

Get the inside scoop and pick up bits of information on a guided walk in the park. Rangers conduct a variety of talks and excursions throughout the day in both the Haleakala summit and Kipahulu areas. The last time we were there, we took a ranger-led hike and learned a lot about the plants and animals that make their home in Haleakala. For example, buzzing wasps are likely to follow along this trail. There are many native insects, too, that crawl on and under the rocks, including the Haleakala flightless moth, one of the rarest insects in the world. Keep your eye out for it as you climb the cinder cone. The small, half-inch-long, silver-gray moth hops along the ground.

Stop by one of the visitor centers for a listing of current programs. You can also pick up information here about the Junior Ranger program for kids ages 7 through 12. See www.nps.gov/hale.

❸ The Top of the Cone   A few more steps up and you'll reach the top of the cone. From its bowl-shaped summit, you'll have sweeping views of Haleakala wilderness and the bottom of the giant basin. Cinder cones erupt from the ashen ground. In the distance, you may be able to see the tallest peaks on the Big Island. Re-trace your steps back down.

PIPIWAI TRAIL ★

Difficulty rating: Moderate

Distance: 4 miles round-trip

Estimated time: 3 hr.

Elevation gain: 800 feet

Costs/permits: $10 per vehicle or $5 per person, valid for 3 consecutive days

Pet-friendly: No

Best time to go: Winter, when the waterfalls are most dramatic

Website: www.nps.gov/hale

Recommended map: The visitor center's free trail map

Trail head GPS: N 20 39.734 W 156 02.727

Trail head directions: Follow the Hana Highway south to the Haleakala National Park entrance at Kipahulu (10 miles south of Hana). The trail takes off from the parking lot, crossing the street and heading to the falls.

This wonderfully scenic trail follows a stream through Oheo Gulch through sweet-smelling guava and dark bamboo forests before reaching 400-foot Waimoku Falls, a truly breathtaking waterfall—and one of the largest on Maui. Be patient on this hike; you'll pass several cascades and a couple of waterfalls along the way, with no access. Keep going through a magnificent bamboo forest until you reach the end: There's swimming!

The well-marked trail starts at the edge of the parking lot, crosses the street, and heads into a sparse forest of guava trees and grasses. In the distance, you'll have views of rolling farmlands and mountain slopes.

❶ Makahiku Falls   The trail gains elevation quickly as it climbs stone steps, before flattening into a sunny clearing. Cut through the level grassy meadow before climbing again. There are some

Kuloa Point Loop

Don't have time and energy to climb the Pipiwai Trail (above)? Consider this half-mile, easy loop trail leading from the Kipahulu Visitor Center down to the ocean at Kuloa Point. You'll pass historic walls and ancient Hawaiian habitation sites. The trail enters a grove of hala trees on the way to beautiful views of the ocean and several large pools and tumbling cascades.

vantage points into Oheo Gulch, with rippling cascades and a series of pools to your right.

At .5 miles, there's a marked overlook to Makahiku Falls. Rocky cliffs and folded mountains serve as a backdrop to the skinny ribbon of silvery water that tumbles down the lush mountain slopes. It's a bit disappointing, as the view of the waterfall is quite far-off and obscured by foliage. There's also no legal access to the water (though it looks like locals have carved several routes down to the water and you can often hear people playing in the stream below). But park warning signs abound. Don't despair—there's plenty of eye-catching scenery to go around, and big falls—with access—coming up.

❷ **Cascades**   Pass through a gate: It's 1.5 miles to the falls from here. In short order, you'll come upon a giant banyan tree straight ahead. Stop for a photo and a walk under its long branches and canopy before continuing on the trail. The trail flattens again with nice views of green mountain slopes ahead. A short, unnamed .2-mile spur trail leads to your right. Go ahead and take it. The trail leads to a stream overlook and then down a rocky path to a further very cool gaze at frothy cascades. The two-tiered cascades drop to a broad ledge and pool and then tumble again to a deeper hole. Hanging stone cliffs, carpeted in jungle-y vines, form a cathedral over the pool. It's a beautiful setting and well worth the short hump down and back out. You probably won't want to linger too long, as this is

a favorite hangout for hungry mosquitoes. There's no water access, but the best swimming hole is yet to come.

❸ **Bamboo Forest**   The trail follows the stream more closely now, with nice views of small cascades and pools to your right. You'll cross two bridges with good views left and right at two waterfalls. After crossing the second bridge, the trail veers left and enters a bamboo forest; it's .8 miles to the big falls from here. Hoof it up a set of stairs, where the trail turns into a wide boulevard through dense stands of bamboo. They're tall, thick, and dark! The bamboo stalks creak and crackle against each other as the wind blows. Take a few moments to look up at the arched canopy, to see it swinging and swaying in the wind, and to listen to the music of the bamboo forest. Wood boardwalks begin taking you further into the bamboo forest. Then, there's a switchback, and it's rock music! The stream is now to your right, splashing and rippling over smooth, water-worn rocks.

❹ **Waimoku Falls**   The trail becomes wetter and the surrounding foliage turns greener, a tangle of ferns and a carpet of mosses. Cross the stream as noted below until you get to the falls—and then retrace your steps back to the start.

Rock-hop the stream, looking left for small cascades. Straight ahead, beautiful Waimoku Falls plunges down the towering rock cliff. In winter, the entire mountain slope is one big wall of gushing water, and the pool at the bottom is huge. But, even in the driest summer months, the falls are

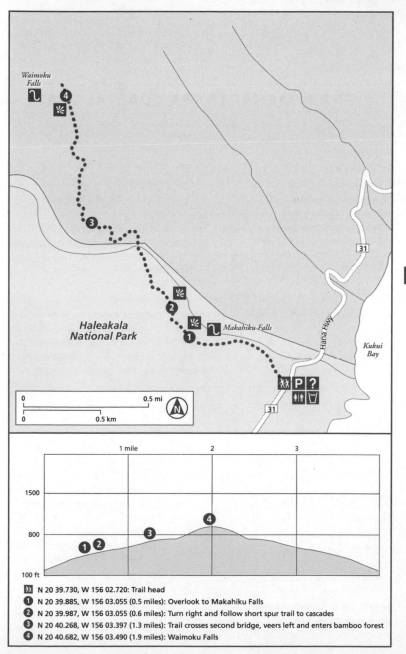

N 20 39.730, W 156 02.720: Trail head
1 N 20 39.885, W 156 03.055 (0.5 miles): Overlook to Makahiku Falls
2 N 20 39.987, W 156 03.055 (0.6 miles): Turn right and follow short spur trail to cascades
3 N 20 40.268, W 156 03.397 (1.3 miles): Trail crosses second bridge, veers left and enters bamboo forest
4 N 20 40.682, W 156 03.490 (1.9 miles): Waimoku Falls

impressive, and the green, lush wall takes on a spa-like feel, with trickling water everywhere.

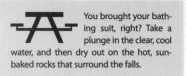 You brought your bathing suit, right? Take a plunge in the clear, cool water, and then dry out on the hot, sunbaked rocks that surround the falls.

HANA-WAIANAPANAPA COASTAL TRAIL

Difficulty rating: Moderate

Distance: 6 miles round-trip

Estimated time: 5 to 6 hr.

Elevation gain: 200 feet

Costs/permits: No entrance fee to the park. Permit needed to camp at Waianapanapa State Park ($5 camping fee).

Pet-friendly: Dogs must be on a leash.

Best time to go: Midweek; avoid weekends when large local crowds congregate at the park.

Website: www.hawaiistateparks.org/parks/maui/waianapanapa.cfm

Recommended map: USGS' "Hana" map

Trail head GPS: N 20 47.225 W 156 00.071

Trail head directions: Take Hwy. 360 (Hana Hwy.), just past mile marker 32. Take a left at the Waianapanapa State Park sign and follow the road to the end. The trail head is clearly marked, near the parking area.

This 122-acre state park is a jewel. Coastal cliffs, stone arches, lava fields, black beaches, blowholes, and ancient temples are part of the highlights of this stunning coastal route, just north of Hana. Parts of this trail follow the original King's Highway, or Piilani Trail, that once circled Maui, connecting villages and sacred spots. The trail, comprised of smooth lava stepping stones, was commissioned by King Pi'ilani, a 14th-century Maui chief.

(*Note:* Consider getting a ride to the state park. That way you can end up in town and avoid retracing your steps on the trail.)

Before you begin the coastal hike, take the half-mile walk down to the black-sand beach; the well-marked path starts left, in front of the office, as you face the water. There's also an ancient burial site near the beach and water views galore. Don't linger too long, as you have a ways to go on the coastal trail and plenty more scenery to savor. Waianapanapa-to-Hana coastal trail begins at the edge of the parking lot and heads southeast.

❶ **Black Beaches and Blowholes** At the beginning of the hike, you'll pass the ancient Hawaiian Honokalani Cemetery, before entering a grove of leggy hala trees. The ancient Hawaiians used the tree in a variety of ways: Leaves were woven into mats and roofing, and the fruits were eaten; leis were made with hala fruits and flowers, and the wood from the tree was used for posts and smoking pipes. The trail leaves the hala forest behind, opens up and skirts the coast. Waianapanapa means "glistening waters," and you'll see it's aptly named.

This is a watery wonderland with powerful surf set against black lava cliffs. Stone arches, formed by the unrelenting surf, jut from the ocean. The trail traverses a deep sink hole; stand for a moment and peer down into the hole of frothy surf. You'll descend into a small cove, lined with a black-sand beach, littered with white coral. Nearby are lava-lined sea caves and black-rock sea stacks, with a backdrop of sudsy

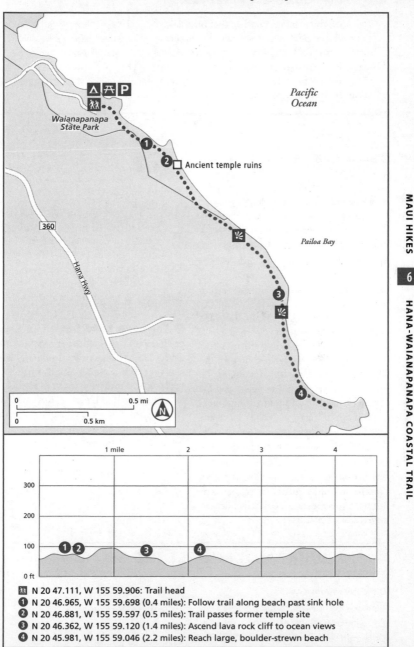

N 20 47.111, W 155 59.906: Trail head

1 N 20 46.965, W 155 59.698 (0.4 miles): Follow trail along beach past sink hole

2 N 20 46.881, W 155 59.597 (0.5 miles): Trail passes former temple site

3 N 20 46.362, W 155 59.120 (1.4 miles): Ascend lava rock cliff to ocean views

4 N 20 45.981, W 155 59.046 (2.2 miles): Reach large, boulder-strewn beach

(Fun Facts) **Don't Take the Rocks!**

We know: You want to scoop up that black lava rock and take it home with you as a souvenir. Don't even think about it! According to Hawaiian legend, removing rocks is disrespect to the goddess Pele, and it really ticks her off. And, making the petulant Pele mad means bad luck for you. In fact, the Hawaiian parks and post offices receive thousands of returned rocks each year along with varying stories of woe. In this case, it's best to leave all stones unturned.

surf. It's a study in black and white, interspersed with the vivid green colors of naupaka plants. Ocean water erupts from a number of blowholes. You'll pass campsite cabins sitting on a hill to your right (see Waianapanapa State Park, under Camping, below). Follow the black-sand and lava-rock trail, hugging the edge of the shoreline.

❷ Ancient Temples A little over a half-mile along the trail, you'll notice another *heiau*. This open mound jutting out to the ocean was a sacred site to the Hawaiians. The rolling mountain ridge and Hamoa Valley are to your right.

The trail begins to gets a little rougher, climbing jumbled, jagged rock to gain the cliff and reach a flat ledge, overlooking the ocean. This was once a popular spot for fishing. Cracked and broken fishing pole holders are still here, as well as the abandoned—somewhat trashed—Luahaloa fishing *hale*. Follow the trail down the ledge.

❸ Stone Arches and Sea Stacks Another stunning coastal landscape coming up! Cross the large lava fields of lichen-covered black rocks.

At about 1.5 miles, you'll climb up and over a lava-rock cliff and have a full view of the ocean, punctuated with stone arches and sea stacks.

The trail weaves along the jagged coastline and becomes more difficult to follow. There are cairns to mark the way—but who can tell? It's all a jumble of rocks! You'll need to pay attention to stay on the trail.

❹ The Long Road Out At 3 miles, you'll reach a large boulder-strewn beach—a nice spot to hang out for a while. This is also your turn-around point if you're hiking back. Or, rock-hop across and look for an unimproved, unmarked dirt road to your right. There's a cluster of rustic homes next to the beach; the road is just before them. Turn right on the dirt road, turn left at the next fork, and follow the road to the main highway leading into Hana.

WAIKAMOI FOREST RIDGE TRAIL

Difficulty rating: Easy

Distance: 08 miles round-trip, 1.5 miles round-trip with the extension

Estimated time: 30 to 60 min.

Elevation gain: 200 feet

Costs/permits: None

Pet-friendly: Dogs must be on a leash.

Best time to go: September to early December

Website: www.hawaiitrails.org/trail.
php?TrailID=MA+13+003

Recommended map: USGS' "Haiku" map

Trail head GPS: N 20 52.521 W 156 11.19

Trail head directions: Take Hana Highway
south, a few hundred yards past mile
marker 9. There is a small parking lot on
the right, at the trail head.

Want to get into the rainforest without having to do much work? This short nature walk, off of scenic Hana Highway, travels through a thick bamboo and fern forest, with valley-to-ocean views of the Keanae Peninsula.

From the parking lot, the trail climbs a ramp and enters the forest, either right or left. Below we describe the hike moving counterclockwise. Interpretive signs mark many of the interesting trees.

❶ **Kukui Trees** It never fails when we're hiking this trail: Someone makes a Johnny Weissmuller jungle call or a "Me Tarzan, you Jane" joke. No wonder, you could definitely film a Tarzan movie on parts of this trail. First you'll walk into a forest of paperbark trees (from Australia) and towering swamp mahogany trees. Big-leafed taro vines smother the trunks of the trees, droop from branches, and snake along the forest floor. Flowering bird-of-paradise plants add vivid color to the jungle scene. The trail continues a gentle ascent through a grove of silvery native kukui trees. The kukui, the state tree of Hawaii, symbolizes hope and renewal, and its nuts were once used to make leis for Hawaiian royalty; kukui-nut leis are still popular today.

❷ **Bamboo Forest** The trail gains a little elevation on even, manmade steps to the first overlook, where you'll find a stone bench.

Enjoy a rest here and the views of the valleys and rolling mountains of the Keanae Peninsula. Now, turn right and follow the root-choked trail as it climbs gently. Dewy, native pala'a ferns overlap the sides of the trail, which is now covered with the thick roots and trunks of the papaya and kepau trees (both native to Hawaii). Walk farther into a dense forest of bamboo and sweet-smelling awa puhi ginger and you'll come up to an enormous mango tree and another peek out to the mountains.

❸ **Picnic Shelter** Turn right and follow the trail; along the way there are a number of short spur paths to the right, leading to ocean and valley vistas. The brilliant red flowers of the awa puhi plants litter the floor and kukui trees line the path. The trail dead-ends in an open, grassy area with a sheltered picnic table, sitting at about 875 feet of elevation. The edge of the ridge has been planted with interesting ornamental arborvite trees from China. Hau trees are also clustered along the ridge, and bamboo crowds the right side of the trail. There are limited views across the trees to the ocean.

MAUI HIKES

6

WAIKAMOI FOREST RIDGE TRAIL

Ⓕ**inds**   **Cloud Forest Climb**

Consider a visit to the Nature Conservancy's Waikamoi Preserve, a wet and wonderful cloud forest that is only open to those on guided hikes led by the Nature Conservancy or park staff. The 3-mile, 3-hour hikes are offered Monday and Thursday at 9am and leave from the Hosmer Grove campground. Call Ⓒ **808/572-4459** for reservations.

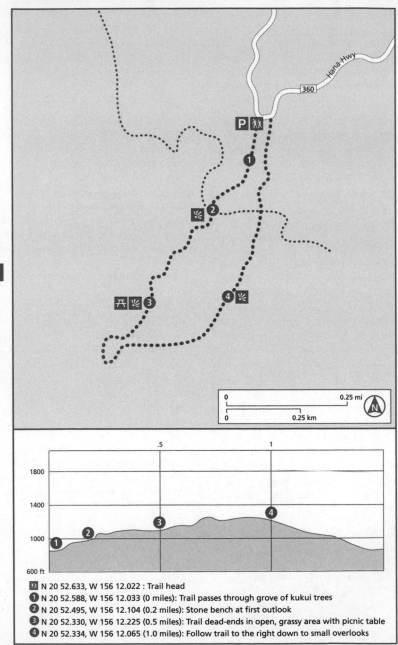

N 20 52.633, W 156 12.022 : Trail head
1 N 20 52.588, W 156 12.033 (0 miles): Trail passes through grove of kukui trees
2 N 20 52.495, W 156 12.104 (0.2 miles): Stone bench at first outlook
3 N 20 52.330, W 156 12.225 (0.5 miles): Trail dead-ends in open, grassy area with picnic table
4 N 20 52.334, W 156 12.065 (1.0 miles): Follow trail to the right down to small overlooks

❹ Valley to Ocean Outlooks Complete the loop hike by retracing your steps to the first lookout. The trail circles left to an unmarked junction. Stay right. The trail descends gently to two small outlets with bench seats. Too bad, Christmas berry trees have invaded and are now obscuring the view, but you'll still get a peek into a deep, forested gulch criss-crossed by the Waikamoi Stream. You'll also see the twisty Hana Highway below. Head down through bamboo forest and stands of red-flamed torch ginger. You'll hear the road noise, and then views of the ocean will open in front of you. And, in a few steps, you're back where you started.

IAO NEEDLE LOOKOUT TRAIL & ETHNOBOTANICAL LOOP IN IAO VALLEY STATE PARK Kids

Difficulty rating: Easy

Distance: 0.6 miles round-trip

Estimated time: 30 min. to 1 hr.

Elevation gain: 100 feet

Costs/permits: None

Pet-friendly: No

Best time to go: Clear mornings, before the afternoon clouds roll in

Website: www.hawaiistateparks.org/parks/ maui/Index.cfm?park_id=36

Recommended map: Visitor center's "Iao Needle and Ethnobotanical Loop" map

Trail head GPS: N 20 52.844 W 156 32.739

Trail head directions: Take Hwy. 32 (Kaa-humanu Rd.) west out of Wailuku in central Maui. This turns into Iao Valley Road. Follow signs to the park. There's plenty of parking.

Iao Valley is one of the prettiest and most sacred sites on the island. A short, paved 0.6-mile walk provides a scenic viewpoint of Kuka'emoku (Iao Needle), rising 1,200 feet from the valley floor. It's believed that the lava-rock formation, surrounded by the forested walls of the Puu Kukui Crater, was once used as a natural altar. The valley is also the site of the battle of Kepaniwai, where the forces of Kamehameha I conquered the Maui army in 1790. Alas, you won't have this place to yourself: This is a very popular tourist stop.

Follow the crowds from the parking lot to the beginning of the trail. Stop at the first set of interpretive signs to learn that Hawaiians gathered here in the valley during their annual Makahiki Festival, to honor and offer sacrifices to Lono, god of fertility. The word "Makahiki" in Hawaiian means "year." The festival marked the new year and took place around mid-November. It lasted about 4 months and was a time of peace for the ancient Hawaiians. Now, walk around the stream.

❶ Ethnobotanical Loop A paved path heads to the left, through an ethnobotanical garden. It'll take about 10 minutes to complete the loop and is a nice introduction to Hawaiian plants with information on how they were used as food, medicine, clothing, tools, construction, and more in earlier times. You'll end up back on the main trail; turn left and follow it to the bridge.

❷ Bridge Crossing & First View of Iao Needle Cross the bridge over Iao Stream; to your right, as you head over the bridge, you'll get your first peek at the unique, foliage-covered rock formation. Climb the paved steps to a perch overlooking the stream. The Battle of Kepaniwai occurred here in 1790, when King Kamehameha

MAUI HIKES

6

IAO NEEDLE LOOKOUT TRAIL & ETHNOBOTANICAL LOOP

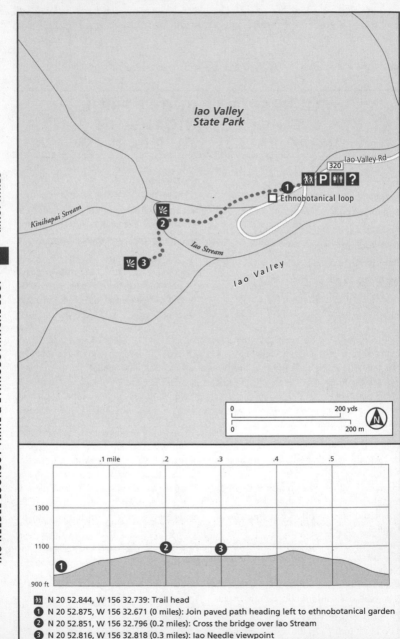

Iao Valley State Park

Iao Valley Rd

320

Ethnobotanical loop

Kinihapai Stream

Iao Stream

Iao Valley

0   200 yds
0   200 m

N

.1 mile   .2   .3   .4   .5

1300

1100

900 ft

🚶 N 20 52.844, W 156 32.739: Trail head

❶ N 20 52.875, W 156 32.671 (0 miles): Join paved path heading left to ethnobotanical garden

❷ N 20 52.851, W 156 32.796 (0.2 miles): Cross the bridge over Iao Stream

❸ N 20 52.816, W 156 32.818 (0.3 miles): Iao Needle viewpoint

Kids in tow? After a peek at the impressive Iao Needle, stop by the Hawaii Nature Center (daily 10am–4pm; $6 adults, $4 children; ☎ **808/244-6500**; www.hawaii naturecenter.org) right next door. Hop on one of the guided rainforest walks offered daily, and explore more than 30 hands-on exhibits, touch pools, and aquariums, showcasing local flora and fauna.

battled Maui's army in his quest to unite the islands. This spot was known as the "damming of the waters." After the battle, it was said that dead bodies clogged the stream and the "river ran red." Notice the old rock-terraced walls that line the stream. Follow the trail to a set of concrete stairs leading to an overlook.

❸ Iao Needle Outlook Climb the 133 steps up for an up-close look at Iao Needle. If you're lucky, the clouds will be gone and you'll have a full view of the looming formation. You'll also have unobstructed views of the sacred valley and Puu Kukui Crater.

WAIHEE VALLEY SWINGING BRIDGE TRAIL

Difficulty rating: Easy

Distance: 5 miles round-trip

Estimated time: 4 hr.

Elevation gain: 650 feet

Costs/permits: Parts of this hike are privately owned. $6 per adult is collected at a roadside trailer near the trail entrance gate. The gate is open from 8am to 5pm.

Pet-friendly: Not prohibited, but would be a tough trip for most dogs crossing the river.

Best time to go: The falls are best after a rain, but watch for flash floods. *Note:* trail closes at 5pm.

Website: www.ecomaui.com

Recommended map: USGS' "Wailuku" map

Trail head GPS: N 20 56.491 W 156 31.447

Trail head directions: Take Hwy. 30 to Wailuku, and make a right on Main Street (Hwy. 32.) Turn left on Market Street, which will become Hwy. 330. At the intersection with Hwy. 340, bear left through Waihee Town. Turn left on Waihe'e Valley Road. Drive about 1 mile and you'll see a small parking area on the right, before you reach the gate.

What could be more fun on a hot Hawaiian day than hiking an impossibly lush rainforest, crossing two swinging bridges, and ending at a perfect swimming hole? Walk through misty and verdant Waihee Valley, with rippling streams, cascades, and waterfalls.

This hike is on the windward, wet side of the West Maui Mountain Range, beginning on a plantation road lined with taro patches, and banana and macadamia nut trees. Walk down the road to the vendor

trailer on the right. Here, you'll pay a $6 fee to cross private property into the valley. There are also drinks, snacks (including packets of local macadamia nuts!) and port-a-potties available. (In any case, you

(Tips) Guided Waihee

One of the best ways to hike Waihee Valley is on a guided hike with **Maui Eco-Adventures** (© 808/661-7720 or 877/661-7720; www.ecomaui.com), which owns exclusive rights for conducting tours on this trail. They'll pick you up at your hotel, take care of fees and permits, and along the way, you'll learn about Hawaiian culture and native plants.

won't go hungry on this hike. Loads of guava, pineapple, banana, and mango trees line the trail, and fallen fruit litters the path and scents the air.)

① Kukui Tree Grove Walk farther and you'll see a grove of kukui trees. The kukui tree is very important to Hawaiians. The nuts are used to make leis, and kukui-nut oil was once used to ignite fires. Sisal, night-blooming cereus, and banyan trees also decorate the way. After a short meander through the woods, you'll have some work to do: The trail widens and starts to climb. It's a huff-and-puff, steady incline, ascending about 460 feet in less than a quarter-mile. The stream, diverted long ago to irrigate taro patches, is on the left, along with hand-dug tunnels and ditches. Follow the path as it veers to the right.

② Swinging Bridges The trail follows the stream as it flows cool and clean from the valley walls. Look for the purple flowers of verbena plants—also known as purple rat's tail—and yellow flowering ginger plants. Soon, you'll reach the first swinging bridge. The cable and wood-plank bridge hangs low, nearly touching the water at certain times. If the river is low, you may be able to rock-hop across the water—but walking the bouncy bridge is a lot more fun! Only a few steps more and you'll be at the second swinging bridge. This one is longer and higher. Take a moment to stop midway on the bridge to look at the river as it tumbles in a hurry down rocks and boulders to the valley floor.

③ Waterfall Viewing A stand of bamboo, brought in by migrant workers a

century ago, has begun to invade the next section of the trail. Follow the path as it makes a short climb uphill. You'll begin to have open views of the West Maui Mountains. If you see or hear helicopters ahead, that's a good sign. It means the falls are flowing—and the tour operators are bringing people to see them. Look for waterfalls tumbling down the mountain slopes.

④ Stream Crossing Listen to rock music—the sound of the stream as it tumbles over water-worn stones—as you walk. The path narrows as it gains elevation gradually and enters a more tropical-looking environment of ferns, ginger plants, and bamboo. The air becomes cooler, and the trail more choked with roots and rocks. You'll pass under a canopy of tall avocado trees before coming to another stream crossing. There's no bridge here, so it's rock-hopping! If the water is gushing, this can be a challenge. In any case, watch your footing on the slippery rocks. After the crossing, the natural inclination is to walk straight, following the stream bed. Don't do this; instead take the trail to the left, climbing the rock steps through a thicket of hau trees. The green-blanketed mountain peaks surrounding Waihee Valley loom ahead.

⑤ Wall of Tears As you hike the rock-strewn, wet trail, look ahead and to your right into the folds of the West Maui Mountains. You'll see a set of twin waterfalls tumbling from the cloud-shrouded peaks. If it's been raining, which is likely, there will be more falls decorating the slopes. This is known as the "Wall of Tears."

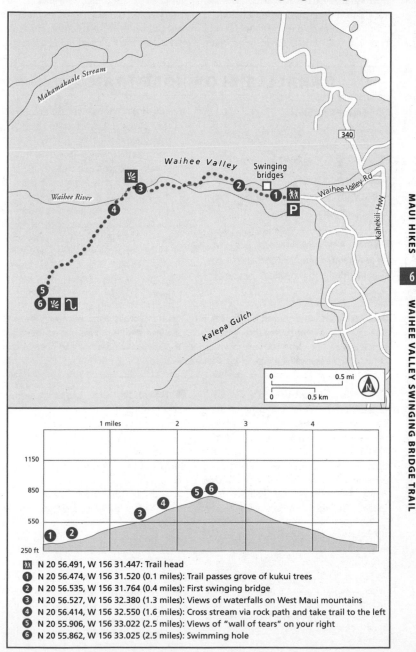

MAUI HIKES

6

WAIHEE VALLEY SWINGING BRIDGE TRAIL

N 20 56.491, W 156 31.447: Trail head
1 N 20 56.474, W 156 31.520 (0.1 miles): Trail passes grove of kukui trees
2 N 20 56.535, W 156 31.764 (0.4 miles): First swinging bridge
3 N 20 56.527, W 156 32.380 (1.3 miles): Views of waterfalls on West Maui mountains
4 N 20 56.414, W 156 32.550 (1.6 miles): Cross stream via rock path and take trail to the left
5 N 20 55.906, W 156 33.022 (2.5 miles): Views of "wall of tears" on your right
6 N 20 55.862, W 156 33.025 (2.5 miles): Swimming hole

6 Swimming Hole In less than a quarter-mile, you'll reach the cascades and small falls and a great swimming hole. The 15-foot-deep pool, lined with boulders, is clear and cool. Locals might be jumping from high tree branches and ledges into the pool; go ahead and join them if you dare. Or, take the easy, slower way into the water, down the gentle slope and over the rocks. This is a nice spot for a picnic, too.

NAKALELE BLOWHOLE TRAIL (Kids)

Difficulty rating: Easy

Distance: 1.2 miles round-trip

Estimated time: 1 hr.

Elevation gain: 245 feet

Costs/permits: None

Pet-friendly: Dogs must be kept on a leash.

Best time to go: When the tides are high and the winds are blowing

Website: www.gohawaii.com

Recommended map: USGS' "Napili" map

Trail head GPS: N 21 01.696 W 156 35.652

Trail head directions: From Lahaina, take Hwy. 30 north to mile marker 38. (Skip the wide turnout parking lot, which is 1/2 mile past mile marker 38 and the more popular trail head to the blowhole.) Instead, park at the small lot at mile marker 38, walk through the yellow gate, and follow the jeep road toward the light beacon, leading to the water's edge; you'll have wide-open views of the ocean and stunning coastline. *Note:* This is a popular tourist stop, but it is privately owned by Maui Land & Pineapple Company. Please be respectful.

Set on Maui's northern coast, Nakalele Point is an otherworldly scene of twisted lava and hissing ocean. Water surges through a hole in the lava shelf, erupting like a geyser and sending seawater some 100 feet or more into the air. Rocky coastline and ocean views abound, and easy walking makes it a good family stop.

1 Walk the Labyrinth We can't imagine a more restful and inspiring place for a labyrinth than this sunny plateau overlooking Maui's northwest coastline. Labyrinths, an ancient pattern that has been used for centuries for mediation and self-discovery, are popping up all over Maui. This one at Nakalele Point is one of the more recently constructed designs.

The labyrinth is made with white coral pieces laid out in a classic design against the green grass. Walk the single path that leads to the center and back out again; along the way, listen to the sound of the surf and sea birds. If nothing else, it's a great place to linger.

2 Nakalele Point Light Continue walking to the edge of the ocean and rock-hop your way along the coastline. Watch your footing; the rocks can be slippery and the drop off is steep. But, the views are fine! There are sea caves, rocky formations, and tiny blowholes along the way. Follow the path, marked by cairns, as it leads to the towering light beacon, set atop a rocky outcropping. The beacon also marks the northernmost point on Maui. Look for sea turtles swimming and feeding in the reefs and rocks just offshore. Descend from the lighthouse, rock-hopping, heading to the right as you face the ocean. The trail is rather informal from here. There are a few scattered white splotches painted on rocks and cairns to show the way, but generally, work your way along the coast.

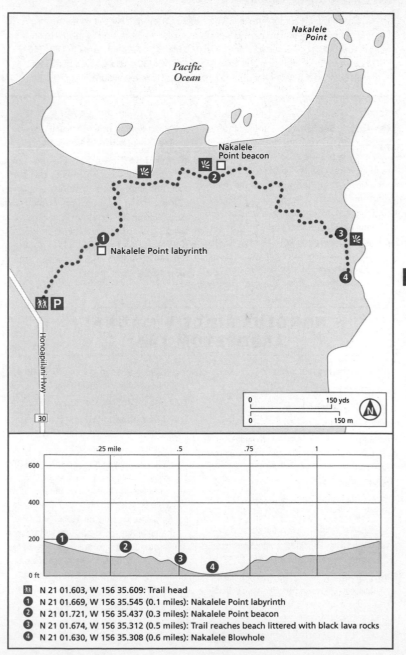

N 21 01.603, W 156 35.609: Trail head

1 N 21 01.669, W 156 35.545 (0.1 miles): Nakalele Point labyrinth

2 N 21 01.721, W 156 35.437 (0.3 miles): Nakalele Point beacon

3 N 21 01.674, W 156 35.312 (0.5 miles): Trail reaches beach littered with black lava rocks

4 N 21 01.630, W 156 35.308 (0.6 miles): Nakalele Blowhole

Consult the Experts

We like to hoof it alone, but we learn a whole lot more if we tail someone else who's knowledgeable about the island's ecosystems, flora, and fauna. Here are two top-notch guide services on the island: **Maui Eco-Adventures** (✆ **877/661-7720;** www.ecomaui.com) and **Hike Maui** (✆ **866/324-6284;** www.hikemaui.com). Both offer a variety of guided trips and custom excursions.

❸ Rocky Sculptures You'll enter a weird wonderland of rocky formations.

The beach is littered with black lava rocks, pockmarked like brain coral. Tall rock formations jut up from the black sand and line the water's edge. Just offshore, you'll see more formations, carved by eons of tidal movement and the powerful surf. Take some time to explore this scenic, multi-colored, multi-dimensional coastal landscape. You've likely roamed for about a half-mile from the car. Nearby, you'll see—and hear—a small blowhole. Snap a few photos and keep going.

❹ Nakalele Blowhole Continue along the jagged coastline, lined with tide pools, rock-hopping toward a windswept plateau in front of you. As you climb the rock shelf, start looking for the spray of seawater and listening for the loud *whoosh* as the tidal waves push water up the hole in a sea cave. Bet you'll want to stick around to witness more of the giant spurts!

HONOLUA RIDGE & MAUNALEI ARBORETUM TRAILS

Difficulty rating: Moderate

Distance: 6 miles round-trip

Estimated time: 3 hr.

Elevation gain: 1,682 feet

Costs/permits: A release form must be filled out at the Kapalua Adventure Center.

Pet-friendly: No

Best time to go: During the annual Kapalua Community Whale-Watching Festival, held each February.

Website: www.kapalua.com/adventures/on-resort-adventures/hiking.php

Recommended map: "Honolua Ridge & Maunalei Arboretum Trail" map (available at Kapalua Resort Adventure Center or online at www.kapalua.com)

Trail head GPS: N 20 58.775 W 156 37.225

Trail head directions: From Lahaina, travel north on Honoapiilani Highway (Hwy. 30) past Napili. Turn left onto Office Road into the Kapalua Resort. Turn right onto Village Road. Kapalua Adventure Center is the second building on the right. The trails are located on private, community land and can only be accessed by the Kapalua Resort shuttle (free). The resort shuttle departs from and returns to the Adventure Center several times a day (approximately every hour and a half starting at 8am with the last shuttle to the trail head at 3:30pm).

This up-and-back hike combines an interesting interpretive trail with ridgeline views of the West Maui Mountain Range and Puu Kukui Preserve. You'll travel through an 80-year-old arboretum of trees and plants collected from around the world, then hike up Honolua Ridge for sweeping views into the Puu Kukui Watershed Preserve, the largest private preserve in Hawaii. In the distance, you'll see the picturesque Honolua and Mokule'ia Bays along the Pacific Ocean and nearby Moloka'i Island.

The well-marked trail begins as a crushed gravel path, lined with guava trees and tall, 100-year-old Cook pines.

① Mokupea Lookout Walk gently uphill, passing a grove of non-native surinam cherry trees, for .3 miles to the first junction. Turn right to the Mokupea Lookout. It's really not much of a lookout, but a peek at the dense forest preserve and ocean in the distance. Nearby, look for the indigenous alahe'e plant and the non-native bo tree. Continue on the Arboretum Trail, turning right at the next junction.

② Banyan Loop It's a pleasant, woodsy walk with a mild incline. Signs point out the prickly-leaved tea tree and the Moreton Bay pine trees flanking the trail. In just a few steps, you'll see the next junction. Turn right again, taking the Banyan Loop Trail. You'll pass a gate, signaling your entrance into the Puu Kukui Watershed Preserve. The preserve is the result of a unique joint initiative between the Maui Land & Pineapple Company, Inc., and the Nature Conservancy, preserving 9,881 acres of the West Maui Mountain Range. The sea-to-mountain nature preserve, the largest private preserve in the state of Hawaii, shelters many rare and endangered species.

Continue on the nearly flat trail under huge New Zealand kauri trees and giant Traveler's palms with their hanging branches. You'll enter a very cool forest of mature banyan trees. The ground becomes a spongy bed of roots; look to your left and it's a fairyland of banyans. Stand among the leggy roots and gnarly trunks

of the trees, and under their dripping aerial roots and branches.

③ Honolua Ridge Trail Turn right at the next junction, onto the Honolua Ridge Trail. The trail, lined with the smooth-barked strawberry guava trees, follows the ridgeline, with some glimpses, to your left, of the Pacific Ocean. The interpretive signs continue, pointing out the endemic carex, manono, maile, and lama plants. Views begin to open up; you'll see Mahana ridgeline across the green valley, with its regal stand of 100-year-old Cook pines, and the ocean beyond.

④ Pu'u Kukui Lookout The trail gets a little steeper, gaining elevation on a series of switchbacks. Clusters of Christmas berry trees line the path, along with the endemic puapuamoa trees and akia and ama'u plants. Make the final push up to Puu Kukui Lookout for a wow view into the preserve. Puu Kukui, meaning "Hill of Enlightenment" in Hawaiian, is home to 300 native plant species, including nine on the endangered species list. From here, you'll have a good view of the West Maui Mountain Range, including the peaks of Keahikauo (2,013 feet); Honolua (2,627 feet); Nakalalau (4,503 feet); Kekaalaau (2,358 feet); and Puu Kukui (5,788 feet), the range's highest. Turn around and retrace your steps back to the trail head, in time to catch the shuttle bus back to the Adventure Center. The shuttle bus leaves the trail head heading back to the center at 9:45 and 11:15am, and at 12:45, 2:15, 3:45, and 5:15pm. (Double check with

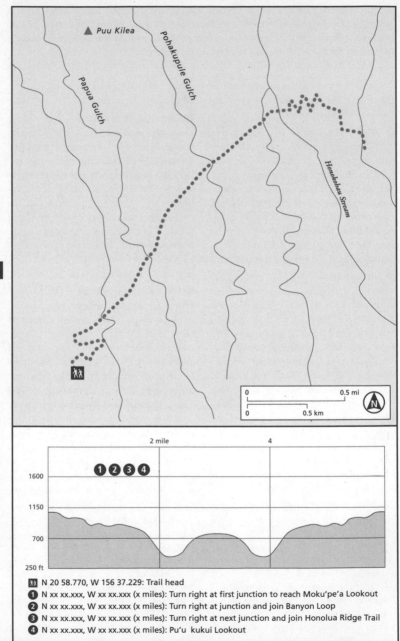

Puu Kilea

Papua Gulch

Pohakupule Gulch

Honokohau Stream

| 0 | 0.5 mi |
| 0 | 0.5 km |

N

2 mile   4

1 **2** **3** **4**

1600

1150

700

250 ft

🏃 N 20 58.770, W 156 37.229: Trail head

1 N xx xx.xxx, W xx xx.xxx (x miles): Turn right at first junction to reach Moku'pe'a Lookout

2 N xx xx.xxx, W xx xx.xxx (x miles): Turn right at junction and join Banyon Loop

3 N xx xx.xxx, W xx xx.xxx (x miles): Turn right at next junction and join Honolua Ridge Trail

4 N xx xx.xxx, W xx xx.xxx (x miles): Pu'u kukui Lookout

Tips Another Option

Instead of re-tracing your steps on this up-and-back hike and catching the shuttle bus back to the Adventure Center, you can opt to hike down the Mahana Ridge Trail. The trail begins at the end of this hike, near the Pu'u Kukui Lookout, and descends 5.75 miles through lush valley forest back to the Adventure Center. You'll have pretty views into Mokupea and Honokahua gulches along the way.

the Adventure Center on shuttle-bus departure times, as they may change.) Or, take the 5.75-mile Mahana Ridge Trail, descending the mountain slope back to the center.

The hike brings you back to the Kapalua Adventure Center, and a short walk away is the fabulous **Sansei Seafood Restaurant and Sushi Bar** (℡ **808/669-6286;** www.sanseihawaii.com). Join the locals (who know a good thing when they taste it) for some of the most creative and tasty sushi that you'll find anywhere.

LAHAINA PALI TRAIL

Difficulty rating: Strenuous

Distance: 5 miles round-trip to the summit peak; 5.5 miles one-way to hike the full length of the trail with shuttle pick-up on one end, 11 miles round-trip to hike the full length of the trail

Estimated time: 4 to 8 hr.

Elevation gain: 1,600 feet

Costs/permits: None

Best time to go: Winter, from December to March, is great for whale-watching.

Avoid high noon/midday, as the trail is exposed and hot.

Website: www.hawaiitrails.org/trail.php?TrailID=MA+06+001&island=Maui

Recommended map: USGS' "Maalaea" map

Trail head GPS: N 20 47.507 W 156 33.820

Trail head directions: From Lahaina, take Hwy. 30 south for 10 miles. The trail head parking lot is at Manawaipueo Gulch, on the right, about ¼ mile north of the Pali tunnel.

It's hot, dry, and rough-going walking on sharp lava rocks. But don't let that stop you! This ancient highway, built more than 200 years ago for horses and foot traffic, zigzags up and over the Kealaloloa Ridge in the West Maui Mountains, with panoramic views of the Pacific Ocean, as well as Kahoolawe and Lanai islands.

The trail starts as a wide boulevard, a cracked, paved road that follows an old foot and horse-and-buggy route. Ahead, you'll see a chain-link fence and a system of cables and wire meshing laid out to stop

erosion and safeguard the drivers below from falling rocks. In a few steps, less than 100 yards, you'll see the Lahaini Pali Trail sign. Take a left here, heading up Kamaohi Gulch. (*Note:* There's a really

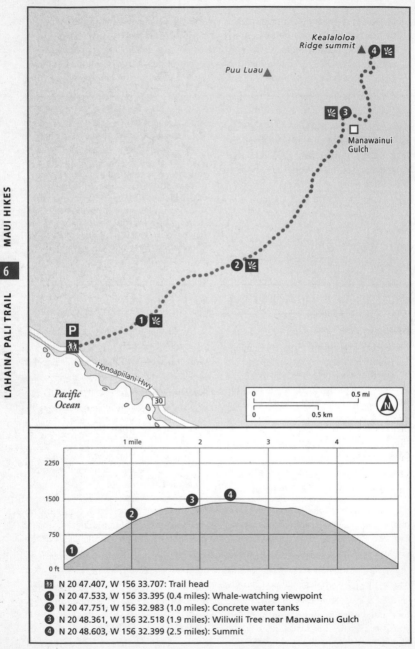

🚻 N 20 47.407, W 156 33.707: Trail head
❶ N 20 47.533, W 156 33.395 (0.4 miles): Whale-watching viewpoint
❷ N 20 47.751, W 156 32.983 (1.0 miles): Concrete water tanks
❸ N 20 48.361, W 156 32.518 (1.9 miles): Wiliwili Tree near Manawainu Gulch
❹ N 20 48.603, W 156 32.399 (2.5 miles): Summit

fine swimming and snorkeling beach near the trail head, but resist. It'll be there when you get back down from this hot hike.)

The entire trail runs 5.5 miles one-way, but we rarely go past the summit of the Kealaloloa Ridge. Start at the trail head parking lot at Manawaipueo Gulch and hike 2.5 miles to the summit; then turn around and return. You'll get the best views on the trail and avoid a shuttle pick-up ride at the eastern end of the trail or the grueling up-and-back 11-mile trek, which makes little sense to us. The 5-mile, up-and-back hike to the summit is what we describe here.

❶ Whale-Watching   It's a thigh-burning, huff-and-puff trek up the exposed, hard-scrabble trail, steadily gaining altitude and views. You'll be hiking through dryland brush and loose rocks; watch your footing, but don't forget to stop and grab a look. Turn around for wide-open ocean views, and perhaps even some whale watching.

❷ Opunaha Gulch   Keep climbing! The rough going gets a little rougher as you gain the ridge of Kamaohi Gulch and head for the steep cliffs of Opunaha Gulch. It's about a mile of heavy breathing and hot sun. You'll see remnants of old retaining walls as you ascend the cliffs. When you see the concrete water tanks, the worst of this climb is over. The water tanks are for the cattle that graze in the area.

❸ Manawainui Gulch   The sun-burned trail eases a bit as it winds through the dusty, rocky gulches. Ahead is **175** Kealaloloa Ridge and the broad and beautiful Manawainui Gulch. The name for this deep gorge translates as "large stream branch."

A lonely wiliwili tree, which has likely welcomed foot travelers for many years, stands guard in the gulch. The wiliwili tree is only found in Hawaii; the wood was traditionally used to make surfboards and canoe outriggers, and the nuts were used in making leis. This is a good spot to catch your breath and grab some shade.

❹ Summit   You'll emerge onto a broad, grassy ridge with endless ocean-to-mountain views as you march to the 1,600-foot summit.

Tag the top and then soak in the scenery. Haleakala, Maui's dormant volcano, fills the eye. From here you'll also have an impressive view of the ocean, Kealia Pond, and Molokini and Kahoolawe islands. The trail continues east to Maalaea as it drops to Maui's wetter, windward side. Instead, hoof it back down the way you came and head to Papalaua Beach Park. Boasting a swath of smooth sand and calm waters, the beach, across the street from the hot Lahaina Pali Trail, is the perfect spot to rest and cool down after the hike. Bring snorkeling gear—there's a small reef and the waters are usually clear.

Whale-Watching

From November through March, hikers get an added dose of remarkable scenery. Locals call it "whale soup," as thousands of humpback whales clog the Maui coastline. The whales migrate from Alaska to the Hawaiian Islands to breed, calve, and nurse their young.

HOAPILI TRAIL & LA PEROUSE BAY ★

Difficulty rating: Easy to moderate

Distance: 5.5 miles round-trip

Estimated time: 4 hr.

Elevation gain: 200 feet

Costs/permits: None

Pet-friendly: Dogs must be kept on a leash.

Best time to go: Early in the day before the tradewinds move in and churn up the water

Website: www.hawaiitrails.org/trail. php?TrailID=MA+18+001

Recommended map: USGS' "Makena" map

Trail head GPS: N 20 35.949 W 156 25.174

Trail head directions: Take Hwy. 31 (Kihei Rd.) south past Makena State Park and Ahihi-Kinal Natural Area Reserve. The road turns into Makena Road, narrows, and becomes rutted but passable; follow it to where it ends at the shores of La Perouse Bay. There's a decent-size lot and roadside parking.

This is an enchanting walk through recent lava fields along the southern coastline, with picturesque coves, secluded beaches, and high surf. Along the way, you'll see remnants of old Hawaiian foundations and *heiau* (religious sites), and have views of the inland foothills of Haleakala and the Pacific Ocean. Bring your bathing suit, snorkeling gear, and rugged hiking boots.

Be alert: The weather and water conditions change rapidly, and the surf can be high and dangerous. Also, bring lots of drinking water, as the biggest chunk of this hike is out in the open, and it can get very hot.

After parking your car, walk back to the road to read the sign that explains some of the ancient ruins that have been found in this area. Then, head toward the ocean and La Perouse Bay. The bay was named for the French explorer Jean-Francois de Galaup, comte de La Perouse, who mapped the area in 1786. In Hawaiian, it's called Keoneoio, and was once the site of an ancient fishing village. Legend has it that the bay was the haunting grounds of *Huaka I po*, also known as Night Marchers. These roaming spirits caused mischief at night—another good reason to hike this trail early in the day!

❶ **Coves & Beaches** Nutrient-rich La Perouse Bay lies just south of the Ahihi-Kinau Natural Area and is the site of Maui's most recent volcanic eruptions, which

occurred in the 1700s. Part of this trail follows remnants of the old King's Highway, a trail that once circled the entire island, and allowed all the king's men to watch over the territory and to collect taxes. The latest volcanic eruptions destroyed much of the original highway. The Hoapili Trail, now traversing cinder fields and lava flows, was improved by Governor Hoapili in the early to mid-1800s.

Poke around the bay's rocky shoreline and the small, sandy cove beach; rock-hop the boulders; and then head up the wide trail, heading north. The trail skirts the bay, as it enters a forest of kiawe. You'll pass several coves and small beaches, strewn with pieces of white coral.

It's a captivating vista of black beaches, scattered boulders, gnarly trees, and frothy surf. The terraced rock walls of a private ranch are on your left, as you follow the broad, dirt- and rock-littered path. Consider spending time along the way exploring the tide pools that gather in the pebbly coves.

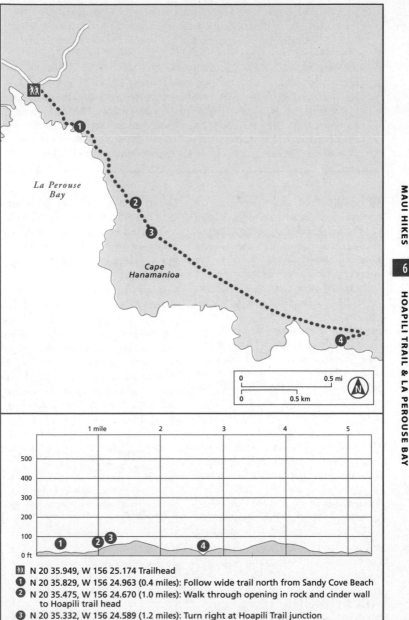

MAUI HIKES

6

HOAPILI TRAIL & LA PEROUSE BAY

🏃🏃 N 20 35.949, W 156 25.174 Trailhead

❶ N 20 35.829, W 156 24.963 (0.4 miles): Follow wide trail north from Sandy Cove Beach

❷ N 20 35.475, W 156 24.670 (1.0 miles): Walk through opening in rock and cinder wall to Hoapili trail head

❸ N 20 35.332, W 156 24.589 (1.2 miles): Turn right at Hoapili Trail junction

❹ N 20 34.824, W 156 23.613 (2.7 miles): Follow trail down to Kanaio Beach

Exploring Polipoli State Park

If you have time to spare and would like a look at Maui highlands and inland forest, consider a visit to this state park. A series of intersecting trails winds through thick stands of redwoods, evergreens, and fruit trees in the Kula Forest Reserve. At the Haleakala Ridge, you'll have views in all directions of central and west Maui. The park, which is popular with local hunters, is not as lush as it used to be due to a recent forest fire, but it's still quite interesting. The road into the park is often rough, and you may require a 4-wheel-drive vehicle to reach the trail head. To get there from Kahului, take Hwy. 37 past Pukulani to Hwy. 377, just before mile marker 14. Turn left on Hwy. 377 for ⅓ mile; then turn right on Waipoli Road. Waipoli becomes Polipoli Access Road as it climbs up the mountain to the state park entrance. See www.hawaiistateparks.org/parks/maui/Index.cfm?park_id=39.

② **Hoapili Trail** An upright pair of surfboards and a handmade memorial sign mark a recent gravesite, overlooking the bay (a grim warning of the dangers of the powerful, shore-breaking surf that can occur in this area). Just past this site, you'll see a barbed fence running through the cinder field to your left. Look for a small opening in the rock-and-cinder wall; beyond you'll see the sign for the Hoapili Trail. Turn left through the opening and walk the straight path to the trail junction ahead. A .8-mile spur trail takes off to your right, leading to the tip of Cape Hanamanioa and a Coast Guard lighthouse perched on a sea cliff at the northern tip of the bay.

③ **Cape Hanamanioa** At the clearly marked Hoapili Trail junction, turn right. The hike can get hot and rough from here as it climbs the lava fields across Cape Hanamanioa, the peninsula that dominates the north edge of La Perouse Bay.

The trail traverses a barren landscape of black lava fields punctuated with toothed boulders before it gains the crest, where you'll have open views of the ocean.

④ **Kanaio Beach** You'll see the stretch of Kanaio Beach, decorated with scattered kiawe trees, ahead of you. Follow the trail down to the beach and take a seat! This is a great place to linger, with views of the ocean and rocky, windswept coastline. Unfortunately, access to the water is tough.

Primitive camping is allowed on the coast beyond the end of the first big lava field at Kanaio Beach. You'll need to backpack in and take plenty of water. No camping is permitted around La Perouse Bay.

Look for the wood-shingled taco truck near Makena Beach. You can't beat their fresh-caught fish tacos topped with roasted habanero pepper sauce made with pineapple and carrots.

SLEEPING & EATING

ACCOMMODATIONS

Best Western Pioneer Inn This plantation-style hotel with verandas overlooking busy streets and the harbor is in the heart of Lahaina's action. The quietest units face the courtyard or the giant banyan tree next door. If you want a front-row seat for the comings and goings on Front Street, book no. 36 or 49.

658 Wharf St. (in front of Lahaina Pier), Lahaina, 96761. (€) **800/457-5457** or 808/661-3636. www. pioneerinnmaui.com. 34 units. $165–$190 double. AE, DC, DISC, MC, V. **Close to:** Lahaina Pali.

★★★ (Kids) **Four Seasons Resort Maui at Wailea**   If money's no object, this is the place to stay. This Hawaiian palace by the sea, in a ritzy neighborhood with great restaurants and shopping, may also be the most family-friendly on the island. Set on a glorious beach, it has a relaxing atmosphere, first-rate amenities, and free kids' programs.

3900 Wailea Alanui Dr., Wailea, 96753. (€) **800/334-MAUI** [6284] or 808/874-8000. www.fourseasons. com/maui. 380 units. $475–$990 double. AE, DC, MC, V. **Close to:** Hoapili Trail and La Perouse Bay.

★ (Value) (Kids) **Kaanapali Beach Hotel**   It's older than its upscale neighbors, but this property, bordering a fabulous stretch of beach, has irresistible charm, along with spacious rooms, lanais facing the courtyard or beach, pool, free culture programs, and free kids' programs. Tiki torches and music create a festive atmosphere nightly in the courtyard.

2525 Kaanapali Pkwy., Lahaina, 96761. (€) **800/262-8450** or 808/661-0011. www.kbhmaui.com. 430 units. $199–$355 double. AE, DC, DISC, MC, V. **Close to:** Nakalele Blowhole, Honolua Ridge, and Maunalei Arboretum.

(Value) **Lahaina Roads**   If you dream of an oceanfront condo but your budget is on the slim side, this place is for you. These small, reasonably-priced units in an older building located in the quiet part of Lahaina have full kitchens; bedrooms face the road, while the living rooms and lanais overlook the ocean.

1403 Front St. (1 block north of Lahaina Cannery Mall), Lahaina, 96761. (€) **800/669-MAUI** [6284] or 808/667-2712. www.klahani.com. 17 units. $150–$225 double. AE, DC, DISC, MC, V. **Close to:** Lahaina Pali.

★ (Finds) **Napili Bay**   One of Maui's best bargains is this small complex on Napili's beach—one of the finest on the coast for swimming and snorkeling. The studio apartments are small, but pack in everything you need, from a full kitchen to a roomy lanai that's great for watching sunsets over the Pacific.

33 Hui Dr. (off Lower Honoapiilani Hwy.), Napili. (€) **877/782-5642.** www.alohacondos.com/maui/napili-bay-condos. 33 units. $120–$315 double. MC, V. **Close to:** Nakalele Blowhole, Waihee Swinging Bridge, and Iao Needle Lookout.

★ (Finds) **Nona Lani Cottages**   Tucked among tropical trees and across the street from a white-sand beach, these cottages offer a wallet-pleasing option in Kihei. They're tiny, but each has a complete kitchen, living room, separate bedroom, and lanai. There's also a garden next to the beach and barbecue area.

455 S. Kihei Rd. (just south of Hwy. 31), Kihei, 96753. (€) **800/733-2688** or 808/879-2497. www.nona lanicottages.com. 11 units. $105–$150. 7-night minimum in high season. No credit cards. **Close to:** Lahaina Pali.

(Value) **Waianapanapa State Park Cabins**   These rustic cabins overlooking Pailoa Bay are the best lodging deal on Maui. They're tucked under a grove of hala trees, with five-star views of coastal cliffs and lava-rock beaches. The cabins come complete with kitchen, living room, bedroom, and bathroom with hot shower. Furnishings include linens, towels, dishes, and basic cooking and eating utensils. Reserve at least 6 months, or up to a year, in advance.

Off Hana Hwy. Reservations c/o State Parks Division, 54 S. High St., Room 101, Wailuku, HI 96793. (€) **808/ 984-8109.** 12 units. $45 for 4 (sleeps up to 6; extra person $5). 5-night maximum. No credit cards. **Close to:** Hana-Waianapanapa Coastal and Pipiwai.

Camping at Haleakala National Park is free (after you pay the $10 park-entrance fee). It's first-come, first-served, and permits are not needed. There are two campsite locations in the park: Hosmer Grove, near the park headquarters, and Kipahulu Campground, along the coastal road 10 miles south of Hana. Primitive campsites are also available at Holua and Paliku. Backcountry cabins at Haleakala require a reservation and cost $75 per night, per cabin, for up to 12 people. Cabin reservations are limited to one group (up to 12 people) and given through a monthly lottery. You must request a reservation in writing 2 months prior to the first day of the month in which you want the reservation.

Paliku Cabin sits in a gorgeous, wild botanical garden, overlooking a cloud forest and surrounded by tropical plants, like akala, ohia, and kolea. The site has camping, pit toilets, and non-potable water. The cabin (reservations required) has a wood-burning stove, propane stove, 12 padded bunks, and cooking utensils.

Camping is allowed at two state parks: Polipoli Spring State Recreation Area and Waianapanapa State Park. Apply for permits, up to a year in advance, from the **Hawaii State Parks Division** (P.O. Box 621, Honolulu, HI 96809; (C) **808/587-0300;** www. hawaiistateparks.org). Permit applications are available online, but must be mailed in. You can check availability by calling the state office. You can also get permits from the **Maui Division of State Parks** ((C) **808/984-8109**). Camping is $5 per campsite, per night.

Kanaha Beach Park in Kahului, and Papalaua Wayside Park in Lahaina, have overnight camping. For Kanaha Beach permits call (C) **808/270-7389;** for Papalaua Wayside permits call (C) **808/661-4685.** Camping is $3 per person, per night. For more information and permit applications, visit www.hi-mauicounty.civicplus.com.

RESTAURANTS

★★★ **The Banyan Tree** ASIAN-INSPIRED   It's hard to top this romantic, oceanfront restaurant for a special night out. The distinctive menu includes dishes like sautéed Kona *kampachi* with mustard greens and poached-shrimp salad, steamed *onaga* with black beans and pineapple emulsion, and roasted duck with snake beans and *enoki* mushrooms. Make a reservation for sunset.

At the Ritz-Carlton Kapalua, 1 Ritz-Carlton Dr. (C) **808/669-6200.** www.ritzcarlton.com/en/Properties/ KapaluaMaui/Default.htm. Reservations recommended. Dinner entrees $34–$55. AE, DC, DISC, MC, V. Tues–Sat 5:30–9:30pm. **Close to:** Honolua Ridge & Maunalei Arboretum, Nakalele Blowhole.

★ (Finds) **Cafe des Amis** CREPES/MEDITERRANEAN/INDIAN   Healthy and tasty meals that are easy on the wallet make this Paia town eatery a find. Crepes are the stars of the menu: spinach with feta cheese, shrimp curry with coconut milk, and dozens more. Dinners also feature authentic Indian curries. Service can be slow, but what's your hurry?

42 Baldwin Ave., Paia. (C) **808/579-6323.** Breakfast $8–$9; lunch $7.25–$9; dinner $11–$15. MC, V. Daily 8:30am–8:30pm. **Close to:** Waikamoi Forest Ridge.

★ (Finds) (Kids) **Cilantro: Fresh Mexican Grill** MEXICAN   This is Maui's best bet for fabulous, made-from-scratch Mexican food at frugal prices. Signature dishes include the citrus-and-herb-marinated chipotle rotisserie chicken, the Mariposa veggie salad, flautas, and lip-smacking adobo pork. Kids' menu items are under $5.

170 Papalaua Ave., Lahaina. (C) **808/667-5444.** www.cilantrogrill.com. Most items $5–$13. DISC, MC, V. Mon–Sat 11am–9pm; Sun 11am–8pm. **Close to:** Lahaina Pali.

★★ (Finds) **Colleen's at the Cannery** ECLECTIC   It's worth the drive to rural Haiku to enjoy Colleen's fabulous culinary creations at wallet-pleasing prices. Try the wild-mushroom ravioli, pan-seared ahi, or filet mignon. There are also smaller meals, such as burgers and fish and chips. Breakfast includes wonderful omelets and mouth-watering French toast made with Colleen's homemade bread.

At the Haiku Cannery Marketplace, 810 Haiku Rd. ℭ **808/575-9211.** www.colleensinhaiku.com. Reservations not accepted. Breakfast $5.75–$9; lunch $7–$15; dinner $10–$33. MC, V. Daily 6am–10pm. **Close to:** Waikamoi Forest Ridge.

★★ **Plantation House Restaurant** SEAFOOD/HAWAIIAN-MEDITERRANEAN   The spectacular 360-degree view here is one of the finest on the island—and the food matches the setting. It's the best place for breakfast in West Maui and a top choice for dinner. You can't go wrong with the daily fresh catch prepared with sautéed crab, or pepper-dusted with olives and caper-berry salsa.

At the Kapalua Golf Club Plantation Course, 2000 Plantation Club Dr. ℭ **808/669-6299.** www.the plantationhouse.com. Reservations recommended. Main courses $26–$42. AE, DC, MC, V. Daily 8am–3pm and 5:30–10pm. **Close to:** Honolua Ridge & Maunalei Arboretum, Nakalele Blowhole.

Restaurant Matsu JAPANESE/LOCAL   Deep-fried *katsu* pork and chicken are the specialties of this casual diner that draws customers from more than 50 miles away. California rolls, cold *saimin,* and bento platters are also popular. The daily specials are a changing lineup of home-cooked classics such as oxtail soup, roast pork with gravy, teriyaki ahi, and miso butterfish.

161 Alamaha St., Kahului. ℭ **808/871-0822.** Most items under $7. No credit cards. Mon–Thurs 10am–3pm; Fri 10am–8pm; Sat 10am–2pm. **Close to:** Waikamoi Forest Ridge, Waihee Swinging Bridge.

★★ (Finds) **A Saigon Cafe** VIETNAMESE   Fans drive from all over the island for the crisp spiced Dungeness crab, steamed *opakapaka* with ginger and garlic, and wok-cooked specials tangy with spices, herbs, and lemon grass. There are also a dozen different soups, cold and hot noodles, and chicken and shrimp cooked in a clay pot.

1792 Main St., Wailuku. ℭ **808/243-9560.** Most dishes $6.50–$17. DC, MC, V. Mon–Sat 10am–9:30pm; Sun 10am–8:30pm. Heading into Wailuku from Kahului, go over the bridge and take the 1st right onto Central Ave.; then take the 1st right on Nani St. At the next stop sign, look for the building with the neon sign that says OPEN. **Close to:** Waihee Swinging Bridge and Iao Needle Lookout.

★★ **Sansei Seafood Restaurant & Sushi Bar** PACIFIC RIM/SUSHI   Perpetual award-winner Sansei offers an extensive menu of Japanese and East-West delicacies, like the mango/crab-salad rolls, panko-crusted ahi sashimi, ahi carpaccio, noodle dishes, Asian shrimp cakes, and creative sauces like ginger-lime chile butter and cilantro pesto. There's simpler fare as well, such as shrimp tempura, noodles, and wok-tossed upcountry vegetables.

Two locations: At the Kapalua Resort, 600 Office Rd., Lahaina. ℭ **808/669-6286;** and 1881 South Kihei Rd., Kihei, ℭ **808/879-0004.** www.sanseihawaii.com. Reservations recommended. Main courses $16–$43. AE, DC, MC, V. Daily 5:30–10pm. **Close to:** Honolua Ridge & Maunalei Arboretum, Nakalele Blowhole (Kapalua location), Lahaina Pali (Kihei location).

Kauai Hikes

by Diane Bair & Pamela Wright

When it comes to outdoor adventure, Kauai may well be the only island you'll ever need. On this 33×25-mile, impossibly lush, volcanic island, you can trek into a canyon, zip-line through a rainforest, explore a cave, and swim in a waterfall—and plan another adventure for the next day! This is an island that deserves exploration, and the best of it is reserved for hikers.

First, realize that more than 90% of the island is inaccessible, so you may want to get an overview via helicopter. As the whirlybird hovers over a caldera, and swoops *this close* to craggy sea cliffs, you'll realize that Kauai got more than its share of jaw-dropping gorgeousness. At some point, you'll stop counting all the waterfalls. The locals, for their part, realize how lucky they are to live here, and constantly tell you how blessed they are to call the Garden Island home.

For the visitor, it's remarkably easy to get acquainted with Kauai. There's basically one perimeter road, which goes *almost* all the way around the island. The road stops at the Na Pali Coast, a stunning series of 2,700-foot spires. It takes about 2¹/₂ hours, one-way, to drive Hwy. 50 to the end.

Need we say the hiking on Kauai is sublime? The island claims more hiking trails than any other Hawaiian island, including the famed Kalalau Trail, considered by many to be one of the finest short hiking trails in the world. Not for the meek, Kalalau Trail humps up and down the stunning Na Pali Coast, ending at a remote beach, bumped up against the sacred Kalalua Valley. Think soaring sea cliffs, caves, hanging valleys, and gushing waterfalls, and you'll start to get the picture.

Don't miss a trek or two in the mountainous, 4,345-acre Koke'e State Park, with more than 45 miles of trails, including a hike across the world's highest rainforest and swampland and a walk through a nutrient forest of tropical plants and trees that grow nowhere else in the world. On your way, you'll see the multi-hued Waimea Canyon, dubbed "the Grand Canyon of the Pacific." A series of switchbacks skirts the canyon, with fabulous outlooks and numerous trail heads along the way.

Also on the west side is Polihale Beach, a 17-mile stretch of sand that's the longest beach in Hawaii. (The rugged road to the beach is an adventure in itself!) It's not the best bet for swimming, but for a long walk on a remote, windswept beach with a backdrop of dunes and frothy surf, you can't beat it.

Even near Kauai's top resort areas, you'll find off-the-beaten-path trails. Take the Mahaulepu Heritage Trail, for example; tucked in behind the Grand Hyatt resort in Poipu, this 4-plus-mile path follows an ancient coastal route, with sea cliffs, secluded coves, sculpted lava formations, and petroglyphs. Walk its length especially in the morning and you're likely to spot endangered monk seals.

As we said: The best of Kauai is reserved for hikers.

GETTING THERE

You'll arrive at the **Lihue Airport (LIH)** (📞 **808/246-1448;** www6.hawaii.gov/dot/ airports/kauai/lih), located about 1.5 miles east of Lihue, on the southeast coast of Kauai. **Hawaiian Airlines** (📞 **800/367-5320;** www.hawaiianair.com) and **go!/Mesa** (📞 **888/ 435-9462;** www.iflygo.com) offer inter-island flights.

VISITOR INFORMATION

There's no walk-in visitor center on Kauai, but you can get online information at www. kauaidiscovery.com and talk with a representative by calling the hotline at 📞 **800/262-1400** or 808/245-3971. You can also mail requests to **Kauai Visitors and Convention Bureau,** 4334 Rice St, Suite 101, Lihue, HI 96766. For camping permits, visit the Division of Forestry & Wildlife office at 3060 Elwa St., #306, in Lihue.

ORIENTATION

It's tough to get lost on Kauai; one major highway nearly circles the island, and well-placed signs and street markers direct visitors to major sites. Both Lihue and nearby Kapa'a are the commercial/tourist centers of the island. In Wailua, make the short drive to Wailua Falls, the twin falls made famous by the TV show *Fantasy Island.* Heading south, you'll reach the go-to beach zone of Poipu, lined with resort hotels. Koke'e State Park is accessed from the far west end of the island and is approximately 90 minutes from Lihue. Both Waimea Canyon Drive (Rte. 550) and Koke'e Road (Rte. 552) head up the canyon and end at Koke'e State Park.

MAPS

You can purchase the **Kauai Recreational Trail Map** at the Kauai Division of Forestry and Wildlife Office in Lihue (3060 Elwa St.; 📞 **808/274-3433**) for $5. You can also get one by mailing a cashier's check or money order in U.S. currency for $6 (for domestic mailings) or $7 (for foreign mailings). Mail checks to the Division of Forestry & Wildlife, 3060 Elwa Street, #306 Lihue, HI 96766.

(**Fun Facts**   **Starring Kauai**

If a few of the scenic spots on Kauai look familiar, it's not because you were a volcano god or goddess in a past life (not that we'd rule that out!). More than 175 movies and 200-plus TV shows have been filmed on this photogenic little island. Just some of the films shot on location here include: *Tropic Thunder* (Ben Stiller has a home here) and *Jurassic Park IV* (also the other three *Jurassic Park* flicks). Harrison Ford showed up for *Raiders of the Lost Ark* and *Six Days, Seven Nights;* Roger Moore did the Bond thing in *The Man with the Golden Gun* (and another ex-007, Pierce Brosnan, has a home on the island); and Elvis partied hearty (and honeymooned with Priscilla) at the now-shuttered Coco Palms Hotel and made movies, including *Blue Hawaii,* on Kauai.

KAUAI HIKES

ESSENTIALS

7

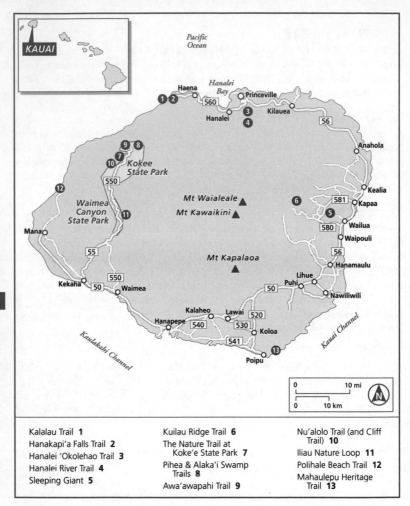

Kalalau Trail **1**	Kuilau Ridge Trail **6**	Nu'alolo Trail (and Cliff Trail) **10**
Hanakapi'a Falls Trail **2**	The Nature Trail at Koke'e State Park **7**	Iliau Nature Loop **11**
Hanalei 'Okolehao Trail **3**	Pihea & Alaka'i Swamp Trails **8**	Polihale Beach Trail **12**
Hanalei River Trail **4**	Awa'awapahi Trail **9**	Mahaulepu Heritage Trail **13**
Sleeping Giant **5**		

WEATHER

The weather forecast on Kauai on any given day is likely to be rain and sunshine. There are nearly always both conditions on the island. The north shore of Kauai is the rainiest, including Mount Wai'ale'ale, the second rainiest spot in the world. On the south shore, it's dry and sunny year-round. The average temperatures range from 73° to 80°F (23°–27°C).

KALALAU TRAIL ON THE NORTH SHORE ★★★

Difficulty rating: Strenuous

Distance: 22 miles round-trip, 4 miles round-trip to Hanakapi'ai Beach, up and back

Estimated time: 14 to 16 hr.

Elevation gain: 1,000 feet

Costs/permits: Permits (free) are required when hiking beyond Hanakapi'ai Beach. Get permits from the Kauai District State Parks office (3060 Eiwa St., # 306, Lihue, HI 96766; ℂ 808/241-3444). There are three authorized camping areas along the way; camping costs $10 per day.

Pet-friendly: No

Best time to go: May through October, when the weather tends to be drier.

Avoid this trail in wet weather, when flash floods may occur.

Website: http://www.hawaiistateparks.org/hiking/kauai/index.cfm?hike_id=13

Recommended maps: The Division of State Parks (see contact info above) has a free map of the trail as well as the "Recreation Map of Eastern Kauai," which provides a general topographical overview of the area.

Trail head GPS: N 22 13.222 W 159 34.960

Trail head directions: The trail head begins at Ke'e Beach at the end of Hwy. 56. The small lot at the beach is often full, but there's an overflow lot about ¼ mile before you reach the beach, on your right.

KAUAI HIKES

7

KALALAU TRAIL ON THE NORTH SHORE

This spectacular trail, arguably one of the best hikes of its length in the country, hugs the rugged and remote Na Pali Coast, providing the only land access to legendary Kalalau Valley. Known the world over, the Na Pali Coast, stretching from Ke'e Beach in the north to Polihale State Park in the west, has inspired poets, artists, and photographers for thousands of years. Some historians believe that this was the first area in Kauai to be settled by the early Hawaiians. The trail is not easy, and rarely level, including some 5,000 feet of cumulative elevation gain and loss. But for the rugged outdoors person, the rewards are worth the hot, grueling effort: sweeping ocean vistas, dewy tropical forests, sea caves, sugar-white beaches, and lush valleys rippled with streams and waterfalls.

"How tough can a hike along a coastline be?" we thought the first time we attempted this trail. We got 2 miles in to Hanakapi'ai Beach and turned back. We'd already fallen more than a few times as soft, water-soaked terra-cotta rocks crumbled beneath our feet and wet roots left no bearing. We were sweating like Miami linebackers in lycra—did we mention it was hot?

We returned the following day, more prepared, with extra water bottles, water purifier, sturdier boots, and less we-can-handle-anything arrogance. Trust us: this hike should not be underestimated. It

doles out unrelenting ups and downs, unforgiving slippery steeps, sweltering heat, and possible flash floods. That said: Its beauty cannot be overestimated.

The well-marked trail starts at the end of Hwy. 560, with a steady climb and likely a steady flow of day hikers. The first 2 miles of the trail make a popular day hike for locals and visitors alike. Switchbacks climb the sea cliffs, and in short time, and less than ½ mile into the hike, you'll get your first jaw-dropping view of the fluted coastline.

KAUAI HIKES

7

KALALAU TRAIL ON THE NORTH SHORE

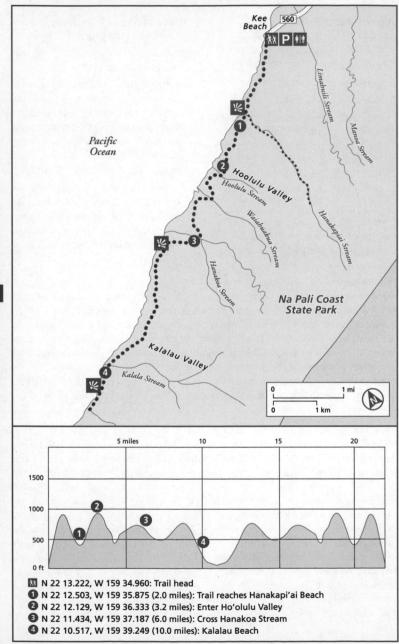

N 22 13.222, W 159 34.960: Trail head
1 N 22 12.503, W 159 35.875 (2.0 miles): Trail reaches Hanakapi'ai Beach
2 N 22 12.129, W 159 36.333 (3.2 miles): Enter Ho'olulu Valley
3 N 22 11.434, W 159 37.187 (6.0 miles): Cross Hanakoa Stream
4 N 22 10.517, W 159 39.249 (10.0 miles): Kalalau Beach

(Tips) Big Views Without the Work

"If you're not up for a hike but want to see the Na Pali, just walk down Ke'e Beach and turn around after about a quarter-mile," advises Peter of **Kauai Eco Tours** (📞 877/538-4453; www.kauaieco-tours.com). "You'll get the same view the ancient Hawaiians saw from their boats."

❶ **Hanakapi'ai Beach** For a short distance, you'll meander through a tropical forest of dewy ferns and sweet-smelling papaya and mango trees, with ocean vistas around nearly every corner. You'll still be climbing, up almost 1,000 feet, before you begin a slip-and-slide descent back to sea level. Two miles and a couple of hours into the hike, you'll reach sugar-white Hanakapi'ai Beach.

Throw your packs on the sand and head for a dunk in the freshwater stream that spills out of the forest and into the ocean and poke around the sea caves that line the Hanakapi'ai shore. This is also where the trail to Hanakapi'ai Falls begins (see "Hanakapi'ai Falls Trail," below). After this stop, you'll be rested and refreshed for the grueling climb out of Hanakapi'ai Valley. (*Note:* Swimming in the ocean here, with strong currents and riptides, can be dangerous.)

❷ **Hoolulu Valley** The trail gets tougher and steeper, climbing another 800 or more feet in the next 2 miles. But the views entering Hoolulu Valley are silly gorgeous. The cliffs of the Na Pali coastline, a tumble of lush, green folds and steep spires, plunge into the blue waters of the Pacific Ocean. Waterfalls tumble into the valleys. Gurgling streams crisscross tropical forests. Go ahead: Gawk and walk. The trail traverses the Hono O Na Pali Natural Area Reserve, through the valleys of Hoolulu and Waiahuakua, and gets narrower and narrower with each step—winding through thick forests and along the canyon walls, before reaching its highest point.

For an outstanding view, stop at the rocky outcropping, perched on the top of a steep cliff, overlooking Hoolulu Bay.

From here, there's a knee-throbbing descent into Hoolulu Valley.

❸ **Hanakoa Valley** Up and down, up and down . . . you need to climb out of Hoolulu Valley before descending (yes, again!) into Hanakoa Valley. The valley is rich with tropical plants, mango and guava trees, stunning views—and water. Streams trickle across the trail; waterfalls gush out of the valleys and down the cliffs; the turquoise Pacific Ocean glistens. You'll cross the Hanakoa Stream before leaving the picturesque valley.

Pack heavy, legs quivering? There's a rustic camping area near the Hanakoa Stream, about 6 long miles into the hike. The campsites—a little tough to find—rest on old coffee-plant terraces, planted in the 1800s. There's also an unmarked .3-mile trail into the valley for a close-up look at Hanakoa Falls.

❹ **Kalalau Beach** There is no rest for the weary on the last 4 miles or so of the trail. In fact, you'll climb into the open (read: no shelter from the sun!), and the trail gets narrower as it traverses the ridgeline. From about 6.5 miles to the 8-mile marker (though it's likely the markers have disappeared; we suspect they're shamelessly taken as souvenirs), you'll be walking on a very steep and narrow cliff edge. Suck it up; put one foot carefully in front of the other, and let the awesome views—sea cliffs plunging to the ocean—move you along. There's one final knee-crunching descent before you cross the Kalalau Stream.

Cool down and wash the trail dust off in the stream. This is also a good place to get fresh water (which needs to be treated!). A few more steps into the mouth of the valley, and you'll reach beautiful and remote Kalalau Beach. Swimming can be dangerous, but there's a waterfall at one end of the beach where you can refresh and get fresh water.

Note: If you see goats at the top of ridge or on the cliffs above, don't go near the waterfall. The goats kick down rocks, and some people have been hurt.

There's camping on the beach and in the shade under the trees behind the beach. During drier summer months, it's also possible to sleep in one of the sea caves. There are some rugged people who do this trail up and back in a day, and more who spend an overnight on Kalalau Beach. We suggest you spend as much time as you can (up to 5 nights of camping are allowed) to explore, relax, and soak in the views. There are sea caves to explore, fellow hikers to meet, and an easy 2-mile trail into the valley, passing ancient taro fields, and ending at a decent swimming hole.

HANAKAPI'AI FALLS TRAIL ★★

Difficulty rating: Strenuous

Distance: 8 miles round-trip

Estimated time: 6 to 8 hr.

Elevation gain: 760 feet

Costs/permits: Permits (free) are required when hiking beyond Hanakapi'ai Beach, to the falls. Get permits from the Kauai District State Parks office (3060 Eiwa St., # 306, Lihue, HI 96766; ✆ 808/241-3444). Camping costs $10 per day.

Pet-friendly: No

Best time to go: Dry, summer months; June through September is best. Don't go if it's raining.

Website: www.hawaiistateparks.org/hiking/kauai/index.cfm?hike_id=13

Recommended maps: The Division of State Parks (see contact info above) has a free map of the trail as well as the "Recreation Map of Eastern Kauai," which provides a general topographical overview of the area.

Trail head GPS: N 22 21.145 W 159 59.448

Trail head directions: You must walk the first 2 miles on Kalalau Trail to access this trail head. Follow the Kalalau Trail (see "Kalalau Trail on the North Shore," above) for 2 miles to Hanakapi'ai Beach. The trail is located at the valley side of the beach, heading inland.

Pack your swimsuits and your rain gear, don sturdy (and preferably waterproof) hiking boots, and bring the camera. Ready? This is the stuff of movies and fantasies: a tromp through a wet, tropical rainforest, dotted with sweet-smelling guava and mango trees, ending at a towering 300-foot waterfall. The misty cloud forest and rushing falls make for a very surreal, jungle atmosphere. Plus, there's a fine swimming hole at the base of the falls. This hike, added on to the Kalalau Trail (above), makes for a super day hike, perfect for those who want a look at the Na Pali coastline—with an added waterfall bonus.

The first 2 miles of the hike begin on the Kalalau Trail (see Kalalau Trail hike description above). The trail climbs the steep *pali* (cliffs), switchbacking for 1 mile across wet rocks and slippery roots. But your reward comes quickly, with views of

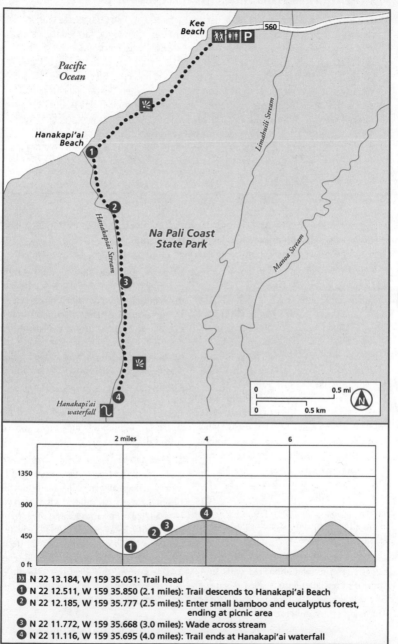

N 22 13.184, W 159 35.051: Trail head

1 N 22 12.511, W 159 35.850 (2.1 miles): Trail descends to Hanakapi'ai Beach

2 N 22 12.185, W 159 35.777 (2.5 miles): Enter small bamboo and eucalyptus forest, ending at picnic area

3 N 22 11.772, W 159 35.668 (3.0 miles): Wade across stream

4 N 22 11.116, W 159 35.695 (4.0 miles): Trail ends at Hanakapi'ai waterfall

Who Are These Folks and Why Are They Here?

The rules say no one can set up house in the famed Na Pali Coast State Wilderness Park. The park was once home to ancient Hawaiians, who farmed the valleys and fished the waters, and to thousands of hippies, who communed, crashed, and checked out in the '60s and '70s. Today, hike your way to Kalalau Beach and you're likely to meet a few longtime rule breakers and colorful characters. These squatters set up camp and then flee into the valley when the official enforcers arrive. The officials destroy their camps and confiscate their supplies, but it doesn't seem to deter everyone. "They have no right to tell us we can't be here," some contend. "The ancient Hawaiians believed that the land could not be owned; it was there for everyone," others argue. We do know this: Spend a night over an (illegal) campfire or cooking stove with the Kalalau "locals" and you'll hear some great stories.

the gorgeous Na Pali coastline. And, in this case, what goes up must come down. The second mile brings an equally steep descent to Hanakapi'ai Beach.

❶ Hanakapi'ai Beach Take a breather; explore the rocky beach and sea caves, and enjoy a wade in the freshwater stream. When you're ready to continue, look to the back, valley-side of the beach for the trail heading inland. The trail follows the west bank of the Hanakapi'ai Stream into the narrow valley. The valley—along with neighboring Hoolulu, Waiahuakua, and Kalalau valleys—was once home to ancient Hawaiians, who planted vast, terraced taro fields. Today, the area is part of the 6,175-acre Na Pali Coast State Wilderness Park and is off limits to permanent inhabitants (see "Who Are These Folks and Why Are They Here?," above). You'll pass guava trees and remnants of ancient stone walls as you climb into the valley.

❷ Mango, Bamboo & Eucalyptus Fed by streams and showered with sunshine, this fertile valley is home to a variety of tropical trees. Walk under a canopy of tall mango trees and enter a small bamboo

and eucalyptus forest, ending at a small picnic area.

❸ Stream Crossings The trail gains elevation, gradually skirting the river and crossing it several times. Depending on the weather, these crossings can be tricky. In high water or threat of rain, it's best to turn back. Even in drought, plan on getting wet, as efficient rock-hopping is difficult, and the easiest way across is often wading your way through the stream. At about 1.5 miles, the trail gets muddier, and the stream crossings get wider, but the scenery is captivating. Rippling cascades and deep, clear pools are surrounded by steep valley walls.

❹ Hanakapi'ai Falls At 2 miles, the trail ends at the base of the stunning, 300-foot Hanakapi'ai waterfall. The thin, white ribbon of water cascades down a steep valley wall, splashing into a large pool. Misty clouds and spray from the falls create a lush, moist atmosphere; mosses, ferns, vines, tropical flowers, trees, and giant boulders crowd the edges of the pool. We never leave without a ceremonious (and refreshing) dip in the pool.

Difficulty rating: Moderate

Distance: 2.5 miles round-trip

Estimated time: 2 to 3 hr.

Elevation gain: 450 feet

Costs/permits: None

Pet-friendly: Dogs must be on a leash.

Best time to go: All year; the drainage is decent, so even during wet weather this trail is doable. We like it best in early morning, before the mercury climbs.

Website: www.hawaiitrails.org/trail. php?TrailID=KA+06+007

Recommended map: The "Recreation Map of Eastern Kauai" is available from the Division of Forestry and Wildlife.

Trail head GPS: N 22 12.102 W 159 28.355

Trail head directions: From Princeville, turn an immediate left after crossing the Hanalei Bridge (approximately 1 mile from Princeville at the bottom of the hill). This is Ohiki Road, but there may not be a sign. Drive ½ mile to the parking lot on the left. The trail head is across the street; walk across the foot bridge with the Okolehao Trail sign bolted on the side.

Lots of native plants line this trail leading to two plateaus on top of Kaukaopua Ridge, where you have near-360-degree, unobstructed views of Hanalei Valley, Hanalei Bay, and the Kauai coastline. It follows an old route established in the days of prohibition, when Okolehao, a Hawaiian liquor, was being distilled from the roots of ti (ki in Hawaiian) plants. You can still see ti plants along the trail.

This trail starts with a bang, an uphill huff and puff on a wide, dirt road. There's wire meshing on some of the trail, which helps prevent erosion but also helps secure footing in the red clay. You'll gain elevation quickly as you slog uphill. Orchids and other tropical plants line the path.

❶ **Hanalei from the First Plateau** The trail keeps climbing to about the 1-mile mark, when you'll reach an open plateau. There's a massive power-line tower to your right, and a good, first look at pretty Hanalei Bay, dotted with sailboats, and the broad Hanalei River, as it weaves through green fields of taro. Below, you'll have glimpses of Hanalei town; the

Na Pali coastline takes off to your left. Beyond, in the distance, are the blue waters of the Pacific Ocean. Bushy, big-leafed ti plants, sacred to the ancient Hawaiians, dot the hillsides. Ti was planted near taro fields to ensure abundant production. It was also used to make Okolehao, a strong liquor. This ridgeline route was a popular place to harvest ti plants during Prohibition. You could stop here on the trail—but don't.

❷ **Tropical Pine Forest** Turn left and head into the woods. The trail, you'll discover, has two distinct sections, and different sets of flora. Native orchids and sunlight decorate its lower elevation, to

KAUAI HIKES

7

HANALEI 'OKOLEHAO TRAIL

ⓘ **Tips** **Short & Sweet**

The trail continues for a 4.6-mile round-trip. However, we describe here a 2.5-mile hike, as the best views are at the 1.25-mile marker.

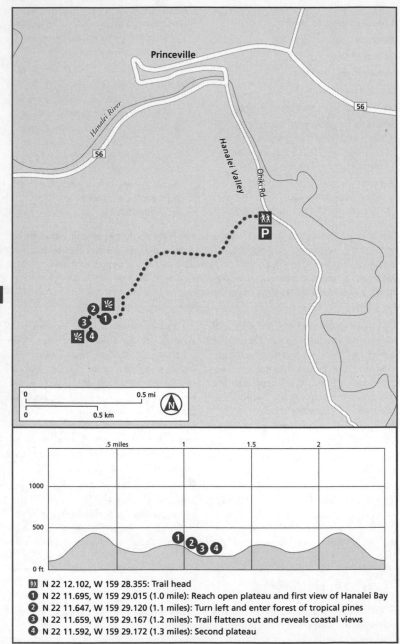

🚶 N 22 12.102, W 159 28.355: Trail head

❶ N 22 11.695, W 159 29.015 (1.0 mile): Reach open plateau and first view of Hanalei Bay

❷ N 22 11.647, W 159 29.120 (1.1 miles): Turn left and enter forest of tropical pines

❸ N 22 11.659, W 159 29.167 (1.2 miles): Trail flattens out and reveals coastal views

❹ N 22 11.592, W 159 29.172 (1.3 miles): Second plateau

this point. Now, just beyond the 1-mile mark, you'll enter a forest of tropical pines and blessed shade. Follow the root-choked trail along the ridgeline route and be on the lookout for a large tree, with a penis-shaped branch sticking out of its trunk. (We have several sophomoric photos of this tree.)

❸ **Coastal Views** The trail veers left, climbing roots and natural footholds as it weaves through the forest, until it parallels the Na Pali Coast. It's a gentle meander from here, a welcome flat section, providing peeks through the trees at the ocean and sea cliffs.

❹ **Hanalei Views from the Second Plateau** At 1.3 miles, there's a last, short-but-steep scramble to an open plateau—and the best views on the trail. Soak up the views, and then re-trace your steps back to the trail head.

> Twirl 360 degrees for a panoramic view of the ocean dropping over the horizon; the green folds of the Na Pali coastline; Hanalei Valley, River, and Bay; and the Kauai coastline as it circles the island. It's a great, bird's-eye look of Kauai.

HANALEI RIVER TRAIL (Kids)

Difficulty rating: Easy

Distance: 2 miles round-trip

Estimated time: 1 to 2 hr.

Elevation gain: 100 feet

Costs/permits: None

Pet-friendly: Dogs must be on a leash.

Best time to go: All year, but we like it best just after a light rain, when it's ultra misty and the cascades and streams are flowing.

Website: www.hi.sierraclub.org/kauai

Recommended map: Contact the Division of Forestry and Wildlife at 3060 Elwa St., Lihue, HI, 96766; ℂ 808/274-3433.

Trail head GPS: N 22 11.116 W 159 27.986

Trail head directions: From Princeville, turn an immediate left after crossing the Hanalei Bridge (approximately 1 mile from Princeville at the bottom of the hill). This is Ohiki Road, but there may not be a sign. Continue 2 miles and park at the end of the road. Straight ahead is a dirt road through the forest. *Note:* There may be no trespassing signs and a fence across the road. The neighbors don't like the visiting hikers, but it's perfectly legal. Be sensitive (read: quiet) as you follow the road into the forest to access the footpath.

This hike offers a tropical, jungle-like experience for little effort, perfect for families with young kids and nature lovers. The trail meanders through dark bamboo forests, leading to the banks of the Hanalei River, Kauai's longest river.

Ignore the NO TRESPASSING signs and the barking dogs and walk quietly past the houses down the dirt road. Hopefully, you've worn your waterproof hiking boots or an old pair of tennies; the road is usually muddy and the footpath muddier still.

❶ **Stream Crossing** Our kids love the towering stands of bamboo that flank the trail. Rock-hop and slosh through the shallow waters of the first small stream crossing before entering an enchanted, dewy forest of mosses, ferns, orchids, and sweet-smelling jasmine.

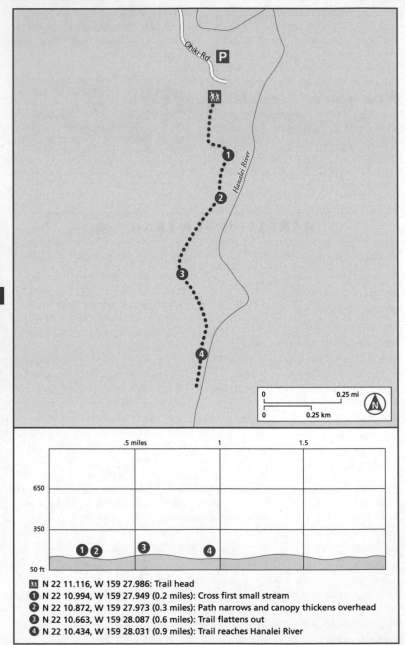

🚶 N 22 11.116, W 159 27.986: Trail head
❶ N 22 10.994, W 159 27.949 (0.2 miles): Cross first small stream
❷ N 22 10.872, W 159 27.973 (0.3 miles): Path narrows and canopy thickens overhead
❸ N 22 10.663, W 159 28.087 (0.6 miles): Trail flattens out
❹ N 22 10.434, W 159 28.031 (0.9 miles): Trail reaches Hanalei River

> **(Finds) Go with a Group**
>
> The local Sierra Club (www.hi.sierraclub.org/kauai) leads group hikes on the Hanalei River Trail, as well as several other trails on the island. It's a great way to learn more about the history, flora, and fauna along the trail, and to connect with local hikers.

❷ **Bamboo Forest** Walk through mud and puddles to the soothing sound of rippling waters and birdsong, and then meander across an open, grass meadow. Now, the path narrows again, and the canopy gets thicker. The bamboo forest becomes dark, dense, and tall. You'll duck under low-lying branches and tangles of vines, as the trail snakes through the lush, wet forest.

❸ **Jasmine & Uluhe Ferns** The trail, following an old pig-hunting path, flattens as it travels through thick forests of bamboo, hau trees, and uluhe ferns and sunlit meadows, dotted with white flowering jasmine. Views are obscured by the dense foliage and tall grasses.

❹ **Hanalei River** After a second stream crossing, at about 1 mile, you'll cross through an open field to the banks of the broad Hanalei River. Here, you'll have views up the river, with green mountains and valleys as a backdrop. Unfortunately, the river is not really accessible for swimming.

Where the official trail ends, you can continue to explore, using a network of pig-hunting trails that follows the river and crisscross the valley.

SLEEPING GIANT (NOUNOU MOUNTAIN EAST) IN THE EAST/KAPA'A/WAILUA AREA ★

Difficulty rating: Moderate

Distance: 3.5 miles round-trip

Estimated time: 3 to 4 hr.

Elevation gain: 950 feet

Costs/permits: None

Pet-friendly: Dogs must be on a leash

Best time to go: All year, early mornings when skies tend to be clearer

Website: www.dofaw.net (Hawaii Division of Forestry and Wildlife) or www.hawaii trails.org/trail.php?TrailID=KA+10+005

Recommended map: Contact the Division of Forestry and Wildlife at 3060 Elwa St., Lihue, HI, 96766; ☎ 808/274-3433.

Trail head GPS: N 22 03.674 W 159 20.795

Trail head directions: From Lihue, drive 6 miles north on Hwy. 56 to Haleilio Road (second intersection after crossing the Wailua River). Look for the Wailua Shell gas station. Turn left and continue about 1 mile to the trail head parking lot on the right.

Hike the Sleeping Giant's chest! This trail is one of three that snake up the sides of Nounou Mountain, known as the Sleeping Giant for its unmistakable ridgeline formation. You'll zigzag through the Nounou Forest Reserve, ending at a picnic area on the chest of the giant. You'll have great views of the Wailua River, the Kauai coastline, and—if the weather cooperates—the summit of Mount Wai'ale'ale. It's a short distance hike with big eye-candy rewards.

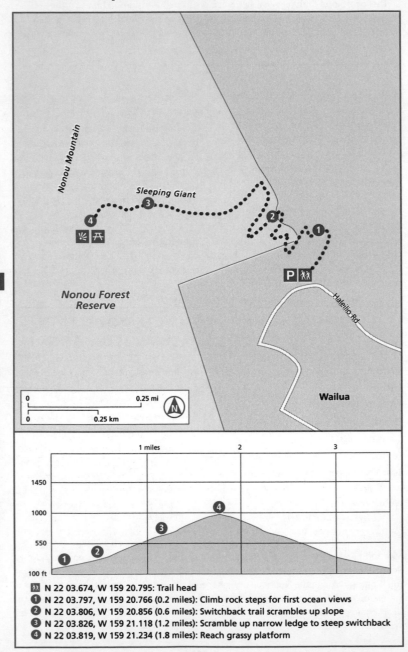

7

KAUAI HIKES

SLEEPING GIANT (NOUNOU MOUNTAIN EAST)

N 22 03.674, W 159 20.795: Trail head
1 N 22 03.797, W 159 20.766 (0.2 miles): Climb rock steps for first ocean views
2 N 22 03.806, W 159 20.856 (0.6 miles): Switchback trail scrambles up slope
3 N 22 03.826, W 159 21.118 (1.2 miles): Scramble up narrow ledge to steep switchback
4 N 22 03.819, W 159 21.234 (1.8 miles): Reach grassy platform

Tips

Kauai Eco-Tours (☎ **877/538-4453;** www.kauaieco-tours.com) offers guided hikes on the Nounou Mountain East and West trails, the Kuilau Trail (see "Kuilau Ridge Trail," below), and others.

① Ocean Views Follow the well-marked red clay path as it gently ascends the body of the giant. You'll climb rock steps, and in a matter of minutes, get your first view of the ocean. The trail then levels, climbs, levels, and climbs at a consistent pace—but not too demanding. About a third of a mile in, you'll have a good view of the giant's profile.

② The Sleeping Giant's Face Switchbacks carve the ridge as you climb to a sharp right and make a scramble up the slope. Here, you'll have a full view of the sleeping giant's giant face and his protruding chin. If you're lucky, the trade winds will pick up and the clouds will block the sun, as you are exposed along this ridgeline and it gets hot.

③ Leggy Tress—and Watch Your Step It's getting fun now! If you have severe vertigo or fear of heights, you may not like the next section. You'll need to

scramble up a narrow, steep ledge, but it's only a few, short steps, and a climb up a steep switchback, before the trail gains the ridge. Stop to rest for a moment and to look at the fairyland-like stand of hala trees.

④ Valley and Coastline Views At 1.8 miles, you'll reach the grassy platform, atop the sleeping giant's chest, with sweeping views of Nounou Mountain; the Wailua River; forested valleys; and, if the skies are clear, a look at the peak of Mount Waialeale.

Grab a seat at one of the two picnic tables; the metal roof overhead provides shelter from the sun. Or, look for the wooden bench, with the word RESPECT carved on it, off to the left. Here, you'll also have a 300-degree panorama of Kauai. Feeling adventurous? There are steep and narrow paths that continue up to the giant's chin; be careful.

KUILAU RIDGE TRAIL

Difficulty rating: Moderate

Distance: 4 miles round-trip to the Moalepe Trail junction

Estimated time: 2 to 3 hr.

Elevation gain: 640 feet

Costs/permits: None

Pet-friendly: Dogs must be kept on a leash.

Best time to go: All year, but the trail can get muddy during winter months, especially January through March.

Website: www.hawaiitrails.org/trail.php?TrailID=KA+07+002 or www.dofaw.net (Hawaii Division of Forestry and Wildlife)

Recommended map: Contact the Division of Forestry and Wildlife at 3060 Elwa St., Lihue Hi ; ☎ 808/274-3433.

Trail head GPS: N 22 04.297 W 159 24.990

> **Finds   Need A Break**
>
> If you're in the Wailua area, check out **Monaco's Taqueria** (© 808/822-4300), located in the Kinipopo Shopping Village. This come-as-you-are eatery serves fabulous fish tacos at wallet-pleasing prices. It's open for lunch and dinner.

Trail head directions: From Lihue, drive 6 miles north on Hwy. 56 to Hwy. 580 (Kuamoo Rd.). Turn left and follow Hwy. 580 for 6.9 miles to the Keahhaa Arboretum. The trail head is just before the parking lot.

Exotic birds, tropical flowers, forests of ferns . . . this trail is the jungle come alive. If you want to see a Kauai rainforest without expending too much effort, this is it. It's a dewy, humid, sweet-smelling, short hike to a fine vantage point, with views of the lush valleys of Kawi, Mount Wai'ale'ale, and Kapehuaala, one of the highest peaks in the Makaleha Mountains. We like to hike it first thing in the morning—it's the best time to hear the symphony of birdsong and catch a glimpse of i'iwi, apapane, elepaio, or amkihi birds that frequent the upland woods and rainforests.

Located in the Lihue-Koloa Forest Reserve, the Kuilau Trail was originally a swath created in 1971 to contain a fire that raged in the region. Today, it's a favorite with guided hiking groups, horseback riders, and mountain bikers.

The well-marked, wide trail takes off from the right-hand corner of the parking lot and heads up the ridgeline. You'll be rewarded immediately with valley views to your left and the sweet, musky aroma of crushed guava leaves and fruit. The ground is likely to be littered with fallen guava fruit; pick a ripe one off a tree for a quick and easy on-the-go snack. We never fail to stop along the way to take yet more close-up photos of the mottled, smooth bark of the strawberry guava trees to add to our collection.

❶ Mountain Vistas You'll begin a gradual ascent up the ridgeline, leaving the roosters that congregate at the trail head—and their noisy crowing—behind. In about a half-mile, the forest becomes thicker and the native forest birds start to provide the background music for this walk. If the weather is decent, you'll also begin to have views of the 5,243-foot Kawaikini summit (Kauai's highest) and

Mount Wai'ale'ale to the west. Straight ahead, to the north, is the rolling Makaleha Mountain Range.

❷ Picnic Shelter The gradual but gentle climb takes you farther up the ridgeline, where the views begin to open up more, with wide vistas of surrounding mountain ranges and green-coated valleys. At 1.5 miles, you'll climb out of the forest-rimmed trail to an open, expansive picnic area, a natural platform for soaking in the views.

There are a couple of picnic tables under a tin roof providing shelter from the sun or rain. You'll want to stay awhile in this amphitheater of sights and sounds. There are sweeping views of the lush valleys of Kawi. Look down to see the Keahua and Kuwi streams. To the east is Nounou Mountain and a view to the ocean in the distance. To the north, you'll see the Makaeha Mountain Range. If the skies are clear, you'll see the high peaks of Kawaikini and Mount Wai'ale'ale and the silver flash of waterfalls tumbling from the forested slopes. Stay awhile, but don't turn back yet.

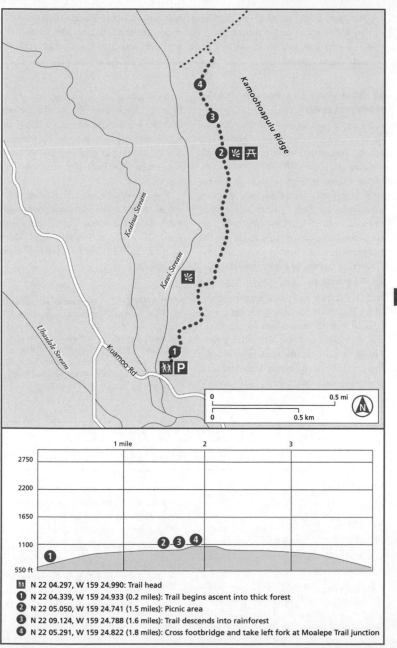

N 22 04.297, W 159 24.990: Trail head

❶ N 22 04.339, W 159 24.933 (0.2 miles): Trail begins ascent into thick forest

❷ N 22 05.050, W 159 24.741 (1.5 miles): Picnic area

❸ N 22 09.124, W 159 24.788 (1.6 miles): Trail descends into rainforest

❹ N 22 05.291, W 159 24.822 (1.8 miles): Cross footbridge and take left fork at Moalepe Trail junction

Let It Rain, Rain, Rain

With an average rainfall of 460 inches per year, Kauai's Mount Wai'ale'ale is one of the wettest spots on the planet. The 5,208-foot mountain gets only a few inches less rainfall than the world's wettest spot, monsoon-drenched Mawsynram, India.

❸ Rainforest Cascades & Scarlet Honeycreepers Head east, leaving the pretty mountain views to your back—for the moment—and gently descend into a lush, tropical rainforest. There's a quick switchback, where you'll have a nice view of the Sleeping Giant (Nounou Mountain) before the trail closes in and you're surrounded by clinging vines and a forest of ferns. Look above in the rainforest canopy for a flash of red; this might be the indigenous i'iwi bird (scarlet honeycreeper), a favorite of birders in Hawaii.

❹ Footbridge Just before the trail ends, it narrows, and you'll hear the sound of trickling water. Look to your right for a peek at a small waterfall and cascades. A few steps more and you'll arrive at a footbridge over the small, trickling Opaekaa Stream and the Moalepe Trail junction. This is a good place to linger and listen to water dripping, birds singing, and insects buzzing. Walk over the footbridge and take the left fork; a few more steps, and you'll have a pretty view of Kapehua'ala, one of the highest peaks in the Makaleha Mountains. Go back the same way you came.

If you have time, visit the Keahua Arboretum next door. There are rivers and pools (and some good places to take a quick dip in the water to cool off), shady picnic areas, restrooms, and pretty grounds to explore.

For homemade sandwiches, snacks, and great, fresh-made poke, stop at the **Ishimura Market** in Waimea, before heading up the Koke'e State Park and Waimea Canyon. You can also pick up bags of ice and a cheap, handy cooler to keep in the car.

THE NATURE TRAIL AT KOKE'E STATE PARK 🅺🆒

Difficulty rating: Easy

Distance: 0.2 miles round-trip

Estimated time: 30 min.

Elevation gain: Minimal

Costs/permits: None

Pet-friendly: No

Best time to go: All year, but especially in the early morning hours, when the flowers are fresh and the crowds are thin.

Website: www.hawaiistateparks.org/parks/kauai/Index.cfm?park_id=7

Recommended map: "Native Plants on the Nature Trail" details plants along the trail and is available on loan at the Koke'e Museum.

Trail head GPS: N 22 07.820 W 159 39.462

Trail head directions: Follow Koke'e Highway or Waimean Canyon Drive to Koke'e State Park. Park at the Koke'e Museum lot. The trail begins from the back of the parking lot.

This sweet, little, self-guided walk is a great way to begin your visit to Koke'e State Park. You'll weave through a native Hawaiian forest, set at 3,600 feet elevation, which includes plants found nowhere else on earth. There are more than 30 plants and trees identified on this walk. Enter the forest and take a look at the koki'o ke'oke'o, a white flowering hibiscus that is found only on Kauai. If it's fall or winter, it might be blooming. You'll pass ohe'ohe trees, halapepe plants and loulu palms before reaching a kauila, which is endemic to Hawaii.

We love this state park, tucked up past Waimea Canyon, with rainforests, swamplands, mountains, and sea cliffs gracing its 4,345 acres. There's a small museum, gift store, restaurant, and picnic pavilion at its entrance, plus eye-candy outlooks and more than 45 miles of trails.

To begin this hike, walk past the large koa tree and the small bushy hibiscus. You'll also notice a fallen log and two tree trunks, decorated with clinging halapepe. Take a few steps more to the endemic kauila plant.

❶ **Kauila**   The strong wood of the kauila was used by early Hawaiians for making spears and weapons, and for shovels and fishing-line weights. As you move on, note the young papala tree, which was once used in fireworks displays because its branches crackle and spark when lit. Walk a short distance past markers denoting a variety of Hawaiian plants until you reach marker 8, the holio plant.

❷ **Holio**   Be sure to take a look at the holio plant. This is the only endemic plant belonging to the avocado family. It's found only on Kauai. Another nearby endemic plant is the laukea, and the very important mokihana tree. The small tree, only found on Kauai, was used in lei making.

❸ **Mistletoe!**   Walk the path, flanked by native fern species, 'ohia lehua, a small maile vine, and a manono coffee plant, and then look up: What's that growing on the bark of the holio tree? It's hulumoa, Hawaiian mistletoe. Walk on.

❹ **Ala'a**   This short study in plants continues as you pass ahakea trees; the wood of the tree was used for making paddles and canoes. You'll also pass uahi a Pele, meaning "Pele's smoke"; 'iliahi or sandalwood, which is endemic to Hawaii; and ala'a or bronze leaf, which was used to treat fevers. As you finish the short loop, look for the tall haha lua plant. This endemic species, found only in west Kauai, can grow up to 40 feet high. The path continues a short distance, completing the 800-foot crescent-shaped trail, putting you back where you started.

KAUAI HIKES

7

THE NATURE TRAIL AT KOKE'E STATE PARK

Ⓚ Kids   Take A Walk

Nothing could be easier or finer than a stroll on the recently constructed Kapa'a Multi-Use Trail. The 6-mile (round-trip) hard-packed walkway skirts the ocean, popular beaches, vendors, and beachfront eateries, stretching from Kealia Beach to Kapa'a. Residents love everything about it, except that dogs—even on a leash—are not allowed. This has caused a bit of a local uproar.

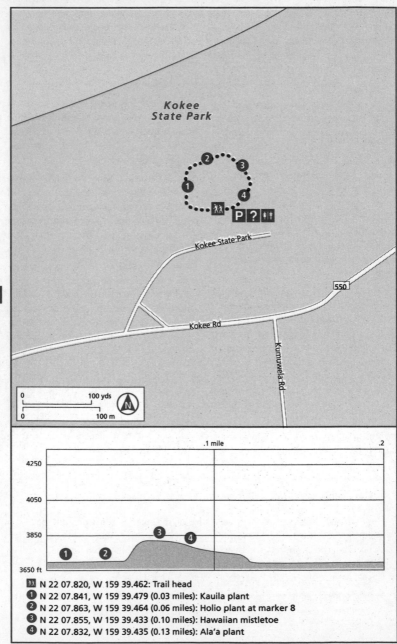

N 22 07.820, W 159 39.462: Trail head
1 N 22 07.841, W 159 39.479 (0.03 miles): Kauila plant
2 N 22 07.863, W 159 39.464 (0.06 miles): Holio plant at marker 8
3 N 22 07.855, W 159 39.433 (0.10 miles): Hawaiian mistletoe
4 N 22 07.832, W 159 39.435 (0.13 miles): Ala'a plant

Difficulty rating: Strenuous

Distance: 7.4 miles round-trip

Estimated time: 6 hr.

Elevation gain: 400 feet

Costs/permits: None

Pet-friendly: Dogs must be on a 6-foot or shorter leash.

Best time to go: March through October, during the dry season

Website: www.hawaiistateparks.org/parks/kauai/Index.cfm?park_id=7

Recommended map: Trail maps are available from Koke'e State Park.

Trail head GPS: N 22 08.859 W 159 37.853

Trail head directions: Follow Koke'e Highway to its end; park at the Puu o Kila Lookout lot.

Take a magical, mystical journey through Old Hawaii! There is no other place quite like this eerie swamp, located on an old caldera floor, created some 6 million years ago. The not-to-be-missed hike travels through dense rainforest and open, muddy bogs—it's the world's highest rainforest and swampland. Along the way, there's opportunity to see rare native plants and birds. You've got to get up early, though, if you have any chance at all of seeing the magnificent views from the Kilohana lookout, at the end of the Alaka'i Trail.

KAUAI HIKES

7

PIHEA & ALAKA'I SWAMP TRAILS

Before hitting the trail, take some time to check out the view at the Puu o Kula lookout, where (if it's not fogged in), you'll have views of the Na Pali Coast and Pacific Ocean. You'll be standing at about 4,240 feet.

The well-marked Pihea Trail starts straight ahead, skirting the ridge between the Kalalau Valley—the largest valley on the Na Pali Coast—and the Alaka'i Swamp. Views of the sheer cliffs dropping to the ocean are spectacular. On clear days, you can see into the canyons, extending to Mount Waialeale. Know ahead of time that you're going to get dirty and wet hiking this trail; it's one of the muddiest on

Kauai and we've heard tales of hiking through ankle-deep muck.

❶ **Pihea Vista** Walk down the wide, red-clay boulevard, pocked with mud holes and slippery steps; it's an easy but consistent up-and-down (baby) roller coaster of a walk. After 1 mile of muddy trekking, you'll reach the Pihea Vista spur trail. Don't even think about skipping this extra jaunt, no matter how wet and mucky it looks. But prepare for a steep climb on dirty rocks (that's part of the fun). It's only a short distance to the lookout, but you'll be scrambling! There are roots for handholds and "steps" formed by thousands of footprints, but still, it's a climb—and worth it. At the

---

Tips Better Together

The 7.4-mile Pihea Trail and the 7-mile Alaka'i Swamp Trail can be done separately. But we like this combo better; it takes in the best of both trails. Also, it eliminates the need for a four-wheel vehicle to access the Alaka'i trail head.

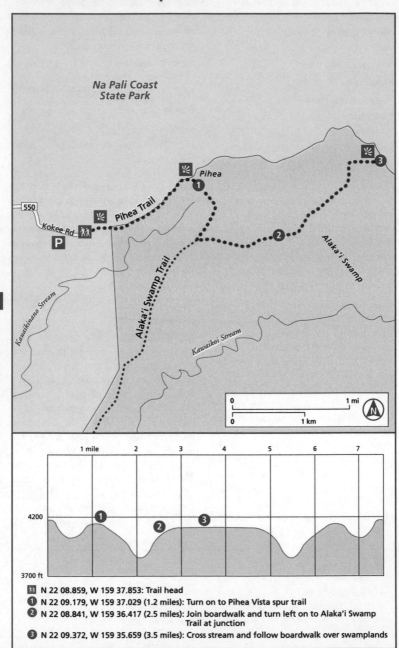

Na Pali Coast
State Park

550

Kokee Rd

Pihea Trail

Pihea

Alaka'i Swamp Trail

Alaka'i Swamp

Kauaikinano Stream

Kawaikoi Stream

0   1 mi
0   1 km

1 mile   2   3   4   5   6   7

4200

3700 ft

N 22 08.859, W 159 37.853: Trail head

1 N 22 09.179, W 159 37.029 (1.2 miles): Turn on to Pihea Vista spur trail

2 N 22 08.841, W 159 36.417 (2.5 miles): Join boardwalk and turn left on to Alaka'i Swamp
Trail at junction

3 N 22 09.372, W 159 35.659 (3.5 miles): Cross stream and follow boardwalk over swamplands

lookout, you'll see a kaleidoscope of colors, as the Na Pali Coast stretches before you. Fern-covered slopes drop down to undulating valleys and the blue waters of the Pacific Ocean. It's not much different than the view at the Puu o Kila Lookout, where you started, but turn in the opposite direction and you'll also have a view into the Alaka'i Swamp. Seeing both views in one spot is quite spectacular.

➋ Boardwalk Hike back to the main trail and start a precipitous descent (with thoughts already of the long haul back up at the end of the day). And, then: What's this?!! A boardwalk! Well-placed, man-made wooden steps and broad boardwalk lead the way to a four-way junction, at 1.7 miles into the hike. Turn left onto the Alaka'i Swamp Trail leading to the Kilohana Vista. The Pihea Trail continues straight ahead to the Kawaikai Camp.

Steps—hundreds of them—now lead down, down, down into a misty rainforest, a haven for rare plants and birds. Be on the lookout for the red-hued apapane bird; if you're lucky, you may also catch a glimpse of the rare, pink-legged puaiohi bird. But even if you can't tell a chicken from a chickadee, you'll appreciate the eerily beautiful atmosphere. Continue on the boardwalk, now straightening, to a small, tannin-colored stream. Although the stream water isn't safe to drink, this is a pleasant spot to grab a seat on a flat rock and take a rest.

➌ Alaka'i Swamp Cross the stream and follow the boardwalks into the open, crossing the primeval swamplands and bogs filled with mosses and algae and dotted with the red-flamed blossoms of o hi a hehua plants, which are endemic to Hawaii.

Hawaiians have a story to explain the creation of this high-altitude rainforest. It's said that a petulant Pele, the red-haired, infamous Hawaiian goddess of volcanoes, threw a tantrum, stomping her foot from the top of Mount Waialeale onto the hot lava a thousand feet below. Her angry footprints created the 16-sqaure-mile swamp. Scientists have other theories, but we like this one.

The boardwalk goes on forever—a fog-shrouded twilight zone—twisting and turning; then straightening, twisting and turning; and straightening as it makes its way to the Kilohana Lookout.

The 4,030-foot-high perch, standing on a steep cliff, overlooks the green-carpeted valleys of Wainiha and Hanalei, fed by the always-wet Mount Wai'ale'ale's slopes. On clear days, you can see all the way down to the shores of Hanalei Bay.

Turn around and re-trace your steps.

AWA'AWAPAHI TRAIL ★

Difficulty rating: Strenuous

Distance: 6.2 miles round-trip

Estimated time: 4 to 6 hr.

Elevation gain: 1,300 feet

Costs/permits: None

Pet-friendly: Dogs must be on a 6-foot or shorter leash.

Best time to go: March through October

Website: www.hawaiistateparks.org/parks/kauai/Index.cfm?park_id=7

Recommended map: Trail maps are available from Koke'e State Park.

Trail head GPS: N 22 08.482 W 159 38.925

Trail head directions: From the Koke'e Lodge and Museum, drive 1½ miles up the canyon to the Awa'awapuhi Trail parking lot on the left, just beyond mile marker 17. The trail leaves from the left-hand side (south) of the parking lot (as you pull in) and ascends gently through a native, red-flowering ohia lehua forest and tall koa trees.

The trail travels through a nutrient-rich forest of endemic Hawaiian plants and trees, with many lookouts of the steep, folded *pali* of the Awa'awapuhi and Nualolo valleys. Ending at a 2,500-foot open ridge, the route gives hikers stellar views overlooking towering sea cliffs and hanging valleys, dropping to the Pacific Ocean. This trail can also be combined with the Nualolo and Nualolo Cliff trails for a great, albeit strenuous, day hike (see tip below).

❶ The Descent Begins   In less than a half-mile from the trail head, you'll begin a continual descent down the Kaunuohua Ridge to the upper slopes of Awa'awapuhi Valley. The forest changes from towering koa to a bushy floor of ferns, kahili ginger, scattered passion fruit trees, and abundant blackberries (now considered an invasive species on Kauai). At about the 1-mile mark, the foliage changes again, becoming drier and more barren.

❷ Valley Views   You'll lose altitude steadily but easily as the trail switchbacks through shrubs of a'ali'i, with a promise of open views to come. Hike to the beat of chattering birds and hovering helicopters. This is a popular route for copters taking tourists for a peek at the Na Pali Coast; you're bound to see and hear them along the trail. Keep an eye out, too, for feral goats that climb and forage around the cliffs. From here, you'll begin to have peeks through the brush at the lush Awa'awapuhi and Noalolo valleys ahead.

❸ Nualolo Cliff Trail Junction   Have your cameras ready. At about 2½ miles into this downward hike, the trees and brush clear to your right, and you have a heart-stopping view of the folded, forested ridgelines of Awa'awapuhi Valley plunging to the blue waters of the Pacific Ocean. You'll reach the Nualolo Cliff Trail junction at about the 3-mile marker. Keep going; there's more to come.

The birds-eye view of the **Awa'awapuhi Lookout** has it all: rolling valleys; trickling streams; ribbons of waterfalls tumbling down verdant slopes; the steep sea cliffs of the famed northern Kauai coast; and, beyond, the Pacific Ocean.

ⓘ Tips   Hiking Awa'awapuhi & Nualolo Trails

For a long but rewarding day hike, we suggest going down the Nualolo Trail and Nualolo Cliff Trail (see description below) and back up the Awa'awapahi Trail. The reverse—down Awa'awapahi and back up Nualolo—adds another 500 feet of elevation to an already tough hike. Park at the Awa'awapuhi trail head and walk 1.5 miles *down* the road to the Nualolo trail head. This way, your car will be waiting when you come out on the Awa'awapuhi Trail (and you won't have to walk *up* the road at the end of the day!). This near-loop is 11 miles long; plan on 6 to 8 hours of hiking.

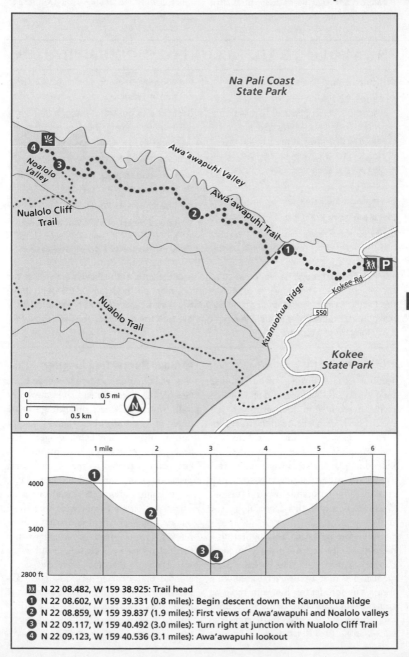

N 22 08.482, W 159 38.925: Trail head
① N 22 08.602, W 159 39.331 (0.8 miles): Begin descent down the Kaunuohua Ridge
② N 22 08.859, W 159 39.837 (1.9 miles): First views of Awa'awapuhi and Noalolo valleys
③ N 22 09.117, W 159 40.492 (3.0 miles): Turn right at junction with Nualolo Cliff Trail
④ N 22 09.123, W 159 40.536 (3.1 miles): Awa'awapuhi lookout

4 Awa'awapuhi Lookout The Nualolo Cliff Trail heads left; you'll turn right, following the ridgeline another .3 miles to the wide-open lookout. After much *oohing* and *ahhing*, turn around and climb back up the ridgeline.

NUALOLO TRAIL & NUALOLO CLIFF TRAIL ★

Difficulty rating: Strenuous

Distance: 7.6 miles round-trip to the Nualolo Cliff Trail junction; 10 miles round-trip combining Nualolo and Nualolo Cliff trails; 11 miles round-trip looping to Awa'awapuhi Trail (see "Hiking Awa'awapuhi and Nualolo Trails," above).

Estimated time: 4 to 6 hr.

Elevation gain: 2,000 feet

Costs/permits: None

Pet-friendly: Dogs must be on a 6-foot or shorter leash.

Best time to go: March through October, as it can be dangerous when raining.

Website: www.hawaiistateparks.org/parks/kauai/Index.cfm?park_id=7

Recommended map: Trail maps are available from Koke'e State Park.

Trail head GPS: N 22.07.750 W 159 39.578

Trail head directions: Park at the Koke'e Museum lot. The trail head is 50 yards back down Koke'e Road, on the right.

You'll descend through native forest to Lolo Vista Lookout, with sweeping views of the Na Pali coastline. Then traverse the rim of the canyon, perched some 3,000 feet above the Pacific Ocean. Mountain-to-ocean views and vistas across the lush Nualolo Valley make this a premier hike in the canyon. Combine with the Awa'awapahi Trail (above) for a day-long, near-loop hike.

The Kuia Natural Reserve Area occupies 1,636 acres and provides critical habitats for a variety of threatened and endangered plants. In recent years, the government has erected steel-mesh fencing in the reserve to keep out pigs, goats, and deer. Browsing and trampling by these animals destroys individual plants and damages native forest systems by destabilizing soils, hastening erosion, and facilitating weed invasion. You'll see some of this fence along the trail.

Follow the trail signs, turning left on a narrow path leading into a shady forest of native koa trees. The trail begins with a gradual 300-foot ascent over Kaunuohua Ridge, but don't let this fool you. You'll be going downhill for most of this hike (until the return!). In ¼ mile, you'll enter the Kuia Natural Area Reserve.

1 Anaki Hunter Trail Junction Grab your walking poles and put on your game face for the steep slip and slide down the trail. Switchbacks descend through dense forest of ferns, strawberry guava, karaka nut, eucalyptus, and kahili ginger. Also, keep your eyes open for iliau plants. This rare plant is related to the better-known silverswords of Maui and the Big Island, but is found only on the island of Kauai. The trail alternates from wide to narrow but continues its relentless descent. About 2 miles in, you'll begin to have views into the Mahanaloa and Kuia valleys and out to sea. Through the trees, you can get a glimpse of the island of Niihau. At 3¼ miles, you'll reach the junction with the Anaki Hunter Trail, leading to the left. Stay right on the Nualolo Trail.

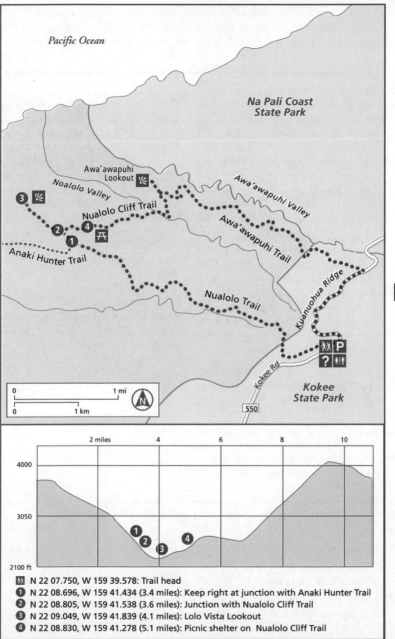

N 22 07.750, W 159 39.578: Trail head
1 N 22 08.696, W 159 41.434 (3.4 miles): Keep right at junction with Anaki Hunter Trail
2 N 22 08.805, W 159 41.538 (3.6 miles): Junction with Nualolo Cliff Trail
3 N 22 09.049, W 159 41.839 (4.1 miles): Lolo Vista Lookout
4 N 22 08.830, W 159 41.278 (5.1 miles): Picnic shelter on Nualolo Cliff Trail

The Koa Tree

The koa is one of the tallest trees in Hawaii, and koa wood was once used by early Hawaiians to make dugout canoes. You'll see a host of koa products and souvenirs throughout the islands, including handmade bowls, vases, platters, sculptures, furniture, and koa-carved ukuleles.

② Nualolo Cliff Trail Junction The trail dips further and the views open up more as you work your way down the knee-throbbing drop to the Nualolo Cliff Trail junction, at 3¹⁄₂ miles. From this spot, you'll have views straight out of a "Best of Hawaii" calendar: the forested Kawaiula Valley to your left, Nualolo Valley to the right, jagged sea cliffs and the Pacific Ocean straight ahead.

③ Lolo Vista Lookout Don't even think about not going out to the Lolo Vista Lookout—unless it's windy or raining, when the wide-open, exposed trail can be dangerous. Otherwise this 0.8-mile up-and-back hike to the edge of the giant promontory that overlooks the Na Pali Coast is worth every extra step.

Crane your neck for a breathtaking look down the remote and rugged coastline, where valleys spill into the ocean, pinched by soaring sea cliffs. In the distance, you'll see Kalalau Beach, a sugar-white swath fronting the green-hued Kalalau Valley.

④ Picnic Shelter After trekking out to the Lolo Vista Lookout, return to the Nualolo Cliff Trail junction and turn left onto the trail. The 2.1-mile trail follows an upper ridgeline in the Nualolo Valley, connecting the Nualolo and Awa'awapuhi trails. The trail is fairly level, traversing grassy meadows, dotted with Kauai hibiscus trees.

About a half-mile in, there's a small picnic area, with views out to the ocean and sea cliffs and into the verdant Nualolo Valley. Continue 1.5 miles to the Awa'awapuhi Trail junction. Turn left and hike another quarter-mile to the wide-open Awa'awapuhi Lookout for more valley-to-sea-cliff-to-ocean views. Turn back and re-trace your steps, or continue on the Awa'awapuhi Trail.

ILIAU NATURE LOOP (Kids)

Difficulty rating: Easy

Distance: 0.3 miles round-trip

Estimated time: 30 minutes

Elevation gain: 40 feet

Costs/permits: None

Pet-friendly: Dogs must be kept on a 6-foot or shorter leash.

Best time to go: All year; we like it best in late afternoon when the setting sun lights up the canyon walls.

Website: www.hawaiitrails.org/trail. php?TrailID=KA+04+005

Recommended map: The "Recreation Map of Western Kauai" is available from the Division of Forestry and Wildlife (3060 Elwa St. #306 Lihue, HI 96766).

Trail head GPS: N 22 03.096 W 159 39.588

Trail head directions: From Waimea, take Hwy. 550 to just before the 9-mile marker. Trail head signs for both the Kukui Trail (see "Kukui Trail," below) and Iliau Nature Loop are on the right. Park on the shoulder of the road.

This easy, roadside stroll traverses a flat plateau with awesome views over the western rim of Waimea Canyon and offers a nice sampling of Hawaii's indigenous and endemic plants. Interpretive signs identify the plants and explain their medicinal and ancient cultural uses. It's a great introduction to some of the plants that you'll spot on other trails.

Note: You can start the trail to the left or right; this description follows the clockwise route.

Start by walking to your left to the first marker, where you'll find an indigenous and useful shrub.

❶ **Pukiawe** The leaves of this indigenous shrub are used to treat colds and headaches. Its red berries are used to make leis. Continue to the shady tree ahead.

❷ **Koa** Endemic to the Hawaiian Islands, the koa tree, meaning "strong and brave," is still abundant throughout the islands. Continue on the path to the 'uki plant.

❸ **'Uki** The hairy, barbed-leaf 'uki plant is endemic to all the Hawaiian Islands except Molokai. Part of the sedge family, it was once used to line the walls of ancient *hale* (houses) and in floral arrangements. The trail veers slightly to the right as you pass a variety of Hawaiian plants marked with interpretive signs. Be sure to stop at the a'ali'i bush.

❹ **A'ali'i** Indigenous to Hawaii, the seed capsules of this shrub are used in leimaking.

There have been fabulous views deep into the Waimea Canyon along the entire trail. But, as you round the bend here, take a moment to savor the sweeping, postcard-pretty vista. Stretched before you are the rainbow-colored ridges and folds of the canyon; in the distance you'll get a glimpse of Waialae Falls across the gorge, as they tumble down the sheer-sided slope.

Follow the path as it hugs the canyon, passing the Kukui Trail junction (see "Kukui Trail" sidebar below). Stop to read the next interpretive plant signs.

❺ **Kawelu & 'Uki'Uki** Kawelu grass is endemic to all the Hawaiian Islands, and was used for house thatching. The 'uki'uki plant is a member of the lily family and also endemic to the islands. Follow the path as it loops back to the trail head. Near the trail head, take note of the iliau plant.

❻ **Iliau** This stunning plant supplies the trail's name. Endemic to only the island of Kauai, it's the feature plant of the loop. It's an ancient member of the sunflower family and a relative of the silversword plant found on Maui and the Big Island. The plant, which can reach 40 feet high, flowers only once in its lifetime—showing off giant, daisy-like flowers—before it dies.

<u>212</u> Iliau Nature Loop

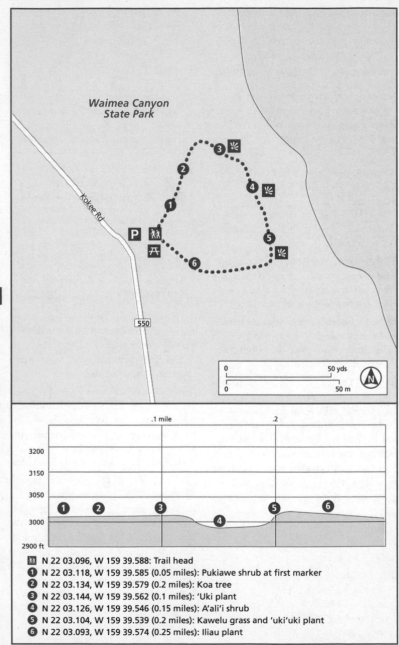

N 22 03.096, W 159 39.588: Trail head
1 N 22 03.118, W 159 39.585 (0.05 miles): Pukiawe shrub at first marker
2 N 22 03.134, W 159 39.579 (0.2 miles): Koa tree
3 N 22 03.144, W 159 39.562 (0.1 miles): 'Uki plant
4 N 22 03.126, W 159 39.546 (0.15 miles): A'ali'i shrub
5 N 22 03.104, W 159 39.539 (0.2 miles): Kawelu grass and 'uki'uki plant
6 N 22 03.093, W 159 39.574 (0.25 miles): Iliau plant

Kukui Trail

For extended, extraordinary views of Waimea Canyon, take the plunge down the steep Kukui Trail. The trail heads for both the Kukui and Iliau Nature trails (see "Iliau Nature Loop," above) are located on Hwy. 550, just before the 9-mile marker. Diehards can hike the entire 2-mile trail, descending 2,300 feet to the canyon floor, but they'll have to hike back up (ouch!). There's no need to punish yourself (unless you want to); hike as far as you like and turn around and come back. There are lookout benches at the quarter- and half-mile marks and stunning viewpoints all the way down. It's okay for kids, but pay attention to how far you're descending. Look back—that's what you have to climb back up!

Consider skipping the stopover at busy Waimea Canyon Lookout, farther up the road; it's a magnet for tourists, bus tours, and guided groups. Iliau is less crowded and the views into the canyon are just as jaw-dropping. There are also picnic tables and benches, making it an ideal roadside stop

Up for more walking? This is also where the Kukui Trail (see "Kukui Trail" above) begins, giving you an option of continuing on into the canyon, on a switchback

descent. Go as far as you like, but remember you have to climb back out!

If you're in the mood for hot and fresh fish tacos or shrimp, don't miss **Waimea Shrimp Station** (9652 Kaumualii Hwy.; *(C)* **808/338-1242**). This roadside shack in Waimea is an inexpensive and tasty option for hikers returning from Koke'e or Waimea Canyon outings.

POLIHALE BEACH TRAIL

Difficulty rating: Easy to moderate

Distance: Wander as long and far as you like, up to 17 miles one-way.

Estimated time: Varies

Elevation gain: 0 to 200 feet

Costs/permits: No permits are required to visit or hike. To camp on the beach, you need a permit from the Division of Forestry & Wildlife. The fee is $5 per person per night.

Pet-friendly: No.

Best time to go: All year. Winter, from November through March, is best for walking, since the beach can be extremely hot at other times. However, the surf is big in the wintertime.

Website: www.hawaiistateparks.org/parks/kauai/Index.cfm?park_id=5

Recommended map: You can get information on Polihale Beach State Park from the Division of State Parks (3060 Elwa St., Rm. 306 Lihue, HI 96766).

Trail head GPS: N 22 05.223 W 159 45.310

Trail head directions: From Waimea, take Hwy. 50 west to the end of the paved road. The beach is located just past the Pacific Missile Range Facility. A sign points to a dirt cane-hauling road that bears to the left. Continue straight on the dirt road for 5 miles to Polihale. The state park is at the north end of the beach. This road is rough and covered with potholes. If you're driving a rental car, review your rental agreement before taking a ride to Polihale, and do not drive on the beach. A four-wheel-drive vehicle is best. After taking the fork to the left of the monkey pod tree, park your car and head north.

This idyllic beach stood in for Bali Hai in the movie South Pacific, so it's no wonder that many locals call it their favorite spot on Kauai. Given that the beach road is poor, and signage skimpy, you may get the sense they want to keep it to themselves. The vast, isolated beach, stretching for 17 miles, boasts sweeping dunes, wild surf, and no crowds. It's the state's longest beach and one of its most serene and picturesque. (According to ancient Hawaiian mythology, Polihale was the gateway to the afterworld.) Enjoy a walk on this magical beach, in the shadows of the Na Pali Coast.

Walk north along the beach and look ahead. At the 3.4-mile mark on the beach road, take a left at the large monkey pod tree to get to Queen's Pond and the south end of the beach. This is a good option if it's a hot day (it usually is!) and you plan to take a swim. Or, take a right and head toward the small, marked parking lot. (If it's closed, park along the road and walk in.) That's the north end of the beach, where your dune-side stroll will take you toward the towering Na Pali Coast. Either way, you'll enjoy miles of luscious beach, 100-foot dunes, and dramatic surf as you wander. Look to the southwest for views of Niihau on a clear day.

❶ **Queen's Pond** You'll see Queen's Pond, a 3,000-foot-wide, encircled reef area. Typically calm, except during winter months when high surf watches over it, this area is the safest swimming zone on Polihale. Since the beach can be scorching hot, you may want to save this experience as a refreshing post-hike reward!

❷ **Campsites** As you walk the beach to the north, you'll see evidence of Polihale State Park: a string of campsites nestled in

the dunes, plus covered picnic pavilions (welcome shade) and restrooms. Talk about a room with a view! Continue past the campsites, taking in the pristine views of windswept sand dunes and crashing surf, as you walk toward the cliffs ahead.

❸ **Polihale Heiau** The ruins of an ancient temple (heiau) sit at the base of Polihale Cliff, located at the northern end of the beach past the campsites. According to Hawaiian legend, this is the place where the dead departed the earth. It's a spiritual spot, a perfect place to reflect upon the beauty of the island—and watch the fiery sun slip into the surf. You'll need to retrace your steps from here back to the car. Once there, you can head south for more beach walking! But, please heed the warning signs.

❹ **Warning Signs** At the state park's parking lot, and at several points along the beach, signs are posted that warn of strong current, high surf, and dangerous shore breaks, plus the favorite local admonition: "When in doubt, don't go out." This isn't just overwrought lawyer-speak; people (mostly tourists) are swept out to sea here

ⓘ **Tips** **Know Before You Go**

Bring lots of water and snacks; there are no vendors here. Also, avoid swimming in the ocean due to dangerous shore breaks, strong currents, and high surf. The protected Queen's Pond lagoon is the safest spot for a dip.

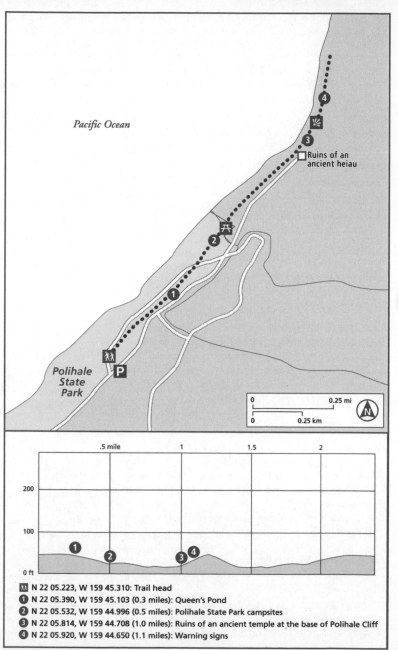

N 22 05.223, W 159 45.310: Trail head
1 N 22 05.390, W 159 45.103 (0.3 miles): Queen's Pond
2 N 22 05.532, W 159 44.996 (0.5 miles): Polihale State Park campsites
3 N 22 05.814, W 159 44.708 (1.0 miles): Ruins of an ancient temple at the base of Polihale Cliff
4 N 22 05.920, W 159 44.650 (1.1 miles): Warning signs

on a regular basis. In winter, in particular, when heavy weather comes in from Alaska, the seas can be unbelievably rough. Even walkers can be swept away in seconds. Err on the side of caution and save the swimming for Queen's Pond—and only there if it's safe. (In winter, Queen's Pond can also be a dicey proposition.)

MAHAULEPU HERITAGE TRAIL ★

Difficulty rating: Easy

Distance: 4 miles round-trip

Estimated time: 3 hr., but plan on more to swim, sunbathe, and linger

Elevation gain: 100 feet

Costs/permits: None

Pet-friendly: Dogs must be on a leash.

Best time to go: November through March, when humpback whales are migrating offshore

Website: www.hikemahaulepu.org

Recommended map: Colored brochures marking points of interest along the path are available from the Poipu

Beach Foundation (☎ 808/742-7444; www.hikemahaulepu.org) and at several major Poipu Beach hotels and resorts.

Trail head GPS: N 21 52.406 W 159 26.136 (at Shipwrecks Beach) N 21 53.564 W 159 24.638 (at Mahaulepu Beach)

Trail head directions: Take Hwy. 50 to Koloa Road (Hwy. 530) and follow to Poipu Road; turn right. Take the left fork toward the ocean. Shipwrecks Beach, where this hike begins, is in front of the Grand Hyatt Kauai. Take the public access walkway between the Hyatt and Po'ipu Bay Resort Golf Course.

This not-to-be-missed, unmarked seaside trail travels the island's southern coastline from Shipwrecks Beach on Ke-one-loa Bay to remote and stunning Mahaulepu Beach near Ka-wai-loa Bay. Along the trail you'll discover rugged sea cliffs, secluded coves, dunes, tide pools, sculpted lava formations, native plants, and petroglyphs. The beach, also the site of a legendary battle during the 1300s, has prime whale-watching in the winter, and is a favorite hangout for endangered monk seals.

Begin this hike at Shipwrecks Beach on Ke-one-loa Bay. The beach was named after a shipwreck that occurred during the 1970s, but the wreck is long gone now. Walk the beach (usually not safe for swimming) and then head toward Maka-wehi Point, the sand dunes at the southern edge of the beach. The path is unmarked, but easy enough to follow along the water's edge. *Caution:* Some of the sand dunes and cliffs are eroded. Stay away from the edges.

❶ **Pa'a Dunes** Continue along the coastline; you'll see Pa'a Dunes straight ahead. If you're here during the winter months, from November through March,

you'll want to stop for awhile at these dunes, since this is a prime humpback whale-watching spot (the endangered whales migrate from Alaska to the Hawaiian Islands to breed). Green sea turtles are also frequently seen swimming and feeding in the waters here.

❷ **Rocky Formations** Walk the sandy path, flanked by ironwood trees and dotted with dainty naupaka flowers. Look ahead, just to the right of the small bay, and you'll see interesting limestone formations. Here, bones from two extinct species of a flightless goose and an owl, and other extinct forest birds, some dating back to 3,000 to 4,000 B.C., have also been

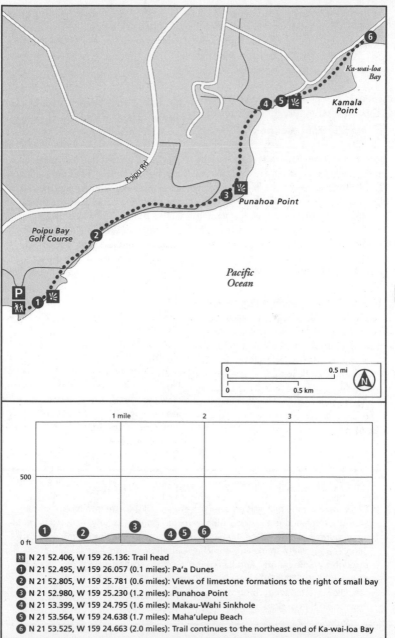

N 21 52.406, W 159 26.136: Trail head

1 N 21 52.495, W 159 26.057 (0.1 miles): Pa'a Dunes

2 N 21 52.805, W 159 25.781 (0.6 miles): Views of limestone formations to the right of small bay

3 N 21 52.980, W 159 25.230 (1.2 miles): Punahoa Point

4 N 21 53.399, W 159 24.795 (1.6 miles): Makau-Wahi Sinkhole

5 N 21 53.564, W 159 24.638 (1.7 miles): Maha'ulepu Beach

6 N 21 53.525, W 159 24.663 (2.0 miles): Trail continues to the northeast end of Ka-wai-loa Bay

found. Circle the pretty cove to the "fishing temple," an ancient place of worship.

❸ Punahoa Point The footpath skirts the cove as it heads to Punahoa Point, formed by swirling sand and wind some 350,000 years ago. They're the oldest sand dunes along this coast. Watch out for the metal and PVC pipes sticking out of the ground. These are fishing-pole holders. This is a popular place for Kauai anglers.

❹ Makau-Wahi Sinkhole The trail meanders under a canopy of tall kiawe trees before coming to a fork. Stay straight and you'll head directly to Mahaulepu Beach. Instead, veer to the left. In a short distance, another worn footpath leads to the right. Stay straight for a peek at a small sinkhole. This is a tiny portion of the largest limestone cave in Hawaii. The trail loops back down toward the ocean, crossing Wai-o-pili Stream and landing at Mahaulepu Beach.

❺ Mahaulepu Beach This beautiful beach is a wide ribbon of sugar-white sand, flanked by lowland shrubs and kiawe trees. There's plenty of elbow room, and it's rarely crowded. The beach was the site of an historic battle in the 1300s when the ruling chief of Kauai defeated the advances of Ka-lau-nui-o-Hua, a Big Island ruler, who had a plan to take over all the Hawaiian Islands.

 This spot is a scenic and peaceful haven. Throw down a beach towel and soak up some sun rays! The water is usually calm enough for swimming, too. But don't stay too long. The best of this coastal trail is up next.

❻ Sea Cliffs, Blowholes & Monk Seals Head northeast, climbing the sand- and pebble-strewn cliff trail, an easy, gradual ascent to Kamala Point. This stretch of trail is the best place to see a beached monk seal. The lumpy monk seals gorge on food all night and then sleep on the warm beach sand during the day (not unlike a lot of Kauai visitors!).

Continue climbing the worn path to Kamala Point, sticking out into Ka-wai-loa Bay, where you'll have up-close views of the powerful surf, which has helped form these coastal sand dunes and shape the coastline. *Whoof!* You'll hear the sound and fury of the surf below as you stand on the ledge.

Keep going, hiking down the ledge, as you begin to circle around Ka-wai-loa Bay. As you descend, look for the spray of a blowhole ahead. Along the way, you may want to spend a few moments poking around the tide pools that line the bay; look for crabs and shrimp scurrying around the rocks.

All the Outdoor Fun You Can Handle, & Then Some

Yeah, we know the hiking is amazing on Kauai, but if you're into multi-sports, consider some of these options: biking, scuba diving, glider flying, horseback riding, mountain tubing (through an old sugar plantation ditch system), river paddling, sea kayaking, snorkeling, stand-up paddling, surfing, and zip-lining through a jungle canopy. And, of course, you can mix-and-match 'em—**Kayak Kauai** (✆ 800/437-3507; www.kayakkauai.com) offers paddle-snorkel and paddle-hike-waterfall swim combos, plus a 6-day multi-sport adventure deal. For rentals and tour options, visit www.kauaidiscovery.com. Knock yourself out!

The trail officially ends at the northeast end of Ka-wai-loa Bay, but several well-worn paths climb Papa-mo-i Point, the tall sand dune in front of you. So, if you haven't yet had enough beautiful views, go for it. Then, turn around and head back to the car. We typically shun up-and-back, re-trace your step trails, but this is not a bad one to repeat.

SLEEPING & EATING

ACCOMMODATIONS

Hanalei Bay Resort & Suites This 22-acre, beachfront resort overlooking the fabled Bali Hai Cliffs and Hanalei Bay recaptures the spirit of Old Hawaii. Rooms are decorated in island style, with rattan furnishings, lanais overlooking the bay, lush grounds, and distant mountains.

5380 Honoiki St., Princeville. HI 96722. ℂ **800/827-4427** or 808/826-6522. www.hanaleibayresort.com. 236 units. $205–$295 double. AE, DC, DISC, MC, V. **Close to:** Hanalei River Trail, Hanalei 'Okolehao Trail.

★ **Kiahuna Plantation Resort** This condo complex consists of several plantation-style buildings loaded with Hawaiian style and sprinkled around a 35-acre garden setting with lagoons, lawns, and a gold-sand beach. Golf, shopping, and restaurants are within easy walking distance. All condo units are spacious, with full kitchens, daily maid service, and lanais.

2253 Poipu Rd., Koloa, HI 96756. ℂ **800/OUTRIGGER** (688-7444) or 808/742-6411. www.outrigger.com. 333 units. $229–$415 1-bedroom. AE, DC, DISC, MC, V. **Close to:** Mahaulepu Heritage Trail.

★ **Outrigger Waipouli Beach Resort & Spa** Nestled on 13 acres between Wailua and Kapa'a, this luxurious beach resort features spacious, high-end condos furnished with top-of-the-line accoutrements (think granite counters, Sub-Zero and Wolf appliances, and flatscreen TVs). There are also an Aveda spa, fitness center, and a saltwater pool, and you're in walking distance to shops and restaurants.

4–820 Kuhio Hwy., Kapa'a, HI 96746. ℂ **800/OUTRIGGER** (688-7444) or 808/823-8300. www.outrigger. com. 196 units. $309–$335 1-bedroom. 2-night minimum. AE, DC, DISC, MC, V. **Close to:** Sleeping Giant Trail, Kuilau Ridge Trail.

Finds **Aloha Sunrise Inn/Aloha Sunset Inn** Set on a 7-acre farm on the North Shore, these cottages have hardwood floors, top-of-the-line bedding, tropical-island decor, full kitchens, and more (including an excellent video and CD library). Close to activities, restaurants, and shopping, yet far enough away to feel the peace and quiet of Old Hawaii.

P.O. Box 79, Kilauea, HI 96754. ℂ **888/828-1008** or 808/828-1100. www.kauaisunrise.com. 2 units (2 people each). $185. Cleaning fee $95. 3-night minimum. No credit cards. **Close to:** Kalalua Trail, Hanakapi'ai Falls Trail.

Waimea Plantation Cottages A good base for exploring Waimea Canyon and Kokee State Park, these lovely beachfront sugar-plantation cottages have been transformed into cozy, comfortable guest units with period rattan and wicker furniture. Each has a furnished lanai and a fully equipped modern kitchen and bathroom; some units are oceanfront.

9400 Kaumualii Hwy., Waimea HI 96796. ℂ **866/774-2924** or 808/338-1625. www.waimea-plantation. com. 48 units. $209–$360 1-bedroom. AE, DC, DISC, MC, V. **Close to:** Pihea & Alaka'i Trails, Awa'awapahi Trail, Nualolo Trail, Polihale Beach Trail.

Value Kokee Lodge   If you plan to spend time hiking Koke'e State Park and Waimea Canyon trails (and you should!), consider staying in one of these cabins. Older cabins have dormitory-style sleeping arrangements, while the new ones have two separate bedrooms each. Both styles sleep six and come with cooking utensils, bedding, and linens.

P.O. Box 819, Waimea. HI 96796. 📞 **808/335-6061.** www.kokeelodgekauai.com. 12 units. $90 double. Cleaning fee $20. Extra person $5. 5-night maximum. AE, DC, DISC, MC, V. **Close to:** Pihea & Alaka'i Trails, Awa'awapahi Trail, Nualolo Trail, Polihale Beach Trail.

Value Poipu Crater Resort   Here's a deal travelers on a budget can't beat: two-bedroom garden-view units for $100 (low season) to $150 a night! Each unit is about 1,500 square feet and comes complete with living area, full kitchen, large lanai, two bedrooms, and two baths. Poipu Beach is about a 10-minute walk away.

2330 Hoohu Rd., Koloa. HI 96796. 📞 **800/325-5701** or 808/742-2000. www.parrishkauai.com. 30 units. $100–$150 2-bedroom. 5-night minimum. AE, DISC, MC, V. **Close to:** Mahaulepu Heritage Trail.

Camping on Kauai

Camping is allowed at three state parks: Koke'e State Park, Polihalie, and Na Pali Coast State Wilderness Park. Apply for permits up to a year in advance from the **Hawaii State Parks Division** (P.O. Box 621, Honolulu, HI 96809; 📞 **808/587-0300;** www.hawaii stateparks.org). Permit applications are available online, but they must be sent via snail-mail. You can check availability by calling the state office. You can also get permits at the **Kauai Division Office** (3060 Elwa Street, Rm. 306 Lihue, HI 96766; 📞 **808/274-3444**). Camping is $5 per campsite, per night; $10 per campsite per night in Na Pali Coast State Wilderness Park.

There are also six small, rustic county parks where camping is allowed: Haena Beach Park, Hanalei Beach Park, Anini Beach Park, Anahola Beach Park, Hanamaulu Beach Park, Salt Pond Park, and Lucy Wright Park. All offer picnic tables and cold showers; some have river and waterfront sites. Permits are available from the **County of Kauai, Department of Parks & Recreation, Parks Permit Section** (📞 **808/241-4463;** www. kauai.gov). Permits cost $3 per adult, per night. Children under the age of 18 camping with an adult are free.

RESTAURANTS

Duke's Kauai STEAK/SEAFOOD   This oceanfront oasis is the hippest spot in town, with a winning combination of a great view, an affordable menu, and popular music. The five or six varieties of fresh fish are popular, as are quesadillas, steaks, and burgers. Hawaiian musicians serenade diners nightly.

At the Kauai Marriott Resort & Beach Club, 3610 Rice St., Nawiliwili. 📞 **808/246-9599.** www.dukeskauai. com. Reservations recommended. Main courses $15–$30. AE, DISC, MC, V. Daily 5–9pm. **Close to:** Mahaulepu Heritage Trail.

Hamura's Saimin Stand SAIMIN   If there was a *saimin* hall of fame, Hamura's would be in it—a renowned *saimin* stand where fans line up to take a spot at a few U-shaped counters that haven't changed in decades. The noodles come heaped with vegetables, won tons, hard-boiled eggs, and sweetened pork.

2956 Kress St., Lihue. 📞 **808/245-3271.** Most items under $7. No credit cards. Mon–Thurs 10am–10:30pm; Fri–Sat 10am–midnight; Sun 10am–9pm. **Close to:** Mahaulepu Heritage Trail.

Kids Hukilau Lanai ISLAND   Fresh, creatively prepared dishes, good portions, decent prices, and a lively, friendly atmosphere are drawing crowds to this casual eatery in Kapa'a. Start with tasty pupus, like ahi poke nachos, followed by one of the locally 221 caught fish entrees. The signature lava flow cake is the must-do dessert.

520 Akela Loop, Kapaa. © **808/822-0600.** www.hukilaukauai.com. Main courses $18–$28. AE, DC, DISC, MC, V. Tues–Sun 5–9pm. **Close to:** Sleeping Giant Trail, Kuilau Ridge Trail.

Mermaids Café HEALTHFUL/ISLAND   A focus on local ingredients and healthy preparations makes this tiny sidewalk cafe a standout. Try the peanut satay made with fresh lemon juice or the seared ahi wrap made with a homemade blend of garlic, jalapeño, lemon grass, kaffir lime, basil, and cilantro. The fresh-squeezed lemonade is made daily.

1384 Kuhio Hwy., Kapa'a. © **808/821-2026.** www.mermaidscafe.com. Most dishes $9–$10. DC, MC, V. Daily 11am–9pm. **Close to:** Mahaulepu Heritage Trail.

Ono Family Restaurant AMERICAN   Hit this place for a hefty breakfast before hitting the trail. Options include several variations of eggs benedict; banana, coconut, and macadamia-nut pancakes; and dozens of omelet choices. And, you gotta love a place that offers fried rice and meatloaf in the early morning hours.

4–1292 Kuhio Hwy., Kapa'a. © **808/822-1710.** Most items under $9. AE, DC, DISC, MC, V. Daily 7am–1:30pm. **Close to:** Sleeping Giant Trail, Kuilau Ridge Trail.

Tidepools SEAFOOD   Splurge-worthy and romantic, a cluster of thatched bunga-lows overlooks a lagoon in this dreamy open-air restaurant. The atmosphere would be reason enough to book a table, but the cuisine is just as outstanding. The restaurant's specialty is fresh fish, such as ginger-marinated ahi or roasted black bean sea bass.

At the Grand Hyatt Kauai Resort & Spa, 1571 Poipu Rd., Koloa. © **808/742-1234.** www.kauai.hyatt.com. Reservations recommended. Main courses $23–$43. AE, DC, DISC, MC, V. Daily 5:30–10pm. **Close to:** Mahaulepu Heritage Trail.

Kids Tip Top Café/Bakery LOCAL   This small, longstanding cafe/bakery serves one of the best breakfast deals in town. Most items are $5 or under, and the macadamia pancakes are renowned throughout Kauai. Lunch ranges from pork chops to teriyaki chicken, but the specialty is oxtail soup.

3173 Akahi St., Lihue. © **808/245-2333.** Breakfast $5 and under; lunch $6 and under. MC, V. Tues–Sun 6:30am–2pm. **Close to:** Sleeping Giant Trail, Kuilau Ridge Trail.

KAUAI HIKES

7

SLEEPING & EATING

Molokai Hikes

by Diane Bair & Pamela Wright

There's the rest of Hawaii, and then there's Molokai. Set in the center of the Hawaiian island chain, Molokai is lovely and aloof, a mysterious island stranger. The 38-mile-long volcanic island is largely ignored by the vacationing masses, and that's just the way the Molokaians want it. Home to more native Hawaiians than any other island, Molokai is aggressively un-touristy. "Come or don't come" is the attitude of most locals, who still cling to old Hawaiian traditions and live a very low-key lifestyle. "We don't want to become another Maui," islanders will tell you.

Suffice it to say that Molokai is not for everybody. If you're looking for luxe resorts, trendy eateries, snap-of-your-fingers-service, or nightlife, don't bother coming. Development is nil, and with the recent closing of Molokai Ranch, accommodations and guided activities are limited. But if you're willing to forego the scene for fabulous scenery—this is the place to go. Molokai is ruggedly windswept gorgeous, home to the world's tallest sea cliffs, Hawaii's longest beach, ancient fish ponds, and sacred sites.

It takes a bit of forethought and sense of adventure to hike on Molokai—a four-wheel-drive vehicle helps, too. Getting around the island on its main, two-lane road is easy and scenic; getting to some trail heads is another story. Who owns the land is a touchy, ongoing battle with island residents; a mish-mash of ancient deeds, traditional beliefs, private plots, and protected lands raises a fair number of access issues and confusion. In some instances, you'll need to join a guided hike or tour, for others, a bumpy, four-wheel-drive and a hike down washed-out dirt roads is required. No matter: It's all worth it.

Maintained and marked trails on Molokai are few and far between, but they're gems! On the rugged, isolated north shore you can descend 2,000-foot sea cliffs to Kalaupapa National Historic Park, home to the infamous Molokai leper colony. On the island's northwest coast, hikers can access one of the last remaining intact beach and sand dunes in Hawaii, a wild, pristine environment for native plants and nesting endangered green sea turtles. In Molokai's northeast corner, a boardwalk trail through Kamakou Preserve traverses a native cloud forest and a high-elevation bog—a misty jungle of rare plants found nowhere else in the world. Finally, a hike through the steep, cathedral-like Halawa Valley takes you past ancient temples to the foot of Mo'oula Falls. The sacred valley, once home to *kahunas* (Hawaiian priests), is considered one of the most culturally significant spots in all of Hawaii.

Much of Molokai is relatively undiscovered and untrammeled. Next time, stay longer, hang with the locals, and who knows? They may take you on one of their favorite—unknown—hikes into Molokai's beautiful wilderness.

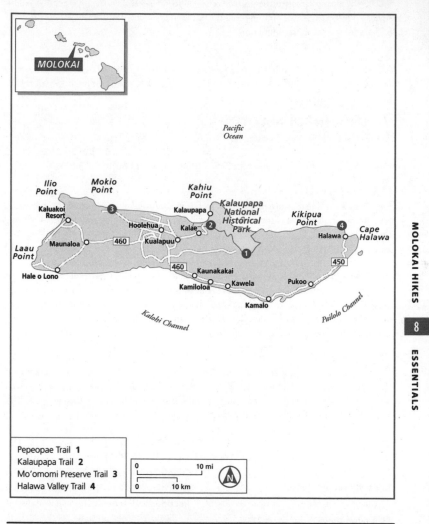

Pacific
Ocean

Ilio
Point

Mokio
Point

Kahiu
Point

Kalaupapa

Kalaupapa
National
Historical
Park

Kikipua
Point

Kaluakoi
Resort

3

Hoolehua

Kalae

2

Cape
Halawa

Halawa

4

Laau
Point

Maunaloa

460

Kualapuu

1

450

Hale o Lono

460

Kaunakakai

Kamiloloa

Kawela

Pukoo

Kamalo

Kalohi Channel

Pailolo Channel

Pepeopae Trail **1**
Kalaupapa Trail **2**
Mo'omomi Preserve Trail **3**
Halawa Valley Trail **4**

| 0 | 10 mi |
| 0 | 10 km |

N

MOLOKAI HIKES

8

ESSENTIALS

ESSENTIALS

GETTING THERE
By Air

Most flights arrive at the **Molokai Airport (MKK)**, located about 4 miles west of
Kualapuu on Maunaloa Highway (© **808/567-6361**; www6.hawaii.gov/dot/airports/
molokai/mkk/index.htm). The airport has two runways that accommodate commuter/
air taxi and general inter-island flights.

Several airlines offer inter-island flights, including **Hawaiian Airlines** (✆ **800/367-5320;** www.hawaiianair.com), **go!/Mesa** (✆ **888/435-9462;** www.iflygo.com), **Island Air** (✆ **800/652-6541** or 808/484-2222; www.islandair.com), and **Pacific Wings** (✆ **888/575-4546;** www.pacificwings.com).

By Ferry

Molokai Princess (✆ **866/307-6524;** www.molokaiferry.com) offers twice-daily ferry service from Lahaina Harbor on Maui to Kaunakakai Wharf on Molokai, aboard a 100-foot yacht accommodating 150 passengers.

VISITOR INFORMATION

There's no walk-in visitor center on Molokai, but you can get online information at www.molokai-hawaii.com. You can also mail requests to Molokai Visitors Association, 2 Kamoi St., Suite 200, Kaunakakai, HI 96748, or phone ✆ **808/553-3876.**

ORIENTATION

First: rent a car. There is no public transportation on Molokai and limited taxi service. A four-wheel-drive vehicle is necessary to access several of the major trail heads, including the Pepeopae Trail in Kamakou Preserve and the Mo'omomi Preserve trails. The good news is that driving on Molokai is a delight. The island, which is 38 miles long and 10 miles wide, has no lights or stop signs. One main highway (Hwy. 450/460) traverses the island from east to west and connects all the major towns and sites. Hwy. 470 provides access to Kalaupapa and the north shore. Sleepy and slow-paced Kaunakakai—a 3-block cluster of small, local stores and markets—is the commercial hub (and pretty much the only place to get food and supplies on the island). It's centrally located on the south shore, and just 8 miles from the airport.

WEATHER

It's nearly always pleasant and warm on Molokai, with average temperatures hovering in the high 70s (low 20s Celsius) to low 80s (high 20s Celsius). The east side of the island is wetter than the west end; clouds, mist, and fog shroud the mountain tops and sea cliffs. On average, January is the rainiest month of the year.

PEPEOPAE TRAIL ★★★

Difficulty rating: Moderate

Distance: 3 miles loop

Estimated time: 1½ hr.

Elevation gain: 600 feet

Costs/permits: No fee unless you join the Nature Conservancy's monthly hike, which is $25 paid in advance.

Pet-friendly: No

Best time to go: During dry weather, from April to October, when the access road is passable (with a four-wheel-drive vehicle)

Website: www.nature.org

Recommended map: Check in with the Nature Conservancy office (✆ 808/553-5236), just outside of Kaunakakai, before entering the preserve. They can provide up-to-date information on road and trail conditions and have a map of the preserve, showing designated trails and boundaries.

Trail head GPS: N 21 07.089 W 156 54.489

Trail head directions: From Kaunakakai, go west on Hwy. 460 for 3.5 miles. Turn right before the bridge at the Homelani Cemetery sign onto Maunahui Road/ Molokai Forest Reserve Road. This turns into a dirt road at about ¼ mile, just past the cemetery. Pass through the Molokai Forest Reserve to about the 10-mile point and the Waikolu Lookout. The Kamakou Preserve begins here. Continue on the rough-going road (a four-wheel-drive vehicle is a must, and still the road may be impassable) until the road splits. Do not turn right; instead stay to the left fork. You may have to walk these last 2 miles to reach the trail head if the road is washed out. The road ends at the clearly marked trail head and lookout platform. The trip to the trail head can take 45 to 90 minutes.

This exquisite trail is located in Kamakou Preserve, in a remote mountainous region of northeast Molokai. The boardwalk trail climbs through dense native cloud forest to Pepeopae Bog, a fragile bog ecosystem. It ends at a stunning overlook into Pelekunu Valley. The 2,774-acre preserve, near the summit of Molokai's highest mountain, is home to more than 250 species of Hawaiian plants, at least 219 of which can be found nowhere else in the world.

Getting to the trail head is the toughest part of this hike, but there are some interesting stops along the way. You'll notice the dry, dusty landscape changes as you ascend the road and enter the forest. Along Maunahui Road/Molokai Forest Reserve Road, on your ride to the trail head, look for the Sandalwood Pit on your left, at about the 9-mile mark. The 75-foot-long hole was dug in the early 1800s by King Kamehameha's men to replicate the cargo hold of a ship. Sandalwood, which grew in the forests above Waikolu Valley, was cut and placed in the pit. When the pit was filled, the wood was carried down to a ship and exported to China.

Farther up the road, less than 1 mile from the pit, is Waikolu Lookout, perched on a ridge at 3,700 feet. Waikolu means "three waters" in Hawaiian, and you'll see why: The green-velvet valley is decorated with waterfalls.

There's a small, primitive camping area near the lookout (see "Accommodations," later in this chapter). The road ends at another lookout, with lofty views of the valley cleft. The well-marked trail begins at 4,000 feet, adjacent to the lookout platform. The boardwalk, built by volunteers to help protect the bog's fragile environment, enters the wet, primeval-looking forest.

Be sure to wear good-gripping boots, as the boardwalk gets very slippery.

❶ The Jungle It's pristine, misty, mystical, and magical! There is nothing quite like this oozy, top-of-the-mountain forest. Follow the always-wet boardwalk through a dense jungle of ferns and flowers, where water trickles and pools everywhere, bugs chirp, and birds—including flocks of apapane birds—flitter. The trail begins to climb gently—watch your footing—as it meanders through the bog. Tree ferns blanket the ground; tree branches are heavily draped in vines and trunks covered in mosses and lichen. Brilliant purple fiddleheads and native violets provide dramatic color against the shades of all-green backdrop. The colors are really amazing, especially as sun rays periodically filter through the canopy.

❷ Open Plateau Follow the twisting boardwalk through the bog until you reach an open plateau—and another world! At about a half-mile, the views open up as you travel across a brilliant landscape of alani and red, yellow, and orange blossoming ohia bushes. Mountain peaks, shrouded in clouds, loom in the distance.

MOLOKAI HIKES

8

PEPEOPAE TRAIL

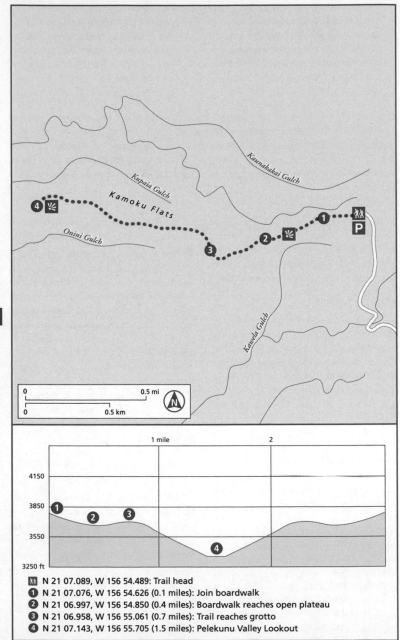

N 21 07.089, W 156 54.489: Trail head
1 N 21 07.076, W 156 54.626 (0.1 miles): Join boardwalk
2 N 21 06.997, W 156 54.850 (0.4 miles): Boardwalk reaches open plateau
3 N 21 06.958, W 156 55.061 (0.7 miles): Trail reaches grotto
4 N 21 07.143, W 156 55.705 (1.5 miles): Pelekunu Valley Lookout

> ### (Finds) Head to the Beach
>
> Guidebooks will direct you to Papohaku Beach in western Molokai. But keep going. About 5 miles past Papohaku Beach Park, turn right at the end of the road, and you'll come to Dixie Maru Beach. Named after a shipwreck, this lovely scoop of tawny sand is one of the only swimmable beaches on the island. There are no facilities here, but there's plenty of shade, sand, and inviting water.

Veer right at the fork in the trail to walk to the first lookout, where you'll have fine views of mountain peaks and deep valley clefts.

Leave the outlook, following the boardwalk as it loops into the enchanted forest of mosses, ferns, and twisty palms.

❸ **Grotto** The trail continues to drop down through the jungle-y forest. It becomes very slippery and slow-going as you maneuver the narrow, wet boards. At about three-quarters of a mile into the hike, you'll come to a very picturesque grotto, surrounded by dripping walls of mosses, ferns, and trickling water.

❹ **Pelekunu Valley Lookout** Just when you think you've seen all this marvelous trail has to offer, you'll reach the second lookout, about 1 mile from your start.

Hope you brought your camera! From a small, grassy perch on the ridge, you'll have a stunning, eagle's-eye look at mountains, valleys, and waterfalls—unless misty clouds are obscuring the view. In any case, you'll want to spend some time here. It's the perfect spot for a lunch break.

The trail continues a steady descent on switchbacks as it makes its way back to the trail head.

Note: Kamakou Preserve is so beautiful that you may not want to leave. Stick around! After completing the Pepeopae Trail, take another hike. The 2-mile long Puu Kolekole Trail begins at the same spot and leads through a cloud forest to the 3,951-foot summit of Puu Kolekole.

KALAUPAPA TRAIL

Difficulty rating: Strenuous

Distance: 4 miles round-trip

Estimated time: 7 to 8 hr., including a 4-hr. required tour of the peninsula

Elevation gain: 1,600 feet

Costs/permits: You'll need to do one of four things: Get permission from the Hawaii Department of Health, be a guest of someone living in the settlement, book a mule-ride tour (see information at the end of this hike review), or book a $40 per person tour with Damien Tours (© 808/567-6171, 7–9am or 5–7pm) before you can hike the trail and enter

the park. No one under 16 years of age is allowed in the park.

Pet-friendly: No

Best time to go: All year, but you'll need to be on the trail by at least 8am to catch the required tour.

Website: www.nps.gov/kala

Recommended map: None

Trail head GPS: N 21 10.299 W 156 59.885

Trail head directions: The trail begins near Palaau State Park close to the end of Hwy. 470, just above the Molokai Mule Ride barn.

MOLOKAI HIKES

8

KALAUPAPA TRAIL

This dramatic trail on a remote peninsula drops nearly 2,000 feet over soaring sea cliffs before reaching Kalaupapa National Historic Park, home to the infamous Molokai leper colony. The disease, likely spread to Hawaii from China, was first thought to be highly contagious (it's not) and incurable (they have since discovered treatment for it). Those inflicted were banished from their homes and sent to fend for themselves on this remote and rugged peninsula. Father Damien deVeuster, a Catholic priest from Belgium, arrived in 1873 and helped the patients build homes and churches and arranged for medical supplies and schooling. Today, Kaluapapa comprises a small settlement situated on the leeward side of the peninsula, and is home to surviving Hansen's Disease patients and their families. The site became a national park in 1980.

The trail begins as a wide swath under a shady forest; it is well marked and easy to follow. However, you'll pass several warning signs at the start, telling you that you must have permission to be on the trail and to enter the Kalaupapa National Historic Park. Alas, you do (see "Costs/permits," above).

Follow the wide path to a sign marking the entrance to Kalauapapa National Historic Park, and a large sign warning you not to enter without permission. The trail turns into a series of hundreds of descending, uneven, concrete-and-rock steps. Someone spent oodles of time and money building these steps, but they make it more difficult to navigate the descent as they don't accommodate your natural gait and rhythm. Oh well; the views, coming up, are worth the extra effort.

❶ First Lookout The trail, which was built as a supply route for mule trains, is marked in switchbacks, 26 in total from the trail head to the end (unlike the typical mile markers). You'll descend the first 10 switchbacks, round a corner, and get your first full view of sea cliffs, sandy beach, and the small settlement below.

❷ Sea Cliffs By now, you've likely picked up a walking stick along the way to help navigate the seemingly never-ending steps down. You'll get into the rhythm: Step down, step down, circle around, step down, step down, circle around. You get the picture.

At around switchback 20, you'll get another good look at the dramatic north shore sea cliffs—the highest sea cliffs in the world. The trail turns a little rocky at the next switchback as it heads to the bottom.

❸ Switchback 26 Blessed relief! The steps end along with the steep descent as the trail flattens and crosses a rock-strewn ridge. Look for goats on the ledges above; to your left, you'll have glimpses of the ocean through the trees. A final, gentle drop lands you on a spectacular beach.

❹ The Beach The trail flanks the wide, smooth swath of straw-colored sand, littered with driftwood and shells. Endangered monk seals are often seen here; many come to the remote, pristine beach to give birth. The trail ends in a clearing, at a dirt road; it takes about 1.5 to 2 hours to hike to this point.

A port-a-potty is to your left. The parking lot where you'll meet Damien Tours is ahead to your right. The Makanalua Peninsula is breathtakingly, eerily beautiful. While generally referred to as Kalaupapa, the peninsula is actually divided into three areas. The Kalawao region sits on the eastern edge of the peninsula; Kalaupapa and the settlement of Kalaupapa is on the west; Makanalua is in the center. The Damien bus tour will not only give you information and background on the history of the settlement, but also a better look at the scenic areas of the peninsula.

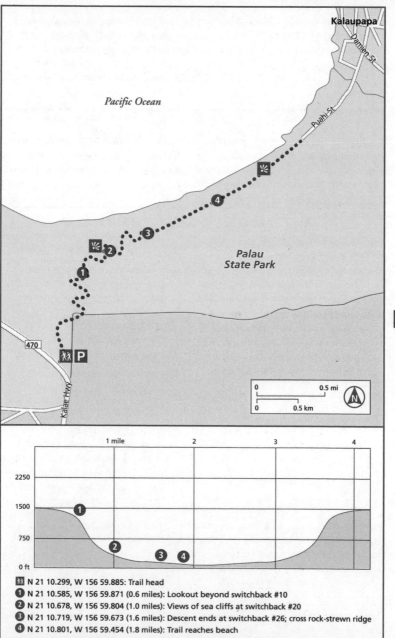

N 21 10.299, W 156 59.885: Trail head
1 N 21 10.585, W 156 59.871 (0.6 miles): Lookout beyond switchback #10
2 N 21 10.678, W 156 59.804 (1.0 miles): Views of sea cliffs at switchback #20
3 N 21 10.719, W 156 59.673 (1.6 miles): Descent ends at switchback #26; cross rock-strewn ridge
4 N 21 10.801, W 156 59.454 (1.8 miles): Trail reaches beach

Tips   Palaau State Park

Not up for the long, 1,500-vertical-foot, up-and-back hike on the Kalaupapa Trail or a muscle-jostling mule ride? You can still get a look at Molokai's steep, north shore sea cliffs and the Kalaupapa Peninsula and settlement at the Palaau State Park (www.hawaiistateparks.org/parks/molokai/Index.cfm?park_id=43). Walk the short trail to Kalaupapa Lookout and Phallic Rock, which was once thought to enhance fertility.

If there's anyone in your group who is not willing or able to hike the Kalaupapa Trail, they can always hop on a mule and meet you at the bottom. **Molokai Mule**

Ride (© **800/567-7550** or 808-567-6088; www.muleride.com) offers guided mule rides on the trail, Monday through Saturday.

MO'OMOMI PRESERVE TRAIL

Difficulty rating: Easy

Distance: 2 miles loop; or 8 miles if you need to walk the road to access the trail head

Estimated time: 2 hr. for trail, another 2 hr. or longer to walk the dirt road to the trail head. (If you join the Nature Conservancy's guided monthly hike—see "Nature Conservancy Hikes," below—you avoid the road walk.)

Elevation gain: Minimal.

Costs/permits: None, but you must pick up a key to the gate and leave a $25 deposit.

Pet-friendly: No

Best time to go: May through September

Website: www.nature.org

Recommended map: The local Nature Conservancy office (© 808/553-5236), just outside of Kaunakakai, can provide up-to-date trail and road conditions and also has a map of the preserve detailing trails and boundaries.

Trail head GPS: N 21 11.794 W 157 09.148

Trail head directions: Take Hwy. 480 to Farrington Road, which turns into Mo'omomi Road when the pavement ends. You'll pass a set of closure signs and a small road heading right into the Department of Hawaiian Homesteads. If the road is too rough, you may have to park here and walk the rest of the way to the trail head. In any case, head down the road toward the beach.

Here you'll be able to walk along the most intact beach and sand dune area in the main Hawaiian Islands. Wild, remote, windswept dunes stretch a mile long and hundreds of feet wide and shelter native grasses and shrubs and nesting endangered green sea turtles. However, getting to the official 2-mile Nature Conservancy trail is confusing and rough-going. It's do-able and worth it.

Here's the story: The Nature Conservancy doesn't really want ordinary folks climbing around the dunes unescorted, so there's no urgency to fix the public road to the trail head. This means, even with a four-wheel-drive vehicle, you'll have to park and walk Mo'omomi Road (up to 3 miles) to the coast and across the beach to the official

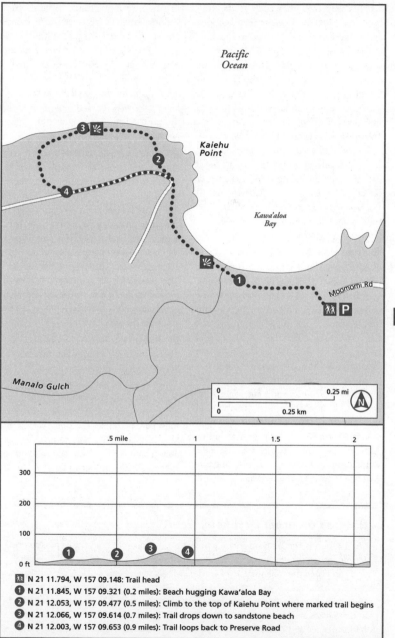

N 21 11.794, W 157 09.148: Trail head

1 N 21 11.845, W 157 09.321 (0.2 miles): Beach hugging Kawa'aloa Bay

2 N 21 12.053, W 157 09.477 (0.5 miles): Climb to the top of Kaiehu Point where marked trail begins

3 N 21 12.066, W 157 09.614 (0.7 miles): Trail drops down to sandstone beach

4 N 21 12.003, W 157 09.653 (0.9 miles): Trail loops back to Preserve Road

trail head (and the prettiest section of the preserve). However, there's an authorized-vehicles-only road that ends at the trail head that Nature Conservancy workers and volunteers use. So, if you join one of their monthly hikes, you'll be able to four-wheel-drive to the trail head, avoid the dirt-road trek, and start at the trail head for an easy 2-mile hike. No question, this is the best way to do it, but you'll need to sign up well in advance for the tour (see "Nature Conservancy Hikes," below).

Follow the red-dirt, pock-marked road straight, heading toward the coast. You'll pass the road on the right, near the water tanks, leading to the Department of Hawaiian Homesteads. Keep straight. The rolling Molokai ranchlands and Manalo Gulch are to your left.

❶ Kaawaloa Bay   You'll pass a couple of cattle gates and two more dirt roads, one to your left, another to your right. Ignore these, stay straight, sights on the coastline ahead. You'll end at a beach hugging Kaawaloa Bay. To your right, in the next cove beyond the bluff, is Mo'omomi Beach, nestled in front of the Hawaiian Homesteads. Walk left, across the beach.

Note: Swimming here is often dangerous, due to the rocky shoreline and strong waves and currents. Locals attempt it in the calmer summer months, but play it safe and leave your bathing suit at home. Also, there are no facilities here, so take water, snacks, sunscreen, and anything else you might need for the day's jaunt.

❷ Kaiehu Point   Make your way up the rocky hill to the top of Kaiehu Point. You'll notice another dirt road and a small parking lot used by the Nature Conservancy. The official, marked trail begins here, entering Mo'omomi Preserve lands. The 921-acre preserve, established in 1988, is home to 22 native Hawaiian plant species and birds. You'll be able to spot Hawaiian owls, sanderlings, plovers, and the great frigate bird. Look for them as you stand on Kaiehu Point.

❸ Secluded Sandstone Beach   Follow the trail west as it drops down to a wild, windswept, sandstone beach, flanked by sand dunes. Deposits of prehistoric bird bones have been found along this coastline and dunes, indicating that at least 30 species lived here at one time.

This is a good place for spotting endangered green sea turtles, just off the coast. The preserve is an important nesting site for the turtles. Keep your eyes peeled and binoculars out: Albatrosses and monk seals also visit the area.

❹ Preserve Road   Continue west, walking under a canopy of kiawe trees to another gorgeous, secluded beach.

We like to hang out here as long as possible—what a view! Standing on this remote beach gives a good sense of what Old Hawaii must have been like. The trail makes a small loop inland, leading back to Preserve Road; a short jaunt up the dirt road takes you back to the trail head at Kaiehu Point.

Nature Conservancy Hikes

Once a month, Nature Conservancy members lead hikes in both the Kamakou and Mo'omomi preserves. Groups meet at the Conservancy's field office in Kaunakakai and carpool to the trail head. Hike leaders will also meet you at the Molokai airport at 8:30am and return you to the airport by 3:30pm if you're only doing a daytrip to the island. Advance reservations are required and there's a $25 fee. Space is limited, and the hikes are often booked several months in advance. Call the Conservancy's Molokai office at ✆ 808/553-5236 or visit their website, www.nature.org.

Return of the Shearwater

For the first time in decades, wedge-tailed shearwaters are establishing new colonies in the Mo'omomi Preserve. The dark brown shearwaters ('ua'u kani) have black-tipped bills and live at sea, but they come to shore to breed. They nest in sand burrows from March through November. Due to an aggressive Nature Conservancy weed- and predator-control program, the new colony is thriving, up from three nests in 1999 to more than 300 today. This is one reason it's important to stay on the Mo'omomi Preserve trail, you don't want to inadvertently disturb the shallow nests.

HALAWA VALLEY TRAIL ★

Difficulty rating: Moderate

Distance: 4 miles round-trip

Estimated time: 4 to 6 hr.

Elevation gain: 500 feet

Costs/permits: Access to the trail crosses private property, so you must hire a local guide. Try the cultural hike led by Lawrence Aki, whose family has lived in the valley for many years. Book his $75 tour through Hotel Molokai (© 808/553-5347; www.hotelmolokai.com)

Pet-friendly: No

Best time to go: If you want to swim in the pools under the falls, go in the summer or fall, from April through October. If you want to see the falls at their fullest, go doing the wetter winter months, from November through March.

Website: www.molokai-hawaii.com

Recommended map: None

Trail head GPS: N 21 09.428 W 156 44.312

Trail head directions: From Kaunakakai, take Hwy. 450 to Halawa. Turn left at the Halawa Valley sign. Guides will meet you at the roadside church parking lot, just before the trail head. The 30-mile (scenic) drive takes about 90 minutes.

Hike into a steep cathedral valley through dense forest and past ancient settlement sites, before reaching the 250-foot-tall Mo'oula Falls. Ancient Polynesians settled in lush Halawa Valley as early as A.D. 650, and archaeologists say it is one of the most culturally significant places in all of Hawaii. The sacred valley is home to 12 of Molokai's 19 ancient temples. Access to the valley continues to be a hot button of controversy. Local residents have erected a gate and nailed up no trespassing signs, in an effort to stop vagrants and disrespectful visitors. Now, to get in, you need an approved guide.

Getting here is half the fun. The scenic road is a gorgeous stretch of hairpin turns that dips into the jungle and out along the ocean. When you book the hike, you'll get exact directions to the meeting spot, but likely you'll park in a small church lot, a few steps from the dirt road heading into the valley. You'll walk past a few homes, restored taro patches, and irrigation ditches. Cross over the ditch, with taro patches to the right, and walk into the green lower valley.

❶ **Ancient Rock Walls** An old house foundation and burial site will be to your right as you walk the path; a rock wall flanks the trail, marking old boundary

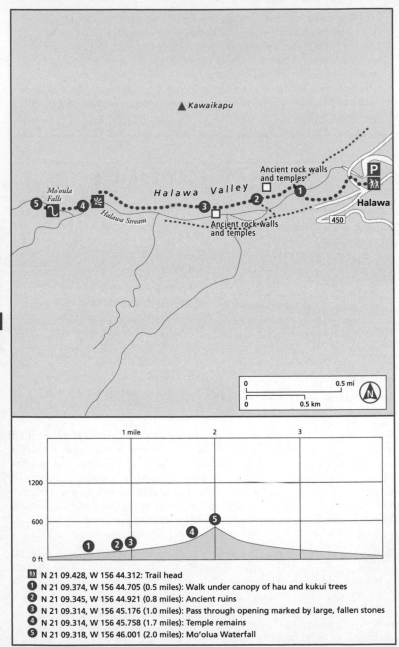

N 21 09.428, W 156 44.312: Trail head

1 N 21 09.374, W 156 44.705 (0.5 miles): Walk under canopy of hau and kukui trees

2 N 21 09.345, W 156 44.921 (0.8 miles): Ancient ruins

3 N 21 09.314, W 156 45.176 (1.0 miles): Pass through opening marked by large, fallen stones

4 N 21 09.314, W 156 45.758 (1.7 miles): Temple remains

5 N 21 09.318, W 156 46.001 (2.0 miles): Mo'olua Waterfall

lines. You'll notice a few white painted arrows on the rocks, pointing the way through the valley. Your guide will point out the first ancient temple on this trail, surrounded by a stone wall. The large, upright rock was a place where offerings to the gods were made. Passing through the rock wall marks the separation from the lower valley to the middle valley.

Pretty bird-of-paradise flowers bloom under a canopy of hau and kukui trees, both important to Hawaiians. The trunk and branches of hau were once used to make tool handles, and hau flowers were used as a dye. Kukui nuts were used for lei making, and the nut oil was good lighting fuel.

Continue along the trail, flanked by large bird ferns, until you pass a small ancestral fireplace. Past the rock wall, you'll also notice a cleared platform. Ancient Hawaiians would go in the center of the clearing to make offerings to the god of fish. There are also remnants of old taro patches on the left, now overgrown.

② Birthing Circle Continue a short way and you'll pass what looks like a bunch of boulders—it's a fertility temple. Different stones represent male, female, and birthing. At the site, women would ask the gods for assistance to conceive. Coupling would take place at this spot, and then, 9 months later, the woman would return to the site to give birth. Beyond the rock wall is a large burial site that covers much of the hillside slope.

③ Circles of Learning After leaving the sacred fertility temple, you'll begin to hear the sound of water. Keep going through an opening marked by a large stone (it's now fallen onto the ground). You're leaving the land of the common people and passing into the land of the priesthood—the kahunas. There are several circles of learning, cleared areas marked by stone fences, where priests taught religion. As you walk from here, you'll get your first glimpse of Mo'olua

Falls in the distance and the scenic Halawa Stream below. You'll also have impressive views of valley's steep walls.

The trail drops down to the boulder-strewn stream and passes another circle of learning; the hula would have been held here, our guides have told us.

④ Temple to Lono Halawa Stream, designated as a Wild and Scenic River, widens and rushes down the valley in a hurry. You'll see small cascades and nearby, six tiers of an old temple dedicated to Lono, the god of agriculture and peace, and another stone wall and opening marking the entrance to the upper valley. The upper levels of Halawa Valley contained royalty graves, the house of the gods and the house of the drum. Traditional Hawaiians would (and many still do) perform a small chant asking permission to enter the upper valley.

The lush upper valley looks exotically jungle-y, draped with fat vines and fringed with wild papaya, apple, banana, and passion-fruit trees. Suriname cherries and kukui nut shells are scattered along the path. Look ahead: Side-by-side towering waterfalls—Mo'olua and Hipuapu—tumble in front of you.

⑤ Mo'olua Falls The two-tiered waterfall, tumbling some 250 feet from the top of the valley wall, is a beautiful site to behold. In the winter, the falls are huge, but the pools beneath them are too dangerous to swim in. We think the falls are impressive even in the driest summer months, and a dip in the water and under the plunging cascades is sublime.

If you're heading to Halawa Valley, make a stop at **Manae Goods and Grindz** (© **808/558-8498**) in Pukoo. There's decent takeout breakfast, lunch, and dinner dishes, and local faves such as dried shrimp or spicy cuttlefish (similar to squid and octopus).

Outdoor Adventures

Swim with sea turtles and dolphins; scuba dive the longest fringing reef in Hawaii; go deep-sea fishing for mahimahi, ahi, and ono; or kayak in the shadows of the world's tallest sea cliffs. **Molokai Fish and Dive** (℃ **808/553-5926;** www. molokaifishanddive.com) offers a variety of outdoor adventure trips on the island.

SLEEPING & EATING

ACCOMMODATIONS

Kids **Country Cottage at Pu'u o Hoku Ranch** Pu'u o Hoku Ranch, an hour's drive from Kaunakakai, spreads across 14,000 acres of pasture and forests, with plenty of room for kids to roam. The comfortable two-bedroom wooden cottage, with breathtaking views of rolling hills and the Pacific, features a full kitchen and a separate dining room on the enclosed lanai. Guided hikes into Halawa Valley and horseback riding trips are offered through the ranch.

Kamehameha V Hwy., at mile marker 25 (PO Box 1889, Kaunakakai, HI, 96748). ℃ **808/558-8109.** www. puuohoku.com. 2 units. $140 double. Cleaning fee $75. Extra person $20. 2-night minimum. No credit cards. **Close to:** Kalaupapa Trail, Pepeopae Trail.

★ Kids **Dunbar Beachfront Cottages** This is one of the most peaceful and elegant properties on the east end—the setting is stunning! Each of these two plantation-style cottages sits on its own secluded, swimmable beach. Both cottages have ceiling fans, comfortable tropical furniture, large furnished decks (perfect for winter whale-watching), and ocean views.

Kamehameha V Hwy., past mile marker 18 (HC 01 Box 738, Kaunakakai, HI, 96748). ℃ **800/673-0520** or 808/558-8153. www.molokai-beachfront-cottages.com. 2 units. $170 cottage (sleeps up to 4). Cleaning fee $75. 3-night minimum. No credit cards. **Close to:** Halawa Valley Trail.

★ **Hotel Molokai** Centrally-located and recently updated with fresh paint and flatscreen TVs, this thatch-roofed, chalet-style motel is the only game in town. Thankfully, it offers decent value for its smallish, modestly furnished rooms; most have balconies, some with views of the beach (not good for swimming). The best part of this place is the on-site bar and restaurant (one of few on the island) and the swimming pool.

Kamehameha V Hwy. Kaunakakai, HI, 96748. ℃ **800/367-5004** from the mainland, 800/272-5275 in Hawaii, or 808/553-5347. www.hotelmolokai.com. 54 units. $159–$219 double; $229 double w/kitchen; from $249 suite. AE, DC, DISC, MC, V. **Close to:** Halawa Valley Trail.

Finds **Paniolo Hale** Tucked into a verdant garden on the dry west end, this condo complex fronts Kepuhi Beach (not safe for swimming). The two-story, old-Hawaii ranch-house design is airy and homey, with oak floors and folding-glass doors that open to huge screened verandas. All units are spacious and well equipped.

Lio Place, next door to Kaluakoi Resort (PO Box 738, Kaunakakai, HI, 96748). ℃ **800/367-2984** or 808/553-8334. www.molokai-vacation-rental.com. 77 units. $120–$150 studio double; $130–$350 1-bedroom apt (sleeps up to 4); $275 2-bedroom apt (up to 6). 3-night minimum; 1-week minimum Dec 20–Jan 5. AE, MC, V. **Close to:** Pepeopae Trail, Mo'omomi Trail.

Camping on Molokai

There's camping at **Palaau State Park** (www.hawaiistateparks.org/parks/molokai/Index. cfm?park_id=43). Camping is free at the park, but you'll need a permit (good for 7 days) from the camp headquarters or from the Division of State Parks on Maui (© **808/567-6618;** www.hawaiistateparks.org). There's beach camping at **Papohaku Beach Park** and **One Ali'i Park** on the west end of the island, where you'll find outdoor showers, picnic areas with grills, drinking water, and restrooms. Get your camping permit, at $3 per person per night, from **Maui County Parks & Recreation** (© **808/553-3204**). Camping is restricted to 3 days, but if no one else has applied for a permit, you can stay longer. There's also a small, primitive camping area near the **Waikolu Lookout** in the Kamakou Preserve. For permits, call © **808/984-8100.**

RESTAURANTS

★ **Hotel Molokai** AMERICAN/ISLAND   Set on the ocean, torches flickering under palm trees, Hotel Molokai's casual dining room evokes the romance of a South Seas fantasy. It offers tasty, uncomplicated fare, running the gamut from salads and sandwiches to burgers, steaks, BBQ ribs, and fresh fish and seafood, of which the coconut shrimp is a must-try.

On Kamehameha V Hwy. © **808/553-5347.** Reservations recommended for dinner. Main courses $8–$15 lunch; $15–$25 dinner. AE, DC, MC, V. Daily 7–10:30am, 11am–1:30pm, and 6–8:45pm (Fri 4–9pm); bar nightly until 10:30pm. **Close to:** Kalaupapa Trail, Pepeopae Trail.

Kanemitsu's Bakery & Restaurant BAKERY/DELI   Morning, noon, and night, this local legend fills the air with the sweet smells of baking. Taro lavosh flat bread is the hot seller, joining Molokai bread—developed in 1935 in a cast-iron, kiawe-fired oven— as a Kanemitsu signature. In the adjoining coffee shop/deli, the hamburgers and egg-salad sandwiches are both popular and cheap.

79 Ala Malama St. © **808/553-5855.** Most items under $5.50. AE, MC, V. Restaurant Wed–Mon 5:30am–noon; bakery Wed–Mon 5:30am–6:30pm. **Close to:** Kalaupapa Trail, Pepeopae Trail.

★ **Kualapuu Cookhouse** AMERICAN/ISLAND   Ask anyone on the island where to eat, and they'll recommend this pleasantly rustic roadhouse where the plain digs belie the good eats. Dinner specials might include baby back ribs in guava sauce or sautéed mahimahi with sweet ginger butter; lunch plates are heaped with stir-fried veggies and meats.

102 Farrington Ave. © **808/567-9655.** Most items under $15. No credit cards. BYOB. Mon 7am–2pm; Tues–Sat 7am–8pm. **Close to:** Kalaupapa Trail, Pepeopae Trail.

Appendix A:
Fast Facts, Toll-Free
Numbers & Websites

1 FAST FACTS: HAWAII

AMERICAN EXPRESS There are two American Express Travel Services offices in Honolulu, Oahu, one at the Hilton Hawaiian Village at 2005 Kalia Rd. (© **808/951-0644**) and another at 677 Ala Moana Blvd., Ste. 100, (© **808/585-3200**). On Maui, there is an office in Lahaina at the Westin Maui Hotel (Shop 101, 2365 Kaanapali Pkwy, © **808/661-7155**).

AREA CODES All the Hawaiian Islands are in the 808 area code. Note that if you're calling one island from another, you have to dial "1-808" before the local number.

AUTOMOBILE ORGANIZATIONS Motor clubs will supply maps, suggested routes, guidebooks, accident and bail-bond insurance, and emergency road service. The **American Automobile Association (AAA)** is the major auto club in the United States. If you belong to a motor club in your home country, inquire about AAA reciprocity before you leave. You may be able to join AAA even if you're not a member of a reciprocal club; to inquire, call AAA (© **800/222-4357**; www.aaa.com). AAA is actually an organization of regional motor clubs, so look under "AAA Automobile Club" in the White Pages of the telephone directory. AAA has a nationwide emergency road service telephone number (© **800/AAA-HELP** [222-4357]).

BUSINESS HOURS Most offices are open Monday through Friday from 8am to 5pm. Bank hours are Monday through Thursday from 8:30am to 3pm and Friday from 8:30am to 6pm; some banks are open on Saturday as well. Shopping centers are open Monday through Friday from 10am to 9pm, Saturday from 10am to 5:30pm, and Sunday from noon to 5 or 6pm.

CAR RENTALS See "Toll-Free Numbers & Websites," p. 245.

DRINKING LAWS The legal age for purchase and consumption of alcoholic beverages is 21; proof of age is required and often requested at bars, nightclubs, and restaurants, so it's always a good idea to bring ID when you go out.

Bars are allowed to stay open daily until 2am; places with cabaret licenses are able to keep the booze flowing until 4am. Grocery and convenience stores are allowed to sell beer, wine, and liquor 7 days a week. Do not carry open containers of alcohol in your car or any public area that isn't zoned for alcohol consumption. The police can fine you on the spot. And nothing will ruin your trip faster than getting a citation for DUI ("driving under the influence"), so don't even think about driving while intoxicated.

DRIVING RULES See "Getting There & Getting Around," p. 15.

ELECTRICITY Like the rest of the United States, Hawaii uses 110–120 volts AC (60 cycles), compared to 220–240 volts AC (50 cycles) in most of Europe, Australia, and New Zealand. Downward converters that change 220–240 volts to 110–120 volts are difficult to find in Hawaii, so bring one with you.

EMBASSIES & CONSULATES All embassies are located in the nation's capital, Washington, D.C. Some consulates are located in major U.S. cities, and most nations have a mission to the United Nations in New York City. If your country isn't listed below, call for directory information in Washington, D.C. (② **202/555-1212**) or check **www.embassy.org/embassies**.

The embassy of **Australia** is at 1601 Massachusetts Ave. NW, Washington, DC 20036 (② **202/797-3000;** www.austemb.org). There are consulates in Honolulu, Houston, New York, Los Angeles, and San Francisco.

The embassy of **Canada** is at 501 Pennsylvania Ave. NW, Washington, DC 20001 (② **202/682-1740;** www.canadianembassy.org). Other Canadian consulates are in Buffalo (New York), Detroit, Los Angeles, New York, and Seattle.

The embassy of **Ireland** is at 2234 Massachusetts Ave. NW, Washington, DC 20008 (② **202/462-3939;** www.irelandemb.org). Irish consulates are in Boston, Chicago, New York, San Francisco, and other cities. See website for complete listing.

The embassy of **New Zealand** is at 37 Observatory Circle NW, Washington, DC 20008 (② **202/328-4800;** www.nzemb.com). New Zealand consulates are in Los Angeles, Salt Lake City, San Francisco, and Seattle.

The embassy of the **United Kingdom** is at 3100 Massachusetts Ave. NW, Washington, DC 20008 (② **202/588-7800;** www.britainusa.com). Other British consulates are in Atlanta, Boston, Chicago,

Cleveland, Houston, Los Angeles, New York, San Francisco, and Seattle.

EMERGENCIES Dial ② **911** for police, fire, or ambulance.

GASOLINE (PETROL) The Hawaiian Islands have some of the highest gasoline prices in the United States. At press time, the cost of gasoline (also known as gas, but never petrol) is $2.50 a gallon. Taxes are already included in the printed price. One U.S. gallon equals 3.8 liters or .9 imperial gallons. Fill-up locations are known as gas or service stations.

HOLIDAYS Banks, government offices, post offices, and many stores, restaurants, and museums are closed on the following legal national holidays: January 1 (New Year's Day), the third Monday in January (Martin Luther King, Jr., Day), the third Monday in February (Presidents' Day), the last Monday in May (Memorial Day), July 4 (Independence Day), the first Monday in September (Labor Day), the second Monday in October (Columbus Day), November 11 (Veterans' Day/Armistice Day), the fourth Thursday in November (Thanksgiving Day), and December 25 (Christmas). The Tuesday after the first Monday in November is Election Day, a federal government holiday in presidential-election years (held every four years; the next is in 2012).

HOSPITALS

On Oahu Straub Hospital (888 South King St., Honolulu; ② **808/522-4000**); Wahiawa General Hospital (128 Lehua St., Wahiawa; ② **808/621-8411**); and Kokua Kalihi Valley Hospital (2239 North School St., Honolulu; ② **808/848-0976**).

On Maui Kula Hospital (100 Keokea Place, Kula; ② **808/878-1221**) and Maui Memorial Medical Center (221 Mahalani St., Wailuku, ② **808/244-9056**).

On the Big Island North Hawaii Community Hospital (67-1125 Mamalahoa Hwy., Kamuela; ② **808/885-4444**).

On Kauai Samuel Mahelona Memorial Hospital (4800 Kawaihau Rd., Kapaa; © 808/822-4961).

On Lanai Lanai Community Hospital (628 Seventh St., Lanai City; © 808/565-6411).

On Molokai Molokai General Hospital (280 Puali St., Kaunakakai; © 808/553-5331).

For information on staying healthy, see "Staying Healthy" in chapter 2.

INSURANCE

Medical Insurance Although it's not required of travelers, health insurance is highly recommended. Most health insurance policies cover you if you get sick away from home—but check your coverage before you leave.

International visitors to the U.S. should note that unlike many European countries, the United States does not usually offer free or low-cost medical care to its citizens or visitors. Doctors and hospitals are expensive, and in most cases will require advance payment or proof of coverage before they render their services. Good policies will cover the costs of an accident, repatriation, or death. Packages such as **Europ Assistance's "Worldwide Healthcare Plan"** are sold by European automobile clubs and travel agencies at attractive rates. **Worldwide Assistance Services, Inc.** (© 800/777-8710; www.worldwideassistance.com) is the agent for Europ Assistance in the United States.

Though lack of health insurance may prevent you from being admitted to a hospital in a nonemergency, don't worry about being left on a street corner to die: The American way is to fix you now and bill the daylights out of you later.

If you're ever hospitalized more than 150 miles from home, **MedjetAssist** (© 800/527-7478; www.medjetassistance.com) will pick you up and fly you to the hospital of your choice in a medically equipped and staffed aircraft 24 hours day, 7 days a week. Annual memberships are $225

individual, $350 family; you can also purchase short-term memberships.

Canadians should check with their provincial health plan offices or call **Health Canada** (© 866/225-0709; www.hc-sc.gc.ca) to find out the extent of their coverage and what documentation and receipts they must take home in case they are treated in the United States.

Travelers from the U.K. should carry their European Health Insurance Card (EHIC), which replaced the E111 form as proof of entitlement to free/reduced cost medical treatment abroad (© 0845/606-2030; www.ehic.org.uk). Note, however, that the EHIC only covers "necessary medical treatment," and for repatriation costs, lost money, baggage, or cancellation, travel insurance from a reputable company should always be sought (www.travelinsuranceweb.com).

Travel Insurance The cost of travel insurance varies widely, depending on the destination, the cost and length of your trip, your age and health, and the type of trip you're taking, but expect to pay between 5% and 8% of the vacation itself. You can get estimates from various providers through **InsureMyTrip.com.** Enter your trip cost and dates, your age, and other information, for prices from more than a dozen companies.

U.K. citizens and their families who make more than one trip abroad per year may find an annual travel insurance policy works out to be cheaper. Check **www.moneysupermarket.com**, which compares prices across a wide range of providers for single- and multi-trip policies.

Most big travel agents offer their own insurance and will probably try to sell you their package when you book a holiday. Think before you sign. **Britain's Consumers' Association** recommends that you insist on seeing the policy and reading the fine print before buying travel insurance. **The Association of British Insurers** (© 020/7600-3333; www.abi.org.uk)

gives advice by phone and publishes *Holiday Insurance*, a free guide to policy provisions and prices. You can also shop around for better deals: Try **Columbus Direct** (📞 0870/033-9988; www.columbus direct.net).

Trip-Cancellation Insurance Trip-cancellation insurance will help retrieve your money if you have to back out of a trip or depart early, or if your travel supplier goes bankrupt. Trip cancellation traditionally covers such events as sickness, natural disasters, and State Department advisories. The latest news in trip-cancellation insurance is the availability of **expanded hurricane coverage** and the **"any-reason"** cancellation coverage—which costs more but covers cancellations made for any reason. You won't get back 100% of your prepaid trip cost, but you'll be refunded a substantial portion. **Travel-Safe** (📞 888/885-7233; www.travelsafe. com) offers both types of coverage. Expedia also offers any-reason cancellation coverage for its air-hotel packages. For details, contact one of the following recommended insurers: **Access America** (📞 866/807-3982; www.accessamerica. com); **Travel Guard International** (📞 800/826-4919; www.travelguard.com); **Travel Insured International** (📞 800/243-3174; www.travelinsured.com); and **Travelex Insurance Services** (📞 888/457-4602; www.travelex-insurance.com).

INTERNET ACCESS On every island, branches of the Hawaii State Public Library System have free computers with Internet access. To find your closest library or to reserve a computer, check www.librarieshawaii.org. There is no charge for use of the computers, but you must have a Hawaii library card, which is free to Hawaii residents and members of the military. Visitors have a choice of two types of cards: a $25 nonresident card that is good for 5 years (and may be renewed for an additional $25) or a $10 visitor card ($5 for children 18 and under) that is

good for 3 months but may not be renewed. To download an application for a library card, go to www.librarieshawaii. org/services/libcard.htm.

To find Internet cafes, check www. cybercaptive.com or www.cybercafe.com.

If you have a laptop, every Starbucks in Hawaii has Wi-Fi. For a list of locations, go to www.starbucks.com/retail/find/ default.aspx. To find other public Wi-Fi hotspots in your destination, go to www. jiwire.com; its Hotspot Finder holds the world's largest directory of public wireless hotspots.

LEGAL AID If you are "pulled over" for a minor infraction (such as speeding), never attempt to pay the fine directly to a police officer; this could be construed as attempted bribery, a much more serious crime. Pay fines by mail, or directly into the hands of the clerk of the court. If accused of a more serious offense, say and do nothing before consulting a lawyer. Here the burden is on the state to prove a person's guilt beyond a reasonable doubt, and everyone has the right to remain silent, whether he or she is suspected of a crime or actually arrested. Once arrested, a person can make one telephone call to a party of his or her choice. International visitors should call their embassy or consulate.

LOST & FOUND Be sure to tell all of your credit card companies the minute you discover your wallet has been lost or stolen and file a report at the nearest police precinct. Your credit card company or insurer may require a police report number or record of the loss. Most credit card companies have an emergency toll-free number to call if your card is lost or stolen; they may be able to wire you a cash advance immediately or deliver an emergency credit card in a day or two. Visa's U.S. emergency number is 📞 800/847-2911 or 410/581-9994. American Express cardholders and traveler's check holders should call 📞 800/221-7282. MasterCard holders should call 🕾 800/307-7309 or 636/722-7111. For other credit cards, call the toll-free number directory at 🕾 800/555-1212.

If you need emergency cash over the weekend when all banks and American Express offices are closed, you can have money wired to you via **Western Union** (🕾 800/325-6000; www.westernunion.com).

MAIL At press time, domestic postage rates were 27¢ for a postcard and 42¢ for a letter. For international mail, a first-class letter of up to 1 ounce costs 94¢ (72¢ to Canada and Mexico); a first-class postcard costs the same as a letter. For more information go to **www.usps.com** and click on "Calculate Postage."

If you aren't sure what your address will be in the United States, mail can be sent to you, in your name, c/o General Delivery at the main post office of the city or region where you expect to be. (Call 🕾 800/275-8777 for information on the nearest post office.) The addressee must pick up mail in person and must produce proof of identity (driver's license, passport, etc.). Most post offices will hold your mail for up to 1 month, and are open Monday to Friday from 8am to 6pm, and Saturday from 9am to 3pm.

Always include zip codes when mailing items in the U.S. If you don't know your zip code, visit www.usps.com/zip4.

MAPS See "Getting There & Getting Around," in chapter 2.

MEASUREMENTS See the chart on the inside front cover of this book for details on converting metric measurements to nonmetric equivalents.

MEDICAL CONDITIONS If you have a medical condition that requires **syringe-administered medications,** carry a valid signed prescription from your physician; syringes in carry-on baggage will be inspected. Insulin in any form should have the proper pharmaceutical documentation.

If you have a disease that requires treatment with **narcotics,** you should also carry documented proof with you—smuggling narcotics aboard a plane carries severe penalties in the U.S.

For **HIV-positive visitors,** requirements for entering the United States are somewhat vague and change frequently. For up-to-the-minute information, contact **AIDSinfo** (🕾 800/448-0440 or 301/519-6616 outside the U.S.; www.aidsinfo.nih.gov) or the **Gay Men's Health Crisis** (🕾 212/367-1000; www.gmhc.org).

NEWSPAPERS & MAGAZINES Daily newspapers in Hawaii are as follows: on Oahu, the *Honolulu Advertiser* (www.honoluluadvertiser.com) and the *Honolulu Star-Bulletin* (www.honolulustarbulletin.com); on the Big Island, *West Hawaii Today* (www.westhawaiitoday. com) for the Kailua/Kona side, and the *Hawaii Tribune-Herald* (www.hilohawaii tribune.com) for the Hilo/Puna side; on Maui, the *Maui News* (www.mauinews. com); and on Kauai, the *Garden Island* (www.kauai world.com).

Publications for visitors include: *This Week Oahu, This Week Big Island, This Week Maui,* and *This Week Kauai* (www.thisweek.com); *Oahu Visitor Magazine, Big Island Visitor Magazine, Maui Visitor Magazine,* and *Kauai Visitor Magazine* (www.visitormagazines.com); and *101 Things to Do* (with separate versions for Oahu, Big Island, Maui, and Kauai).

Lifestyle magazines include *Honolulu Magazine* (www.honolulumagazine.com), while business publications include *Pacific Business News* (www.bizjournals.com/pacific) and *Hawaii Business* (www.hawaii business.com).

PASSPORTS The websites listed below provide downloadable passport applications as well as the current fees for processing applications. For an up-to-date, country-by-country listing of passport requirements around the world, go to the "International Travel" tab of the U.S. State Department at **http://travel.state.gov**. Allow plenty of time before your trip to apply for a passport; processing normally takes 4 to 6 weeks (3 weeks for expedited service) but can take longer during busy periods (especially spring). And keep in mind that if you need a passport in a hurry, you'll pay a higher processing fee.

For Residents of Australia You can pick up an application from your local post office or any branch of Passports Australia, but you must schedule an interview at the passport office to present your application materials. Call the **Australian Passport Information Service** at ℭ **131-232,** or visit the government website at www.passports. gov.au.

For Residents of Canada Passport applications are available at travel agencies throughout Canada or from the central **Passport Office,** Department of Foreign Affairs and International Trade, Ottawa, ON K1A 0G3 (ℭ **800/567-6868;** www. ppt.gc.ca). *Note:* Canadian children who travel must have their own passport. However, if you hold a valid Canadian passport issued before December 11, 2001, that bears the name of your child, the passport remains valid for you and your child until it expires.

For Residents of Ireland You can apply for a 10-year passport at the **Passport Office,** Setanta Centre, Molesworth St., Dublin 2 (ℭ **01/671-1633;** www.irlgov. ie/iveagh). Those under age 18 and over 65 must apply for a 3-year passport. You can also apply at 1A South Mall, Cork (ℭ **21/ 494-4700**) or at most main post offices.

For Residents of New Zealand You can pick up a passport application at any New Zealand Passports Office or download it from their website. Contact the **Passports Office** at ℭ **0800/225-050** in New Zealand or 04/474-8100, or log on to www. passports.govt.nz.

To pick up an application for a standard 10-year passport (5-year passport for children under 16), visit your nearest passport office, major post office, or travel agency, or contact the **United Kingdom Passport Service** at ℭ **0870/521-0410** or search its website at www.ips.gov.uk.

POLICE Dial ℭ **911** for police.

SMOKING It's against the law to smoke in public buildings, including airports, shopping malls, grocery stores, retail shops, buses, movie theaters, banks, convention facilities, and all government buildings and facilities. There is no smoking in restaurants, bars, and nightclubs.

Most bed-and-breakfasts prohibit smoking indoors, and more and more hotels and resorts are becoming nonsmoking even in public areas. Also, there is no smoking within 20 feet of a doorway, window, or ventilation intake (so no hanging around outside a bar to smoke—you must go 20 feet away).

TAXES The United States has no value-added tax (VAT) or other indirect tax at the national level. Every state, county, and city may levy its own local tax on all purchases, including hotel and restaurant checks and airline tickets. Hawaii state general excise tax is 4%, and the City and County of Honolulu (which is the entire island of Oahu) adds an additional .5% on anything purchased there. Hotel tax is 11.4%. These taxes will not appear on price tags.

TELEGRAPH, TELEX & FAX **Telegraph and telex services** are provided primarily by **Western Union** (ℭ **800/325-6000;** www.westernunion.com). You can telegraph (wire) money, or have it telegraphed to you, very quickly over the Western Union system, but this service can cost as much as 15% to 20% of the amount sent.

Most hotels have **fax machines** available for guest use (be sure to ask about the charge to use it). Many hotel rooms are wired for guests' fax machines. A less expensive way to send and receive faxes may be at stores such as **The UPS Store.**

TELEPHONES Many convenience and grocery stores and packaging services sell **prepaid calling cards** in denominations up to $50; for international visitors these can be the least expensive way to call home. Many public pay phones at airports now accept American Express, Master-Card, and Visa credit cards. **Local calls** made from pay phones in most locales cost either 25¢ or 35¢ (no pennies). Most long-distance and international calls can be dialed directly from any phone. **For calls within the United States and to Canada,** dial 1 followed by the area code and the seven-digit number. **For other international calls,** dial 011 followed by the country code, city code, and the number you are calling.

Calls to area codes **800, 888, 877,** and **866** are toll-free. However, calls to area codes **700** and **900** (chat lines, bulletin boards, "dating" services, and so on) can be very expensive—usually a charge of 95¢ to $3 or more per minute, and they sometimes have minimum charges that can run as high as $15 or more.

For **reversed-charge or collect calls,** and for person-to-person calls, dial the number "0" then the area code and number; an operator will come on the line, and you should specify whether you are calling collect, person-to-person, or both. If your operator-assisted call is international, ask for the overseas operator.

For **local directory assistance** ("information"), dial *C* **411;** for long-distance information, dial 1, then the appropriate area code and 555-1212.

TIME The continental United States is divided into four time zones: Eastern Standard Time (EST), Central Standard Time (CST), Mountain Standard Time (MST), and Pacific Standard Time (PST). Alaska and Hawaii have their own zones.

For example, when it's 9am in Los Angeles (PST), it's 7am in Honolulu (HST), 10am in Denver (MST), 11am in Chicago (CST), noon in New York City (EST), 5pm in London (GMT), and 2am the next day in Sydney.

Daylight saving time is in effect in the U.S. from 2am on the second Sunday in March to 2am on the first Sunday in November, **except in Hawaii,** Arizona, the U.S. Virgin Islands, and Puerto Rico. Daylight saving time moves the clock 1 hour ahead of standard time.

TIPPING Tips are a very important part of certain workers' income, and gratuities are the standard way of showing appreciation for services provided. (Tipping is certainly not compulsory if the service is poor!) In hotels, tip **bellhops** at least $1 per bag ($2–$3 if you have a lot of luggage) and tip the **chamber staff** $1 to $2 per day (more if you've left a disaster area for him or her to clean up). Tip the **doorman** or **concierge** only if he or she has provided you with some specific service (for example, calling a cab for you or obtaining difficult-to-get theater tickets). Tip the **valet-parking attendant at least** $1 every time you get your car.

In restaurants, bars, and nightclubs, tip **service staff** 15% to 20% of the check, tip **bartenders** 10% to 15%, tip **checkroom attendants** $1 per garment.

As for other service personnel, tip **cab drivers** 15% of the fare; tip **skycaps** at airports at least $1 per bag ($2–$3 if you have a lot of luggage); and tip **hairdressers** and **barbers** 15% to 20%.

TOILETS You won't find public toilets or "restrooms" on the streets in Hawaii, but they can be found in hotel lobbies, bars, restaurants, museums, department stores, railway and bus stations, and service stations. Large hotels and fast-food restaurants are often the best bet for clean facilities. Restaurants and bars in resorts or heavily visited areas may reserve their restrooms for patrons.

Dept. of State Travel Advisory: ℂ **202/
647-5225** (manned 24 hrs.)

U.S. Passport Agency: ℂ **202/647-
0518**

U.S. Centers for Disease Control International Traveler's Hotline: ℂ **404/332-
4559**

Also see Visitor Information contacts and numbers listed in chapter 2.

VISAS For information about U.S. Visas, go to **http://travel.state.gov** and click on "Visas." Or go to one of the following websites:

Australian citizens can obtain up-to-date visa information from the **U.S. Embassy Canberra,** Moonah Place, Yarralumla, ACT 2600 (ℂ **02/6214-5600**) or by checking the U.S. Diplomatic Mission's website at **http://usembassy-australia.state.gov/consular.**

British subjects can obtain up-to-date visa information by calling the

U.S. Embassy Visa Information Line (ℂ **0891/200-290**) or by visiting the "Visas to the U.S." section of the American Embassy London's website at **www.usembassy.org.uk.**

Irish citizens can obtain up-to-date visa information through the **Embassy of the USA Dublin,** 42 Elgin Rd., Dublin 4, Ireland (ℂ **353/1-668-8777;** or by checking the "Consular Services" section of the website at **http://dublin.usembassy.gov.**

Citizens of **New Zealand** can obtain up-to-date visa information by contacting the **U.S. Embassy New Zealand,** 29 Fitzherbert Terrace, Thorndon, Wellington (ℂ **644/472-2068**), or get the information directly from the website at **http://wellington.usembassy.gov.**

WATER Safe water is readily available throughout the Hawaiian Islands from taps and fountains. Do not drink the water from rivers or lakes without treating it first.

---

2 TOLL-FREE NUMBERS & WEBSITES

MAJOR U.S. AIRLINES
(*flies internationally as well)

Alaska Airlines/Horizon Air
ℂ 800/252-7522
www.alaskaair.com

American Airlines*
ℂ 800/433-7300 (in U.S. and Canada)
ℂ 020/7365-0777 (in U.K.)
www.aa.com

Continental Airlines*
ℂ 800/523-3273 (in U.S. and Canada)
ℂ 084/5607-6760 (in U.K.)
www.continental.com

Delta Air Lines*
ℂ 800/221-1212 (in U.S. and Canada)
ℂ 084/5600-0950 (in U.K.)
www.delta.com

Hawaiian Airlines*
ℂ 800/367-5320 (in U.S. and Canada)
www.hawaiianair.com

Northwest Airlines
ℂ 800/225-2525 (in U.S.)
ℂ 870/0507-4074 (in U.K.)
www.flynaa.com

United Airlines*
ℂ 800/864-8331 (in U.S. and Canada)
ℂ 084/5844-4777 (in U.K.)
www.united.com

US Airways*
ℂ 800/428-4322 (in U.S. and Canada)
ℂ 084/5600-3300 (in U.K.)
www.usairways.com

MAJOR INTERNATIONAL AIRLINES

Air Canada
☏ 888/247-2262 (in U.S. and Canada)
www.aircanada.com

Air France
☏ 800/237-2747 (in U.S.)
☏ 800/375-8723 (in U.S. and Canada)
☏ 087/0142-4343 (in U.K.)
www.airfrance.com

Air New Zealand
☏ 800/262-1234 (in U.S.)
☏ 800/663-5494 (in Canada)
☏ 0800/028-4149 (in U.K.)
www.airnewzealand.com

Hawaiian Airlines
☏ 800/367-5320 (in U.S. and Canada)
www.hawaiianair.com

Japan Airlines
☏ 012/025-5931 (international)
www.jal.co.jp

Korean Air
☏ 800/438-5000 (in U.S. and Canada)
☏ 0800/413-000 (in U.K.)
www.koreanair.com

North American Airlines
☏ 800/359-6222
www.flynaa.com

Quantas Airways
☏ 800/227-4500 (in U.S.)
☏ 084/5774-7767 (in U.K. or Canada)
☏ 13 13 13 (in Australia)
www.quantas.com

WestJet
☏ 800/538-5696 (in U.S. and Canada)
www.westjet.com

INTER-ISLAND AIRLINES

go!
☏ 888/435-9462
www.iflygo.com
(Hawaii based)

Hawaiian Airlines
☏ 800/367-5320
www.hawaiianair.com

Interisland Airlines
☏ 800/652-6541
www.interislandair.com

Mokulele Airlines
☏ 808/426-7070
www.mokuleleairlines.com

Pacific Wings
☏ 888/575-4546
www.pacificwings.com

CAR-RENTAL AGENCIES

Advantage
☏ 800/777-5500 (in U.S.)
☏ 021/0344-4712 (outside of U.S.)
www.advantage.com

Alamo
☏ 800/GO-ALAMO (462-5266)
www.alamo.com

Avis
☏ 800/331-1212 (in U.S. and Canada)
☏ 084/4581-8181 (in U.K.)
www.avis.com

Budget
☏ 800/527-0700 (in U.S.)
☏ 087/0156-5656 (in U.K.)
☏ 800/268-8900 (in Canada)
www.budget.com

Dollar
☏ 800/800-4000 (in U.S.)
☏ 800/848-8268 (in Canada)
☏ 080/8234-7524 (in U.K.)
www.dollar.com

Enterprise
✆ 800/261-7331 (in U.S.)
✆ 514/355-4028 (in Canada)
✆ 012/9360-9090 (in U.K.)
www.enterprise.com

Hertz
✆ 800/645-3131
✆ 800/654-3001 (for international
    reservations)
www.hertz.com

National
✆ 800/CAR-RENT (227-7368)
www.nationalcar.com

Payless
✆ 800/PAYLESS (729-5377)
www.paylesscarrental.com

Rent-A-Wreck
✆ 800/535-1391
www.rentawreck.com

Thrifty
✆ 800/367-2277
✆ 918/669-2168 (international)
www.thrifty.com

MAJOR HOTEL & MOTEL CHAINS

Best Western International
✆ 800/780-7234 (in U.S. and Canada)
✆ 0800/393-130 (in U.K.)
www.bestwestern.com

Clarion Hotels
✆ 800/CLARION (252-7466) or 877/
    424-6423 (in U.S. and Canada)
✆ 0800/444-444 (in U.K.)
www.choicehotels.com

Comfort Inn
✆ 800/228-5150
✆ 0800/444-444 (in U.K.)
www.comfortinnchoicehotels.com

Courtyard by Marriott
✆ 888/236-2427 (in U.S.)
✆ 0800/221-222 (in U.K.)
www.marriott.com/courtyard

Crowne Plaza Hotels
✆ 888/303-1746 (in U.S.)
www.ichotelsgroup.com/crowneplaza

Days Inn
✆ 800/329-7466 (in U.S.)
✆ 0800/280-400 (in U.K.)
www.daysinn.com

Doubletree Hotels
✆ 800/222-TREE (8733) (in U.S. and
    Canada)
✆ 087/0590-9090 (in U.K.)
www.doubletree.com

Econo Lodges
✆ 800/55-ECONO (553-2666)
www.choicehotels.com

Embassy Suites
✆ 800/EMBASSY (362-2779)
www.embassysuites.com

Fairfield Inn by Marriott
✆ 800/228-2800 (in U.S. and Canada)
✆ 0800/221-222 (in U.K.)
www.marriott.com/fairfieldinn

Four Seasons
✆ 800/819-5053 (in U.S. and Canada)
✆ 0800/6488-6488 (in U.K.)
www.fourseasons.com

Hampton Inn
✆ 800/HAMPTON (426-7866)
www.hamptoninn.com

Hilton Hotels
✆ 800/HILTONS (445-8667) (in U.S.
    and Canada)
✆ 087/0590-9090 (in U.K.)
www.hilton.com

Holiday Inn
✆ 800/315-2621 (in U.S. and Canada)
✆ 0800/405-060 (in U.K.)
www.holidayinn.com

Howard Johnson
✆ 800/446-4656 (in U.S. and Canada)
www.hojo.com

Hyatt
℃ 888/591-1234 (in U.S. and Canada)
℃ 084/5888-1234 (in U.K.)
www.hyatt.com

InterContinental Hotels & Resorts
℃ 800/424-6835 (in U.S. and Canada)
℃ 0800/1800-1800 (in U.K.)
www.ichotelsgroup.com

La Quinta Inns and Suites
℃ 800/642-4271 (in U.S. and Canada)
www.lq.com

Loews Hotels
℃ 800/23LOEWS (235-6397)
www.loewshotels.com

Marriott
℃ 877/236-2427 (in U.S. and Canada)
℃ 0800/221-222 (in U.K.)
www.marriott.com

Motel 6
℃ 800/4MOTEL6 (466-8356)
www.motel6.com

Omni Hotels
℃ 888/444-OMNI (6664)
www.omnihotels.com

Quality
℃ 877/424-6423 (in U.S. and Canada)
℃ 0800/444-444 (in U.K.)
www.QualityInn.com

Radisson Hotels & Resorts
℃ 888/201-1718 (in U.S. and Canada)
℃ 0800/374-411 (in U.K.)
www.radisson.com

Ramada Worldwide
℃ 888/2-RAMADA (272-6232) (in U.S.
and Canada)
℃ 080/8100-0783 (in U.K.)
www.ramada.com

Red Carpet Inns
℃ 800/251-1962
www.bookroomsnow.com

Red Lion Hotels
℃ 800/RED-LION (733-5466)
www.redlion.rdln.com

Red Roof Inns
℃ 866/686-4335 (in U.S. and Canada)
℃ 614/601-4075 (international)
www.redroof.com

Renaissance
℃ 888/236-2427
www.renaissance.com

Residence Inn by Marriott
℃ 800/331-3131
℃ 0800/221-222 (in U.K.)
www.marriott.com/residenceinn

Rodeway Inns
℃ 877/424-6423
www.rodewayinn.com

Sheraton Hotels & Resorts
℃ 800/325-3535 (in U.S.)
℃ 800/543-4300 (in Canada)
℃ 0800/3253-5353 (in U.K.)
www.starwoodhotels.com/sheraton

Super 8 Motels
℃ 800/800-8000
www.super8.com

Travelodge
℃ 800/578-7878
www.travelodge.com

Vagabond Inns
℃ 800/522-1555
www.vagabondinn.com

Westin Hotels & Resorts
℃ 800/937-8461 (in U.S. and Canada)
℃ 0800/3259-5959 (in U.K.)
www.starwoodhotels.com/westin

Wyndham Hotels & Resorts
℃ 877/999-3223 (in U.S. and Canada)
℃ 050/6638-4899 (in U.K.)
www.wyndham.com

Appendix B: The Hawaiian Language

Almost everyone here speaks English. But many folks in Hawaii now speak Hawaiian as well. All visitors will hear the words *aloha* and *mahalo* (thank you). If you've just arrived, you're a *malihini*. Someone who's been here a long time is a *kamaaina*. When you finish a job or your meal, you are *pau* (finished). On Friday it's *pau hana*, work finished. You eat *pupu* (Hawaii's version of hors d'oeuvres) when you go *pau hana*.

The Hawaiian alphabet, created by the New England missionaries, has only 12 letters: the five regular vowels (*a, e, i, o,* and *u*) and seven consonants (*h, k, l, m, n, p,* and *w*). The vowels are pronounced in the Roman fashion: that is, *ah, ay, ee, oh,* and *oo* (as in "too")—not *ay, ee, eye, oh,* and *you,* as in English. For example, *huhu* is pronounced *who-who*. Most vowels are sounded separately, though some are pronounced together, as in Kalakaua: Kah-lah-*cow*-ah.

WHAT HAOLE MEANS   When Hawaiians first saw Western visitors, they called the pale-skinned, frail men *haole* because they looked so out of breath. In Hawaiian, *ha* means *breath*, and *ole* means an absence of what precedes it. Today the term *haole* is generally a synonym for Caucasian or foreigner and is used without any intended disrespect. If uttered by an angry stranger who adds certain adjectives (like "stupid"), the term can be construed as a racial slur.

THE HAWAIIAN ALPHABET

The Hawaiian alphabet, created by missionaries in the early 19th century as they tried to capture a non-written language in print, consists of just 12 letters: a, e, I, o, u, k, l, m, n, p, and w.

The following is a very general guide to Hawaiian pronunciation:

      a — ah, as in far: *hale*
      e — ay, as in way; *nene*
      i — ee, as in see; *pali*
      o — oh, as in no: *taro*
      u — oo as in moon; *kapu*

COMMON HAWAIIAN TERMS

As you explore the islands, you'll probably encounter some common Hawaiian words and sayings. Here's a brief list of the local lingo, organized alphabetically.

ahi   Hawaiian tuna fishes, especially the yellowfin tuna

ahupua'a   land division usually extending from uplands to the sea

aina   land, earth

akamai   smart, clever

Alii   chief, chieftess, king, queen, noble, royal, kingly, to rule or act as chief

aloha love, mercy, compassion, pity; greeting; loved one; to love; to greet, hail; greetings; good-bye

anuenue rainbow

aole no, not; to have none

apu coconut shell cup

aua stingy

ewa crooked, out of shape, imperfect; place name for area west of Honolulu, used as a directional term

hahalua manta ray

haiku flower

hailepo sting ray

hala the pandanus or screw pine

halau long house, as for canoes or hula instruction; school

hale house or building

hale pili house thatched with pili grass

hale pule church, chapel

haleu toilet paper; to wipe, as with toilet paper

hana hou to do again; repeat; encore

hanai foster child; adopted child

haole white person; formerly any foreigner; introduced, of foreign origin

hapa portion, fragment, part; person of mixed blood

hapa haole part white person; of part-white blood; part white and part Hawaiian, as an individual or phenomenon

hau kea snow

haupia pudding made from coconut cream, formerly thickened with arrowroot, now usually with cornstarch

heiau Hawaiian temple or place of worship

kahuna priest or expert

hele to go, come, walk; to move, as in a game; going, moving

hele mai come

hele wale to go naked; to go without fixed purpose

heap idiot

hihimanu various sting rays and eagle rays; lavish, magnificent, elegant

hoa hele traveling companion, fellow traveler

holo hele to run here and there

holoholo to go for a walk, ride, or sail; to go out on pleasure

honu general name for the turtle

ho'o-haole to act like a white person, to mimic the white people, or assume airs of superiority

hooilo winter, rainy season

hui club, association, firm, partnership, union; to form a society or organization; to meet

hukilau seine; to fish with a seine

hula   Hawaiian form of dance

iwi   bone; shell, as of coconut, candlenut, gourd, egg, shellfish

iwi po'o   skull

kahu   honored attendant, guardian, keeper, administrator, pastor of a church; one who has a dog, cat, or any pet

kahuna   priest, minister, sorcerer, expert in any profession

kai   sea, seawater

kamaaina   old-timer; native born

kanaka   human being, man, human, mankind, person, individual, subject, as of a chief; Hawaiian

kane   male, husband, male sweetheart, man

kapa   tapa, bark cloth

kapakahi   one-sided, crooked, lopsided; biased

kapu   taboo, forbidden

keiki   child

koa   brave, fearless; soldier; an endemic forest tree, the largest and most valued of the native trees

koko   blood; rainbow-hued

kumu   bottom, base, foundation; teacher

kupuna   respected elder

lanai   porch or veranda

lau   leaf

laulau   wrapping, wrapped package; individual servings of pork or beef, salted fish, and taro tops, wrapped in ti leaves of banana leaves, and baked in a ground oven, steamed, or broiled

lei   garland, wreath; necklace of flowers, leaves, shells, ivory, feathers, or paper; any ornament worn around the neck

limu   general name for all kinds of plants living underwater

loa   distance, length, height; distant, long, far, permanent

lolo   feeble minded

lomilomi   massage; kneaded, worked until softened; in cuisine, raw fish is softened through the use of an acidic marinade, like ceviche

lua   hole, pit, grave, den, cave, mine, crater; toilet

luakini   large *heiau* where ruling chiefs prayed and human sacrifices were offered

luau   young taro tops, especially baked with coconut cream and chicken or octopus; Hawaiian feast

mahalo   thank you

mahimahi   broad-headed game fish called dolphin

maile   a native twining shrub, with tiny fragrant leaves, a favorite for decorations and lei

makahiki   ancient festival beginnings about the middle of October and lasting about 4 months, with sports and religious festivities and *kapu* on war

Makahiki Hou   New Year (Hau'oli Makahiki Hou: Happy New Year)

makai   a direction, toward the sea

make to die, defeated, death

malama to take care of, care for, preserve, fidelity, loyalty

malihini stranger, newcomer, guest, one unfamiliar with a place or custom

mana supernatural or divine power

manini small, stripped sturgeon fish; stingy

maoli native, indigenous, genuine, true, real

mauka inland; a direction, toward the mountains

Menehune legendary race of small people, who worked at night building fish ponds, roads, temples; if the work was not finished in one night, it remained unfinished

muumuu loose-fitting gown or dress

nalu wave, surf, full of waves

noni Indian mulberry, a small tree or shrub formerly useful to Hawaiians as a source of dyes, food, and medicine

nui big, large, great, important

ohana family

oheo a small, native shrub, in the cranberry family, bearing small, red or yellow **edible** berries

ono delicious

opala trash, rubbish

opu belly, stomach, abdomen

pali cliff, steep hill

paniolo Hawaiian cowboy(s)

pau finished, over, completed, all done

Pele lava flow, volcano eruption; the colcano goddess

Piko navel, umbilical cord, genitals; summit of a hill or mountain, crown of the head, ear tip, end of a rope

Pipi beef, cattle

Poi the Hawaiian staff og life, made from cooked taro corms

Pono goodness, morality, moral qualities, correct or proper procedure; right, just, fair

Puka hole

Pule prayer, church service, to pray

Pupu relish, snack, hors d'oeuvre

Umi umi whiskers, beard

Wahine woman, lady, wife, female, feminine

Wai water or liquid of any kind, other than sea water

Wiki, wikiwiki to hurry, hasten; quick

PIDGIN: 'EH FO'REAL, BRAH

If you venture beyond the tourist areas, you might hear another local tongue: pidgin English, a conglomerate of slang and words from the Hawaiian language. "Broke da mouth" (tastes really good) is the favorite pidgin phrase you might hear; "'Eh fo' brah" means "It's true, brother." You could be invited to hear an elder "talk story" (relating myths and memories). But because pidgin is really the province of the locals, your visit to Hawaii is likely to pass without your hearing much pidgin at all.

Appendix C: Outdoor Activities A to Z

Here's a brief rundown of the many other outdoor activities available in Hawaii.

BIRDING

Many of Hawaii's tropical birds are found nowhere else on earth. There are curved-bill honeycreepers, black-winged red birds, and the rare o'o, whose yellow feathers Hawaiians once plucked to make royal capes. When you go birding, take along *A Field Guide to the Birds of Hawaii and the Tropical Pacific*, by H. Douglas Pratt, Phillip L. Bruner, and Delwyn G. Berett (Princeton University Press, 1987).

Kauai and Molokai, in particular, are great places to go birding. On Kauai, large colonies of seabirds nest at Kilauea National Wildlife Refuge and along the Na Pali Coast. Be sure to take along a copy of *The Birds of Kauai*, by Jim Denny (University of Hawaii Press). The lush rainforest of Molokai's Kamakou Preserve is home to the Molokai thrush and Molokai creeper, which live only on this 30-mile-long island.

For more on birding, see the wildlife guide at the front of this book.

BOATING

Almost every type of nautical experience is available in the islands, from old-fashioned Polynesian outrigger canoes to America's Cup racing sloops to submarines. You'll find details on all these seafaring experiences in the individual island chapters that follow.

No matter which type of vessel you choose, be sure to see the Hawaiian Islands from offshore if you can afford it. It's easy to combine multiple activities into one cruise: Lots of snorkel boats double as sightseeing cruises and, in winter, whale-watching cruises. The main harbors for visitor activities are Kewalo Basin, Oahu; Honokohau, Kailua-Kona, and Kawaihae on the Big Island; Lahaina and Maaalea, Maui; Kaunakakai, Molokai; and Nawiliwili and Port Allen, Kauai.

BODAY BOARDING (BOOGIEBOARDING) & BODYSURFING

Bodysurfing—riding the waves without a board, becoming one with the rolling water—is a way of life in Hawaii. Some bodysurfers just rely on hands to ride the waves; others use hand boards (flat, paddlelike gloves). For additional maneuverability, try a boogie board or body board (also known as belly boards or paipo boards). These 3-foot-long boards support the upper part of your body and are very maneuverable in the water. Both bodysurfing and body boarding require a pair of open-heeled swim fins to help propel you through the water. The equipment is inexpensive and easy to carry, and both sports can be practiced in the small, gentle waves. See the individual island chapters for details on where to rent boards and where to go.

CAMPING

Hawaii's year-round balmy climate makes camping a breeze. However, tropical campers should always be ready for rain, especially in Hawaii's wet winter season, but even in the dry summer season as well. And remember to bring a good mosquito repellent. If you're heading to the top of Hawaii's volcanoes, you'll need a down mummy bag. If you plan to camp on the beach, bring a mosquito net and a rain poncho. Always be prepared to deal with contaminated water (purify it by boiling, through filtration, or by using iodine tablets) and the tropical sun (protect yourself with sunscreen, a hat, and a long-sleeved shirt).

There are many established campgrounds at beach parks, including Kauai's Anini Beach, Oahu's Malaekahana Beach, Maui's Waianapanapa Beach, and the Big Island's Hapuna Beach. Campgrounds are also located in the interior at Maui's Haleakala National Park and the Big Island's Hawaii Volcanoes National Park, as well as at Kalalau Beach on Kauai's Na Pali Coast and in the cool uplands of Kokee State Park. For more details on getting regulations and camping information for any of Hawaii's national or state parks, see "Visitor Information" at the beginning of this chapter.

Hawaiian Trail and Mountain Club, P.O. Box 2238, Honolulu, HI 96804, offers an information packet on hiking and camping throughout the islands. Send $2 and a legal-size, self-addressed, stamped envelope for information. Another good source is the Hiking/Camping Information Packet, available from Hawaii Geographic Maps and Books, 49 S. Hotel St., Honolulu, HI 96813 (© **800/538-3950** or 808/538-3952), for $7. The University of Hawaii Press, 2840 Kolowalu St., Honolulu, HI 96822 (© 888/847-7737; www.uhpress.hawaii.edu), has an excellent selection of hiking, backpacking, and bird-watching guides, especially The Hiker's Guide to the Hawaiian Islands, by Stuart M. Ball, Jr.

GOLF

Nowhere else on earth can you tee off to whale spouts, putt under rainbows, and play around a live volcano. Hawaii has some of the world's top-rated golf courses. But be forewarned: Each course features hellish natural hazards, like razor-sharp lava, gusty trade winds, an occasional wild pig, and the tropical heat. And greens fees tend to be very expensive. Still, golfers flock here from around the world and love every minute of it. See the individual island chapters for coverage of the resort courses worth splurging on (with details, where applicable, on money-saving twilight rates), as well as the best budget and municipal courses.

A few tips on golfing in Hawaii: There's generally wind—10 to 30 mph is not unusual between 10am and 2pm—so you may have to play two to three clubs up or down to compensate. Bring extra balls: The rough is thick, water hazards are everywhere, and the wind wreaks havoc with your game. On the greens, your putt will always break toward the ocean. Hit deeper and more aggressively in the sand because the type of sand used on most Hawaii courses is firmer and more compact than on mainland courses (lighter sand would blow away in the constant wind). And bring a camera—you'll kick yourself if you don't capture those spectacular views.

HORSEBACK RIDING

One of the best ways to see Hawaii is on horseback; almost all islands offer riding opportunities for just about every age and level of experience. You can ride into Maui's Haleakala Crater, along Kauai's Mahaulepu Beach, or through Oahu's remote windward valleys on Kualoa Ranch, or you can gallop across the wide-open spaces of the Big Island's Parker Ranch, one of the largest privately owned ranches in the United States. See the individual island chapters for details. Be sure to bring a pair of jeans and closed-toed shoes to wear on your ride.

KAYAKING

Hawaii is one of the world's most popular destinations for ocean kayaking. Beginners can paddle across a tropical lagoon to two uninhabited islets off Lanikai Beach on Oahu, while more experienced kayakers can take on Kauai's awesome Na Pali Coast. In summer, experts take advantage of the usually flat conditions on the north shore of Molokai, where the sea cliffs are the steepest on earth and the remote valleys can be reached only by sea.

SCUBA DIVING

Some people come to the islands solely to take the plunge into the tropical Pacific and explore the underwater world. Hawaii is one of the world's top 10 dive destinations, according to Rodale's Scuba Diving Magazine. Here you can see the great variety of tropical marine life (more than 100 endemic species found nowhere else on the planet), explore sea caves, and swim with sea turtles and monk seals in clear, tropical water. If you're not certified, try to take classes before you come to Hawaii so you don't waste time learning and can dive right in.

If you dive, go early in the morning. Trade winds often rough up the seas in the afternoon, especially on Maui, so most operators schedule early-morning dives that end at noon. To organize a dive on your own, order The Oahu Snorkelers and Shore Divers Guide, by Francisco B. de Carvalho, from University of Hawaii Press.

Tip: It's usually worth the extra bucks to go with a good dive operator.

SNORKELING

Snorkeling is one of Hawaii's main attractions, and almost anyone can do it. All you need is a mask, a snorkel, fins, and some basic swimming skills. In many places, all you have to do is wade into the water and look down at the magical underwater world.

If you've never snorkeled before, most resorts and excursion boats offer snorkeling need lessons, however; it's plenty easy to figure out for yourself, especially once you're at the beach, where everybody around you will be doing it. If you don't have your own gear, you can rent it from one of dozens of dive shops and activities booths, discussed in the individual island chapters.

While everyone heads for Oahu's Hanauma Bay—the perfect spot for first timers—other favorite snorkel spots include Kee Beach on Kauai, Kahaluu Beach on the Big Island, Hulopoe Bay on Lanai, and Kapalua Bay on Maui. Although snorkeling is excellent on all the islands, the Big Island, with its recent lava formations and abrupt drop-offs, offers some particularly spectacular opportunities. Some of the best snorkel spots in the islands—notably, the Big Island's Kealakekua Bay and Molokini Crater just off Maui—are accessible only by boat.

Some snorkeling tips: Always snorkel with a buddy. Look up every once in a while to see where you are and if there's any boat traffic. Don't touch anything; not only can you damage coral, but camouflaged fish and shells with poisonous spines may also surprise you. Always check with a dive shop, lifeguards, or others on the beach about the area in which you plan to snorkel and ask if there are any dangerous conditions you should know about.

SPORTFISHING

Big-game fishing at its best is found off the Big Island of Hawaii at Kailua-Kona, where the deep blue waters offshore yield trophy marlin year-round. You can also try for spearfish, swordfish, various tuna, mahimahi (dorado), rainbow runners, wahoo, barracuda, trevallies, bonefish, and bottom fish like snappers and groupers. Each island offers deep-sea boat charters for good-eating fish like tuna, wahoo, and mahimahi. Visiting anglers currently need no license.

Charter fishing boats range widely both in size—from small 24-foot open skiffs to luxurious 50-foot-plus yachts—and in price—from about $100 per person to "share" a boat with other anglers for a half-day, to $900 a day to book an entire luxury sport-fishing yacht on an exclusive basis. Shop around. Prices vary according to the boat, the crowd, and the captain. Also, many boat captains tag and release marlin or keep the fish for themselves (sorry, that's Hawaii style). If you want to eat your mahimahi for dinner or have your marlin mounted, tell the captain before you go.

Money-saving tip: Try contacting the charter-boat captain directly and bargaining. Many charter captains pay a 20% to 30% commission to charter-booking agencies and may be willing to give you a discount if you book directly.

SURFING

The ancient Hawaiian practice of hee nalu (wave sliding) is probably the sport most people picture when they think of Hawaii. Believe it or not, you, too, can do some wave sliding—just sign up at any one of the numerous surfing schools located throughout the islands. On world-famous Waikiki Beach, just head over to one of the surf stands that line the sand; these guys say they can get anybody up and standing on a board. If you're already a big kahuna in surfing, check the island chapters for the best deals on rental equipment and the best places to hang ten.

TENNIS

Tennis is a popular sport in the islands. Each island chapter lists details on free municipal courts as well as the best deals on private courts. The etiquette at the free county courts is to play only 45 minutes if someone is waiting.

WHALE-WATCHING

Every winter, pods of Pacific humpback whales make the 3,000-mile swim from the chilly waters of Alaska to bask in Hawaii's summery shallows, fluking, spy hopping, spouting, breaching, and having an all around swell time. About 1,500 to 3,000 humpback whales appear in Hawaiian waters each year.

Humpbacks are one of the world's oldest, most impressive inhabitants. Adults grow to be about 45 feet long and weigh a hefty 40 tons. Humpbacks are officially an endangered species; in 1992, the waters around Maui, Molokai, and Lanai were designated a Humpback Whale National Marine Sanctuary. Despite the world's newfound ecological awareness, humpbacks and their habitats and food resources are still under threat from whalers and pollution.

The season's first whale is usually spotted in November, but the best time to see humpback whales in Hawaii is between January and April, from any island. Just look out to sea. Each island also offers a variety of whale-watching cruises, which will bring you up close and personal with the mammoth mammals; see the individual island chapters for details.

Money-saving tip: Book a snorkeling cruise during the winter whale-watching months. The captain of the boat will often take you through the best local whale-watching areas on the way, and you'll get two activities for the price of one. It's well worth the money.

WINDSURFING

Maui is Hawaii's top windsurfing destination. World-class windsurfers head for Hookipa Beach, where the wind roars through Maui's isthmus and creates some of the best windsurfing conditions in the world. Funky Paia, a derelict sugar town saved from extinction by surfers, is now the world capital of big-wave board sailing. And along Maui's Hana Highway, there are lookouts where you can watch the pros flip off the lip of 10-foot waves and gain hang time in the air.

Others, especially beginners, set their sails for Oahu's Kailua Bay or Kauai's Anini Beach, where gentle onshore breezes make learning this sport a snap.

INDEX

See also Accommodations and Restaurant indexes, below.

Explore over 3,500 destinations.